African Politics in Comparative Perspective

This book reviews fifty years of research on politics in Africa. It synthe-sizes insights from different scholarly approaches and offers an origi-nal interpretation of the knowledge accumulated over the years. It dis-cusses how research on African politics relates to the study of politics in other regions and mainstream theories in comparative politics. It focuses on such key issues as the legacy of a movement approach to political change, the nature of the state, the economy of affection, the policy deficit, the agrarian question, gender and politics, and ethnicity and conflict. It concludes by reviewing what scholars agree upon and what the accumulated knowledge offers as insights for more effective political and policy reforms. This book is an ideal text in undergrad-uate and graduate courses in African and comparative politics as well as in development-oriented courses in political science and related dis-ciplines. It is also of great relevance to governance and development analysts and to practitioners in international organizations.

Goran Hyden is distinguished professor in political science at the University of Florida. His publications include *Beyond Ujamaa in Tanzania* (1980); *No Shortcuts to Progress* (1983); *Governance and Politics in Africa*, coedited with Michael Bratton (1992); and *Making Sense of Governance*, coauthored with Julius Court and Kenneth Mease (2004). He served as president of the African Studies Association in 1995. He has also served as a consultant on African development to many international agencies.

African Politics in Comparative Perspective

GORAN HYDEN

University of Florida

CAMBRIDGE
UNIVERSITY PRESS

CAMBRIDGE UNIVERSITY PRESS
Cambridge, New York, Melbourne, Madrid, Cape Town, Singapore, São Paulo

Cambridge University Press
40 West 20th Street, New York, NY 10011-4211, USA

www.cambridge.org
Information on this title: www.cambridge.org/9780521856164

© Goran Hyden 2006

First published 2006

Printed in the United States of America

A catalog record for this publication is available from the British Library.

Library of Congress Cataloging in Publication Data

Hydén, Goran, 1938–
African politics in comparative perspective / Goran Hyden.
    p.   cm.
Includes bibliographical references and index.
ISBN-13: 978-0-521-85616-4 (hardback)
ISBN-10: 0-521-85616-7 (hardback)
ISBN-13: 978-0-521-67194-1 (pbk.)
ISBN-10: 0-521-67194-9 (pbk.)
1. Political science – Africa.   2. Africa – Politics and government – 1960–
3. Comparative government.   I. Title.
JA84.A33H92   2005
320.96 – dc22   2005018124

ISBN-13   978-0-521-85616-4 hardback
ISBN-10   0-521-85616-7 hardback

ISBN-13   978-0-521-67194-1 paperback
ISBN-10   0-521-67194-9 paperback

Contents

Acknowledgments

This book has been long in the making. Due to many other commitments, not the least being to finish a number of joint projects with other scholars, the opportunity to complete this manuscript was constantly pushed backward. I am glad that during the spring of 2004 I was able to finish a first draft and, subsequently during the second part of the year, revise it in the light of comments received from colleagues and reviewers.

This project is a celebration of fifty years of political science research on Africa. It is also a humble attempt on my part to summarize it and draw my own conclusions from the knowledge that has been accumulated over the past five decades. Many colleagues over the years have been very helpful in shaping my own thinking about Africa, whether or not they have agreed with the conclusions I have drawn. It is appropriate that I first mention my three most important intellectual mentors – individuals who have inspired my curiosity and also helped me develop as a professional. The late James S. Coleman, perhaps the foremost Africanist of the early generation of scholars, gave me intellectual encouragement and leadership at a time in my young career when I was still looking for direction. So did Colin Leys, whom I had the benefit of interacting with at Makerere and Nairobi Universities in the late 1960s and early 1970s. I also count Robert W. Kates among those who have helped form my thinking about Africa and the world. Bob and I were both at the University of Dar es Salaam, but our intellectual encounters came especially in the late 1980s and early 1990s when Bob was director of the Alan Shawn Feinstein World Hunger Program at Brown University in Providence, Rhode Island, and I had the fortune of serving – on a part-time basis – as his associate director.

Over the years I have also benefited greatly from comments and advice from many political science colleagues. I cannot list them all, but I would like to mention especially Professor Emeritus Crawford Young at University of Wisconsin; Professor David Leonard, University of California, Berkeley; Professor Joel Barkan, University of Iowa; Professor Nelson Kasfir of

Dartmouth College; Frank Kunz, Professor Emeritus at McGill University; Professors Rene Lemarchand and Michael Chege, University of Florida; Dr. Norman Miller, an independent scholar based in Norwich, Vermont; and Mette Kjaer, an associate professor at the University of Aarhus, Denmark.

For a more recent and immediate contribution, I also want to thank the graduate students in my African Politics seminar in the spring semester 2004 who all participated in discussions of the issues in the first drafts of each chapter and in many instances returned their marked-up copies of drafts for my consideration. They are, in alphabetical order: Idrissa Abdourahmane, Kenly Fenio, Jennifer Forshee, Aaron Hale, Karsten Jørgensen, Joseph Kraus, Fredline McCormack, Shannon Montgomery, Elisabeth Porter, and Li Zhen.

I also want to express my gratitude to Branoslav Kovalcik who served as my research assistant during the spring semester 2004. Not only did he assist in some of the more tedious tasks of looking up references, but he also took the time to offer helpful comments on my drafts. The same applies to Ms. Elsebeth Søndergaard, who very ably served as my research assistant when I revised the manuscript while I was a guest professor in Political Science at the University of Aarhus during the fall semester 2004. I am most grateful to the four external reviewers who provided useful and constructive comments on earlier drafts of this manuscript.

A special thanks goes to the staff at the Center for African Studies at the University of Florida, most notably its current director, Dr. Leonardo Villalon, for providing a congenial atmosphere for the study of Africa at the University of Florida. Together with the support from the current dean of the College of Liberal Arts and Sciences, Dr. Neal Sullivan, African studies at the University of Florida has reached a national and international pinnacle.

Finally, this list of acknowledgments also includes my eldest son, Michael, who has kept me alert to and interested in the concerns of the world of nongovernmental organizations working in Africa, and, not the least, my wife of almost forty years, Melania, who has not only provided a source of stability in my life, but in her own way has also offered important insights into the subject matter discussed in this volume.

Aarhus, Denmark and Gainesville, Florida
December 2004
Goran Hyden

I

The Study of Politics and Africa

What do we know about politics in Africa after fifty years of research on the subject? How does the accumulated knowledge fit into the rest of the discipline of political science and especially the field of comparative politics? What, if any, are the practical implications of this knowledge for Africa's development prospects? These are the three questions that this volume addresses. It is informative and analytical as well as policy-oriented. It speaks to newcomers to the subject by providing basic data about the continent and its politics. It appeals to the more informed students of politics in Africa by analyzing and discussing key issues that feature in current research. It also invites policy analysts and practitioners to examine the issues discussed in this volume by showing how politics bears directly on development on the continent.

Africa in this volume refers to the region south of the Sahara Desert – usually called "sub-Saharan Africa." It is a region of great cultural and geographic diversity. But with a few exceptions, like Botswana, Mauritius, and South Africa, countries in the region share the common fate of being among the poorest in the world. In the context of the current global economy, they are marginal. Various explanations have been provided for this miserable state of affairs: colonialism, traditional values, lack of capital – human as well as financial – and so on. This book takes a critical look at the character of African politics. It suggests that its still untamed nature is a significant part of the explanation of Africa's current predicament. The accumulated knowledge that political scientists have generated over the years, therefore, is of special significance for the issue of how to understand and deal with the continent's plight.

How Political Scientists Do Their Science

Making generalizations about the conditions in Africa is always hazardous. Anthropologists and historians, for example, will rightly point to the differences that exist in the microsocial or temporal context. Their own scholarship, focusing as it does on the peculiar and exceptional rather than on the general, offers important contributions to knowledge. It enriches our understanding of phenomena that otherwise would be only little known. Whereas they aim at a holistic understanding of a specific case, their ability to generalize from their empirically rich case study is limited. Understanding context is more important than being able to place the case in a comparative perspective. I acknowledge that local actors in Africa handle their predicament in multiple ways. In fact, the rich variety of ways in which they do it is truly fascinating.

Political scientists typically operate differently from historians and anthropologists in that they are more ready to engage in generalizations and comparisons. Because their ambition is to generalize, they often overlook the wealth of knowledge that is contained in the many case studies of specific countries or events that scholars in neighboring disciplines, such as anthropology and history, produce. This theoretical ambition may not be as high as economists who believe that they possess a lawlike knowledge of reality. Most political scientists are less pretentious although many are fond of trying to imitate economists. Several political scientists do, of course, become specialists: Some study only elections, others only government institutions, yet others only policy, and so forth. Knowledge generation in political science itself, therefore, tends to be fragmented. It comes in spurts, often in response to fads within the political science discipline or empirical events that attract the interest of many scholars. For instance, the demise of the Soviet Union and the end of the Cold War – none of which was predicted by the discipline – caused a major reorientation of scholarship toward peace and democracy. It had significant reverberations across fields in the discipline.

This book has been written because, at least for a long time, no one has tried to aggregate the knowledge that political scientists have generated about politics in Africa. More than ever, such a review is needed to demonstrate to the discipline as well as to others – not least those involved in development policy and governance – the common foundation on which political science builds its scholarship about Africa. The more specialized research that has been carried out over the years has enhanced our knowledge of specific aspects of it, but it has also tended to overemphasize some issues at the expense of others. This inevitably happens in the social sciences where theories come and go in response to specific problems or issues that members of the discipline deem important at a particular time. In order to overcome the limits inherent in specialized research and the rotation in theoretical orientation that characterizes the discipline, I have adopted a fifty-year perspective, through which I present a holistic analysis of politics in Africa that does not exist anywhere else. It brings together bits and pieces of important findings that are rarely fully integrated into a systematic overview. It tries to identify underlying factors that are common to African societies and economies and that determine the nature of politics in the region. It avoids putting all the blame on one or two variables, for example, clientelism, corruption, bad leadership, or ethnicity. As this volume shows, the relationships between different factors in the African situation are much more complex than the often unicausal accounts of the continent convey. The knowledge that Africanists share comes from many different streams; they flow together in a powerful, but still multifarious current that is difficult to tame or ride. Whether deemed successful or not by others, I attempt to do exactly that.

Africa's position as an area of interest in the discipline has come and gone. When I started my own career in political science in the early 1960s, Africa was the center of attention in the discipline. Thanks to systems analysis and structural functionalism, comparative politics had emerged as the essence of a new political science. The new states of Africa constituted its most prominent empirical realm. This distinction gradually disappeared, as other paradigms came to dominate, rendering comparative politics at large and African politics, in particular, much more marginal to the mainstream of the discipline. The bottom may have been in the late 1990s, when the value of area studies in American political science had reached its lowest point.

Fortunately for those interested in comparative studies, there is a growing recognition that knowledge about specific regions of the world cannot be neglected, that the study of American politics is just another area study, and that, therefore, its exceedingly privileged position in the discipline limits our understanding of what is going on, not only in other countries of the world, but in the United States itself. In short, area studies are an integral part of comparative politics, the latter an integral part of the study of American politics. Not everyone buys this thesis, but a greater number of scholars than before are ready to accept these connections today. More specifically, the study of African politics has benefited from two recent trends in the discipline. One is the growing recognition of – some would say respect for – a methodological pluralism. The other is the increasing interest not only in formal, but also in informal institutions as determinants of political choice.

Anyone studying comparative politics is aware of the continuous tension between comparability and contextuality. How does one compare a phenomenon in a distant part of the world with what is known from one's own country without losing sight of potential differences? Are there categories for analytical purposes that simultaneously do justice to African as well as American – or European – realities? As this volume demonstrates, most of us have come to acknowledge that compressing African data into preconceived boxes deduced from empirical evidence elsewhere is often problematic. African realities force the honest scholars into an inevitable stretching of the discipline's more universally accepted concepts. It is easy to make the case for an African exceptionalism. This, however, is not the position I take here. African realities may be different in many respects, but they are so as a matter of degree, not kind. In this respect, Africa is no more exceptional than Asia is – or the United States, for that matter – to the rest of the comparative politics field.

This statement is not an endorsement of the position that all that counts in comparative politics are cross-sectional surveys. These have become fashionable within the field in recent years and they make their own contribution to knowledge. Relying on such type of studies, however, is never enough, whether it is the study of Africa, Asia, Europe, or the United States. As the emerging subfield of American political development indicates, even those who study the United States recognize the importance of a historical perspective on the present.

Reductionism is an integral part of science. The question is rather how far the study of politics can rely on it alone. There are two issues of immediate concern: One is the nature of the data on which such studies depend. The second, what the data really capture. Comparativists need common data sets in order to be able to do their job. They seem to disagree, however, about which sets are really fundamental. New data sets keep cropping up all the time, typically justified by a redefinition of the research agenda. This is inevitable because political and social reality keeps changing. It shows the limits to relying on quantitative data analysis alone. This becomes especially true for countries around the world, including many in Africa, where national statistics are incomplete and often unreliable, where few scholars have produced their own alternative sets, and where the conditions for scientific sampling are far from ideal. The validity and reliability concerns that we all share in our research are important, but these methodological ambitions are impossible to fully realize except in those situations, for example, of decision making, where the basic premises are identical and can be held constant. These are rare in political contexts and they are usually the least interesting, because the outcome could be predicted without an elaborate formal model.

The second is what data sets really capture. Because they are a simplification of reality, they inevitably examine only what may be called the tip of the iceberg. It is inevitably partial. The cross-sectional survey, therefore, is a snapshot that leaves out a number of issues and fails to capture temporal changes. Even if some of these are controlled for in the analysis, such surveys are never anything more than one contribution of many to the answers we look for. The study of the relationship between economic development and democracy – one of the more popular themes in comparative politics – is a case in point. It has been studied on and off ever since Lipset (1959) did his study almost fifty years ago. Many scholars have added their own twist to the interpretation of this issue, showing an ever-increasing number of correlations that were overlooked in Lipset's original work. This is not the place to dwell on this issue at length, only to acknowledge that what looked like a convincing correlation in the late 1950s is now much more complex and multidimensional. The conclusion that political scientists must be ready to draw, therefore, is that the more we know, the less certain we are of making predictions; the more specialized we become, the less relevant we are to the social and political issue around us. We do not accumulate knowledge in the linear fashion of physical scientists. Nor can we claim, like pioneers in medicine, that our findings or the methods we used to generate them have implications for the human body. Our research is inevitably more fragmented, but also society-oriented. It tries to rein in variation, not what is already offered to us by nature as common to all. Therefore, we are more like the pharmacologist who recognizes that there is a general recommendation for how many pills and how often patients should take them, but also knows that humans vary genetically and therefore the effects are bound to differ from one person to another. The fact that some people are better than others in remembering to take their pills adds another element of uncertainty. The reality of the pharmacologist captures best the circumstances in which students of politics try to pursue their science. It is full of yes-buts.

This book is produced in that spirit. I recognize that all knowledge in political science is partial and rests on porous ground. With this in mind, it becomes especially important that all this knowledge is occasionally brought together into a comprehensive framework for stocktaking. The frame of this book is built on as much political science research that I have been able to read and interpret, and is complemented by a range of studies from neighboring disciplines that political scientists have often cited in their own work on Africa. The frame no doubt has its holes, but I try to demonstrate what the shared knowledge is on which I base my own analysis.

Why Africa Matters Today

Themes and geographical regions come and go within the field of comparative politics. Africa held center stage in the 1960s. In the 1990s Latin America had grabbed that position, because of its own transition to democracy, a theme that became popular throughout the field in recent years. The study of both economic and political reform since the 1990s has focused on the role of institutions. The new institutional economics (NIE), drawing on scholars like North (1990), has been highly influential in both economics and political science. As it has continued to permeate the two disciplines, however, it has become increasingly clear that the premises on which the theory rests often have to be relaxed, especially in the study of economies and polities outside the more developed industrial societies. This drift has now proceeded far enough that there is a growing recognition that formal institutions do not explain everything. Much agency in both economics and politics relies on informal behavior and institutions. Agency so inspired may sometimes contradict the operations of formal institutions and contribute to increased transaction costs. But it may also have the opposite effect: reducing such costs and making organizations more effective.

Informal institutions, therefore, are ubiquitous. Their role can be studied in many different contexts, for example, business management, market trans-actions, political decision making, electoral campaigning, and bureaucratic problem solving. These institutions may have positive or negative conse-quences, but the important point is that scholars can really not ignore them. They constitute a new research frontier in political science and, increasingly in economics, especially among those who work with policy. For instance, frustration is growing in the international finance institutions and among bilateral donor agencies because their models do not really have much impact. They lack political traction in many countries, not the least in Africa. It is for this reason that the role of informal institutions is important also for development-policy analysts.

Africa is the best starting point for exploring the role of informal institu-tions that have become increasingly important around the world for at least four good reasons. One is globalization and the growing challenge it poses to states and thereby formal institutions. Another is the growing disparity between rich and poor that follows in the wake of economic liberalization of national economies. The third is postmodernism and the decline of foun-dationalism in favor of fundamentalism. Modernization may have had its weaknesses both as theory and development practice. We are now beginning to see the same with postmodernism. Its relativism and notion that what is right and wrong must be interpreted in a context takes away the sense of right and wrong that used to prevail in policy circles. The fourth reason is the growth of global terrorism. Terrorist groups are informal institutions that threaten not only states, but also innocent citizens. Nonetheless, so are many of the responses to terrorism. For instance, fear in the United States has given rise not only to a growing importance for Christian evangelism, but also to the desire to seek security in informal institutions based on face-to-face reciprocities. These institutions tell us that formal institutions are not forever and that when faced with threats to our day-to-day existence, we tend to resort to the *Kernkultur* of immediate and direct reciprocities. What so many American citizens have experienced in recent years is pre-cisely what many people in Africa encounter daily. The world has become smaller in the sense that the challenges facing people in the developing world are also becoming part of the reality of people in the developed world. This has implications for political science research. No region is necessarily more important than any other when it comes to determining what research is important. Right now, with the growing interest in informal institutions, Africanists have a golden opportunity to prove their region's significance to the rest of the field of comparative politics and beyond.

Several factors help explain why informal institutions have been largely ignored in the past. One factor is the inclination in mainstream political science to ignore the private realm. Researchers do not have to be feminists or postmodernists to acknowledge the role power plays outside the public realm or that power relations have political implications beyond the mere social. Politics is not autonomous of society, nor is society just made of organized interests. It is in the interaction between state and society, between things public and private, that increasingly important institutional developments take place. Although those in power may have an interest in formalizing these institutions, they do not always succeed. There is certainly a significant informalization going on in every society, developed as well as developing. The process may manifest itself primarily in incidental informal behavior, such as when people pay contractors under the table to avoid paying the value-added tax to the state. Once this behavior is regularized and more than a few individuals practice it, informal institutions emerge. Individuals behaving this way respond to an unwritten rule that can be described as rational. Individuals paying their contractors escape the burden of the state; the latter agree to the deal in the hope that they will get more business that way. The parties engage in morally hazardous behavior, but they take the chance because there is no outsider able to punish them. The emergence in this case of informal behavior and institutions is a manifestation of the invisible power that exists in society and helps share outcomes.

The line between institution and culture, between public and private, therefore, is much less clear-cut than our mainstream theories assume. Culture cannot be dismissed as irrelevant to political scientists because it is the foundation on which not only formal, but also informal institutions arise. The degree to which informal institutions are manifest, and thus easy to study empirically, differs from country to country, but they can never be ignored altogether. Formal institutions, although limited in their longevity, reflect culture as much as informal institutions do. Informal institutions challenge their legitimacy when a discrepancy occurs between the cultural norms guiding formal and informal institutions. This is nowhere more apparent than in African countries. That is why there is a reason to think about informal behavior and institutions as a system driven by a social logic that is different from market economics or the way the modern state operates. I have referred to it as the economy of affection (Hyden 1980).

The new emphasis on informal institutions recognizes that political economy choices are socially and culturally embedded. Economy and culture are no longer two separate spheres, but analytically as well as empirically are understood as one. This interest has been empirically nurtured in recent years by changes in the global economy that exacerbate conflicts between capital and people. For instance, the many corporate scandals around the world indicate that this conflict is no longer merely between capital and labor, as understood in the orthodox Marxian political economy, but one that manifests itself in terms of strict adherence to formal rules as opposed to creative formation of informal rules that circumvent the former. This type of conflict is evident also in the contradiction between free capital and bound labor (Sassen 1998). Because movement of people across borders is strictly regulated, informal behavior and institutions develop to cope with these formal restrictions. The point is that this new research frontier is present in many everyday situations both in developed and developing societies. Again, though, informality is the mainstay of life in Africa. How it operates there is of both intellectual and strategic significance.

This becomes especially apparent as one turns to the link between politics and development in Africa. For several decades now, the region's development concerns have been part of the research agenda of economists, political scientists, and often also of anthropologists and geographers. This connection has helped shape the research agenda in all these disciplines partly by the policy concerns it has raised, partly because of the funding it provides. This means that what social scientists interested in Africa have done is to adjust their scholarly interests to fit the priorities expressed by the key agencies in the international development community. A brief recapitulation of how this has affected research may be in order.

It began in the 1960s with the emergence of a new field – development economics. In the perspective of these economists, development in the emerging states of what has since become the Third World would be best achieved through transfers of capital and technical expertise (Rapley 1996). This philosophy prevailed in the last days of colonial rule and in the early years of independence in Africa. Lodged in a modernization paradigm – implying that development is a move from traditional to modern society – this approach was characterized by great confidence and optimism. Although it was not reconstruction (as with the Marshall Plan in Western Europe after the Second World War) but development that was attempted in Africa, the challenge looked easy. Defined largely in technocratic terms, development was operationalized with little or no attention to context. The principal task was to ensure that institutions and techniques that had proved successful in modernizing the Western world could be replicated.

The second phase began in the latter part of the 1960s, when analysts and practitioners recognized that the assumption that development would trickle down from the well endowed to the poor, thus generating ripple effects, proved mistaken. Convinced that something else had to be done to reduce global poverty, the international community decided that a sector approach would be more effective. The important thing in this second phase, therefore, became how to design integrated programs that addressed the whole range of what analysts identified as basic human needs. Human capital mattered. Whereas capacity building in the first phase had been concentrated on the elite, the second phase focused on such areas as adult education and universal primary education under the assumption that these measures were integral parts of a poverty-oriented approach to development (Kuznets 1955).

At the end of the 1970s there was another shift, this time of even greater consequence than the first. It was becoming increasingly clear that governments typically could not administer the heavy development burden that had been placed on them. This was very apparent in sub-Saharan Africa, where the state lacked the technical capacity, but this was acknowledged also elsewhere because of bureaucratic shortcomings. Government agencies simply did not work very efficiently in the development field. Placing all development eggs in one basket, therefore, was being increasingly questioned as the most useful strategy. So was the role of the state in comparison with the market as an allocating mechanism of public resources (Meyer et al. 1985). As analysts went back to the drawing board, the challenge was no longer how to manage or administer development as much as it was identifying the incentives that may facilitate it.

The World Bank, mandated by its governors, took the lead on this issue and with reference to sub-Saharan Africa, the most critical region, produced a major policy document outlining the proposed necessary economic reforms (World Bank 1981). This report was to serve as the principal guide for structural adjustment in Africa in the 1980s, although the strategy was also applied in other regions of the world. These reforms, combined with parallel financial stabilization measures imposed by the International Monetary Fund, were deemed necessary to get the prices right and to free up resources controlled by the state that could be potentially better used and managed by other institutions in society – particularly the private sector. However, this period also witnessed the increase in voluntary organizations around the world and preliminary efforts to bring such organizations into the development process. With more responsibilities delegated to the market, private and voluntary organizations could play a more significant role in working with people to realize their aspirations, whether individual or communal (Schumacher 1973; Korten and Klauss 1985). Even though the economic reforms tended to create social inequities, the basic premise was that nongovernmental organizations could do with the people what the government had failed to do for the people.

The new thing since the 1990s has been the growing recognition that politics and development are not two separate and distinct activities. Development analysts, especially economists, had always treated development as independent of politics. Out of respect for national sovereignty, donors and governments upheld this separation for a long time. Although the new creed in the international development community is controversial in government circles in the Third World, there has been a growing recognition that getting politics right is, if not a precondition, at least a requisite of development. The implication is that conventional notions of state sovereignty are being challenged and undermined by the actions taken by the international community, both international agencies and bilateral donors. For example, human rights violations, including those that limit freedom of expression and association, are being invoked as reasons for not only criticizing governments of other countries, but also for withholding aid if no commitment to cease such violations and improvement is made. Underlying this shift toward creating a politically enabling environment is the assumption that development, after all, is the product of what people decide to do to improve their livelihoods. People, not governments (especially those run by autocrats), constitute the principal force of development. They must be given the right incentives and opportunities not only in the economic, but also in the political arena. They must have a chance to create institutions that respond to their needs and priorities. Development, therefore, is no longer a benevolent top-down exercise.

As long as politics and development were treated as two separate phenomena, what political scientists had to say about development was at best of secondary interest. Since the 1990s, however, this has changed. The result is that political scientists have increasingly focused their work on issues of democratization and regime transition. The question that must be raised at this point, however, is: Are we really helping to get politics right?

Working under the mantle of the international development agencies has its own costs. The agencies wish to see results quickly and they look for a blueprint for their interventions. Much of what has happened in recent years under the rubric of "good governance" reflects these problems. The main ambition has been to carry out transfer of institutions from the north to the south, based on the assumption that somehow they realign the incentive structures to foster improved forms of governance. The emphasis on strengthening civil society, free and fair elections, and more transparency and public accountability in the public sector are noble aims – and they enjoy support in certain circles in African countries. The way these attempted transfers have occurred, however, has typically ignored the social and political realities on the ground in Africa.

For this reason, there is need to take a step backward and reflect on why these proposed incentive structures do not work in Africa. The study of politics in Africa over the years has generated an enormous amount of insights that cannot be just cast aside at this point. It is precisely because of incorporating past knowledge with new that we can better understand and advise those with responsibility for making policy in and/or for Africa. I hope to bring a comprehensive and also broader perspective on politics in Africa thereby showing not only the opportunities, but also the limits to what can be done. This book is meant to bring a dose of realism to the debate about the African plight without falling into the trap of Afro-pessimism.

STUDYING AFRICA

Africa is both huge and complex. Any attempt to write a review of what is happening on the continent faces challenges and difficulties. This volume is no exception. The problem begins at the level of data collection. What kind of information is available? How reliable is it? These are questions that most scholars in our information-rich age never have to – or bother to – address. Data available from formal institutions in developed societies are usually taken for granted. They are trusted to be objective descriptors of reality. Scholarship on Africa can never start from such a premise. Much of what happens in African economies and societies is not captured in national statistics. Even information gathered for such purposes is fraught with methodological weaknesses (Yeats 1990; van de Walle 2001). For instance, sampling is very difficult in situations where civil administration data are nonexistent or only partially developed. National population censuses, accordingly, have to be taken with a grain of salt, as one has to treat public opinion surveys and other studies drawing on available civil administration data. These are significant provisos that both reader and researcher must bear in mind.

Nonetheless, a scholarly analysis of Africa cannot avoid facts and figures. Limitations notwithstanding, data constitute important markers of both description and analysis. The official information that is available constitutes the common ground on which analysts base their arguments. One relies on it, but there is reason to keep a healthy distance from it, realizing its shortcomings.

Although facts and figures are being collected at a country level and included in national accounts and statistics, the real data banks for Africa – especially its economic and social development – are hosted by international organizations. In other words, the summary information that covers the continent as a whole is most easily found in agencies like the World Bank, United Nations Children's Fund (UNICEF), or the United Nations Development Programme. The latter, for instance, publishes an annual Human Development Report with information that transcends the more economistic data sets provided by the World Bank. Fortunately for today's students and researchers, most of this information is also available on the web through various sites and search engines. For more country-specific information, some African governments – or parliaments – have websites on which some public information is available. These sites, however, are still in need of development, both in terms of content and style of presentation.

Africa's Geography[1]

The landmass of Africa is approximately 25 percent larger than that of North America, including Canada and Alaska. It is roughly the same as Europe and South America together. With three-quarters of its landmass situated between the tropic of Cancer and the tropic of Capricorn, Africa is mostly tropical with hot summers and mild winters. Elevation moderates the climate especially in eastern and southern Africa. Africa's two highest mountains – Mount Kilimanjaro in Tanzania and Mount Kenya in Kenya – are situated in the immediate vicinity of the equator and have caps covered with snow.

Africa is one of the fastest urbanizing regions of the world. The urban residents as percentage of the total population rose from 23 percent in 1980 to 36 percent in 2002. Lagos, the former capital of Nigeria and its most important port city, is the single largest metropolitan area in sub-Saharan Africa with over ten million people. The second is the Pretoria/Witwatersrand/ Vereeniging (PWV) conglomeration around Johannesburg in South Africa with over seven million people. Third is the Kinshasa/Brazzaville area that spans the lower Congo River with close to six million people. Because so many people are not officially registered as residents, the total number is difficult to know in these areas as well as in others. Yet, there are many metropolitan areas that accommodate two million people or more, for example, Cape Town and Durban in South Africa, Maputo in Mozambique, Abidjan in Ivory Coast, Nairobi in Kenya, and Dar es Salaam in Tanzania.

Over 700 million people live in sub-Saharan Africa. More than 1,000 languages are spoken across the continent. Arabic, which dominates in the countries north of Sahara, is also spoken in countries in the Sahel belt immediately south of the desert, notably, Mauritania and Sudan. Mandinke, Yoruba, and Hausa are dominant languages in West Africa; Swahili is most prominent in eastern Africa; Zulu, Sotho, and Xhosa are the most commonly spoken languages in southern Africa. Many countries have chosen the language of their former colonial power for official and business purposes. Thus, French is the official language in twenty-one countries, English in twenty, and Portuguese in five. Cameroon and Mauritius use both English and French as official languages.

Apart from local animistic religions, which continue to exist on the continent, Christianity and Islam are the most important religions. Orthodox Christianity reached northeastern Africa from Syria in the fourth century after Christ. Much later Catholicism was brought to Africa by Portuguese and Dutch seafarers, some of whom also settled in the southern parts of the continent. The Republic of South Africa was established by descendants of these early settlers in the beginning of the twentieth century. Islam came to

---

[1] For information presented in this subsection, I have relied on de Villiers (2003).

the countries south of the Sahara via North Africa, partly through trade, partly through warfare (*jihad*); both Christianity and Islam have grown in numbers at the expense of believers in animistic forms of religion. Within Christianity, Catholicism remains the dominant denomination, but protestant churches have been successful in proselytizing and have significant followings in many countries. Today, Christianity dominates in nineteen countries, Islam in eleven.

Geography has played its part in shaping the African predicament in three important ways. One is through the width of the Saharan desert that separates sub-Saharan Africa from the rest of the continent, which instead was connected to Europe through trade across the Mediterranean Sea. To be sure, there were long-distance trade routes through the desert, but technology available in precolonial days limited the opportunities for indigenous Africans to create banking houses and other finance institutions that became so important in developing the Mediterranean region. The second geographic barrier is the climate and vegetation that discouraged the movement of people and animals across long distances in much of Africa. Not only did these factors hinder trade among Africans, but it also locked them out of the innovations in Europe and the Middle East that helped spur the modernization of those regions. For instance, neither oxen nor horses were introduced into African agriculture. Without these draft animals, Africans were also deprived of access to the plow – another modernizing influence in both Europe and Asia. The third barrier can be found in the main rivers of the continent – including the Nile, Congo, Niger, and Zambezi – which have been difficult to travel for exploring the hinterland. Thus, prior to colonialism in the beginning of the twentieth century, the interior of Africa remained largely unknown. Much of it was surrounded by myths that suited the Western image of Africa as the Dark Continent.

Africa's History[2]

Africa's history does not begin with European colonization, as is sometimes assumed. In fact, much of human history that is still to be uncovered can be found in sub-Saharan Africa. Scientific discoveries of early humans have already been made in both eastern and southern Africa. These indicate that Africa may well have been the cradle of humankind. Even though paleontologists and other scientists still disagree among themselves on some critical points regarding the origin of people, there is no doubt that Africa is central to their work. In this respect, Africa is the real Old World. This is not the place for a lengthy review of the continent's history. Suffice it to mention a few salient features of the colonial period.

---

[2] For the information presented in this section, I have relied most heavily on Middleton et al. (1996), Young (1994), and Brown (2004).

The latter part of the nineteenth century witnessed a surge of interest in Africa among Europeans. Industrialization and urbanization in Europe had created demands for new products that were grown in Africa, for example, palm oil. Improved communications like the steamship facilitated travel; the telegraph paved the way for new information flows. The opening of the Suez Canal in 1869 made travel to and from the African continent easier. Growing knowledge of tropical medicine and the onset of geographical exploration also helped open the interior of Africa to outsiders and their interest. Much of it centered on the continent's natural and mineral resources. The discovery of diamonds in Kimberley in South Africa in 1867 was one such milestone. Britain and France were most active among the European powers during this scramble for Africa.

The colonial period in Africa began officially with the Berlin Conference in 1884–85, during which the African continent was divided into colonies between the principal European powers at the time: Britain, France, Germany, Belgium, Italy, Portugal, and Spain. Ambition and power allowed Britain and France to grab control of the majority of these new colonies. Some of the smaller countries like Portugal were able to retain control of territory in Africa thanks to the diplomatic support of Britain in its attempt to fight off pressures from France and Germany. Effective control in many of these places was established only much later, in some cases not until the beginning of the twentieth century. The colonial interlude – as historians typically describe it – lasted until 1960, although the continent was not fully liberated until thirty years later when the white apartheid regime in South Africa agreed to majority rule. It was quite brief. For instance, Kenya's first president was born in 1896 before the British had established full control of that colony. He served as president from 1963 to 1978. In other words, in his own lifetime he had experienced the full length of the colonial period and also ruled his own country for no less than fifteen years!

The European colonization of Africa was carried out using both carrot and whip. Many African chiefs realized that they could not defeat the European invaders and they preferred to strike a deal, often on very unfavorable terms. Other African chiefs – or groups of people – did engage in resistance and warfare. As military control gave way to civil administration in the colonies, economic issues became more important. Infrastructural investments were made in railways, roads, and harbors in order to facilitate exportation of crops and minerals. Taxation was used as a means of inducing smallholding farmers to engage in cash crop production. Although wage labor became important over time, conscription of labor by force was common in less developed areas, like the Portuguese colonies, until the 1960s. Concessionary companies and white settlers, especially in southern Africa, were also important actors on the agricultural scene in colonial days.

Where settlers monopolized land and resources, colonialism tended to bear harshly on traditional African life. Elsewhere, however, the direct

European impact tended to be much less. The very small number of European colonial officials in these places necessitated reliance on African intermediaries. This system, indirect rule, meant that African chiefs were incorporated into the colonial system of rule. Despite this form of integration of local African rulers into the administration, the British colonial doctrine emphasized the separateness of its colonies from the imperial power. Within the extension of this doctrine was the notion of political independence for the colonies in the distant future. The French practiced a different doctrine, which envisaged the assimilation of Africans as citizens of a greater France, although little was done to put this into reality until after the Second World War. These contrasting principles were important in shaping the process of decolonization and, subsequently, postcolonial relationships.

Racial discrimination was deeply resented by those Africans who had been educated during colonial days. It was especially pronounced in the British colonies where the notion of separateness was put into practice both in official and social contexts. In some places, workers protested or revolted for the same reason. In other instances, revolts were caused by disputes over taxes. Especially well known and studied is such a riot by women in eastern Nigeria in 1929.

African resistance to colonialism was initially focused primarily on improving the conditions for the indigenous people. Many of the initial organizations were so-called welfare societies, trade unions, social clubs, and sports clubs (Hodgkin 1956). Only after the Second World War did the aspirations begin to include political objectives, initially self-government, and soon thereafter full political independence. Developments in the French colonies were especially important. In 1944 the government-in-exile led by General de Gaulle, which was based in Congo-Brazzaville, one of the French colonies, had promised Africans a new deal. In 1946, Africans were given the right to elect their own representatives in the French National Assembly. The political parties active in France established their own branches or associates in the colonies and Africans were elected on party tickets that were linked to these French parties. Loi Cadre in 1956 was meant to guarantee universal suffrage to all African colonies, but to the dismay of many African nationalists, it was applied in such a way that the two federations – one for west and a second for equatorial French Africa – were withered away. The British began their decolonization in West Africa. Although a series of incidents in the Gold Coast (now Ghana) and Nigeria helped trigger nationalist sentiments, the transfer of power in both countries went relatively smoothly. Without wishing to take anything away from those who so gallantly fought for political sovereignty on the day of political independence, the ceremony was first and foremost pomp and circumstance.

The most important aspect of the decolonization process for the purpose of this volume is the acceleration of the progress to independence that took place in the 1950s. The colonial governments had not anticipated such a quick transition. To the extent that they were planning a peaceful transition during which they could make Africans familiar with principles of governance associated with their own democratic states, they never got time to put it into practice. The result was that political organizations remained movements that were more interested in overturning the whole regime than to participate within the specific parameters of parliamentary rule.

Africa's Economy[3]

The majority of the African economies are both small and fragile, and there is evidence that the region south of the Sahara is being increasingly left behind in the global economy. Details of this will be provided in some of the subsequent chapters. The most important information to share at this point is that poverty is rampant in Africa. As many as 40 percent of the population live on less than one U.S. dollar a day, while as many as 75 percent live on less than two U.S dollars a day. Africa's share of the poorest people in the world increased from 25 to 30 percent during the 1990s. Unlike all other developing regions, output per capita in Africa was lower in 2002 than it was thirty years earlier. This does not mean that Africa lacks wealthy people. They are also on the increase and with that process in full swing the gap between rich and poor is also growing. Only Latin America has a more unequal distribution of income than Africa.

Another piece of factual information that cannot be ignored is that economic growth in Africa during colonial times and in the first few years after independence was at par with other regions of the world. For instance, between 1960 and 1973 – in most African countries coinciding with the first decade of political independence – the region's economic growth was no different from that of South Asia. Africa's inability to keep pace with the rest of the world, therefore, has occurred mainly since the early 1970s. To put this in perspective: In 1957, when Ghana became independent, it was more prosperous than the Republic of Korea (South Korea). Today, Korea's economy is eighty times larger than that of Ghana. In 1965, the economic output in Indonesia and Nigeria was roughly the same. Thirty-five years later, that of Indonesia was eight times bigger.

The Gross Domestic Product (GDP) per capita in many African countries has declined since the 1970s. The average GDP per head in 2001 was U.S.$567 compared with U.S.$660 in 1980. In some of the least developed countries like Niger, Togo, and Zambia, the decline during that period was as high as 30 percent. The poorest countries were in fact poorer in 2003 than they were forty years earlier at political independence, despite an economic recovery in the late 1990s. It is no surprise, therefore, that out of the

---

[3] For information in this section I have relied primarily on *African Development Indicators 2004*, published by the World Bank (2004), *The Economist* (2004), and Sparks (2004).

forty-nine countries classified by the United Nations as least developed in 2001, thirty-four were in sub-Saharan Africa.

Africa's poverty is not because the continent is short of natural resources. To be sure, the soils in the region vary in quality and in many places are not very fertile. Yet, agriculture was developed even on poor soils in colonial days but has been allowed to degrade in recent decades, making Africa the only region where per capita agricultural production has been going down. Africa's real wealth to date is buried in its old rocks. The region has a diversity of minerals that exceeds that of most other regions of the world. Countries like South Africa, Ghana, and Tanzania, together with Russia, are among the top producers of gold in the world. Angola, Botswana, Democratic Republic of Congo, Sierra Leone, South Africa, and Tanzania are all principal suppliers of diamonds in the world market. Strategic minerals that are used in the defense industries in the United States and around the world are also in generous supply in Africa. Finally, oil and natural gas are becoming increasingly important to the region's economic growth and export. Nigeria is a main supplier to the United States, as is Angola. Gabon and Cameroon are strategically important to France as producers and exporters of oil. Chad, Equatorial Guinea, and Sudan are among other countries in Africa that have recently entered the world market as significant exporters of oil.

Despite its riches, African countries have not been very successful in wooing investors to the continent. Globalization in the past twenty years has generated more intense competition for capital. Developing countries raised their share of foreign direct investment (FDI) from 21 percent in 1988 to 42 percent ten years later. The bulk of this money has gone to Asian countries. Africa's share in 1988 was only 5 percent of all FDI going to developing country regions. FDI as percentage of Gross National Income (GNI) was less than 1 percent. Twenty-nine states in Africa did not even manage to attract U.S.$50 million in foreign investment. Nigeria received by far the most – U.S.$1,800 million – primarily for developments in the petroleum sector.

A significant bottleneck for economic development in many countries of the region is its poor physical infrastructure. Essential services such as electric power, water, roads, railways, ports, and communications have been neglected, especially in the rural areas. In addition to long distance, it is often the poor state of the physical infrastructure that makes transportation costs in the region exceedingly high. Whereas such costs have gone down in all other regions of the world, they have gone up in Africa. To put this in perspective: Excluding South Africa, the whole region has fewer paved roads today than Poland, one of the poorest member countries of the European Union!

For the purpose of this volume the most important things to reiterate about the region's economy is that it remains undeveloped and is becoming increasingly marginalized in a competitive global economy where other

TABLE 1. *Intervals for Political Independence in Africa*

Interval	Number of Countries
1955–59	3
1960–64	26
1965–69	6
1970–79	9
1980–89	1
1990–99	2

developing regions are making the fastest headway. Africa continues to rely on exporting primary commodities. It cannot generate enough investment capital from within and is largely failing to attract foreign investments. Its countries often have to sell themselves cheap in the global market in order to attract investors.

Political Facts about Africa[4]

Sub-Saharan Africa consists of forty-eight independent states.[5] All but two are former colonies. Ethiopia is the oldest country in the region. It was never colonized. Liberia was established as an independent republic with the assistance of the United States in 1847. South Africa gained political independence under white minority rule in 1910, but shifted officially to majority rule in 1994. All other states gained their independence after 1956, with Sudan the first and Ghana the second in 1957. As Table 1 shows, the majority became politically sovereign in the 1960s. Virtually all countries belonging to the British and French empires gained their independence in the 1960s; the only exception was Rhodesia, now Zimbabwe. Like the white minority in South Africa earlier, the European settlers in Rhodesia declared unilateral independence in 1965, but fifteen years later they were forced by African liberation movements to transform the system into majority rule. The rise in number of independent states in the 1970s is explained by the demise of the Portuguese empire. Its five colonies – Angola, Cape Verde, Guinea-Bissau, Mozambique, and Sao Tome and Principe – all gained their independence in 1975 soon after the fascist regime in Lisbon had been overthrown in a military coup. The last country to gain independence is Eritrea, which broke away from Ethiopia.

---

[4] The presentation in this section relies primarily on *The Economist* (2004), Gleditsch et al. (2003), and Sparks (2004).

[5] Algeria, Egypt, Libya, Morocco, and Tunisia are considered part of Africa north of the Sahara. In international politics, they are considered part of the Middle East region.

TABLE 2. *How African Leaders Left Office, 1960–2003*[6]

Cause	1960–69	1970–79	1980–89	1990–99	2000–03	Total
Overthrown in coup, war, or invasion	27	30	22	22	6	107
Died of natural or accidental causes	2	3	4	3	0	12
Assassination (not part of coup)	1	1	1	1	0	5
Retired voluntarily	1	2	5	9	2	19
Lost election	0	0	1	12	6	19
Other (interim or caretaker regime)	6	8	4	14	1	33

In 1999, a fifth of all Africans lived in countries battered by war. Warfare has been common in Africa since the 1970. The twenty-eight wars fought in the region between 1970 and 2004 resulted in more than seven million refugees. The single most devastating in terms of human life is the thirty-year-old civil war in Sudan, which cost two million people their lives between 1972 and 2002. As many as one million people were killed in the fighting between Tutsis and Hutus in Rwanda in 1994. The civil war in Angola that lasted twenty-seven years caused the death of at least half a million people. It must be recognized that most warfare in Africa has been within, rather than between, states. Despite the artificiality of the region's political boundaries, which were established by the colonial powers over the heads of the local people and their leaders, they have remained intact since independence. In fact the only real interstate war has been between Ethiopia and Eritrea. Ironically, it was fought over the validity of a particular map drawn by the Italians as they tried to occupy the Horn of Africa in the late nineteenth century.

When African countries became independent, with a few exceptions like the ex-Portuguese colonies, they inherited the basic principles of a parliamentary system. To be sure, Africans were never really given time to adopt it as their own. They abandoned it soon after independence in favor of a presidential system, the assumption being that it would give the new states the strong executive they needed in order to stay together and develop economically. These systems soon turned highly authoritarian. Many became dysfunctional. The result was that between 1960 and 1979 no fewer than fifty-nine heads of state were toppled or assassinated. Only three retired peacefully.

[6] This table is borrowed from *The Economist* (2004), which in turned got it from Dr. Arthur Goldsmith of Harvard University.

The introduction of multiparty politics and competitive elections in most countries since the early 1990s means that being voted out of power is an increasing possibility. Eighteen heads of state have lost elections and been replaced by someone else. This new political dispensation, however, has also exacerbated conflict in some countries and some rulers have found it hard to accept the prospect of losing an election. The overall picture of how politics is being conducted in Africa, therefore, is mixed.

If a public opinion poll carried out by the Afrobarometer[7] in 2003 is anything to go by, there are strong objections to nondemocratic government and strong support for democracy as the least bad system of government. Although the poll was conducted in only in one-third of all forty-eight countries,[8] it provides an indication of individual preferences among Africans when interviewed in private. Seventy-seven percent of the respondents disapprove of coups, 76 percent reject dictatorship, and 67 percent object to one-party rule. On average, however, more than one out of five respondents believed that what kind of system of rule a country has doesn't make a difference to ordinary folks like themselves. One of five South African respondents also thought that opposition parties should be barred from standing for office.

These figures do not translate into public pressure on leaders to behave more democratically. There is no such thing as an effective public opinion that operates with a view to changing regime or policy. The only pressure in such a direction comes from the international community, mainly through the diplomatic missions and development assistance agencies of OECD countries.[9] In response to the new political circumstances that have emerged since the 1990s, some African governments have also been active in taking the initiative to create a better political and administrative framework for the region's social and economic development. The New Partnership for Africa's Development (NEPAD) is very ambitious in its effort to holistically and comprehensively tackle the continent's many obstacles to development. More specifically, its priorities include (a) creating peace, security, and stability, (b) investing in people, (c) promoting industrialization, (d) increasing the use of information and communications technology, and (e) developing basic infrastructure.

---

[7] The poll was conducted in 2003 by a consortium of African and American social scientists. See www.afrobarometer.org.

[8] The countries included in the survey were Botswana, Cape Verde, Ghana, Kenya, Lesotho, Malawi, Mozambique, Namibia, Nigeria, Senegal, South Africa, Tanzania, Uganda, and Zambia. I have referred to "one-third" in the text because the actual number – fifteen – is approximate enough to that.

[9] OECD is the acronym for the Organization for Economic Cooperation and Development, which is made up of all the industrialized countries in Europe and North America as well as Japan and Korea.

NEPAD is heralded as an African initiative and has attracted initial support because of the promise by many, if not all, of Africa's leaders to include a regular review of their governance performance. It is too early to say how far this – the latest – initiative aimed at addressing the African development quandary will go. International donors wish to believe that this is different from previous attempts but remain guarded with regard to how genuine the commitment is among African government leaders to the new governance agenda.

ORGANIZATION OF THIS VOLUME

This volume is made up of twelve chapters and there is logic to its organization. The second chapter introduces a common thread in African politics ever since the days of struggle for independence from the colonial powers: the effort by its political leaders to shape a future based on Africa's own cultural idioms. This ambition has both a temporal and a spatial dimension. In the days of decolonization and immediately thereafter, the objective of Africa's leaders was to distance themselves as much as possible from the values and institutions of the colonial state. Some political leaders emphasized this more than others, but they all shared the idea that Africa could be recreated in the image of its own indigenous traditions using – paradoxically – the rhetoric of modernism. Thus, whereas I accept that remnants of colonialism have continued in African societies after independence, I differ from the arguments of several other authors who imply that colonial influences were formative long after independence. Chapter Two, The Movement Legacy, discusses the role that nationalist movements came to play in shaping postindependence politics in Africa. Organized underground to fight an external enemy – the colonial power – it required both secrecy and informality to be successful. Once in power, these movements retained much of their original momentum and never became just another set of political parties. Instead, they claimed monopoly of the political arena while keeping the reins of power in the hands of a very small group of people. This chapter also shows how the movement legacy has lived on and served as a model for political renewal in countries that suffered chaos, tyranny, or other types of decline.

Chapter Three, The Problematic State, reviews the literature on the state in Africa and places it in a comparative perspective. It shows how this institution lacks a social base and thus fails to serve as an instrument in the hands of a particular ruling group or class, and how officials ignore both roles and rules and thus render the state both weak and soft. It further discusses the implications for Africa's chances of making progress in the future. The Economy of Affection, Chapter Four, brings in a discussion of the political economy in Africa that prevails because of the rudimentary social formations that still dominate the continent, and highlights why the state fails to play the role of a corporate body serving society. Above all, here I show the rationale for the significance of informal institutions and how it can be best understood with the help of social exchange theory.

So in the absence of a functioning state, how do African countries govern themselves? The answer is suggested in the title of the next chapter: Big Man Rule. It discusses the phenomenon of neopatrimonialism and how leaders in Africa have typically seen themselves as standing above and beyond the rule of law. Instead of relying on formal institutions, they fall back upon a personalized system of rule in which informal institutions prevail. The second part of this chapter focuses on recent efforts in many African countries to constitutionalize rule into more democratic forms of governance. It shows how unofficial or informal mechanisms nonetheless tend to prevail and create uncertainties regarding which rules apply and to whom.

Where politics dominates, economics takes the back seat. Such is the policy-making reality in African countries. Policy makers tend to make their decisions based on an expressive value rationality rather than on a more instrumentalist calculation of costs and benefits, feasibility, or sustainability. Chapter Six, The Policy Deficit, discusses how African officials approach policy and what its consequences tend to be. It provides an understanding of why policy in African countries rarely leaves behind a living legacy that society can build on and why African governments are not real policy governments.

Having identified the basic features of politics in Africa, the next three chapters more closely examine its underlying dimensions. The Agrarian Question, Chapter Seven, deals with trends in African agriculture since independence and discusses how what was once considered the economic backbone of the continent now has become its Achilles heel. It shows how economic policies have had little positive effect on agricultural production and how peasant households have become increasingly dependent on off-farm sources of income. This chapter discusses how people rely on the economy of affection to pursue strategies that ignore official policy and the work of formal institutions. It compares the position of peasants in African countries with that of peasants in Asia in order to illustrate the problems of replicating a Green Revolution there.

Chapter Eight, Gender and Politics, focuses on how the economy of affection influences the issue of gender and politics. It locates the gender issue in its cultural, social, and economic context showing how it differs in Africa from what is found in Eurasian societies. It discusses the heavy economic burden that African women carry and how, much as a result, their potential outside the household remains underutilized. The chapter concludes by discussing some of the headway African women have made in the economy and in politics despite the heavy odds against which they work.

Ethnicity and Conflict, Chapter Nine, traces the way the concept of ethnicity has featured in the study of African politics and how, more recently, it has been examined, especially in the context of the growing number of intrastate conflicts in the region. It argues that neither ethnicity per se nor access to economic enclave resources is enough to explain the frequency of conflict. Instead, the cause of conflict must be sought in the political realm and especially in the inclination among leaders to demonstrate that they have prestigious followings that give them power and influence in the political game.

The movement legacy has survived because political leaders in Africa have continued to view themselves as engaged in a battle against external forces, often more specifically identified as neocolonialism or The West. Chapter Ten, The External Dimension, argues that external factors are important because they condition the circumstances in which Africans make decisions. They are not determinants, however, because a determining factor implies agency and thus must be attributed to humans acting individually or in concert. This chapter compares the literature on Africa's economic dependence on the world economy in the 1970s with the more recent literature on globalization, and demonstrates that the region is more marginal today than it ever was in the 1970s. This has definite repercussions on how Africans behave and make choices, including how they sustain the movement legacy.

The last two chapters pull things together. Chapter Eleven, So What Do We Know?, shows what the accumulated knowledge of politics in Africa really is. It discusses ten propositions on which there seems to be full agreement in the discipline of political science. Based on this consensus, I offer my own concluding interpretation of the subject matter of this book, discussing its implications for further research and showing how it relates to ongoing interests in the discipline. Chapter Twelve, Quo Vadis Africa?, raises the question of where Africa is going from here. The question arises from the accumulated knowledge demonstrated in this volume and is being answered with some practical policy advice on what to do. Without falling into the trap of providing yet another blueprint, I give some suggestions about the kind of reforms that may be necessary both in African political systems and in the relationship between African governments and their international donor partners.

CONCLUSIONS

Finally, for those familiar with my earlier writings, let me confirm that this book may be seen as a sequitur to *No Shortcuts to Progress*, which came out in 1983. More than twenty years have passed. It is interesting to reflect on differences between then and now. The early 1980s was a time when a strong measure of development optimism still prevailed. The challenge was largely that of shifting the burden from state to market, from public to private and voluntary organizations. There was an accompanying shift in the literature from development administration to development management that recognized development was not merely the prerogative of a public service, but a responsibility that had to be shared by multiple agencies. Today, there is growing awareness that there are no easy institutional fixes. Underlying structural forces limit the extent to which policy provides answers to Africa's predicament. This message is not a cause for pessimism, but only one of caution regarding Africa's development prospects. What it does mean, however, is that governments in Africa and international development agencies have to think outside the box, if they wish to be more effective in pushing the continent forward.

2

The Movement Legacy

This chapter – and the full volume, for that matter – begins from the premise that those of us who study politics in Africa have usually underestimated the symbolic power of the collective experience of colonialism. Few, if any, have lived through these conditions. We have never been treated in the often dehumanizing and certainly derogatory manner in which the colonial masters approached their African subjects. In short, we have difficulties in fully grasping the power of both imagery and rhetoric associated with the first generation of nationalist leaders in Africa. The vehicles for gaining independence were not conventional political parties but social movements that demanded control not only of parliament, but also of society at large. To the Africans fighting for independence, it was a battle in black and white. You were either for us or against us. There was little room for reconciliation with the enemy. This willingness and ability of the early nationalists to stand up to a stronger outside force has continued to appeal to subsequent generations of Africans. They set the tone for others to follow: the notion of the supremacy of politics in defense of colonized people.

To the extent that we look for agency among African leaders, we should focus on their wish to conquer the political kingdom and reverse or oppose the agenda that has been set for them by outsiders, be they the colonial powers as in the past or members of the international community as in more recent years. To fully appreciate this story of fifty years of independence politics, it is appropriate to begin this volume with an analysis of how the supremacy of politics emerged and has since manifested itself, beginning with the early years of independence and moving forward to more recent times. Drawing on the literature on political parties and their relationship to the state, this chapter argues that the nationalist movements left behind a legacy that has made a transition to conventional party politics difficult on the continent.

THE RISE AND PRACTICE OF POLITICAL SUPREMACY

It is no exaggeration that the name of Kwame Nkrumah should feature prominently in any analysis of how the political dynamic in Africa after independence would evolve. As Prime Minister and later the first President of what had been the Gold Coast and is now Ghana, he was directly more responsible than any other person for the wind of change that began to blow over colonial Africa in the 1950s. He was the charismatic and articulate representative of a new generation of West African intellectuals and politicians ready to break with the colonial past. Demands for better wages or more educational opportunities were seen as too deferent and conservative; so was the call for self-government. The only thing that counted in the minds of his generation was full political independence. Drawing on a biblical metaphor, Nkrumah demanded nothing less than the whole political kingdom.[1] With it, he dreamed, everything else would be added onto them. He was the undisputed leader of the Convention People's Party that had defeated the opposition in preindependence elections. Nkrumah came to set the tone, both ideologically and organizationally, for much of the rest of Africa. He helped radicalize the political demands by Africans across the continent. Although his ideas, like those of other African nationalists, had been shaped by exposure to European philosophy, their political claim was to recreate a future for Africa that signified a break with the colonial past. This call has continued to echo throughout the region to this day despite the fact that Nkrumah himself was toppled from power in 1966, only nine years after having led the country to independence.

The full impact of the movement legacy across Africa has not always been appreciated. The more common approach has been to look at the colonial legacy as a prime determinant of development, both economic and political, after independence. The argument here is that, through nationalist movements, it is the response of Africans to the colonial legacy that is most important. This does not take away the role that colonialism has played, but it makes its impact indirect rather than direct. It has conditioned agency on the continent, but it cannot be labeled a determinant factor. The latter requires agency and colonialism itself is not an agent, only a structural legacy. As this chapter also demonstrates, the movement legacy has lived on as a source for political renewal in African countries in more recent times. Political and economic reform, therefore, has come through the renewal and energy that movements can produce. Africa's reliance on movements rather than on formal political parties, however, is associated with its own challenges and problems. Foremost of these are the nature of its agenda and how it can

---

[1] Nkrumah was prone to using religious and other metaphors in his political speeches. For further detail, see for example, Nkrumah (1961) and Apter (1963).

TABLE 3. *The Supremacy of Politics by Period, 1955–Present*

Years	Main Feature	Main Objective
1955–1968	Party state	Order
1969–1981	Development state	Progress
1982–Present	Contracting state	Control

sustain its legitimacy. Africa's history since independence is full of examples of how movements have become liabilities or have been overthrown.

In examining the literature on African politics, it is possible to discern three rather distinct phases during which the supremacy of politics has been exercised with different objectives. I suggest that during the first decade or so after independence, the ultimate aim of politics was to create and sustain a new order. Nationalist leaders, though optimistic about the future, had no experience of exercising power. They were anxious to secure their own position at the helm of the state; hence the rise of what has since been referred to as the party state. In the late 1960s and throughout the 1970s, the objective shifted from order to development. The political leaders realized that they needed to show their ability to develop their countries; hence their interest in grabbing control of the state for purposes of guiding progress. The party state was replaced by the development state. The third phase began in the 1980s and has continued to date. These past two decades have been characterized by international efforts aimed at contracting the state and, therefore, limiting the supremacy of politics, which for the political leaders in these countries has been an affront to their position as heads of sovereign nation-states. This challenge has often had the effect of making the leaders even more anxious to exercise their supremacy, if for no other objective than to ensure their own control of the political process. The main features of the three periods are summarized in Table 3.

I am not arguing that from the perspective of each country, this periodization is set in stone. For some countries, especially those that were late in gaining political independence, these periods have been compressed. Some Africanist scholars may also disagree because they use a different definition of key terms. For example, Widner (1992) writes about the rise of a party state in Kenya, arguing that it was consolidated in that country only during the Moi regime that began in 1978. Admittedly painting in somewhat broad strokes, the main reason for my periodization is to capture the ideological shifts that took place in the postcolonial years and which are reflected in the objectives associated with exercising political supremacy. In this perspective, the notion of a party state with an emphasis on order is the first of three major scenarios that characterize politics after independence in sub-Saharan Africa.

The Party State

The evolution of politics after independence was very much determined by the extent to which the nationalist struggle had been carried out under one or more banners. Because the colonial power was viewed as a common enemy, nationalists in many African countries managed to unite into one dominant political movement. It happened in Ghana and was repeated in most French-speaking countries and later also in Tanganyika, Malawi, and Zambia. As Wallerstein (1961:95) noted, this was the standard pattern. There were other countries, however, where the pattern was less clear-cut. Nigeria had three major political parties, each representing a major ethnic constellation. In Kenya, the nationalists were divided in two major organizations, one representing the two largest ethnic groups, the other drawing support from the smaller ethnic groups in the country.

The first generation of students of African politics tended to treat the nationalist organizations as political parties. There was an understandable inclination at the time to assume that once independence was gained, these organizations would become political parties occupying different sides in the parliament. That they would have difficulty in accommodating themselves to the rules of parliamentary politics was not a major concern in the early literature on Africa's political organizations in the postindependence era. The primary concern was how parties tended to differ in terms of their organization and mode of operation. The concepts used to highlight these differences varied, but pointed in the same direction. Morgenthau (1961) distinguished between mass parties, on the one hand, and cadre or patron parties, on the other. In her view, mass parties claim to represent all the people, have strong institutional leadership, are quite disciplined, and are singularly focused on building a new nation by using organization as a principal instrument. Patron parties, by contrast, rely on personal leadership, are less disciplined, and do not make the same concerted effort to foment a new nation. Another prominent scholar at the time, Hodgkin (1961:69), made a similar distinction between mass and elite parties, the latter reflecting the structure of society as it is, the former trying to impose its own new type of structure upon society. This initial classification was further refined in what became the most influential publication at the time, an edited volume on political parties and national integration (Coleman and Rosberg 1966). With specific reference to criteria such as ideology, popular participation, and organizational aspects, the contributors to this volume agreed that the two dominant patterns among African political parties are best classified as pragmatic-pluralistic and revolutionary-centralizing. The former corresponds to the elite or patron parties listed above, whereas the latter are the equivalents of the mass-party category.

There are at least two reasons why the revolutionary-centralizing pattern became dominant after independence. One is the sense of insecurity that many nationalist leaders experienced once they were in power. The second is the interest leaders had in showing that they could make a difference to their country. The first may be called the challenge of horizontal integration. The nationalist political organizations were typically urban-based and led by members of a relatively small, educated elite. It fell on their shoulders to hold the emerging new nation together as the campaign for independence, manifested in preindependence elections and other political pursuits like protests, strikes, and demonstrations, mobilized mass support based on ethnic loyalties (Geertz 1963; Coleman and Rosberg 1966). Bringing representatives of all significant groups on board the nationalist bandwagon was not particularly difficult during the days of decolonization because there was the perception of a common enemy. After independence, however, the task of holding the coalition together became more challenging. This process had gone out of control in several countries, notably the Congo, where Lumumba had attempted to command a nationalist movement along revolutionary-centralizing lines, but due to a number of factors, including his own personality and intervention by outside agencies, for example, the U.S. Central Intelligence Agency (CIA), had been repelled, captured, and eventually brutally murdered by his Congolese opponents. Events like that no doubt made an impression on political leaders elsewhere on the continent.

Lumumba's intention to create a revolutionary political organization may have been an overstretch in the sense that a country with such ethnic diversity but generally poor communications didn't easily lend itself to such a strategy.[2] For purposes of control and integration, however, the events in the Congo did not deter other nationalist leaders from adopting a revolutionary-centralizing approach to rule. Many of them had been exposed to Marxist-Leninist ideas about political organization, and recognized the importance of uniting under a common ideological banner. In the context of decolonization and building new states, nationalism in Africa was the ideology of the oppressed, not as in Europe, where the bourgeoisie had domesticated that ideology in the nineteenth century (Gellner 1983). Thus, instead of being imbued with a liberal content, it increasingly took on socialist ingredients. This happened at independence or soon thereafter in several West African countries, notably Ghana, Guinea, and Mali. It eventually spread to eastern

---

[2] For interested outside observers and actors, the political rhetoric seemed to matter more than political reality. They were feeling either threatened or inspired by the revolutionary language of Lumumba and his supporters. Even after he had been killed, the image of a country ripe for revolution remained in the minds of many external actors, including governments in the West as well as the East. To the Belgians and the Americans, Congo continued to invoke images of revolutionary savagery. To the Chinese and the Cubans, it constituted a hotbed for revolution. To learn how far this image, based on the original revolutionary rhetoric of Patrice Lumumba and his supporters, was removed from reality, see the publication of Che Guevara's posthumous account of his experience in trying to repeat the Cuban revolutionary success in eastern Congo (Galvez 1999).

and southern Africa, where nationalist parties in Tanzania and Zambia as well as liberation movements in countries that were still colonies adopted a decisively Leninist-inspired approach to political organization, emphasizing the vanguard role of the leadership in mass political parties.

Not all leaders shared this radicalization of the nationalist cause. The difference between the revolutionary and pragmatic approaches to political supremacy became a source of division on the continent.[3] The more pragmatic-pluralist approach to horizontal integration relied on a combination of carrots and sticks. Some leaders of particular ethnic groups were co-opted by being given important positions in the party or the government. Others who refused to be bought were detained. As the cases of Kenya under Kenyatta (1963–78) and Malawi under Banda (1964–1994) suggest, the two nationalist leaders tried to establish their personal hegemony immediately after independence by intimidating or rewarding followers in ways that neutralized others. The extent to which this approach provided for more pluralism than the revolutionary-centralizing version seems to have varied from one country to another. Some scholars have suggested that Kenya under Kenyatta was, relatively speaking, more open than it was in later years when his successor, Daniel arap Moi, was in power (e.g. see Barkan 1994). Given that both used similar methods (but Kenyatta relied more on the state machinery than the party organization), this point can easily be contested. Certainly, the case of Malawi – and several others in the pragmatic-pluralist category – indicates that the supremacy of politics tended to produce authoritarian tendencies. Regarding the challenge of horizontal integration, therefore, there is little evidence to suggest that the more pragmatic approach produced more scope for political pluralism.

The second reason for the revolutionary-centralizing approach becoming predominant is best understood in the context of the challenge of vertical penetration. The notion of political penetration was quite commonly used in the literature in the 1960s and 1970s (e.g. Cliffe, Coleman, and Doornbos 1977). It aimed at capturing the extent to which the party state reached out into society to make a difference. I am modifying the concept by highlighting its specific objective: that of allowing for a vertical penetration by central authority, whether lodged in the ruling party or in the state machinery, or a combination of both as was especially the case in countries that had adopted the revolutionary-centralizing approach.

---

[3] For instance, within the Organization of Africa Unity (OAU) that had been established in Addis Ababa, Ethiopia, in 1963, this difference manifested itself in two blocs, one revolutionary, called the Casablanca group, another pragmatic, called the Monrovia group. All claimed to be nonaligned, but the former leaned much more toward the Communist camp, while the latter had closer ties with Western countries.

The issue of vertical penetration became significant after independence because in the days leading up to independence, the political leadership had emphasized the importance of expanding political participation. One of the battle cries of the nationalist campaign was one person, one vote. Universal suffrage was only extended in the last few years before independence. Most colonies in Africa were able to organize only one or two elections using this principle before political independence was granted. The campaign itself, however, had raised political interest and expectations among members of the public, who initially had been afraid of challenging colonial authority. Once nationalist leaders demonstrated that this authority could be challenged, others were ready to follow because most of them had no problem finding a reason to oppose the occupying power. As Zolberg (1966:21) argues, as participation was extended, most people hitherto uninvolved in politics identified with the dominant party unless there was a strong reason – usually involving primary group ties – for not doing so. The public was open to leadership – and by implication – penetration of central powers in the period that followed independence. Comparing the African voters in the early days of independence with the portrait of their American counterparts provided by the most influential study on the topic at the time (Campbell et al. 1960), Zolberg saw some similarity: regardless of cultural context, the voters would respond to the most powerful available stimulus, whether it was personality or ideology that attracted them. He laments the fact that no empirical study was carried out in West Africa to further probe this issue, but it is worth noting here that my own study on the subject in northwestern Tanzania in the mid-1960s confirmed two important things: one that supports Zolberg's thesis, another that complements it. Villagers in this distant part of Tanzania had indeed joined the bandwagon of the ruling party – Tanganyika African National Union (TANU) – but they also demonstrated a remarkably high level of knowledge both of political personalities and issues (Hyden 1969). Penetration, therefore, was not just ad hoc and confined to influencing the minds of people to vote in a particular way; it had also laid the foundation for a deeper understanding of the situation in which political participation was being encouraged. Furthermore, whether the villagers lived close to the main urban center, had access to education in their immediate vicinity, or were actively involved in commerce made no difference when it came to political knowledge. This observation is important because it contradicts the argument that was commonly applied to West African countries in the 1960s: The nationalist movement was capable of mobilizing the public only at times of elections. The situation that I found in northwestern Tanzania in 1965 was evidence of a strong political organization that had made a difference of both political awareness and orientation.

Tanzania may be an exception because of the relative absence of ethnic rivalries and the possibilities of developing ties cutting across ethnic lines as well as the outstanding ability of the country's foremost nationalist leader, Julius Nyerere, to use cultural idioms that made sense to local people. This was especially well documented in a study by Miller (1970), who demonstrated how the ruling party at the local level got involved in an almost endless number of petty issues that, from a legal perspective, were private rather than public. Miller concludes that in the villages he studied in the mid-60s, the new nationalist movement acted with what amounted to parental authority. Such empirical evidence is not unique. Wherever else the nationalist leaders insisted on establishing a party state, vertical penetration tended to affect people's perception of the relationship between rulers and ruled in line with prevailing cultural idioms. Politics was indeed supreme, even on matters that from a Western horizon would be called the private realm.

The impact of politics in countries where leaders adopted a pragmatic-pluralist approach was generally less dramatic, but it would be wrong to assume that it was not there. It may have been less ideological and more personally discretionary, but there was also a sense that politics was the means to achieve a change in their conditions. It was the question of what this change should be all about that came to the fore in the late 1960s and shifted the concerns from political order to national development.

The Development State

The emergence of a more explicit focus on development was, to a great extent, the result of a failure of the nationalist leadership to meet popular expectations about what political independence was supposed to imply. The nationalists themselves had promoted the idea that the essential experience during the colonial period was exploitation of the local people. By implication, they promised a different state of affairs after independence. By the end of the 1960s, the political leaders had little to show for themselves. The party state had not delivered much, if any, tangible improvement in the lives of the common people. Concern with development, therefore, became paramount for enhancing the political legitimacy of those in power. People expected progress, not decline.

The supremacy of politics suited this new orientation quite well. The late 1960s and the 1970s were the heyday of Keynesian thinking in development economics. The latter implied the role that government plays in managing demand in the economy by providing funding for projects that put money into the pockets of people. Much the same way that the Marshall Plan had helped governments after the Second World War in Western Europe, African governments were seen as being helped by transfers of capital that would raise demands for local products. Although foreign aid had begun already at independence, it was only in the late 1960s and early 1970s that it became a major feature of African development. Foreign aid was viewed as first and foremost a government-to-government transfer. Most of it went straight from one treasury to another with few, if any, questions asked. For instance, no one really questioned whether the state in African countries had the capacity to play the same role that it had in Western Europe after 1945.

The new focus on the development state provided a rationale for continuing the supremacy of politics. Although questions had been raised about the integrity of the political leadership and its interest in public issues during the party-state period, these concerns seemed peripheral to the international community because it promoted the notion of a development state as the mechanism for enhancing progress on the African continent. Bilateral and multilateral donor agencies alike defended this new logic. The World Bank during the time the former U.S. Secretary of Defense Robert McNamara was its president (1968–80) played a pivotal role in promoting and supporting the development-state model.

This model also justified a strong central authority. The distinction that scholars had made during the first period between revolutionary-centralizing and pragmatic-pluralist types of political parties was now replaced by the extent to which the state followed socialist or capitalist policies. The premises of the development state were more in tune with socialism than with capitalism because it implied a strong central authority and guidance. It is no surprise, therefore, that an increasing number of African states became organized along socialist rather than capitalist lines. During this second period, socialist states were generally regarded as being better equipped than capitalist ones to achieve progress. Socialism also provided a stronger rationale for the perpetuation of the movement legacy. Attention during the 1970s shifted from West to East Africa. What happened in the three East African countries of Kenya, Tanzania, and Uganda stands out as most significant during this period.

Tanzania was in many respects the prototype of the development state. President Nyerere had paved the way for socialism by having his ruling party adopt the Arusha Declaration in 1967. It led to nationalization of the major means of production and trade. The Tanzanian state became a virtually monopolistic actor in the country's economy. The ruling party was meant to mobilize the peasantry against bureaucratization much like the so-called Red Guards in China, but state officials, especially after authority had been decenetralized to regional and district levels in 1972, continued to prevail. Decentralization only reinforced what was already a rigid top-down approach to managing development (Coulson 1982). What made the Tanzanian approach especially interesting, however, was Nyerere's ability to justify his new policies with reference to indigenous African values, notably the notion of *ujamaa* – literally, familyhood, but more generically meaning "sharing." This language took away some of the rougher edges that Western analysts associated with a Marxist-Leninist approach to development. During a ten-year period beginning in 1968, Tanzania earned a lot of respect in development circles and was able to translate this into an unusually great influence on the world scene, first in the context of the attempts by Third World countries to establish a new international economic order (NIEO) and later on in the context of so-called south-to-south development efforts.[4] Tanzania during the 1970s was a living example that the supremacy of politics inherent in the movement legacy paid off.

In the shadow of the light shed on Tanzania, neighboring Kenya received much less attention from those interested in funding development. Although the Kenyan government laid claim to having adopted African socialism, its policies looked disingenuous in comparison to the more serious and comprehensive attempt to build socialism in Tanzania. There was a much stronger presence of foreign and domestic capital in Kenya and there was the beginning of a genuine domestic middle class. During the 1970s this trend was castigated as being bad for the country. Relatively little appreciation was expressed in spite of Kenya's ability to show constant economic growth through the 1970s. The approach to development, however, differed more in degree than in kind with what was going on in Tanzania. Kenya was also embracing the development-state approach, albeit more pragmatically than its southern neighbor (Barkan 1984). It attracted foreign funding and it provided the basis for political patronage – an important factor for earning legitimacy. The political leadership, in spite of its interest in building wealth for itself, needed the development state to reproduce itself. Like their Tanzanian counterparts, members of the Kenyan political elite needed access to a state treasury that was seen as engaged in funding development. It is no coincidence that in both countries, almost simultaneously, government committed itself to universal primary education and primary health care in the mid-1970s.

Although Uganda in colonial days had been portrayed as the pearl of Africa, its status in East Africa after independence was overshadowed by what happened in Kenya and Tanzania. Its first president, Milton Obote, never developed the strong profile of Kenya's Kenyatta or Tanzania's Nyerere. In fact, to the extent that Obote had a policy at all for his country, it was a less articulate version of what Nyerere was attempting in Tanzania. He never rose high enough above the rest of the political elite to command its respect. Instead he turned to the army to help him keep control of the country in the late 1960s, a strategy that backfired because the person that Obote had himself promoted to lead the army – Idi Amin – staged a coup in January 1971 and forced the president into exile in Tanzania. Once in

---

[4] President Julius Nyerere served as Chairman of the South Commission in the mid-1980s, when the ideas that he had propagated in the 1970s, however, had already lost much of its luster and relevance.

power, Amin turned out to be an unpredictable and cruel maverick. He tried to sustain some level of legitimacy by expelling the Asian minority that controlled the country's commercial sector in 1972. Most of them ended up in the United Kingdom, Canada, or the United States. His maniacal behavior in power, however, went too far when he decided in 1978 to invade the northwestern corner of Tanzania, claiming that it was part of Uganda. Together with groups of Ugandan fighters resisting Amin, the Tanzanian army fought the invaders back, and forced the tyrant into exile in Saudi Arabia in April 1979 after six months of hostilities. The lesson from Uganda is that even when the nationalist movement collapsed because of inadequate leadership, its legacy of political supremacy continued. In fact, in the absence of a strong political organization, any shackles on the use of politics for discretionary purposes were removed. Its supremacy became a definite liability.

The war with Uganda was an important turning point for Tanzania, because it meant that the country had to allocate much of its scarce resources for military rather than development purposes. Nyerere defended himself, arguing that the donors should not punish him for having tried to defend his country's sovereignty. However, to the donors, the war against Amin became an eye-opener that called into question the extent to which the development state was a sustainable institution in countries with scarce resources that are not always used very efficiently. Because Tanzania had served as an authoritative example of the development state, it also became the first to be effectively scrutinized by the international community in 1979. An initial team from the International Monetary Fund (IMF) visiting Tanzania that year raised a serious warning that the development state was no longer a viable proposition, especially when occupying a monopolistic position in the economy and society. Thus, the first steps toward redefining the development – and by extension, political – agenda for Africa was taken in Tanzania in the wake of ten years of socialism and the war against Amin that left the international community in doubt whether to continue funding a fully state-centered approach to development.

The trends in East Africa had their parallel in West Africa. Guinea and Mali came closest to resembling the socialist model adopted by Tanzania. Ivory Coast and Senegal adopted development patterns similar to those of Kenya. Countries like Chad, Upper Volta (later, Burkina Faso), Central African Republic, and the Republic of Congo, following military coups, came to follow the downward trend of Uganda.

The Contracting State

The new period really began with the publication of the World Bank's report on *Accelerated Development in Sub-Saharan Africa* (World Bank 1981). It was a generally upbeat report about the prospects for accelerated development on the continent – provided governments were ready to take measures to reduce the role of the state in development, generally, and in the economy, particularly. It emphasized the importance of getting the house of public finance in order by reducing inflation and overvalued local currencies, getting the state out of production and trade, and providing price incentives to local producers. African governments initially reacted with strong opposition to the proposed measures. Under the auspices of the United Nations Economic Commission for Africa (UNECA), they tried to come up with their own somewhat softer agenda – the Lagos Plan of Action (Browne and Cummings 1984). Unlike the World Bank report, which was backed by conditional loans, the latter initiative had no real material support. Not surprisingly, therefore, the Lagos Plan was never implemented.

The bottom line during this most recent period is that African governments have become increasingly dependent on policy advice and funding for economic reform from external sources. The generous flow of resources from bilateral donors that characterized the development-state period has significantly dried up. Instead, the international finance institutions – the World Bank and the IMF – have come to occupy center stage in the development of African countries. This doesn't mean, however, that politics has lost its supremacy in these countries. It is just that it has become more defensive than assertive, more reactive than proactive. The challenge, therefore, for African leaders has been how to balance the external conditions and demands for economic reform, on the one hand, and retain control of the political process that since the new pressures for democracy in the early 1990s has become more open and thus harder to master.

The idea behind a leaner state apparatus has been to reduce the amount of public resources that are subject to political patronage. The accompanying call for multiparty politics – and thus more competition – however, tends to reinforce the need for central government control. Balancing these two conflicting demands is not easy. Not all African political leaders have succeeded.

The contracting state period has produced two major political trends in Africa: (1) the on-and-off reform sequence, and (2) the state-disintegration cycle. The first trend is most pronounced in countries that have been able to avoid civil violence that disrupts regular state functions. It is treated in the literature on economic and political reform as the "new broom" phenomenon (e.g. Haggard and Kaufman 1992; Nelson 1994); the assumption is that a new leader is better able to initiate change than someone who has been there for a long time. The reasoning is that the new leader cannot be held responsible for past government failures and will therefore find it easier to introduce reforms. Another reason is that the leader is assumed to be less tied in by patronage networks. As the international finance institutions call for economic liberalization, therefore, the best-placed leaders are those that are new in office (Bienen and Herbst 1996). Without implying that other leaders have ignored the demands for economic and political reform, there is a distinct pattern in Africa whereby the enthusiasm for change in policies falters as their consequences are felt in society and the costs of holding the country together politically rise. Kjaer (2002), for instance, has demonstrated how efforts to reduce the size of government cabinets in Tanzania and Uganda have proved difficult because of the perceived need to co-opt people who constitute a threat to the ruler and his immediate supporters. Many prominent members of the opposition cannot be ignored because they have their own power base, typically within their own ethnic group. Others, however, ride on the wave of popular discontent that has developed in the wake of reduced public services and other benefits that people used to take for granted in the development-state period. The task of horizontal integration has, if anything, become more complicated and costly after the introduction of multiparty politics with implications for both policy and political order.

The international donor community may try to reduce the supremacy of politics, but they lack the means by which this can be enforced in sovereign states, however poor they may be. Thus, we have seen Ghana serving as the World Bank's showcase of success in the 1980s, Uganda through much of the 1990s, and Tanzania and Mozambique in recent years. Although no one wishes to deny the relative success of these countries in terms of economic and public sector reforms, the supremacy of politics continues to loom as a threatening cloud in these places. The tendency to think – and act – in movement terms continues to be there, threatening the evolution of an institutional pattern built on the separation between party and state or the private and public.

The second trend has been more ominous and indicative of the vulnerability of African states as they try to adopt a more pluralist pattern of politics while at the same time reducing the role of the state in development. The tendencies toward disintegration have occurred in two separate settings. One is where there is very little in material terms to fight over, but where symbols and power over people matter particularly much as in nomadic Somalia. The other is where the natural resource endowment is concentrated in the form of a valuable mineral, for example, diamonds (Collier and Hoeffler 1998; Leonard and Strauss 2003). This has allowed groups of people with access to arms to challenge state control over these resources, take it over, and use it to finance their own political pursuits. This has been a serious threat to countries such as Angola, Congo, Liberia, and Sierra Leone. What all these cases have in common is that the original nationalist movement had collapsed altogether or lost so much control of national territory that the voids could be easily filled by individuals focusing their attention on gaining control of the country's most valuable natural resources.

THE LIBERATION MOVEMENTS

This account would be incomplete without reference to the liberation movements. They may qualify as even more representative of the movement legacy than the nationalist movements that were rewarded with political victory without physical struggle. With the exception of the movement that liberated Cape Verde and Guinea-Bissau from Portuguese rule,[5] all the liberation movements operated in the southern part of the continent: Angola, Mozambique, Namibia (Southwest Africa), and Zimbabwe. South Africa may also be included here, although it was nominally already an independent country under white minority rule. The liberation movement was thus focused on gaining majority rule for the country.

The liberation movements date back to the same period as the first nationalist movement, but their protracted struggle for independence lasted into the 1990s with Namibia and South Africa having taken their position as independent countries under majority rule. The former Portuguese colonies gained independence in 1975 as the Portuguese military staged a coup in Lisbon following extensive dissatisfaction with the fighting in the colonies. Zimbabwe became independent under majority rule in 1980, following a Unilateral Declaration of Independence by the white minority in 1965.

The big difference between the nationalist and the liberation movements is threefold. The first is that the latter had to operate in exile and often in underground conditions. It did not have the same access to the majority of the population as the nationalist movement had when it campaigned for independence. For this reason, the liberation movement tended to be a relatively small organization with an exclusivist orientation. It could not afford an open-door policy, because there was always the risk that opponents would try to infiltrate its ranks. Liberation movements were generally more secretive about their operations. Even sympathizers had difficulty gaining access to information about what they were doing. Once they came to power after the struggle was over, these movements were forced to deal with this legacy of secrecy. It has never been easy. To this day, the former liberation movements have had great difficulty in adhering to such principles as transparency and public accountability.

The second difference is that liberation movements relied on military means to achieve their objectives. They did not come to power by way of a popular ballot, but by way of the barrel of a gun. Compared to the nationalist movements, this military component made the liberation movements

---

[5] Sao Tomé e Principé is another former Portuguese colony on the western coast of Africa that gained independence at the same time as the other Portuguese colonies but unlike the others, it did not have a characteristic liberation movement paving the way for its independence.

more disciplined but also more rigid when dealing with dissent. This part of the movement legacy has also been a challenge because it has been obliged to adjust to international calls for greater respect for human rights and democratic forms of governance. A few countries like Mozambique and, to a lesser extent, Namibia have managed to make this adjustment without too much turbulence, but Angola, Guinea-Bissau, and Zimbabwe have all faced serious problems in transcending the military component of the movement legacy.

The third difference is that the nationalist movement could take on the challenges of order, development, and control in sequential order. Not that all countries succeeded in handling this triple challenge, but they had the time to sort out one after the other. Countries that have proved politically stable like Tanzania have generally done well in sorting them out, one at a time. The liberation movements never had that opportunity because they were latecomers to independence. They had to cope with all three in compressed time. This is one reason that they have run into political difficulties after independence. Whereas the liberation struggle had produced a hard core of committed and disciplined leaders, their ability to make a difference after independence soon faltered. The story of FRELIMO – the liberation movement in Mozambique – is a case in point: It started off with a very ambitious Marxist-Leninist agenda for development in 1975, but because it failed to adjust to the day-to-day realities of Mozambique after its Portuguese minority had left, its independent actions soon caused more destruction than improvement.

RENEWAL OF THE MOVEMENT IDEA

Although the movement legacy has a pedigree dating back all the way to the initial campaigns for independence some fifty years ago, it is important to emphasize that it has been reactivated in recent years in the struggle against tyranny and misrule by African leaders. The National Resistance Movement (NRM) in Uganda is the first case of a group of Africans taking to the bush to fight misrule in their country in the same fashion as the nationalist and liberation movements fought for independence. Yoweri Museveni, the incumbent president of the country, was the chief architect behind NRM. However, he could call on a number of fellow countrymen and women in exile to join NRM and begin liberating territory from government control. To be sure, NRM was assisted by Tanzanian troops fighting in Uganda to get rid of Idi Amin, but that does not take any credit away from Museveni and his group who quite effectively revived the movement idea and put it to successful use.

Three other countries have experienced a similar revival of the movement idea. As an extension of the NRM, many Rwandans in exile in Uganda – some having occupied key leadership positions in the NRM – created their own Rwanda Patriotic Front to fight their way to power in their own country. Although this invasion was one factor that sparked the genocide in the country in 1994, its disciplined leadership and ranks helped it conquer and retain power. It still runs Rwanda very much along the lines of a movement in which political considerations are supreme.

The other two countries are Ethiopia and Eritrea. The Marxist-Leninist model of rule that prevailed in Ethiopia after the emperor had been overthrown in 1974 created its own opposition in exile and on the ground. The Eritrean People's Liberation Front (EPLF) and the Tigrayan People's Liberation Front (TPLF), based in the northernmost provinces in Ethiopia, led this battle. These movements derived their inspiration from Maoist ideas about the power of the people. Like NRM and RPF, they liberated parts of the country's territory until it became too costly for the government army to retain control. EPLF eventually led the struggle in Eritrea to independence in 1991, whereas the TPLF became the core of a broader alliance of movements that was renamed the Ethiopian People's Democratic Revolutionary Front (EPDRF). EPLF has continued to rule Eritrea without opposition, although there have been cracks in its leadership in recent years due to alleged heavy handedness on the part of the movement's leader. In Ethiopia, the Front continues to control the country although it has officially allowed for the establishment of a multiparty system. The parliamentary election in 2005 showed that the opposition constitutes a challenge to EPDRF.

The young leaders of these four countries have once been referred to as a new generation of African leaders contrasting them with the old nationalist guard. They are different because they have succeeded in overthrowing domestic dictators. They are also seen as a fresh start because they are not only educated, but people with cosmopolitan experience. Although this applied to some of the old nationalist leaders too, for example, Julius Nyerere and Jomo Kenyatta as well as Leopold Senghor and Felix Houphouet-Boigny, they were deemed to bring a more correct Western governance to their country. This does not mean that they agree with all the republican values that many outside observers wish to see put into practice in African countries as part of improved governance. For instance, they have been reluctant to let political parties be institutionalized at the expense of the control and influence that the movement enjoys. They maintain a fine balance between what gives them legitimacy by adhering to a global governance agenda and what brings them popularity by responding to domestic expectations. The international community no longer endorses everything they do, but they thrive in power by reinventing modes of governance that draw on both African and international sources.

In this respect, these four leaders differ from some of the others who have applied the movement model to deal with their country's domestic political problems. President Laurent Gbagbo of the Ivory Coast has in recent years been forced to invent the notion of Ivoirité as a way of creating a new rallying point for support. The problem is that the concept excludes a large part of the population in the Ivory Coast who lives in the northern part of the country. It has become a means of dividing the country into two parts and fueling a civil conflict. The leader of the opposition, Alassane Ouattara, himself from the north, has been accused of not being born to Ivoirian parents. Despite the fact that he has DNA evidence to prove his Ivoirian origin, he is not recognized as a legitimate leader of the opposition (Akindés 2004). The result is that the political struggle is fought in the streets of the country's major cities rather than in the national legislature.

Much the same applies to Zimbabwe, where the political opposition is being forced to fight in the streets because of President Mugabe's attempt to make this fight equivalent to previous liberation wars (*chimurenga*). He knows that by resorting to a movement approach to solving the problem of his legitimacy in power, he stands a better chance of winning than if he tries to fight the opposition within the confines of parliamentary rule alone. Like the Ivoirité movement in the Ivory Coast, the attempt by President Mugabe to revitalize ZANU as a movement is exclusivist and has the inevitable effect of deeply dividing the country.

Movements in Africa are ubiquitous, but differ in their orientation and organization. The old nationalist movements were the most embracing because they fought a common enemy. The liberation movements were more exclusive, because they relied on a disciplined vanguard. The more recent movements that have been created to deal with power challenges within African countries are of two kinds: (a) those that strive for a broad-based reform of the political regime inspired at least in part by a cosmopolitan outlook, and (b) those that face challenges to their power from within and as a result become reactive and vindictive, causing civil conflict. Movements in Africa are a mixed blessing; their legacy is both positive and negative.

MOVEMENTS IN PERSPECTIVE

It is important to place the political movements in Africa in a comparative perspective. There is a considerable literature on social movements derived from experience in North America, Europe, and Latin America, ably summarized by Tarrow (1998). The difference is that social movements in those three regions of the world are typically not calling the political regime into question, but focus on a cause that can be achieved without first having to overthrow the whole regime. A movement differs from an interest group or a nongovernmental organization (NGO) in the sense that it goes beyond simply lobbying in parliamentary and governmental circles. A social movement is a membership organization that derives its strength from both numbers and ideas. The environmentalist movement is a case in point. The interesting thing about it is that once its ideas have become mainstream, its members have decided to form a political party of their own to ensure that their cause stays on the public agenda.

African countries, with the possible exception of South Africa, do not really have a legacy of social movements. It has proved very difficult to create such movements around a particular issue or social cause. However, African countries have been dominated by political movements to the point that other organized actions have sometimes been discouraged, if not outright banned. Although its dominance varies from one country to another, it is there and constitutes a feature of the African political scene that is fundamental to understanding the prospect for its economic as well as political development.

It is also important with regard to Africa to make a distinction between political party and movement. Political parties in Africa are still in formation. Party systems are far from being institutionalized. There is fluidity in the role that parties play. Many parties come and go like fashion changes, partly as a result of the personalized style of conducting politics in these countries. Many individuals in politics believe that they are nothing unless they lead their own party. This fluidity is also the result of the movement legacy. It informalizes the conduct of politics by taking the moral high ground. For instance, they refer to their role in defeating the colonialists. Even though this is much less influential today, political incumbents seek other reasons for making such claims, for example, their responsibility in achieving political renewal in a situation of civil conflict or economic decline. African political parties, therefore, have yet to settle into their role as instruments of aggregating interests in the parliamentary political arena. As the rest of this volume will discuss further, the structural conditions that make such an evolution a spontaneous part of the process of democratization are not really in existence. To be sure, there is some variation across the continent. It would be interesting, therefore, to do further research on the issue of the extent to which – and how – movements transform themselves into conventional political parties. Such a transformation would entail shifts that the following table illustrates:

TABLE 4. *Differences between Political Movements and Parties*

Variable	Movement	Party
Orientation	Cause	Issues
Level of operation	Regime	Government
Main arena of operation	Society	Parliament
Method of operation	Mobilization	Persuasion
Member orientation	Diffuse	Specific
Claims to resources	No formal limits	Constrained by rule of law

Attempts have been made in recent years to distinguish African countries in terms of how successfully they are transiting to democracy. Because of the fluidity and ambiguity of the transition process itself, it has been difficult to agree on specific patterns and which country belongs to which pattern. Van de Walle (2001) decided that it was possible to make a meaningful distinction among three categories: (a) old, (b) new, and (c) nondemocracies, basing the classification on Freedom House Index scores for 1999.[6] Leaving alone any quibbling about the classification itself, the author comes to the conclusion that level of democracy does not explain economic performance.

His analysis like that of others of the political transition in African countries (for example, Lewis 1992; Monga 1993; Callaghy 1994) shows that there are very few, if any, organized interests exercising influence over policy. The political leadership drawing on the legitimacy that comes from a catch-all organization sets policy in a discretionary manner. As further discussed in Chapter Six, this discretionary style of policy making is based on a political rather than on an economic rationality. This dominance by the political incumbents has not precluded others from starting their own political parties with the ambition to one day become rulers. On average, twelve political parties participated in the first two competitive elections that were held in Africa in the 1990s (van de Walle 2001:258). Despite this proliferation, only half of them gained seats in parliament. What is more, the biggest political party in the elections received close to or more than two-thirds of all votes. A qualified majority of two-thirds is typically required for a constitutional amendment. The ruling party in many African countries enjoys such a qualified majority.

The big question mark that hangs over Africa today is the extent to which it can make progress toward democratic consolidation. It is clear that only a few countries may be deemed close to achieving it. The most optimistic assessment is a recent survey of African elections by Lindberg (2004). He shows what he calls the power of elections by demonstrating that the more free and fair elections a country is capable of organizing, the greater the prospect that civil liberties and political rights will be respected. In short, elections are key contributors to democratic consolidation.

STRUCTURAL CONSTRAINTS

Agency matters in Lindberg's analysis and although questions can be raised about his model and the assumptions underlying it, it is encouraging to see

---

[6] Old democracies include Botswana, Gambia, Mauritius, Senegal, and Zimbabwe; new democracies are Benin, Cape Verde, Central African Republic, Congo, Guinea-Bissau, Lesotho, Madagascar, Malawi, Mali, Niger, São Tomé, Seychelles, and Zambia; nondemocracies include Burkina Faso, Cameroon, Comoros, Equatorial Guinea, Gabon, Ghana, Guinea, Ivory Coast, Kenya, Mauritania, Nigeria, Swaziland, Tanzania, Togo, and Uganda.

that there is a positive trend in Africa. Nonetheless, also taking into consideration the structural realities in Africa, some caution is still warranted. When looking back over the experience Africa has had with the priority given by their leaders to the political kingdom, there are two things that, in a comparative perspective, stand out as especially important. The first is the continued presence of a premodern social formation. The second is the absence of a civic public sphere.

Modernization Revisited

One important interpretation that is relevant to the contemporary African situation is provided by Anthony Giddens in his analysis of the consequences of modernity (Giddens 1991). His ideas on the subject have something in common with earlier writers on modernization in the 1950s and 1960s (for example, Lerner 1958; McLelland 1961; LeVine 1966; Inkeles and Smith 1974), but Giddens transcends the limitations of modernization theory, especially as it was applied in political science by placing Western democracy – especially its U.S. version – as the ultimate station of political development. With his help, it is time to revisit modernization.

In structural terms, modernization implies differentiation; in cultural terms, it involves rationalization. Giddens identifies at least three consequences of these processes that are important for understanding the African situation: (1) the disembedding of institutions, (2) a new perception of risk and trust, and (3) the evolution of a reflexive consciousness. I shall briefly recapitulate his main points in reference to these consequences.

Disembedding is itself a consequence of the separation of time and space by fostering relations between people who are locationally distant from any given situation of face-to-face interaction. Locales become effectively penetrated and shaped by social influences quite distant from them. Disembedding, therefore, according to Giddens, means the lifting out of social relations from local contexts of interaction and their restructuring across infinite spans of time and space. Money is an important medium in the process of modernization because it allows the exchange of anything for anything regardless of whether the goods share particular substantive qualities with one another. In short, money provides for the enactment of transactions between actors widely separated from each other.

Money is not the only disembedding mechanism. What Giddens calls expert systems is another type. By the term, he means systems of technical or professional expertise that laypersons become increasingly dependent upon as society modernizes. People consult lawyers, engineers, doctors, or architects because these professionals have specialized knowledge that others don't have. Expert systems are disembedding in the sense that they remove social relations from the immediacies of context. They provide guarantees of expectations across time and space. Standards are universalized and sustained through impersonal mechanisms such as tests and, if violated, by public criticism. Expert systems, like money – and the exchange institutions it gives rise to – standardize values at the expense of local uses and know-how.

With modernity comes also a change in perception of risk and trust. Drawing especially on Luhmann (1988), Giddens distinguishes between trust and confidence, arguing that trust presupposes awareness of circumstances of risk, whereas confidence refers to a more or less taken-for-granted attitude that familiar things will remain the same (Giddens 1991:30–31). An individual who does not consider alternatives is in a situation of confidence, whereas someone who acknowledges alternatives and the risks associated with each option engages in trust. In a situation of confidence, a person reacts to disappointment by blaming others; in circumstances of trust, the person must at least partly shoulder the blame and may regret having placed trust in someone or something. In conditions of modernity, therefore, trust exists in the context of the general awareness that human activity is socially created rather than given in the nature of things or by divine influences; and also the vastly increased transformative scope of modern social institutions. Trust intertwines with risk in that it normally serves to reduce or minimize the dangers to which particular types of activity are subject. What is perceived as acceptable risk, that is, the minimization of danger, varies from one context to another and from individual to individual, but it is usually central in sustaining trust.

A third consequence associated with modernity is the rise of reflexivity. The latter refers to the fact that social practices are constantly examined and reformed in the light of incoming information about those practices, thus constitutively altering their character. In the context of modernity, the sanctioning of a practice merely because it is traditional is not good enough. Tradition can of course be justified even in modern society, but only in the light of knowledge that is not authenticated by tradition. The latter, however, is not wholly static because it has been reinvented by a new generation as it takes over the cultural heritage from those preceding it. What is important about tradition is not that it resists change, but that it pertains to a context with few separated temporal or spatial markers in which change can have any meaningful form. Change becomes meaningful and potentially progressive once these markers, associated with the disembedding of institutions, come into place and provide opportunities for new initiatives. Modernization sets in motion a search for accumulation of knowledge that is reflexively constituted and therefore always subject to revision. Even those thinkers like Popper (1962) who have defended science's claim to certitude are ready to acknowledge that in science, nothing is certain and nothing can be proved once and for all, even if scientific endeavor provides us with the most dependable information about the world on which we can rely on.

With these insights into the consequences of modernity, it is easier to understand the supremacy of politics in African countries after independence. The process of institutional disembedding has not proceeded far enough to give rise to rules that rein in political action. Nor has trust replaced confidence as the principal factor determining behavior. State-society relations, according to this perspective, remain blurred because politics is still locational, that is, driven by a variety of locale-specific interpretations of reality that have not been standardized and co-opted by institutions that are independent of these perspectives. In short, the state is easily penetrated by locale-specific concerns and thus captured by political patrons representing these constituencies much the same way that special interests capture public authority in the United States. The big difference between Africa and the United States is that the markers for performance in the latter are related to change and growth, whereas in Africa they are related to stability and redistribution.

The Absence of a Public Sphere

Politics rather than economics remains supreme in Africa in the beginning of the twenty-first century. Even though most African countries nowadays have individuals who have accumulated large amounts of money, their influence is limited, especially regarding establishing the rules and organizations that make a market economy function reliably and predictably. African countries lack the civic public sphere that Habermas (1979) has identified as such a key ingredient in the evolution of bourgeois democracy in Western Europe.

The notion of a public sphere is an antidote to political power, because it involves the sharing of ideas in a mutually reflective atmosphere. This is how one writer in the tradition of critical theory describes the concept:

A public sphere is brought into existence whenever two or more individuals... assemble to interrogate both their own interactions and the wider relations of social and political power within which they are always and already embedded. Through this autonomous association, members of public spheres consider what they are doing, settle how they will live together, and determine...how they might collectively act. (Keane 1984:2–3).

Historically speaking, the creation of public spheres was part of the bourgeois challenge of traditional and hierarchical authority that characterized premodern or prebourgeois society. In short, it was an integral part of the effort to mobilize public opinion against the royal and aristocratic establishment.

The latter was never really that significant in African societies and during colonial times, the social and political establishment was really made up of foreigners. The historical anomaly of the African continent in the mid-twentieth century was that it lacked an indigenous or national bourgeoisie. To the extent that these countries had a class of private owners of capital, it was composed largely of non-African minorities. The Lebanese constituted the strongest such minority in West African countries, whereas Asians, that is, immigrants from India and Pakistan, made up the vast majority of businesspeople in eastern and southern Africa. European settlers were prominent in southern Africa, but elsewhere the vast majority of white people were either administrators or missionaries. When the economically powerful departed or were forced out, as happened in the majority of countries at or soon after political independence, there was no such historical enemy to fight on the ground. The political elite saw little reason to slow down its nation-building ambitions by creating autonomous spheres within which issues shared by members of the public could be critically discussed.

The point is that without the kind of respect for rules in public that a bourgeois class, historically speaking, has been in the forefront of creating, politics is difficult to tame. Movement-type political organizations are likely to arise to challenge incumbent governments; governments under threat will resort to movement approaches to solving problems rather than relying on formal means of solving problems Such are the social and political realities in African countries today. Progress is being made, but it is still a matter of touch-and-go.

CONCLUSIONS

Reflecting on the conditions in the party states in West Africa in the mid-1960s, Zolberg (1966:6) asked the question whether Africa suffers from too much or too little authority. His reflection is a good starting point for the conclusions to this chapter. I have deliberately not used the word "authority" in this chapter, but rather have referred to "power." This distinction is intentional. The former implies a form of power that is prescribed by rules. It is legalized – if not legitimate – power.

The analytical story line of this chapter has been that agency in African politics is embodied in movement in which the exercise of power is not limited by rules, only by countervailing powers. Political actors prefer to operate in the informal context of a movement in which formal rules can be ignored in the interest of achieving a particular overarching objective. Such movements are typically most effective when faced with a common threat or enemy as the case was at the time of decolonization, because in such situations they tend to be inclusive of all. That is why African political leaders are inclined to find such threats or enemies. Once the enemy is inside the country, however, the movement approach becomes much more controversial. In this chapter, we have discussed the stories of the countries in which leaders have resorted to the movement approach to deal with perceived or real threats from within.

The results are mixed. Some leaders are more successful than others, but the revitalization of social and political action that is attempted comes at a cost.

It is a primary paradox of African politics that whenever a country wishes to make headway, it has to do so by first mobilizing political support against a perceived threat or enemy, even if such action is subsequently rendered irrelevant by stronger external forces being brought to bear on the African realities. At the time of independence the rest of the world, including the former colonial masters, were willing to give Africa a chance to prove its capacity to develop on its own terms. In the beginning of the twenty-first century, such a generosity does not exist. The international development community, directly or indirectly, is much more involved in the continent's destiny. It has not been easy under these circumstances for African governments to experience ownership of policy. It is instructive, however, that those governments that have been relatively successful in economic policy terms, notably Ghana, Tanzania, and Uganda, are all countries that began by mobilizing people against the international finance institutions – the perceived enemy – only to find that out of such opposition came the political legitimacy and energy to gradually accept the new economic wisdom and turn it into their own.

The movement as a dominant phenomenon in African politics resembles what Greif and Laitin (2004) call a self-enforcing institution. It acquires its dynamics from responses to exogenous factors, real or perceived. When there is no real external enemy in sight, one is constructed. The interesting thing that has occurred in Africa in recent years is that this exogenous variable is not only located in the global economy but also in the political realm within individual countries. The introduction of multiparty politics has generated a situation in which a movement flourishes thanks to its ability to paint the opposition, e.g., as a threat to stability. In this respect, African countries still have some way to go before the new party politics turns into a functioning party system. The movement tends to dominate at the expense of the emergence of true political parties devoting their activities to the parliamentary arena.

As self-enforcing institutions, movements in African politics differ from the conventional notion of rational, game-theoretic behavior. The latter assumes autonomous individual actors and predictable rules. The movement legacy contributes to giving African politics a different foundation. Because rules are informal – embedded as they are in personal reciprocities – strategic action is more complex and requires consideration of implications not so much for objective as subjective outcomes. An African politician would be more concerned about the effects of his choices for relations he has with other political actors, including supporters, than what happens in terms that can be measured objectively. To be sure, this is not a uniquely African phenomenon, but it is definitely more pronounced there than it would be elsewhere, including the United States with its own version of "pork barrel" politics. In other words, independent choice tends to be confined to the movement leaders – sometimes just *the* leader. This lack of a set of rules that is independent of individual actors gives African politics its relative instability. The movement becomes a necessary response to this personalist form of politics and the organization that offers an element of stability and predictability that would otherwise not be there.

3

The Problematic State

Students of American politics rarely, if ever, encounter the concept of the "state." The separation of power that characterizes the American political system invites the use of a different terminology than the one associated with political systems that emerged in the Old World and the regions of the world colonized by these powers. The state, therefore, is a concept that is more prominent in the fields of comparative politics and international relations. Occasional efforts to avoid the use of the concept in comparative politics, for example, by the comparativists in the 1960s using a structural-functionalist approach, have never succeeded. It has always rebounded and continues to be prominent in the study of politics in all regions outside the United States.

A state emerges in response to needs that groups in society have. These needs may emanate from problems with security, welfare, or resolving conflicting demands on scarce resources. Those who occupy positions in the state do so in ways that make them different from the public because their positions carry an element of authority whether that authority was delegated to them or grabbed in the course of dealing with the problem. States historically differ in complexity. Early historical states were quite rudimentary, often the mere extension of the household of a king. More recent examples, notably the welfare state in developed societies, are intricate creations in which citizens as a collectivity have delegated responsibility for much of their daily lives to officials whom they trust will act in their common interests.

States are hierarchical organizations; they are systems of power that are legitimized for specific functions that they are supposed to carry out. State officials are expected to perform particular roles within those systems. In this respect, officials are giving up personal interest to act in the public interest. This line between the personal and the official, the private and the public, is not always easy to draw in ways that satisfy everyone. Some state organizations become too bureaucratic, that is, the officials become too preoccupied with blindly following procedures. Others display the opposite characteristic: The officials tend to favor their own interests at the expense of the public.

The state as an object of study in political science straddles several fields. Students of international relations analyze it in the context of international politics by which the state is generally considered the principal actor. Public administration examines the organizational aspects of the state. Comparative politics tends to take the most comprehensive approach to the study of the state, typically focusing on the role of the state in relation to both economy and society. In other words, in that field there is both a political economy and a political sociology of the state.

The more specific study of the state in Africa is particularly important because it helps to throw light on how states come about. It puts other states in a useful perspective, showing that states cannot be taken for granted. Certain conditions need to be fulfilled before what is supposed to be public authority becomes statelike in the sense of serving as an instrument in the hands of society whether that means the public at large or just the elite. By placing the study of the state in Africa in a comparative perspective, this chapter highlights what it has in common with states elsewhere as well as its differences stemming from the particular conditions prevailing on that continent. It points to a weak indigenous state tradition and the challenges that have emanated from colonial states. These states lacked legitimacy among nationalist politicians for whom control of people was more important than control of territory. To most Africans, local community institutions carried much greater legitimacy than the civic institutions established by the colonial powers. Therefore, as a useful precursor to the analysis of the state, the first section of this chapter will discuss the notion of community and compare it with collectivity, the concept that is more often used in the study of modern industrial society. The second section discusses three separate perspectives on the study of the state that bears on our understanding of the state both in Africa and elsewhere. The last section discusses state and power in the African context.

COMMUNITY IN THEORY AND PRACTICE

Historically, there has often been a tension between community and state. In the history of Western Europe, community is frequently portrayed as standing in the way of both individualism and a strong sovereign state. Capitalism and the modern state grew together in those societies. Capitalism rarely launched direct attacks on the local communities. It could live with some aspects of what they were really all about. Just the same, it was uneasy with social entities that lay between the individual and the global market. Communities were potentially dangerous, because they provided an identity based on locality, land, language, or sect that might limit people's mobility and reduce their willingness to become part of a factory-based, city-dwelling workforce. In the nineteenth century, therefore, community was more like an obstacle to be cleared than an institution to be valued for its identity-forming qualities. Even those who were generally critical of capitalism typically shared this view. Marx and his followers, for example, treated consciousness of community instead of class as false consciousness.

This aversion toward community remained in Western Europe and North America well into the twentieth century. When, at the end of the Second World War, strategies were devised to bring about decolonization and development in Africa neither the liberal-capitalist nor the Marxist school of thought was ready to give prominence to community. For example, modernization theorists in the late 1950s and early 1960s saw the community in African countries as a barrier that had to be hurdled as a condition for progress, especially when the community took the form of a clan or ethnic group (Geertz 1963). Primordial ties had to be loosened and identification with the state and its central institutions encouraged if these countries were going to develop in an orderly fashion. Similar ideas could also be found among the Marxists. Warren (1980) agreed that capitalist penetration of countries in the developing world might be painful but it was inevitable and desirable. Attempts to preserve incompatible historical formations, including traditional communities, were merely romantic folly.

The first scholar to really question these perspectives in the social sciences was Peter Ekeh, a Nigerian sociologist who argued that in the absence of a nation-state, where the boundaries between community and state would tend to coincide, African countries were characterized by much more tension between community and state (Ekeh 1975). In fact, he went as far as claiming that Africans have no loyalty to the civil institutions of the state – what he calls the "civic" public realm – but instead nurture their membership in a local community based on a primary social organization such as lineage, clan, or tribe. It is this primordial public realm, as Ekeh calls it, that commands loyalty in African societies. The result is that the institutions that were inherited from the colonial powers at independence are essentially milked of material resources to feed communities.

Ekeh's perspective on this set of issues was that Africans had resorted to their community identity as a response to the threats posed initially by slave trade and later by the colonial state. He criticized the notion of an evolutionary trend toward greater identification with the state and argued instead that community-state relations in African countries have remained contested. With independence, leaders of particular communities were able to take over state power but because they had no loyalty to it, their natural reaction was to treat it as prey. His study is crucial to understanding the problematic nature of the state in Africa.

It is important to also point out that officials in the colonial state did little to shake up social relations. The colonial state had been a relatively efficient vehicle for social control and economic exploitation because those in power were foreigners and largely isolated from the social organization of indigenous society; thus, separated from the fabric of local community ties, few limits existed on the extent to which colonial officials could dictate policy priorities on their own. At the same time, however, the costs involved in administering the colonies (Young 1994) made the colonial powers practice indirect rule, that is, running the countries through traditional rulers from the indigenous communities wherever possible. Their promotion of customary law further solidified the legitimate standing of norms inherent in local communities and the way they were traditionally ruled. The contradiction that African countries inherited on the eve of independence was an arrangement whereby the state ruled in a discretionary manner without attempting to turn its subjects into citizens (Mamdani 1996).

Thus, it is not necessary to go as far back as precolonial days to find the reasons why Africans preferred social exchange outside of formal state structures. Primary forms of social organization such as family, lineage, and even tribe provided meaning and significance to people in ways that the foreign symbols associated with the state did not. The important thing in the African context is that it is the norms associated with a nondistanciated place that have shaped the ways individuals relate to each other and develop shared expectations about behavior and choice.

To appreciate this point fully, the distinction between community and collectivity may be helpful. The former is constituted through what I call "primary reciprocities" in which rules are self-enforced, that is, there is no need for a third party to intervene. *Community*, as defined here, then, refers to a group of persons who are drawn together by a sense of affective solidarity and meaningful participation in reciprocal exchanges within the group. *Collectivity* refers to a group of people who have decided to work together to achieve specific objectives. In such social entities, rigid cultural prescriptions do not hold sway over members, as they tend to in communities. Instead, group values are malleable and open to reorientation in response to changing circumstances and new opportunities. This distinction between community and collectivity bears some resemblance to Durkheim's notions of mechanical and organic forms of solidarity. What matters most here, however, is the point that one prevails in local space where place and space have not been separated, whereas the other exists in distanciated space and time. This point is important for understanding the relations between community and state in Africa, as indicated in Table 5. The relative strength of community in these countries is also attributable to the relatively weak penetration by capitalist relations of production. Trade was not unknown to Africans before the Europeans came, but it was the colonial powers that brought the world market to the region. The extent to which capitalist relations of production

TABLE 5. *Differences between Community and Collectivity*

Type	Origin	Objective	Method	Behavior
Collectivity	By choice	Achieve specific good	Voice	Autonomous
Community	By birth	Achieve generalized benefits	Loyalty	Interdependent

were introduced, however, varied. Their presence were strongest wherever white settlers by seizing or buying land removed Africans from their community and forced them into new social collectivities. Elsewhere, Africans remained only marginally affected by the market. They increasingly traded in the market, but their base was still a homestead and family farm where a subsistence ethos prevailed. It is in this respect that the African economies at independence were first and foremost peasant economies over which state officials had only a limited control.

Although there has always been variation among African societies because the precolonial and colonial heritages were not identical, equally interesting is the fact that at the base, so to speak, these societies have a lot in common. They have all relied on rudimentary forms of agricultural technology. Their level of sociopolitical complexity has been generally quite low in comparison with other regions of the world. Most notably, with a couple of exceptions such as Ethiopia, there was no real indigenous state tradition. Economic relations were embedded in social organization. Rudimentary state formation occurred within the confines of local communities. Once the colonial powers left Africa some forty years ago, Africans – leaders and followers alike – preferred a return to what they were most familiar with from home. This has left Africa with two features that are much more pronounced there than in societies with more advanced agricultural technologies and higher levels of sociopolitical complexity (Mueller et al. 2002).

The first is that politics is more about control of people than of land or territory. Land was never individually owned. It belonged to a lineage, clan, or ethnic group with the chief or a group of elders holding it in trust. The purpose of politics in precolonial society was to accumulate subjects in order to rule, not land (Fairley 1987:91–100). Whether these societies had the initial trappings of a state or not, the purpose of government was to represent the powers of lineage groups, that, in turn, had corporate control of specific land areas, a point that anthropologists have repeatedly made (see e.g. MacGaffey 1970; Kopytoff 1987). Success was measured not in terms of territorial but, instead, in popular reach.

This takes us to the second feature, which is that there was no border, only a frontier. Rulers did not really seek to stake out territorial boundaries in the way that their counterparts tried to do in Europe and Asia.

The Americas had an open frontier,[1] but it was different, especially in the north. There independent individuals engaged in technological and economic entrepreneurship used survival and ingenuity to push the frontier in new directions and, in the process, establish new territorial borders. In Africa, by contrast, this entrepreneurship was sociopolitical. It manifested itself in three different ways. The first was for rulers to acquire new adherents. Such acquisitions came with conquest, not of land but of people who would become slaves and women who would add to the prestige and power of the ruler. A second was for rulers to seek alliances with other rulers in order to strengthen their position vis-à-vis neighboring enemies. Diplomacy was an important means to maintain peace in precolonial Africa. A third was for people to desert the ruler to whom they had pledged loyalty in the past. Some of these migrants established themselves on land where no existing lineage claimed control; others sought refuge under the protection of another ruler. In short, as Africanist historians emphasize, precolonial social formations in Africa were quite fluid, as were social identities (Vansina 1990; Isaacman 1993).

Much has, of course, changed in postcolonial times, but ever since Ekeh produced his thesis about the two publics in Africa, there has been a growing recognition that this lineage orientation survives in contemporary Africa. Whether in politics or in the marketplace, it manifests itself through enduring bonds of family ties, restructuring of kinship relations, patron-client networks, and other forms of primary reciprocities founded upon affective and oftentimes highly moral criteria. As the many studies of the pragmatic use of ethnic entrepreneurship suggest, such frontier methods are an integral part of how politics in Africa is being conducted (Young 1976; Kasfir 1979).

Community-centered networks are not atavistic remnants of the past, but conscious creations by individuals seeking to enhance their political fortunes or social status in society. They reflect the embedded structural realities of Africa's political economy, in which vertical class relations have not yet replaced horizontal kinship relations. This provides individuals in African societies with a scope for social mobility that is not available in places where class relations have been institutionalized. Thus, for instance, the prospects for the poor in countries like India to get out of poverty are very dim indeed. What is more, the poor rarely, if ever, contemplate it. The situation in Africa is different. Kinship and other forms of affective relations offer hope of getting out of poverty. Africa may be the poorest region of the world, but individuals never give up looking for the way out. That is why, for instance,

---

[1] The notion that it was open is, of course, misleading in several respects because there were indigenous peoples who were removed or killed to provide space for the expansion of new immigrants moving further inland.

so many young men who grow up in the rural areas, faced with the boredom of hand-hoe agriculture and low returns on labor, move to the urban areas.

The prevalence of a community-centered orientation in contemporary Africa can only be fully understood against the background of the embeddedness of its political economy (Sangmpam 1995). It leads to at least two of the aspects that characterize African politics. The first is the tendency to rely on informal rather than on formal institutions. In societies where face-to-face relations and primary forms of reciprocity prevail, there is no need for external rules and impersonal authorities to enforce social action. Communities take it upon themselves to enforce rules. The second aspect is the tendency of politics to become centrifugal; there is little respect for the formal rules associated with a higher authority such as the state. The abstract nature of the system underlying the ideal of a rational-legal type of bureaucracy is ignored in favor of the locale-specific pressures and interests associated with individual communities. This doesn't mean that utilitarian rationality is unknown in Africa. It is being pursued by individuals there as anywhere else. The difference, however, is that these pursuits are not autonomous of what others think and do. Self-interest is mediated by considering what a particular choice means for others. In fact, rational action in the context of primary reciprocities involves investing time and effort in nurturing particular social relationships. That is why Africans don't see themselves as acting irrationally when they behave in ways that undermine formal bureaucratic norms or other rules associated with a technical definition of rationality. That is also why the informal character of a movement becomes a more congenial forum for action than the formality of public institutions.

THE STATE IN THEORY AND PRACTICE

This takes us to a discussion of the state in Africa. It has been described as variably weak or soft. Much of the literature since the 1980s has referred to it as being in crisis. The problem with what has been said about the state in Africa is its preference for a one-dimensional interpretation of the institution. Thus, for instance, Bates (1981) was interested in how the state was used by the elite to transfer resources from the rural to the urban areas. Callaghy (1984) was largely interested in the question of why states in Africa did not undergo the same process of rationalization as in Europe during earlier periods. Rothchild and Chazan (1988) focused their attention on how state and society interacted. Migdal (1988) wrote with a similar objective in mind, arguing that where societies are weak, states are necessarily strong. Young's (1994) concern was with the legacy of the colonial state, one that Mamdani (1996) further developed in his notion of the bifurcated state that African countries inherited from the colonial powers. The notion of bifurcation refers to his argument that the state was organized differently in urban and rural areas. In its urban manifestation, the state spoke the language of civil society

TABLE 6. *Different Theoretical Perspectives on the State*

Perspective	Premise	Focus	Approach
Marxian	Conflictual	Class relations	Instrumentalist
Durkheimian	Organicist	Division of labor	Relational
Weberian	Historicist	Organization	Authoritative

and civil rights; in the rural areas, the language of community and culture prevailed.

All these observations and argument are valid, but none on its own is enough to explain the crisis of the state that has afflicted Africa since independence. It is important, therefore, to examine three different conceptualizations of the state, all of which together allow us to achieve this objective. Each conceptualization draws on a theoretical perspective that has been influential in the literature on the state: (1) the Marxian notion that the state serves as the instrument of the ruling class, (2) the state-society relations literature, drawing in many respects on Durkheimian ideas, with its focus on the legitimacy of the regime guiding these relations, and (3) the Weberian focus on the role of bureaucracy in the state. The principal distinctions between these three perspectives are summarized in Table 6.

State and Class

Marx's assertion about the state rests categorically on the premise that the economic structure of society is the real foundation on which a legal and political superstructure arises (Marx 1970). In the beginning of history, there was no state because society did not need it. When history comes to an end with the arrival of a true communist organization of social relations there would, again, be no need for a state. As his foremost collaborator, Friedrich Engels, put it, "the interference of the state power in social relations becomes superfluous in one sphere after another, and then ceases of itself. The government of persons is replaced by the administration of things and the direction of the processes of production" (Engels 1939:307).

Their idea that a classless society that had existed before capitalism could be recreated after the defeat of capitalism was especially attractive to many African nationalists. Drawing on indigenous ideas about the precolonial legacy in Africa, they saw the recreation of a classless community as their mission after independence. It featured in the minds of such prominent African leaders as Kwame Nkrumah, Sekou Toure, and Julius Nyerere. The latter, however, was the only leader who tried to take African communalism from theory to practice with his policies of *ujamaa*. For him, it would provide a historical shortcut to a more egalitarian society.

African leaders who propagated the notion of a return to a classless society after independence were roundly criticized by neo-Marxists scholars in
the 1970s. They argued that economy and society in Africa changed enough
during colonialism so that the only way to understand it is in the context
of the capitalist world economy. Classes already existed or certainly were
in formation, according to critics like Cliffe and Saul (1973), Shivji (1976),
and Mamdani (1976). The importance of class was also highlighted by others who were less closely wedded to a strict Marxist interpretation of the
political economy in Africa, for example, Markovitz (1987) and MacGaffey
(1988). Although African leaders may have exaggerated the role of agency,
their critics tended to overemphasize structure. To be sure, African economies
had changed during colonialism, but had the process reached a point where
capitalist social relations were effectively dominant? In a contemporary perspective, it is clear that the neo-Marxists engaged in wishful thinking, seeing
class where there was none. Neither the objective conditions for class formation nor the subjective consciousness of class had really taken root to the
point where the social class dynamics that Marx identifies with capitalism
were a force of social transformation. Attempts to degrade the African bourgeoisie by referring to it as petty or bureaucratic, because it was functioning
in the periphery of the world economy, did little to make the neo-Marxist
position more credible. Their line of argument was too reductionist to survive
a closer scrutiny of the realities on the ground in Africa.

Marx himself had argued with reference to the difference between the
state in Europe and North America that there is a need to see its trajectory
in historical perspective, recognizing that the past in each country provides
the impetus for different stories. Thus, Marx was aware of the importance
of the feudal origins of the modern state in European countries. Societies
like Germany and France that have known a feudal past tend to engender a
bureaucratized state capable of dominating civil society rather than a state
that is a mere instrument of a ruling bourgeoisie. By controlling such key
resources as the military and the police, the state in ex-feudal societies tended
to acquire a certain measure of autonomy from society.

With reference to the United States, Marx argued that bourgeois society did not develop on the foundation of a feudal system but developed
rather from itself, that is, American society is not the remnant of a centuries-
old movement but rather the starting point of a new movement. As a
result, the state was right from the beginning in U.S. history subordinate
to bourgeois society and to its production. It could never pretend, as the
case was in France and Germany, to be autonomous or an end in itself.
Because it started as an instrument of the bourgeoisie, the state in the
United States in comparison with continental Europe has always remained
minimal and much more responsive to demands from civil society and
business.

So what does this suggest for our attempt to understand the state in Africa? Without the presence of a corporate ruling class like the bourgeoisie, one would expect a scenario similar to that of France or Prussia – a strong and centralized state. Such was the scenario in colonial days, when European officials ruled African territories in response to bourgeois interests in the metropolitan countries. The colonial state enjoyed a definite measure of autonomy because it was sanctioned, not by African society, but by foreign interests.

Scholars who emphasize the continuity between colonial and postcolonial rule tend to go wrong because they overlook the completely different social basis of the state that emerged after independence as African nationalists took it over. They had the vision of restoring a form of development that reflected African values. What is more, they took charge of the state, not as a corporate class, but as representatives of different ethnic group interests. Even though the struggle against colonialism had brought them together in a more or less united front, their arrival at the gates of the state after independence forced upon them the challenge of working out a governance formula that accommodated these many contending group interests. This was not always easy. In Kenya, for instance, the Kikuyu who had led the Mau Mau movement against the British in the 1950s claimed a larger share of the cake after independence. When Zimbabwe turned to majority rule in 1980, the Shona, affiliated with Robert Mugabe's ZANU party, demanded a similar deal. In other countries, the process of gaining control of the state entailed similar issues of bargaining for advantages and preferences.

In this context, it is difficult to suggest that the state served as an instrument in the hands of a class that had identical interests. The vertical divisions along ethnic and other similar lines that characterized African countries turned the state into an arena where conflicting group interests had to be resolved. The main preoccupation of the political leaders was not to use state power to pursue a common interest that they shared as members of a ruling class. Instead, they were bringing to the state demands that originated in the communities that they represented and thus could bargain for the best possible deal. In this respect, the state in postcolonial Africa resembles that of the United States rather than continental Europe. It was weak, because it acted in response to society. Bringing home the pork is a common measure of political success in the United States as well as Africa. The big difference, however, is that the state in the United States is an instrument in the hands of a corporate class, whereas in Africa it is an arena from which to draw as much resources as possible. Patronage, although present in the United States, is therefore severely constrained by state formalism; in Africa it is liberally practiced because formal rules do not have the same significance as in the United States.

There are, of course some variation on this theme, even some exceptions. The most significant is the state in Ethiopia. It is special because Ethiopia was never colonized and its institutions were allowed to emerge in an organic fashion. Thus, Ethiopia did develop feudal institutions and an attempt by the emperor to control the class of landlords by strengthening the state along lines similar to those in Prussia, where the model of modern bureaucracy first emerged. Because of the presence of a state tradition in Ethiopia, kinship and community structures have been weakened, especially in the heartland. The presence of relatively articulate class relations provided the impetus for the Ethiopian revolution in the early 1970s, which swept away not only the feudal landlords, but also the imperial regime. The interesting thing about Ethiopia in a comparative African perspective is that the notion of the state as an instrument in the hands of the rulers has prevailed there. In the postrevolutionary period, despite the introduction of a federal constitution, community interests have not been allowed to guide state action. It has remained in the hands of the revolutionary movement – the Ethiopian People's Democratic Revolutionary Front (EPDRF). This way, political leaders have used state power in discretionary ways with much more direct effects on the population. For instance, there has been a more systematic attempt to eliminate anyone opposed to the political leadership. Secondly, state-peasant relations have been much harsher than anywhere else on the African continent. The rural population has been forced to feel the full weight of the state without any mediating patrons or groups (Kebbede 1992). The result is that to this day, Ethiopian peasants are the only ones in Africa that tend to see their opportunities in life confined to the land. Unlike other places where the social frontier remains open and people leave the rural areas in search of a better life in the cities, the tillers of the land in Ethiopia come closest to being a true peasant class.

State and Society

If Marx is the quintessential theoretician of conflict, Durkheim is the apostle of the peaceful and stable development of society. The latter believed, contrary to Marx, that the division of labor is the principal force behind the transformation of a social system. His organicist thinking was very much a product of prevailing systems of ideas in the latter part of the nineteenth century thus, social history could be explained by the division of labor; like biological systems, societies develop because of the constantly increasing specialization of their organs, each of which is responsible for performing certain specific functions. Division of labor, in this perspective, is not only an instrument of modernity, but it is also a source of new social structures and hence new forms of power.

Foremost among those new forms of power is the modern state. In fact, Durkheim believed that the greater the development of society, the greater also the development of the state. With societal development, the state is being asked to take on more and more functions and thus bring them together in a centralizing and unifying fashion. Advances in centralization parallel advances in civilization. This was such a self-evident proposition to Durkheim that he claimed that no historical law is more firmly established than that one (Durkheim 1975). In short, the necessity of division of labor gives rise to a centralizing state. He contrasted the modern centralized state with societies where division of labor is unknown. There, he argued, solidarity cannot arise from the division of labor. Instead, it must be produced by strong external constraints imposed by custom and religion. The state in such societies is not distinct and thus is insignificant in determining development. This observation is highly applicable to the African situation today.

This point is especially important in the sense that Durkheim saw the rise of the state as a mechanism of weakening the hold groups have over individuals. He went as far as arguing that the essential function of the state is to liberate individual personalities (Richter 1964). The implication was that with the rise of the state, citizens would gain freedom from the control of such institutions as community and church. Whereas Marx treated bureaucracy as a phenomenon that must be combated, Durkheim treated it as progressive because the agents of the state act in the general interest.

Durkheim's worry stemmed from another source. Like Tocqueville who a generation earlier had warned of the tyranny of the majority, he saw the roots of despotism lying in the emergence of an atomized mass society in which no primary or intermediary group and no association or corporation is available to limit the power of the institutionalized state. Thus, while he clearly saw more in state-society relations than his organicist perception of development typically allowed, he failed to address these concerns in a way that would cast new light on his thesis about the relationship between advances in civilization and advances in state control.

The main problem with applying Durkheim's analysis to Africa is that the state, with the exception of Ethiopia, never developed in response to a spontaneous division of labor driven from within Africa. To be sure, the colonial state was meant to perform civilizing functions such as reducing the control that communities had over individuals, but foreigners performed this task. Their ability to institutionalize such social changes had its own limits. That is why, at independence, political leaders and civil servants, filling the gap left by the departing colonial officials, embarked upon a process of bringing the community back in. Even though African society, even in colonial days, had been far from the atomistic entity that Durkheim foresaw as a threat, the emphasis since independence was to reinvent and strengthen communitarian ties that had been deliberately weakened by colonial policy. From a Durkheimian perspective, it appears as if they decided that taking one step backward was necessary in order to take two steps forward. In other words, a return to a more endogenous approach to development would, in the long run, facilitate a division of labor that was more truly reflective of African society than anything that had been institutionalized under colonial rule.

What has happened across the African continent since colonial days is a shift from one crisis of legitimacy to another. During colonialism, the crisis that eventually emerged in these societies was the discrepancy between the values underlying the operations of the state and the norms guiding African communities. The success of nationalism brought about a change so that after independence the crisis that has come to dominate the political scene on the continent is the inability of the state to operate as a distinct institution free from the constraints of community and church. Even in those instances where the military has seized power of the state with the intention to suppress tribalism and other such manifestations of communitarian identity, the efforts have largely failed.

Especially instructive are the various programs that were initiated by military rulers in Nigeria. The military government under General Murtala Muhammed in the late 1970s established investigative tribunals under the auspices of the Corrupt Practices Investigation Bureau and dismissed some ten thousand civil servants for alleged acts of corrupt enrichment. The government also created a National Youth Service Corps that required all graduates from higher educational institutions to work for one year in a Nigerian community not of their own origin with a view to establishing a national culture that would erode parochial identities (Agbaje and Adisa 1988). The civilian Second Republic (1979–83) brought an end to all these programs but they were reinstated with vigor by the military government that seized power in 1983. General Muhammed Buhari's government tried to go even further by implementing the War Against Indiscipline (WAI) aimed at instilling discipline, patriotism, and eradicating corruption (Joseph 1987). These and other vigorous programs to place state above society in Nigeria as well as elsewhere have failed to institutionalize the kind of modernization that Durkheim had in mind.

State and Bureaucracy

Whereas class and society were more important concepts to Marx and Durkheim than the state, the latter was central to Max Weber, the father of modern political sociology. He is the first to treat political institutions as having a logic and history of their own. Weber was interested in such concepts as domination, power, and authority. His own interpretation of history was based on looking at the transformation in the mode of government. For example, feudalism in Weber's eyes could be explained by how the control over the material means of domination is exercised, which, notably, is through a regime of private property in the instruments of violence and in diffuse appropriation of the means of administration.

Weber recognized the importance of history but did not embrace the notion that it is evolutionary or dialectic. Instead, his main concern was to identify historical types of domination across social boundaries. His main contribution along these lines was to identify three ideal types of legitimate domination: (1) charismatic, (2) traditional, and (3) rational. No claim is made that these forms of domination succeed each other in any particular order, although subsequent generations of scholars, for example, those embracing modernization theory like Apter (1965), have tried to provide an ordering that implies a move from traditional to rational means of legitimate domination with a brief spell of charismatic authority prevailing in the moment of transition.

The interesting thing about the African state in this perspective is that it follows the reverse order of what happened in Europe. Historically, according to Weber, states arose in connection with efforts to deal with problems inherent in traditional systems of domination in which the hereditary power of a lord or a king prevailed. The latter maintains control over his underlings, whose help he needs to administer his territory, either by feeding them at his own table, remunerating them in kind, or awarding them a fief. The state as we know it today in its rational and legal form of domination came about in response to countering the patrimonial approach to domination, which is inherent in the traditional type. Weber was convinced that the rise of rational bureaucratic forms of administration was what gave state – and society – its modern character (Badie and Birnbaum 1983:20). Modern societies are characterized by the emergence of exclusive legal domination that is revealed chiefly through the formation and development of an institutionalized bureaucracy, which, literally, is the instrument of the modern state.

This transition from traditional to modern forms of domination did not always happen without conflict and violence. In fact, a look at European history suggests that it was almost always characterized by both forward and backward movements. It was in such contexts that the charismatic form of domination often arose. It relied on personal rather than traditional or rational authority. Among the instances of charismatic domination in European history that Weber cites are Cromwell, Robespierre, and Napoleon, all of whom established plebiscitary forms of democracy in which their own authority provided guidance. Charismatic authority, however, is difficult to sustain over long periods because it calls into question the relevance of economic calculation. As a result, it always gives way to other forms of legitimizing power.

A rational and legal form of domination constitutes the essence of the modern state; however, by the concept of state, Weber went a step further by suggesting that it refers to a set of political institutions that is capable of enforcing its rules and regulations, and thus exercises a monopoly of legitimate force over a territory. He shows how feudalism ended as a result of the concentration of military power and the use of an army that no longer depended on ties of vassalage because, as soldiers of the lord, it received regular wages (Gerth and Mills 1958). Subsequent studies of state formation in Europe, for example, by Tilly (1990), have also emphasized the way in which the modern state expropriates the independent private forces that rival it in possession of administrative power. A state becomes modern, then, when it puts an end to all patrimonial aspects of office and severs all ties between the performance of civil and military duties for the state and all title to the profits derived from the exercise of office (Badie and Birnbaum 1983:20–21). With the end of patrimonialism, the state becomes a distinct institution within society. It differentiates itself from society and becomes institutionalized. In order to complete this process successfully, however, the state must be able to compensate its servants so that they truly identify with their functions and, as far as their roles are concerned, sever their ties to other social groups.

Although the colonial state in Africa was a poor replica of the modern state that had taken form in Europe toward the end of the nineteenth century, it was in a historical perspective, as Young (1994) points out, the first colonial state to include the features of a rational-legal bureaucracy. The history of the modern state in Africa began where the state in Europe had ended. Its modern features became increasingly pronounced as colonial rule was effectively institutionalized. It was very much an institution distinct from society. Colonial officials were adequately compensated and administered the African territories in accordance with what they saw as their modernizing mission.

The independence of the colonial state from African society eventually became an issue, as nationalist leaders called into question not only how their territories were being ruled but also what kind of policies were being imposed upon the population. The nationalist leaders were heroes who could call upon their personal charisma to lead. Like Cromwell and Robespierre before them, they could appeal to the notion of a plebiscitary democracy in which their command of the masses would be particularly important. The difference, however, was that Nkrumah, Nyerere, and the others who led nationalist movements in Africa did not question traditional forms of domination, but did challenge its modern forms; the impersonal rather than the personal nature of the state was the issue.

Once the charisma of the nationalist leaders was routinized after independence, therefore, it was not in the direction of a rational-legal form of domination, but one that relies more on the discretionary power of the lord and his ability to distribute patronage to his underlings. This is reflected in the vast literature on neopatrimonialism – to be discussed further in Chapter Five – and related concepts such as prebendalism (Joseph 1987) that has emerged in the study of African politics since the 1980s. The latter refers to a practice, once prevalent in Europe, whereby public offices are competed for and then utilized for the personal benefit of office holders as well as their support group. This practice was pursued across Africa, but became particularly pronounced in countries such as Nigeria – the public revenue from oil provided an especially generous basis for dispensation of patronage. Diamond (1983) relates how state governors in the Second Republic inflated public employment and started a large number of state-financed schemes, only to have these funds diverted by politicians with the aid of government officials and private contractors. Although these practices within the frame of rational-legal forms of authority are illegitimate and criminal, they were typically understood in Nigeria as a legitimate means of fulfilling patronage obligations within the community idiom. These and other similar examples from across the African continent confirm that the trajectory of the state in Africa has been from being autonomous to becoming increasingly embedded in society. More specifically, its own logic is being subordinated to that of the community.

STATES AND POWER IN AFRICA

Drawing on the discussion in the previous section and additional literature on the subject, for example, Villalon and Huxtable (1998) and Forrest (2003), it can be argued that the state in Africa is problematic for three specific reasons. It lacks the autonomy from society that makes it an instrument of collective action. Instead, it tends to respond to community pressures and demands that undermine its authority as a public institution. It fails to operate as a corporate entity – as a system. A second reason is that state officials do not adhere to the formal rules that constitute public authority. They prefer not to distinguish between what is private and what is public, the result being that citizens lose confidence in their readiness to act in the public interest and instead look at these officials as primarily motivated to feather their own nests using public resources. The third reason is that individuals appointed to public office rarely subordinate their personalities to the definitions of the role that they are expected to perform. They do not allow themselves to be reduced to the notion of a cog in a machine but insist on upholding their personal esteem and dignity in ways that often go contrary to the demands of a rational-legal type of bureaucracy. In short, the state in Africa is not an independent system of power that operates predictably and provides guidance to society. It is not the kind of "development machine" that nationalist leaders had hoped for and international donors have expected to find in place for their funding.

The literature has concentrated on two explanations for this rather anomalous situation. One is that in historical comparison, the state in Africa is still at a stage of evolution that compares with previous periods in the history of other regions of the world, notably Western Europe, which is – rightly or wrongly – most commonly used as a point of reference. In other words, the patrimonial and prebendal features of state institutions correspond to what happened in Europe in earlier historical periods. It also corresponds to what we know about the state in other regions at earlier points in history. The second explanation is that the state in Africa is problematic because nationalist leaders have intentionally sought to eliminate the modern features of the state that were brought to the continent by the colonial powers. They have preferred to mold the state in the image of African society and are thus creating a situation in which the values prevailing in local communities have been elevated to hegemonic status. The problem with these values in the current context is that they are tied to local places and are parochial, that is, difficult to apply as universal principles for state action.

State formation in Africa, therefore, is characterized by a contradiction that is no longer as apparent in other regions of the world: there is not enough state power to project to all corners of the national territory. This is the argument of a recent book on states and power in Africa (Herbst 2000). He takes issue with a number of assumptions prevailing in the literature on the state in Africa. For instance, he maintains that the problem with African boundaries is not that they are artificial and too weak, but rather the opposite: that they are too strong and at the same time integral to the broadcasting of power in Africa. He comes to this conclusion after showing how boundaries in precolonial Africa were a true reflection of how far the power of the state could reach. Given rudimentary technologies and undeveloped infrastructure, the reach of the state was inevitably quite limited hence the prevalence of small political entities. The main change that the colonial powers brought to Africa was the introduction of a system of territorial boundaries that became consequential because they were backed by a state system that respected them. One of the things that African nationalists did not change after independence was the system of boundaries that they inherited from the colonial powers. At the first meeting of the Organization of African Unity (OAU) in 1963, they dedicated themselves to respecting existing state boundaries. By insisting on the integrity of the colonial boundaries, African leaders have been able to hide the weakness of their state institutions. The empirical absence of the state in much of the hinterland has had little, if any negative, effect because the state system set up under the auspices of the OAU reduces the risk of exposing failures to establish effective control in these areas. African states are what Jackson (1990) calls "quasi states," because they are sustained not by of their empirical strength, but by a state system that gives them juridical recognition as sovereign entities. Even so, Herbst maintains, they do survive and have strengthened their buffer mechanisms by introducing national currencies and citizenship laws that increase the salience of national boundaries.

The contradiction of states with incomplete control of their hinterlands but full claims to sovereignty, however, was too fundamental to remain hidden for long. The continuous weakening of the state through neopatrimonialism and urban biases in resource allocation left the hinterland increasingly exposed. The liberation movements in southern Africa already had demonstrated state weakness in the days of colonial rule, but, as mentioned in Chapter Two, it was Yoweri Museveni's National Resistance Movement in Uganda that constituted the first serious postcolonial challenge to the state powers, which had been artificially sustained by the OAU. As will be discussed further in Chapter Nine, similar challenges to government authority have subsequently been launched in many other countries, for example, Liberia, Sierra Leone, Somalia, and more recently also in the Ivory Coast, long considered one of the few African countries with an effective state.

Herbst contrasts the process of state formation with that of Europe and argues that better comparisons may be found elsewhere in the world. This point seems to rest primarily on the assumption that this process took place in Europe in the context of high population densities, whereas in Africa it has occurred while population densities have been low. Thus, national boundaries were contested in Europe because land was valuable and it therefore was worth sacrificing men and treasure to control. The African dedication to fixed boundaries was a way of ensuring stability in the absence of effective control of a population that was dispersed over wide spaces in the hinterland.

Two questions come to mind when reading Herbst's account of state consolidation in Africa. The first is the extent to which it is land or people that factors most importantly in power calculations in Africa. The second is whether it is high or low population density that lies behind the breakdown of state authority in Africa.

The literature in anthropology emphasizes the important role that the notion of rule over people rather than rule over land plays in African social and political relations. Because people rather than land was in shortage, the search for adherents was always more important than the appropriation of land (Goody 1971). Kopytoff (1987:43) expands on this subject when he writes that African kin groups had an almost insatiable demand for people and jealously guarded those they already had. It is no coincidence, he argues, that over half of all cases in customary courts have to do with disputes over marriage, divorce, and bridewealth (*lobola* in southern Africa) – matters that all involve the social appropriation of progeny. Rights in persons, therefore, are considered more important than rights in land or other property. These rights, however, vary over time and place and Kopytoff stresses the versatility of kinship systems in managing such rights. They acquired new members not merely by reproducing their own kinsmen, but also by adopting new adherents, purchasing slaves, and attracting strangers.

The kinship idiom served as a way of organizing political relations along lines that were based on generalized loyalty rather than on a functionally specific one. The services a person sought from another member could not be reduced to a contractual agreement. This way of looking at politics has resurfaced after independence with a growing emphasis on community rather than on collectivity. The feudal phase in Europe that paved the way for capitalism was contractual and functionally specific, permitting, for example, a vassal to owe obligations to more than one suzerain. Allegiance in African societies was – and continues to be – functionally diffuse and indivisible involving the kind of primordial allegiance to which kinship ties easily lend themselves (Kopytoff 1987:58–49).

This brief review of what anthropologists have had to say about the nature of rule in precolonial Africa and its implications for the present is to highlight the embedded nature of state institutions in Africa. The difficulties that the African state has had to broadcast its powers to the peripheral corners of its territory, as Herbst calls it, are very much a result of the premium that leaders pay on controlling people rather than territory. Because the state is not really an instrument but an arena for accommodating competing community interests, the issue of consolidating power over territory takes on only secondary importance in relation to acquiring and controlling followers. The logic behind the exercise of power in Africa is not focused on broadcasting over territories but on informal exchanges aimed at acquiring and sustaining followers.

The other question relates to Herbst's suggestion that the peripheral parts of the territory are characterized by low population density hence they count little to those having access to state power. The point about the recent challenges to the African state, however, is that they have occurred in high-density areas and they have been as much over control of people as over control of territory. The political turmoil that has afflicted the Great Lakes region of Africa – Uganda, Rwanda, Burundi, and the Democratic Republic of Congo – takes on some of the same features as wars in Europe. In this respect, these more recent events appear to question Herbst's point that Africa's states are underdeveloped because they have not been formed through war (Reno 2000). It is worth noting, however, that unlike Europe, the wars have been fought without demands to change existing state boundaries. Instead, in the light of growing uncertainty, efforts to build stronger ties among the Tutsi/ Hima aristocracy in the region have been a major cause of these interstate and intrastate conflicts. Again, there is reason to emphasize the demographic rather than the geographic dimensions of the problems the state in Africa faces in consolidating its powers.

So how does the state in Africa compare with states elsewhere in the world? Herbst has suggested that comparing it with Europe alone is not very helpful, because the process of state consolidation in Africa has been so different. I suggest that in order to make this assessment, it is necessary to examine two dimensions of the state: (a) its executive capacity, and (b) its legality or adherence to rules. States differ in their capacity to act autonomously: a strong state is one that is capable of shaping society rather

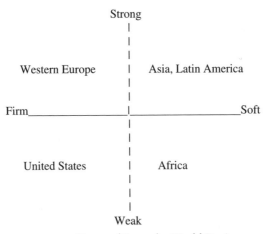

FIGURE 1. Types of States by World Region.

than being shaped by it; a weak state is the opposite – it fails to exercise such control. States also differ in terms of how closely officials adhere to rules, be they procedures, laws, or constitutions. A state is firm when its officials act in accordance with formal rules and thus provide a measure of certainty as to what can be expected. A state is soft when officials do not follow these formal rules but find ways of circumventing or subverting them on their own or in collusion with outsiders. To be sure, most states in the world display more or less of these qualities, but it may still be possible to create a typology that arranges states by region in ways that indicate their predominant features. Figure 1 is an attempt to provide such a typology. This typology goes beyond the categorization of states that Migdal (1988) provides in his analysis of weak states and strong societies. The problem that states face in their interaction with society is not just in terms of their capacity to exercise social control of groups in society. It is also, as the figure suggests, a matter of how easily the state can be penetrated by groups in society using informal means to acquire influence. Thus, the states in both Asian and Latin American countries tend to have the capacity to control society, but they are not immune to the deals that are indicative of efforts by individuals or groups, for example, private corporations, to collude with officials to obtain benefits or services. In Africa, the state is not only weak as an organizational instrument, but it is also open to undue influences by political patrons representing communities whose interests cannot be ignored.

It is in these dual respects that the state in Africa is more problematic than it is elsewhere. Because it is so deeply embedded in societal relations that remain locally specific and inadequately integrated into an abstract system of rules that can be manipulated by officials, the state lacks the preconditions that Scott (1999) associates with the modern state. Most notably, society in Africa lacks the organization and civil statistical information that makes the state's development function legible. In this respect, therefore, the state in Africa is like a blind man sensing his way around and responding to constraints and opportunities set by others rather than an instrument of development charting – and sustaining – new ways forward. That is also why the study of the state in Africa must include not just its formal institutions, but also the way informal networks operate and influence policy outcomes.

CONCLUSIONS

Most countries of the world are engaged in a process of state consolidation. The issues that they face relate to how it can be made more efficient, more accountable, and transparent. The vast majority of countries in Africa are first and foremost preoccupied with state formation. The most important issues relate to how to secure more effective control over existing territory, and how to integrate communities that continue viewing themselves as more legitimate political entities than the public institutions that are the state. States in Africa tend to be different in this respect from what is found elsewhere in the world. This leads to a concluding question: are the structural conditions that must prevail for consolidation present in Africa?

The study of the state in Africa tells us that certain structural underpinnings help it modernize and become consolidated. Foremost among these is the emergence of a corporate class of independently wealthy individuals who do not have to rely on public resources to become rich. With such a group in power, the state becomes an instrument that molds development in the image of economic reasoning. A calculative and instrumentalist approach to policy analysis and policy making emerges. With it comes the notion of systems thinking and a new approach to governing the public realm. The state in Asia and Latin America shares some of the shortcomings we have discussed in this chapter but despite their softness, they act as corporate bodies ensuring that corruption does not get in the way of national development. Unlike Africa, corruption in these other regions is merely a by-product of national development programs.

The important thing to acknowledge is that although structural conditions in Africa are less hospitable to progress in the modern sense of the word, there is no absolute hindrance to change. Botswana has shown that it is possible to embrace modernization and move ahead without threat to political stability. In fact, it is precisely because its leaders have followed such an approach that the country counts as not only one of the more stable, but also one of the more democratic countries. Scholars argue about the reasons for its exception, but they agree that in addition to the wealth of the country's cattle-owning elite and ethnic homogeneity – the Tswana constitute some

90 percent of the population – a principal reason for its stability is that that the government embraced advice from the West instead of rejecting it (e.g. Holm and Molutsi 1992). In order to understand why the vast majority of African leaders have rejected a complete wooing of modernity and have at best had only a schizophrenic relationship with it, it is necessary to take a closer look at the political economy of these countries.

4

The Economy of Affection

The previous two chapters have suggested that relations of power in African countries are predominantly personal and in that sense, informal. They are not just indicative of odd behavior that goes contrary to formal authority. They are in fact the social structures that hold society together. As the discussion of the movement legacy indicated, agency occurs in the context of informal relations. The informal has been institutionalized to the point where it tends to dominate the way formal institutions operate. Formal rules, for instance, are often bent to serve informal institutions. The informal institutions are not unique to Africa, but their significance is particularly noticeable there. Nowhere else can they be studied more extensively than in African countries.

Because these institutions permeate social and political life, one can rightly speak of the presence of a fundamental social logic. This logic centers on direct, face-to-face reciprocities to get things done. Its core principles are that (a) whom you know is more important than what you know, (b) sharing personal wealth is more rewarding than investing in economic growth, and (c) a helping hand today generates returns tomorrow. Such is the essence of the informal political economy that I call the "economy of affection" (Hyden 1980).

This economy differs from capitalism as well as socialism. Money is not an end in itself, nor is the state the primary redistributive mechanism. It relies on the handshake rather than the contract, on personal discretion rather than official policy to allocate resources. It coexists with capitalism or socialism, often helping individuals to get around the rough edges of such systems. Exchanges within the economy of affection do not get officially registered. It is an invisible economy that conscientious policy makers have no taste for and economists find no real way of effectively incorporating into their conventional forms of analysis.

This chapter will discuss the parallel institutions that Africans have created in order to avoid the whims of the market and the arm of the state. As

Herbst (2000) notes in his analysis of the state, this arm is neither long or strong. There are plenty of ways to circumvent it, even if one gets caught. This set of issues is important not only because class relations as well as the miracle of the market (Bates 1989) have faded as principal lenses of analysis in political science. These issues are also important because the interest in Africa's informal institutions has continued to grow. Not everyone has thought of the subject in terms of an economy of affection, but whichever other concept has been used, the legacy of this original notion of how people behave and make choices in African society is still very much alive.

The failure to recognize the prevalence of an economy of affection and its robustness in Africa compared to formal institutions is one of the biggest – if not *the* biggest – challenge to scholars and policy analysts alike. Because of our strong desire to standardize and compare, the natural inclination has been to look only at the formal institutions and how they can be reformed. Even though they may generate statistics that lend themselves to quantitative modes of analysis and measurement, they do not tell more than part of the story at best. The light that these figures offer is limited in range and quite dim, because the collection and aggregation of data are usually of questionable quality. Thus, if we wish to understand – and explain – what happens on the scene in Africa, the informal institutions must be given highest priority (Chabal and Daloz 1999).

This chapter begins by discussing what the economy of affection is all about and what kind of informal institutions it gives rise to. It continues to discuss the nature of informal institutions and how they differ from formal ones. The third part will place the economy of affection in its proper theoretical context – social exchange theory. The last section will provide illustrations of how the economy of affection operates and the implications it has for attempts to create civic forms of governance on the continent.

THE ECONOMY OF AFFECTION

Definition

The easiest way of describing the economy of affection is to suggest that it is constituted by personal investments in reciprocal relations with other individuals as a means of achieving goals that are seen as otherwise impossible to attain. Sought-after goods – whether material or symbolic such as prestige and status – have a scarcity value, that is, they may be physically available, but not accessible to all, so people invest in relations with others to obtain them. Many such investments are incidental or may be a form of regularized behavior, but not necessarily an institution. For instance, people who approach officials to illegally obtain licenses or a piece of property are not part of an informal institution, but engaging in affective behavior to achieve their goals. An informal institution in the economy of affection arises when a group of people agree voluntarily on doing something together; they let a code of unwritten rules develop to guide their activities and their dealings with those who breach these rules.

The economy of affection is not an expression of irrationality or altruism. Nor does it have anything to do with romantic love. It is a practical and rational way of dealing with choice in contexts of uncertainty and in situations where place, rather than distanciated space, dictates and influences people's preferences. People engage in affective behavior and create informal institutions for a variety of reasons. They may do so from a position of either strength or weakness. They may do it when faced with opportunity or constraint. Four motives for engaging in affective behavior are to (a) gain status, (b) seek favor, (c) share a benefit, and (d) provide a common good.

As discussed in the previous two chapters, status and wealth in African societies has always depended on the ability to accumulate dependents and followers. Gaining status, therefore, through such measures as hired labor, many wives, and acquisition of clients has continued to be an important aspect of social structuration in Africa. As Barber (1991:183) writes about Yoruba society in southwestern Nigeria:

[Yoruba society was] animated by a dynamic, competitive struggle for self-aggrandisement, which permeated the society from top to bottom. There was scope for people to create a place for themselves and expand it by their own efforts. Like the "Big Men" of New Guinea, they did it through the recruitment of supporters. A Yoruba proverb says, "I have money, I have people, what else is there that I have not got?" Money was one of the principal ways of gaining public acknowledgement as a big man; but "having people" constituted that acknowledgment itself.

Spending money conspicuously therefore was an act of sharing while it also amounted to gaining status – and influence. Parkin (1972) provides interesting insights of this in his study of a Giriama community on the Kenyan coast. He shows how individuals who have recently acquired their wealth spend lavishly on such private ceremonies as funerals and weddings to demonstrate their commitment to local institutions of kinship, and to earn enough respect to testify before elders on their behalf in disputes over rights to land and trees. Much the same happens in contemporary political contexts, especially at times of election. Candidates may try to say the right thing about their opinion of specific policy issues, but they know that what they say has much less importance than what they do to demonstrate that they have a following. To make a gain, therefore, they have to invest in dispensing monetary and other forms of tangible rewards to prospective supporters. Studies of elections in Africa, ever since the first study of one-party elections in Tanzania (Cliffe 1967) till more recent ones by, for example,

Lindberg (2003), confirm the extent to which political actors operating in the economy of affection are ready to go to furnish individual perks to potential followers. This stands in contrast with candidate behavior in democratic elections in the United States or Western European countries where promises are verbal and generalized. In the economy of affection, accountability at election time is immediate; the candidate must demonstrate personal generosity as part of the process of campaigning. In Western democracies, it is deferred and exercised only if the candidate wins and comes into office.

Illustrations

The importance of sharing in the economy of affection does not only generate clientelism among leaders and other important people in society. It also engenders an expectation on the part of the less well endowed that seeking a favor from someone with resources is quite legitimate. Such favors are most often pursued within family structures, but with growing social mobility, the boundaries for this form of behavior are being extended. The point about the economy of affection, regardless of who is involved, is that the inclination is to approach problem solving by seeking out another person for help rather than finding a solution on one's own. A couple of examples will do. Perhaps the most relevant illustration comes from the literature on urban-rural transfers (Little 1965; Caldwell 1969; Weisner 1976; Moock 1978; Sandbrook 1982). Rural households across Africa have always struggled to make ends meet working the land alone. Relying on a rudimentary manual technology and unpredictable climate, having someone earning an income from other sources is important. As will be further discussed in Chapter Eight, this orientation prevails to this day. With agriculture increasingly failing to generate income for rural households, off-farm sources of income have in fact grown in significance. Urban migrants may try to negotiate ways of ensuring that their burden of transferring money back home to family and community does not become too heavy, but they have great difficulty escaping these expectations and social pressures without losing their status in the eyes of those at home. For urban residents, therefore, life in town is very much tied to demands, both specific and general, from relatives and friends in the countryside who see themselves as having an entitlement to claim part of the money that their urban-based kin generate while away from the farm.

The other illustration comes from the field of credit. African development programs are full of stories about problems of securing repayment of loans. The reasons for low rates of loan repayment vary and include credit programs for development initiatives that stand a very little chance of succeeding in the first place. Thus, loan repayment problems cannot be blamed on the economy of affection alone. It does, however, play an important part in explaining the issue. The idea of loan and that it needs to be repaid in agreement with a contract is foreign to the economy of affection, where reciprocity is not really negotiated. Reciprocity includes the possibility of nonpayment because someone with money or resources is expected to share his wealth. Whether or not this comes through an institution such as a bank makes no difference. There is always the possibility of explaining to the bank clerk that things didn't go as planned (Shipton 1990). Microfinance schemes may be better designed to deal with this issue, but problems of getting people to repay their loans exist even in such programs. For most people seeking credit, obtaining a loan is perceived as a favor, and paying it back, therefore, makes much less sense than trying to redefine the situational boundaries in order to escape it. The result is that formal lending institutions in Africa are inundated with excuses rather than repayments.

The economy of affection, however, is not only about conspicuous consumption or prostrating behavior. For many, the most important association with the concept is the creation of a common good. Because the economy of affection relies on primary forms of reciprocity, it tends to function best in small-scale, face-to-face contexts. Local communities provide natural organizations for institutionalizing affective norms. African countries are full of examples of local communities that cater to their own needs through self-help efforts. So-called *stokwel* projects aimed at building and managing water holes for cattle in southern Africa are cases in point. So is the *harambee* – literally "pull together" – movement in Kenya. Although politicians eventually appropriated it for their own ends, it began – and continues to exist at local level – as a truly genuine self-help organization. This pooling of efforts is common in the rural areas, but exists also among urban migrants, who find themselves faced with needs that they cannot cope with on their own. Even though mutual aid societies in the cities are no substitute for the social security system provided by the modern welfare state system, they are meaningful bodies because they give assistance to members in sickness, bereavement, and other unforeseen crises. Many of these informal institutions take the form of rotating credit institutions, known as *esusu* among the Yoruba, *adaski* among the Hausa of northern Nigeria, *djana* among the Fang of Cameroon, and *ndjonu* in Benin (Little 1965:51–52). The reciprocity involved in lateral social interaction such as those discussed here tends to be both immediate and reliable. This form of fund-raising is important because it provides a ready sum of money that can be used to acquire goods for trading, to build a house, or to pay school fees.[1]

---

[1] Little (p. 48) quotes the example of Nanemei Akpee (Society of Friends), an organization that, in the 1960s, had branches in many towns in Ghana. Its motto was "Love Is the Key," that is, the key that opens the door to brotherhood.

Urban-rural transfers do not only go to meet the needs of individual rural households. They also play an important role in rural development. The hometown associations among the Yoruba provide an especially interesting illustration. Urban-based individuals, as Trager (2001:168) notes, participate in local community development in three ways. The first, and most common, is to contribute to organizational and community fund-raising for specific projects. The second is for an individual to establish a presence of some sort in the community, typically by forming an economic enterprise that serves the community at large. The third way is to engage in local philanthropy by donating something for the use of the entire community. The establishment of community banks throughout much of Yorubaland in the 1990s is one of several manifestations of the dynamics of this sharing of resources with one's home community.

Similar urban-rural linkages exist in other parts of Nigeria and Africa, although they may differ in scope and intensity. The economy of affection and its informal institutions are the mechanisms by which resources are allocated. The significance of urban-rural linkages, however, goes beyond its economic significance for local development. Geschiere and Gugler (1998) emphasize that an increasing number of individuals in African countries function not in one but in both of these locations. They function in a multilocal space; what shapes their identity is not a set of impersonal and formal institutions, but an affective network based on identification with community. The glue that holds African societies together tends to be affective rather than civic. It is more fluid and opportunistic than civic-mindedness because the latter is based on principle.

The economy of affection is not just an African phenomenon. It is ubiquitous. It's found in rural communities elsewhere in the world. Sil (2003) has analyzed it with reference to the Japanese *mura* and the Russian *mir*. He shows that the legacy of these two forms of peasant community although significantly altered by land reform and collectivization, respectively, has been important in shaping formal institutional practices in recent years. Scott (1976), with his notion of a moral economy, comes close to arguing the same thing when he suggests that peasants band together in defense of their lifeworld as the forces of modern capitalism impinge on their livelihoods. The moral economy is a subtype of the economy of affection that mediates the relations peasants and other marginal groups in society have with state or market.

The economy of affection is present in many other contexts as well as in modern society. The idea that one can make gains by nurturing a good relationship with another person is not foreign to what we may witness in U.S. society. Even though it is not institutionalized, opportunistic behavior based on affective relations is quite common, for example, when it comes to getting a job, being promoted, or securing a contract. Some of the corporate scandals in the United States in recent years are cases in point. In many

European countries, the economy of affection has developed as a substitute for formal channels that are too cumbersome or costly. It is present there as well as in the United States among immigrant groups that have yet to be fully acculturated into their new society. Finally, terrorist groups that operate clandestinely do so according to the principles of an economy of affection; their threat to others stems from their ability to function as informal institutions eluding, in their case, the attempt by formal institutions to capture them.

The economy of affection, therefore, may have either positive or negative consequences. It typically helps those ready to participate in it, but may pose a threat or be a cost to others. Because it is informal, it operates as a black market or in a gray zone between morality and law. Some people get away with their behavior, others do not, mainly because there is a general trust in the ability of modern society to discover such attempts at breaking the formal rules. Experience in recent years, however, has shown that getting a handle on informal institutions of an affective nature has proved much more difficult than what officials expected. For instance, the presence of these institutions constitutes a challenge to the principles of good governance, notably public accountability and transparency, and not only in developing countries, but also in developed societies.

INFORMAL INSTITUTIONS IN PERSPECTIVE

The discussion so far has suggested that the economy of affection is a function of direct reciprocal relations that may be either vertical or lateral. It has also indicated that these reciprocal relations may be either inclusive or exclusive. These two dimensions provide the parameters of the social space that the economy of affection covers. As Figure 2 shows, this distinction also serves as the basis for identifying its primary institutional manifestations.

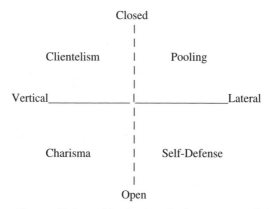

FIGURE 2. Types of informal institutions in the economy of affection.

Types of Informal Institutions

These four types of informal institutions are analytical categories. They are not mutually exclusive in the empirical realm. For instance, groups that rely on pooling may also contain elements of clientelism. Similarly, groups that oppose others may rely on a charismatic leader. Furthermore, institutions may shift over time from one type to another. In other words, these are not necessarily stable social entities, but shift character in response to changing circumstances. I shall briefly discuss each type below.

Clientelism. This is one of the most prolific informal institutions around the world. Judging from the literature, it certainly is pervasive in Third World societies, both in and outside of politics. Although it is not gender-specific, it is typically associated with masculine figures of power. Lemarchand (1972) rendered the first systematic account of clientelism in African politics. His treatment of this informal institution was quite appreciative: A political patron brought to the political center a large following that facilitated national integration. In retrospect, one may argue that Lemarchand's treatment of clientelism was the informal equivalent of Lijphart's consociationalism, the political order found in some multicultural countries in Western Europe (Lijphart 1977). Even in these European countries, the political center has been held together by a series of deals among representatives of cultural groups sharing state power.

This positive account of clientelism has gradually become more critical, if not negative. Neopatrimonialism – the ultimate form of clientelism in politics – has become the principal concept in Africanist political science. Political rulers treat the exercise of power as an extension of their private realm. The prevalence of clientelism in African politics is evidence that formal institutions are weak. As suggested in Chapter Two, it appears that the introduction of multiparty politics has only reinforced affective relations because competition for power and resources has intensified in the new political dispensation (Bratton and van de Walle 1997). Clientelism is deemed problematic, especially in circles that are concerned with improving governance in African countries. It keeps African countries barely afloat, but it does not help them swim forward.

Pooling. This concept is sufficiently general to serve as a generic classification of all forms of cooperation in groups that are organized along voluntary and self-enforcing lines. These groups are not sanctioned by law. Instead, they are constituted by adherence to unwritten rules. Examples include criminal organizations like the Mafia and Chinese tongs, where the closure of the group is very strict. In each example, breaking the informal code may result in death. The blood oaths that members of these organization generally take to certify their unquestioned loyalty serve as surrogate kinship bonds; all of them swear to trust one another in situations in which betrayal is very tempting (Fukuyama 1995:101).

The family is the basic social organization and it features – directly or indirectly – in many of the examples of lateral informal institutions that are found around the world. Informal institutions in which the family is important prevail in cultures where voluntary associations such as schools, clubs, and professional organizations have yet to acquire influence in society. As Fukuyama (1995:62–63) also notes, cultures in which the primary avenue to sociability is family and kinship rather than in secondary associations have a great deal of trouble creating large, durable economic organizations; therefore, they look to the state to support them, a point that has also been made by others, e.g. Putnam (1993).

China is a good example of where family has continued to play a very important role in economic life. Although the family in China, as Mueller et al. (2002) also demonstrate, tends to be smaller but vertically strong – especially in the relationship between father and son – it is a closed unit that operates to maximize its own gains. The relatively exclusive nature of the Chinese family allows it to enjoy initial success in business, but limits its success once the business calls for organizational expansion. Formalization, through professionalization, is inhibited by the relative strength of the informal relations prevailing within the family.

The African family is more extensive and generally open to cooperation with others. Kinship relations dominate, facilitating solidarity across family lines. In addition to the rotating credit societies, groups sharing labor are quite common forms of small-scale informal organizations in rural Africa. Groups like these, however, are not necessarily as effective today as they used to be. Integration into the global economy means that resources needed for one's livelihood involves transaction outside the local community. Hoon (2002) reports on what he calls the verticalization of personal relations in a study of farming groups in eastern Zambia. Wealthier individuals in the community become brokers with the outside world and use this role to build a position of power. Pooling gives way to clientelism.

Lateral groups bound together by affective ties often coexist with formal structures. Studies of the Japanese conglomerates referred to as *keiretsu*, for example, Mitsubishi, indicate that lateral informal relations are very important in the management of these multipurpose, large-scale corporate entities (Gerlach 1992). The significance of informal relations has also been demonstrated in the sociology of organization literature describing management patterns in the United States (e.g. Gouldner 1954; Ouchi 1981). Much more remains to be done on the issue of how informal rules influence political life. Fenno (1966) and, more recently, Gordon (2003) are among those who have discussed the importance that informal relations play for reaching consensus among legislators, for example, in the House Appropriations Committee of the U.S. Congress. To the extent that such behavior is regularized and takes on a self-enforcing quality, it becomes institutional.

Self-Defense. This refers to informal institutions that mobilize support against a common threat or enemy – whether real or perceived. Affection is a powerful instrument to achieve this. It binds people together across narrower organizational boundaries. As discussed in Chapter Two, modern African history is full of examples of how affection has been used to generate movements for defense of what is perceived as an African lifestyle.

Informal behavior or institutions for self-defense have their own problems because they tend to view issues in straight black-and-white terms: You are either with me or against me. The OAU is a case in point. Meetings of heads of state were always behind closed doors. This way they could avoid criticizing each other in public. As Herbst (2000) argues, this was important because they could not politically afford for it to be showed that they were accused of having weaknesses in the way they governed their respective countries. The informal character of this club was institutionalized and it eventually contributed to the OAU losing its credibility. Under the reorganized African Union, African heads of state have agreed to a self-monitoring system to ensure improved governance on the continent, but it is far from clear that this formal agreement will erase the informal behavior and institutions that exist within the organization.

The use of affection in self-defense is a more pronounced phenomenon in Africa than in Asia. A major reason is that Asian societies have been permeated by a single religion or philosophy. For example, Confucianism has defined social relations in China over two thousand years. Even though its ethical principles have not been in the form of a national constitution, Chinese, regardless of social status, have internalized these principles (Rozman 1991). In Africa, customary norms were never universal and only confined to small-scale societies. Although similarities did exist among these societies, they were not enough to form the basis for a national constitutional and legal framework. Instead, what held the new nation-states together was a perceived need to guard against an enemy from within or without. This was done through affective ties that were generated as complement to the formal structures in place.

Charisma. Charisma, one may argue, is the ultimate informal institution. *Charismatic,* according to Weber (1947:242), is defined as "devotion to sanctity, heroism, or exemplary character of an individual person, and the normative patterns or order revealed or ordained by him." Although the origin of the concept is different,[2] Weber applied it broadly to refer to all individual personalities endowed with supernatural, superhuman, or, at least, specifically exceptional powers or qualities. Such people included a great variety of heroes, saviors, prophets, shamans, and even demagogues. Weber himself is not easy to understand on the issue of what charismatic authority really is, but, in short, his treatment of the concept is meant to capture the revolutionary moment in history. At the same time, he makes the point that charisma is not sustainable without routinization. In the study of law and administration, scholarship has treated the role of charisma as instrumental in transforming traditional or customary authority into a new type that in Weber's language is rational-legal authority. In Africa, the story of charisma is different. It seems important especially in terms of filling the gap that exists between formal institutional structures, on the one hand, and customary and informal institutions, on the other.

Charisma, like self-defense, is inclusive, but the charismatic leader occupies an unquestioned position of authority. The interesting thing about Africa is that charisma typically works to reestablish traditional rather than rational-legal authority. The affinity with the modern common or civil law that was brought to Africa by the colonial powers is virtually nonexisting, except in professional legal circles. What counts are the principles of the past that a charismatic figure – a politician or a cleric – can invoke to gain followers. By wishing to reinvent something genuinely African, these persons seek legitimacy based on the sanctity of age-old rules and powers. This is inevitably a process of informalization. Compliance in this scenario is not owed to enacted rules but to the persons who occupy positions of authority or who have been chosen for it by a traditional master. Galvan (2002) provides an intriguing and empirically rich case study of how this process works among the Serer in rural Senegal. Innovations or adaptations, even if they lead to syncretistic institutions, are legitimized by disguising them as reaffirmations of the past.

Charisma blurs the line between person and rule. It assumes a reciprocal exchange in which the authority of the charismatic figure is accepted without question. These exchanges are essentially affective in nature. No attempt is made to reflect on a particular principle before accepting authority because charisma makes such reflection superfluous. Many African nationalists were charismatic figures. No one succeeded more than Julius Nyerere in trying to disguise his modernist policies regarding the sanctity of past rules. He developed socialist policies with a modern economy in mind, but legitimized every initiative he took in that direction with reference to recreating an ideal of the African past (*ujamaa*). The result was that he became a very successful

---

[2] Weber borrowed it from the German legal historian, Rudolph Sohm, who used charisma to refer to the concept of sacramental grace, which underlay the law of the church prior to the twelfth century (Berman 1983:549).

political patron, but like all prophets or heroes, his relations with others was based on affection rather than cognitive reflections about the feasibility of the new policies. There was never any room for criticism of the proposals that he made. In short, the informal institutions that he created under his leadership inhibited a critical examination of his policies from within. Instead, they fostered conformity and compliance. In the end, it required intervention from the international community, including his political friends – notably the Scandinavians – to literally force a policy change on the political leadership in Tanzania.

The role of charisma is not necessarily confined to modernization processes alone. It springs up in different modern contexts as well. For example, an element of affection is often brought into more routinized settings to make it more dynamic. A political leader, a corporation executive, or a trade union boss may use charisma to mobilize support for a new policy. Charisma is by definition temporary and informal, but it forms an important part of the institutional landscape of every society. It may help to overcome a political hurdle, to transform an organization, or help emancipate a lot of downtrodden people. Thus, the setting for charisma exists everywhere and in any period. Yet, in a contemporary perspective with so many problems and so much uncertainty facing the continent, it is no coincidence that charisma is an especially important example of informal institutions in Africa.

Formal and Informal Institutions

The rationality of affective behavior needs an explanation. The autonomous, self-maximizing individual is no longer the model of human that even economists work with. There is a broad agreement that institutions, although helping to overcome market failures, nonetheless are constraining individual choice. Rationality is bounded by formal rules. Thus, firms can make the market operate better while at the same time set boundaries for what individuals can choose or do (Williamson 1985). Individual choice and behavior, however, is not constrained merely by formal rules. Informal ones matter too. And they may be more influential in determining human behavior and choice than the formal ones. An individual is not just an organization man. Thus, rationality in the economy of affection is socially embedded in the sense that it presupposes personal interdependence. For instance, A seeks out B as a shortcut to obtain a good otherwise out of reach. But it is also rational for B to accept the request, because B gains influence over A (or a credit that can be called upon in the future). An informal deal is often preferable because it does not entail the wait and uncertainty associated with formal collective action. Nor does it carry the threat of a free ride that Olson (1965) discusses. It rests on the assumption of shared expectations, not the maximization of a particular goal that relies on the organizational reconciliation of an N range of individual preferences.

The economy of affection modifies, but does not contradict the notion of maximizing one's gains. In this sense, it relaxes the assumptions underlying rational choice theory. It does so by assuming that personal, face-to-face reciprocities or exchanges are sometimes preferable to reciprocity inherent in an individual's interaction with a distant actor, be that a state institution or a trading partner. The latter, which Oakerson (1988) calls the essence of rule of law – that is, the trust a person has in the system – is replaced in the economy of affection by an interpersonal trust that is more immediate and exclusively reliant on unwritten rules in use. Tobler (1998), analyzing Swiss-born and immigrant youth, makes the distinction between those who rely on a primary form of reciprocity – a *Kernkultur* – and those who feel comfortable relying on the impersonal and more distant institutions of the state.

The economy of affection makes a lot of sense for individuals in many circumstances, be they characterized by constraint or opportunity. Poor people would act together or seek out a patron to help them achieve what they could not do on their own. Entrepreneurs, in economics as well as in politics, would take advantage of opportunities available to them to seek and dispense favors. Like the market economy, therefore, the economy of affection deals with growth and redistribution, innovation, and safety. The difference is that in the latter, contractual agreements are not needed. There is no standard, like money, to gauge the value of specific exchanges. Terms are never precise, always ambiguous. That is why the economy of affection is more political than economic in the strict sense that the latter, economics, is being interpreted in the neoclassical version of the market.

It may be useful at this point to set the informal institutions discussed here in the comparative context of their formal counterparts. Table 7 summarizes the extent to which the economy of affection relaxes the standard assumption underlying the neoinstitutionalist theories. With regard to

TABLE 7. *Comparison of Formal and Informal Institutions*

Variable	Formal Institutions	Informal Institutions
Type of exchange	Impersonal	Face-to-face
Approach to rules	Rule of law	Rules in use
Character of rules	Written	Unwritten
Nature of exchange	Contractual	Noncontractual
Time schedule	Specified	Nonspecified
Actor premise	Organizational goal adherence	Shared expectations
Implications of agreement	Precise compliance	Ambiguous execution
Transparency	Potentially open to scrutiny	Closed and confidential
Conflict resolution	Third-party body	Self-enforcement

Africa, the most important point to make here is that because the social formations continue to rely on rudimentary forms of technology, social and political action is not collective in the sense that those familiar with modern society imply. People do not share goals that stem from common interests. They do not think in terms of reconciling private preferences to make a public choice. Those social dilemmas that are a mainstay of neoinstitutionalism and require an ordering of preferences so suboptimal solutions can be found that benefit everyone – the win-win formula – are not part of the mental map of Africans when they make decisions. They share expectations about what is appropriate behavior: that is, reciprocity in all exchanges, even if this does not mean giving back exactly what one received, or responding within a specified time. The political economy equations in Africa, therefore, are more rudimentary and are best captured in social exchange theory.

ECONOMY OF AFFECTION AND SOCIAL EXCHANGE THEORY

The peculiar social logic of the economy of affection is most easily comprehensible through social exchange theory. Emerson (1962) and Blau (1964) are among the most influential scholars behind the theory of power that emphasizes mutual dependence as its principal source. Their view of power differs from those who assume that power is an attribute of a person or a group. It challenges the conventional view that A affects B in a manner contrary to B's own interests because A possesses resources that allow exercising influence over B. In this respect, it also differs from the theories that emphasize conflicts of interest. In short, social exchange theory departs from mainstream definitions of power in political science offered by Weber (1947) and Dahl (1957). Social exchange theory assumes that power can be balanced in a social relationship. Power, therefore, is not a requirement for the exercise of power. When power is unbalanced – and that is, of course, the more common scenario – conflict is can be seen as inherent in the unequal dependencies that created the imbalance. Because B is more dependent on the exchange than A, their preference for an exchange will not be the same. It may or may not imply willful exercise of power or willful resistance to that power, but the core of the social exchange theory approach to power is that the power is manifest in different degrees of dependence on the exchange itself. Power, therefore, is not as absolute as other theories assume.

At first glance, social exchange theory approaches power in a benign fashion. Because it downplays the intentional imposition of one person's will over another as well as willful resistance, it comes closer to accepting that power exists in all social relations, even intimate ones, as postmodernism would also claim. This doesn't mean, as Molm (1997) convincingly argues, that coercion needs to be absent in social exchange theory. Social exchanges are not just exchanges of rewards or positive power, but often entail punishment or negative power. Certainly reward power can be used coercively, although it may not always be easy.[3] Thus, in the economy of affection, reciprocities may entail both rewards and punishment. Examples of use of coercive power include patrons denying their clients rewards because of lack of full support, but also the opposite: voters denying political patrons support because they have not delivered on promise of reward. Each party typically has some degree of power over the other, although the degree of it varies (Baldwin 1978).

This takes us to the issue of structure and agency in the use of power. Is it structurally induced or is it strategic, that is, reflective of an actor's intention? Exchange theorists such as Emerson (1962) would argue that even in the absence of any conscious or intentional use of power, an actor who possesses a structural advantage will, over time, obtain more rewards at lower cost. The structural characteristics of the exchange relations, rather than motives of the actors, cause a power imbalance. Some actors have advantages over others as a result of these structural determinants. Therefore, they can pursue exchanges with others without necessarily giving them all they want. By withholding rewards – and either intentionally or unintentionally punishing them – they exercise power over them. In the course of doing this, they drive up the cost of obtaining the rewards they control, while lowering their own costs of obtaining rewards from their exchange partners. In short, as Molm (1997:36) points out, actors with a power advantage are likely to pursue exchange with their more available or more valuable alternatives, and in the process they inadvertently make their disadvantaged partners pay higher costs for their rewards. Reciprocities, as the case is in the economy of affection, do not have to be equal, nor immediate. Powerful actors may withhold giving something back to an unspecified later point, or may even ignore such a reciprocal act altogether, leaving the disadvantaged persons with nothing in return for their own effort at social exchange.

Reciprocal exchange relations in the economy of affection are largely non-negotiated, that is, individuals perform actions that produce rewarding or punishing outcomes for their partners and respond sequentially to the outcomes produced by their partners. They do not bargain over the terms of exchange. Their contingent use of rewards or punishments becomes part of a continuing relation – an informal institution – that is likely to be driven by one of three types of transaction: (a) mutual rewards, (b) mutual punishment, or (c) coercion. Transactions based on mutual rewards have the greatest chance of producing positive outcomes, whether they are symmetrical or asymmetrical in nature. Mutually punishing transactions are much less stable and tend to produce conflict. Coercive transactions are explicitly

[3] A classical example of this would be the Greek drama, *Lysistrata*, in which the women declare a sex strike until the men make peace.

asymmetrical, involving the potential flow of punishment from one actor, for example, in the form of withholding rewards, and the potential flow of reward from another.

Both economic and social exchange are based on a fundamental characteristic of social life: Much of what we need and value in life, like goods, services, companionship, approval, status, and information, can only be obtained from others. People depend on one another for such valued resources, and they provide them to one another through the process of exchange (Molm 1997:12). Social exchange departs from economic exchange, however, in two important and related respects. Whereas classical microeconomic theory assumes that there are no long-term relations between exchange partners, social exchange theory assumes that more or less enduring relations between exchange partners do exist. Secondly, classic microeconomic theory assumes that actors engage in sets of independent transactions that are aggregated into markets. Social exchange theory, in contrast, is built on the premise that actors engage in recurring interdependent exchanges with specific partners over time. In short, what distinguishes social exchange theory from microeconomics – and psychology, for that matter – is its emphasis on social structure as the framework within which exchange processes take place and the structural change that results from those processes.

There have been attempts in recent years to bring microeconomic theory closer to social exchange theory. Scholars like Granovetter (1985) have pointed to the embedded nature of choice and thus the importance of social structure in shaping what individual actors do. The neoinstitutionalist approach that draws its inspiration from rational choice has also contributed to a modification of microeconomic theory by pointing to the importance that rules have in setting the parameters of choice (North 1990; Ostrom 1990). Although North acknowledges the role that both informal and formal institutions play, he does not pay enough attention to the possibility that they may be in conflict with each other. Informal institutions exist not just where formal institutions are absent; nor are these informal institutions mere complements that reinforce the functioning of formal institutions. They are also often at odds with formal institutions and undermine their ability to function effectively. Unlike North, who treats informal relations merely as constraints that can be done away with, the economy of affection considers them to constitute the very social fabric on which action is based.

Social exchange theory, more than neoinstitutional approaches, helps us understand what is going on where an economy of affection prevails. It captures the consequences of interdependent social transactions that involve direct reciprocity. They are informal, nonnegotiated, and hence driven not by adherence to an abstract norm or rule, but by the dynamics of exchanges involving rewards and punishments in different degrees and at different intervals. Social trust in these exchanges is limited to face-to-face contexts and they do not need the trust in formal institutions such as money and expert systems that Giddens (1991) describes as the essence of modernity. In fact, the economy of affection more often than not subverts the trust in rules that are distant and abstract. For instance, in Africa, people engage in social exchanges because they treat them as more reliable and often as shortcuts to obtaining the goods, services, or other valued things that they desire.

There are many reasons why this type of social exchange prevails in Africa at the expense of rules that grow out of microeconomic or neoinstitutionalist theories. One is the historical experience of these societies, which is based on exchanges that are limited in space and time. The reach of social trust has always been short – even in the instances of long-distance trade. It has involved only a small number of persons and exchanges that has been direct. There is no indigenous legacy of abstract institutions that operated independently of society. Africa's precolonial states were all rudimentary formations in which rulers engaged in direct reciprocal transactions rather than relying on formal rules and independent courts.

Another reason Africans have been particularly prone to engage in simple and direct reciprocal exchanges is the relative uncertainty and insecurity that pertains to their living. This was once interpreted as a consequence of the prevalence of traditional belief systems. Africans felt insecure because they lacked the positivist and scientific knowledge that would allow them to explain things through objective factors. This rather simplistic analysis has since been abandoned because it is increasingly obvious that modernization and globalization processes do not eliminate this sense of insecurity and uncertainty, but rather reinforce it. The interdependence between global and local modes of production and the accompanying challenges to existing belief systems accentuate tensions in the minds of people, regardless of social status, education, or gender (Geschiere 1997; Comaroff and Comaroff 1991). Thus, globalization tends to create a situation in which Africans look for answers in modes of thought and organization that they are already familiar with. For instance, it is no coincidence that many individuals resort to the charismatic leadership of prophets or evangelists (Faure 2000), and it is no surprise that occult beliefs are on the rise (Geschiere 1997; Kohnert 2002). So, what is happening to the economy of affection in contemporary Africa?

ECONOMY OF AFFECTION IN CONTEMPORARY AFRICA

In the absence of a welfare state set of institutions aimed at providing citizens with a measure of social security, Africans have always relied on informal social support systems such as the extended family, neighbors, or community at large. Osseo-Asare (1991) has documented the frequency with which members of these local networks engage in some form of support, be that material or immaterial, for example, counseling and personal visits to relieve stress of others. It is clear from her study that people devote quite a lot of their time to obligations associated with the economy of affection. At this most fundamental level of pooling, the economy of affection continues to be very much alive.

Another, more recent study (Morris MacLean 2003) argues in a comparative study of Ghana and the Ivory Coast that the core of the economy of affection is really under threat because of years of economic crisis. Her point is that in a context of increased poverty, people's capacity to support others is diminishing to a point where affective networks break down. As she writes, the economy of affection appears to be narrowing in both Ghana and the Ivory Coast, but the trends are not identical. The comparative strength of the state in the Ivory Coast (at least until relatively recently) seems to have had the effect of fostering a nuclearization of the family, whereas in Ghana, with a weaker state, the affective networks have become more diverse. She also shows that the amount of support being offered is quite small in both countries relative to the cost of living and coping with such problems as hospital visits and school fees.

Morris MacLean's study confirms the argument in the literature that as the state becomes stronger and more important in allocating resources in society, the relative importance of kinship networks diminishes (e.g. Mueller et al. 2002). The state in the Ivory Coast has been able to substitute the support that originally was provided by members of extended families; hence the process of nuclearization of the family structure. She notes, however, that in both the Ivory Coast and Ghana, there is a continued tendency to rely on informal ties to ensure state support. It cannot be taken for granted that the formal institutions will deliver without the prodding of well-placed persons in government who are ready to serve as patrons for local clients. Informal networks shift from being largely horizontal to becoming more vertical, a shift within the economy of affection that has also been noted by others (e.g. Hoon 2002). Pooling is increasingly becoming clientelism.

Morris MacLean's study also indicates that Ghanaians are more willing than the Ivorians to engage in new types of horizontal exchanges that transcend the boundaries of the extended family. Many are ready to seek benefits from other villagers and people ready to reciprocate. This confirms another trend in Africa: the inclination to seek benefits from increasingly distant sources. Her data from Ghana also show that as resources within many extended families have diminished in recent years – in addition to nuclearization – there has been a process of diversification. Going outside the conventional networks means asking others – many of whom may be even strangers – to provide support in situations of crisis. This search for new sources of support is associated with a higher degree of moral hazard. The chance that these others will reciprocate is lower and the time devoted to seeking their support may turn out to be a waste. Such is the predicament, however, of many African families that they have to venture into such new exchange relations. This is becoming more and more common because of the harm that HIV/AIDS is causing to existing social structures in many African countries.

The AIDS epidemic competes with globalization as the main cause of social change in Africa today. It is especially serious, because it hits more directly than economic forces at the very core of the continent's social structures. The latest figures from the United Nations and UNAIDS reveal that sub-Saharan Africa remains by far the hardest hit of all regions in the world. By the end of 2001, it was estimated that some forty million people were living with HIV/AIDS, 71 percent of them in sub-Saharan Africa. Moreover, 78 percent of the children orphaned by the epidemic were in sub-Saharan Africa. With regard to deaths from AIDS, three-quarters of the global total was in sub-Saharan Africa (UNAIDS 2002). In sub-Saharan Africa, as in parts of the Caribbean and Latin America, heterosexual intercourse is the principal mode of transmission. Social science explanations of the epidemic in Africa fall into three categories: (a) cultural, (b) economic, and (c) sociological.

The cultural explanation attributes infection to such factors as polygamy, which drives women to seek sexual fulfillment outside marriage, and the high value placed on children, which also drives people to indiscriminate sexual activities. Some researchers such as Caldwell et al. (1989) go as far as suggesting that sexual promiscuity, particularly among women, is the norm in Africa. Lack of control of women's sexuality, therefore, is the key to the AIDS epidemic in the region. This conclusion is drawn from an unrepresentative documentary review and completely ignores the fact that the sexual behavior of women in African is subject to a great deal of social control. Nor does it acknowledge the variation in norms that exist across the continent. For instance, one study found that premarital sexual activity was virtually absent in Burundi, where only 4 percent of never-married females had had sex, but very prevalent in Botswana where more than 75 percent of never-married women aged 15–24 had had sexual experience (Gage-Brown and Meekers 1993).

The economic explanation draws heavily on assumptions about human behavior according to which individuals act in order to maximize their interests through the calculation of costs and benefits. For instance, Philipson and Posner (1995) suggest that personal decisions to participate in risky sex are rational. Looking at what they identify as prostitutes as the main source of infection in Africa, they argue that the AIDS epidemic has reduced the nominal price of prostitution and, consequently, these women have to engage in more rather than fewer sexual activities to make the same monetary gains as before. They also argue that since infection is already rampant among these so-called prostitutes and females in nonmonogamous relations, there is little incentive for safe sex. The more likely one is to be infected, the smaller the expected benefits from safe sex. The authors also argue that the lower life expectancy also reduces the perceived benefits from safe sex, because the number of years lost through HIV infection means less than in societies where life expectancy is high. The problem with this type of explanation is that it ignores the pressures that characterize everyday activities. For example, as Hughes and Malila (1996) argue, the risk of loss of income or rejection is more consequential than the more abstract risk of death in the future.

The sociological explanation focuses on such factors as poverty and migration to the urban areas. Using world systems theory, Hunt (1989) explains the spread of HIV by assuming that cities are where most jobs can be found. Poverty in the rural areas induces people to move to the cities. As migrants to these places, they live away from their wives and turn to prostitutes for sexual gratification. Periodically, they return to their home village and spread HIV to their wives. Thus, the epidemic has hit especially hard in southern Africa where migration to the cities is also most common. The poverty, which inordinately affects women, also contributes to the spread of the virus. Because women generally have to depend on men for a living, they often have to obtain resources by providing services, such as sex for men. Conversely, men feel that they have the right to demand sex from wives and partners whenever they want.

A sociological explanation – even without the world systems theory – comes close to providing the relevant analytical framework for understanding the extent to which social, cultural, or economic factors contribute to the spread of HIV/AIDS in Africa. As one Cameroonian analyst has noted, in African societies it is taken for granted that in order to earn something, a person must first give. In this kind of nonnegotiated exchange, the reciprocal act may be postponed – even for good. Yet, even if there is nothing in return for what is being given, it is nonetheless an assertion of sociability that people think will have its payoffs in future social exchanges (Etounga-Manguelle 2002). It is important to appear as doing the socially correct thing. A pervasive issue in the context of the AIDS epidemic is that women engage in sexual activities from a position of weakness. They are no more promiscuous than women anywhere else but women, especially if they are single, are often forced to engage in unwanted sex to obtain money for their livelihood. This gives men a tremendous advantage, which they typically use by ignoring much of what the women ask for, that is, the use of condoms or reasonable payments as a show of appreciation. By denying women their rewards, men exercise their power over them.

Power is not formally institutionalized, but manifest in myriad informal exchanges in which structural power is the outcome of relations of dependence. Thus, the economy of affection differs from relations of power in other types of political economy, where social relations are disembedded from their origin in local places. The economy of affection makes no claim to providing universal values. Instead, it emphasizes pragmatism: the idea of being able to adapt and cope with shifting conditions over which people

TABLE 8. *Comparison of Civic and Affective Spaces of Communication*

Type of Space	Action Level	Interaction Behavior	Claims of Validity	Effects
Civic	Principles	Discursive	Universal	Enhancing citizen voice
Affective	Concrete action	Compliant	Local	Strengthening loyalty

have little control. Validation claims are made in the local arena wherein reciprocity can be seen and evaluated. People do not strive for the right to speak out and challenge authority, as is the case in the ideal type of civic communicative space that Habermas (1979) refers to. Even though the widespread disillusion with government in African countries has produced an interest in professional and other circles in creating a civic culture, the fledgling civil society in these countries is still under the influence of the economy of affection. Power relations remain personal rather than institutional. The many new associations that have been established since the 1990s find emancipation from relations of affection a harder challenge than speaking out to authorities. The challenges facing civil society actors in African countries, therefore, are not only the willful use of state power, but also how to turn their own associations from being havens for affective relations into more civic-minded entities. Table 8 summarizes a comparison between civic and affective spaces of communication. As mentioned in Chapter Two, a civic public space is in opposition to the use of power because it involves the sharing of ideas in a mutually discursive or reflective way. In order to be able to enhance the voice of all citizens, a civic public space inevitably depends on a set of principles or rules that have a universal claim to validity. It applies to everyone and to every place regardless of circumstance. This is the kind of space that those opposed to the way political power is currently exercised in Africa are looking for. They find, however, that associations operate under a very low ceiling. Dissenting views are rejected as threatening, and compliance rather than mutual reflection tends to prevail in these organizations. Leaders strive to ensure highest possible loyalty. Performance is measured in the delivery of gains in concrete terms, such as money. The claim to validity is local in the sense that it is made with reference to key actors, rivals, or patrons, with whom they interact on an everyday basis. The civic values that are so important for democratic forms of governance, therefore, are still to emerge in African societies. Those who try to do it are faced with a sizable political challenge.

CONCLUSIONS

The rudimentary social formations on the African continent explain to a very large extent why the economy of affection and its informal institutions are so dominant there. Its social logic expresses itself in a preference for a movement over a state approach to development. It rests on communal rather than collective action in that persons band together not as autonomous individuals trying to achieve a common goal, but as people interdependent on each other and anxious to satisfy each other's sense of fairness. Although the moral hazard involved in affective relations increases as goods and resources are seen as difficult to obtain without engaging more distant intermediaries – as the examples of HIV/AIDS infection illustrate – informal behavior and institutions continue to flourish and prevail over formal ones. As the next chapter demonstrates, this applies not the least to how these countries are being ruled.

Finally, it is important to recognize that not everything beyond the boundaries of formal institutions can be treated as cultural residue that is beyond what a political scientist can or should explain. Informal institutions are created out of culture in the same way formal institutions are. They are part of what determines efficiency and effectiveness in every society. Usually our models limit us from grasping the significance of informal institutions. The premises on which these models rest must be relaxed if we are going to become more effective in not only understanding, but also in predicting what happens in Africa.

5

Big Man Rule

If informal institutions are so dominant and the state so weak and soft, how do countries in Africa govern themselves? This is an issue that occupies a significant place in the literature. Price (1974; 1975) as well as Jackson and Rosberg (1982) were among the first to argue that individuals and organizations do not engage in politics to win the right to govern or to influence government policy within an overall framework of legitimate rules. Instead, politics in most African states is rather like politics in the international arena where the unsanctioned use of coercion and violence takes place in the absence of agreed-upon rules. Consequently, politics in Africa are less restrained and more personalized than in places with formalized systems of rule. The results, as the three authors argue, are higher stakes and greater risks for those who engage in the political game and greater uncertainty for the general public.

Personal rule remains prominent in Africa. Many perceive it as highly problematic. The international donor community wishes African countries could transcend its limits. So do some citizens who are disgruntled with the way in which politics is being conducted and with politicians who believe they are above the law. The unbound nature of African politics has raised the question of how rules can be made more effective in holding leaders to the norms and principles of modern institutions.

The purpose of this chapter is to trace the issues associated with Big Man rule and how far efforts in the past decade and a half have succeeded in bringing about a more formally institutionalized rule. It begins by providing an account of the main contributions to the literature on Big Man rule, including a discussion of neopatrimonialism, an especially common way of analyzing it. It proceeds to discuss the need for theorizing our understanding of Big Man politics in ways that capture its particular logic. The final section deals with an analysis of the constitutional reform efforts that have taken place in Africa and what results they have achieved.

THE FOCUS ON PERSONAL RULE

The question of what matters in African politics was clearly shifting in favor of an emphasis on personal factors in the early 1980s. To be sure, there were still some who maintained a focus on the formal rules, for example, what types of political regime exist in Africa. Collier (1978) distinguished between different subtypes of authoritarian rule, looking at the preindependence experience as a determining factor of what kind of regime would evolve after independence. Berg-Schlosser (1984) linked regime type to development performance and concluded that what he calls polyarchic systems have a better track record than socialist and military regimes.[1] Confirming the shift in analytical interest is the fact that these two contributions, although published in a main comparative politics journal, have been very little cited by other scholars.

The interest in personal rule raised an important question: What is the most relevant theory for analyzing this phenomenon? Judging from the literature on African politics in the 1980s, there was a strong preference for applying the language of Max Weber's historical types of rule, notably his concept of patrimonialism. Given its significance, it is worth quoting Weber (1978:1028–29) verbatim on the subject:

> The patrimonial office lacks above all the bureaucratic separation of the "private" and "official" sphere. For the political administration, too, is treated as a purely personal affair of the ruler, and political power is considered part of his personal property.... The office and the exercise of public authority serve the ruler and the official on which the office was bestowed; they do not serve impersonal purposes.

Weber's original points of reference were societies that were traditional in the sense that the authority of the ruler stemmed from divine or other such nonsecular sources. Thus, medieval kings and religious rulers like sultans in Muslim societies would serve as illustrations of Weber's patrimonial type. The problem with the once many kingdoms that had existed in Africa was that few had survived European colonization or the attacks of the new nationalist elite after independence. The only example of a truly patrimonial system of rule in the 1970s was Emperor Haile Selassie's Ethiopia, but he was subsequently overthrown in 1974 and replaced by a military junta. Nonetheless, an account of Haile Selassie's way of ruling his country is instructive:

> He combines his appeal to divine right with an intense personal grasp of power.... High on Haile Selassie's list of essential skills is his ability to play on the aims and characters of others in order to secure their dependence on himself – for example,

---

[1] It must be noted that Berg-Schlosser uses a rather generous definition of polyarchy, which includes semicompetitive systems. Thus, virtually all one-party systems that were not socialist fall into this category.

by appointing antipathetic rivals to complementary posts, or encouraging officials to appeal direct to the palace over the heads of their superiors. (Clapham 1969: 115–16)

Scholars realized, however, that despite the disappearance of patrimonial systems of rule in Africa, the norms associated with such systems survived among the leaders of the new nation-states. They behaved much like medieval kings or sultans without carrying such titles. It is this similarity that gave rise to the concept of neopatrimonialism. The latter, like the former, assumes the presence of personal rule, in which the authority of the leader, who is beyond question, is personally in control of running the affairs of the state. Patrimonialism in Africa after independence is new in that it is backed by the resources of a modern state, including funds provided from external sources (Medard 1982). Neopatrimonialism, therefore, thrives on a resource base that gives the rulers plenty to work with. The relevance of patrimonialism is demonstrated in the work of Callaghy (1984; 1988), in which he studies not only the role that it plays in sustaining political order, but also how it affects the prospects for economic development. With regard to the latter, Callaghy refers to capitalism in Africa as being patrimonial in kind, that is, individuals with access to state power are able to accumulate private wealth by virtue of their public office. In this type of capitalism, it is the political rather than the economic logic that comes first. Given the weakness of an indigenous merchant and industrial group or class, patrimonial capitalism is seen as structurally inevitable in Africa at least in a transitional period. His own assessment of what will happen to it is that it could go either way: Patrimonial capitalism may continue as it is or it may move in the direction of modern capitalism (Callaghy 1988:88).

Joseph (1987), writing about the Second Republic in Nigeria, breaks with those who use the concept of patrimonialism, but does not depart from Weber. Instead, he borrows yet another concept – prebendalism – that comes out of Weber's historical sociology. Criticizing others for using patrimonialism as a catch-all concept referring to all types of exchange of favors or resources, Joseph believes that prebendalism captures more accurately what is going on: offices of state are allocated and then exploited as benefices by the officeholders, and legitimated through satisfaction of demands of specific subsets of the general population. In short, prebendalism allows officers of the state to enjoy the benefits that justifiably come with the office, but only as long as they share the spoils with their communities. Joseph's analysis comes close to what Lemarchand (1972) has called patrimonial clientelism that, in his usage, means the "doling out of offices in return for administrative and political benefits."

Neopatrimonialism and prebendalism in ruling circles in Africa are not only the creation of individual leaders, but also the response of members of the public who see the need for a powerful intermediary to help them solve their everyday problems. In a situation of insecurity and uncertainty, as Sandbrook (1972) has noted, it is not surprising that individuals seek attachment to "big men" capable of providing protection and even advancement. No one has documented more extensively the role that big men play in African politics than Bayart (1993). He recognizes the role that colonialism had in paving the way for the emergence of a system of rule that entails accumulation of wealth through the use of public office. He echoes a point made several years ago by a French anthropologist that participation in power provides a hold over the economy, much more than the opposite (Balandier 1971). Bayart's main point is that there was a lot of both extraction and extortion by the colonial administration. This was especially true in what is now the Democratic Republic of Congo, formerly Zaire, where during the colonial period it had been a free state for a long time under King Leopold's personal rule. Thus, President Mobutu's decision on November 30, 1973, to nationalize all property belonging to foreigners was a mere imitation of what had happened in colonial days. As one account tells of what happened as a result of this policy intervention, the lion's share of the property was distributed to leading politicians at different levels of the system (Schatzberg 1980; 2002). They, in turn, distributed it to followers in order to boost their local support.

Although the memory of colonialism may have been a factor in the decisions made by nationalist leaders in the wake of independence, these decisions seem to have been made also in response to more immediate trends or events. The first generation of nationalist leaders had often been able to rely on the charismatic authority that they acquired by virtue of their heroism in leading the struggle against colonial rule. By the 1970s much of this authority had vanished and in many countries, such as Zaire, the head of state had come to power through a coup rather than a struggle. Acquiring legitimacy through a movement approach, as Mobutu tried in the 1970s with his indigenization campaign, proved more difficult in these circumstances, and certainly more expensive. The idea of acquiring foreign-owned property to redistribute to members of the political elite, therefore, was one way of placating clients who otherwise would be restless and prove a threat to the head of state.

Assets owned by foreigners were the primary target, but as these opportunities were exhausted, the public purse became the next natural target. The story of Uganda during Idi Amin's term is instructive in this context. Much of the Ugandan economy at independence was controlled by Asian businessmen, most of them owning small- to medium-sized enterprises. A large number of this minority had acquired Ugandan citizenship after independence. No one had anticipated the turn of events that followed Idi Amin's coup d'état in 1971. Amin seized power from Milton Obote, a civilian politician who had ousted the first president of the country, Kabaka Mutesa – also king of Buganda – in 1966 with the help of the same Amin acting in his capacity as chief of the military. In 1972, only a year after coming to power, with little to show, Amin made a sudden decision to force members of the Asian minority – all of them originally from India and Pakistan – out of the country. They were left with no chance to really dispose of their assets in Uganda, which were expropriated and distributed by Amin to his followers as a way of demonstrating his power and ability to be a generous patron. Once these freebies had been distributed, Amin had to turn to the state for patronage resources. This meant taxation of the citizens, and also a costly appropriation of public money to share with political followers who could not necessarily be fully trusted (Mamdani 1976). The invasion of northwestern Tanzania in 1978 was Amin's ultimate attempt to rally support for his regime. The sequence described above was repeated, albeit less brutally, in many other countries in Africa, where nationalizating or indigenizing constituted the first move to secure an expanded patronage base and plundering of the state the inevitable next step.

Jackson and Rosberg (1982) offer the most extensive comparative study of the Big Man phenomenon in Africa. They place their study in the context of the classical notion of political institution as a union of rules and behavior; that is, institutions are neither only rules nor only behavior, but rather conduct in respect of rules. In an effectively formalized state, everyone respects the rules, no matter how important the individual may be. In a state without effective institutions, formal rules are defied or ignored. Officeholders are not bound by office and they are able to change its authority and power to suit their own personal and political needs or preferences. This is the case in Africa, where abstract constitutions and formal institutions exist on paper, but they do not shape the conduct of individual actors, especially those in power. In short, political leaders in Africa have had a very instrumental view of constitutions and formal institutions, treating them seriously only when it has suited them.

A political system of personal rule is not a system that responds to public demands and support by means of public policies and actions, as will be further discussed in Chapter Six. Nor is it, as Jackson and Rosberg (1982:18) point out, a system in which the ruler aims at policy goals and steers the governmental apparatus by information feedback and learning. Borrowing from Michael Oakeshott, the British philosopher, they suggest that governance in African countries is more a matter of seamanship and less one of navigation – that is, staying afloat rather than going somewhere. Personal rule is a system of relations linking rulers not with the citizens but with patrons, clients, supporters, and rivals, who constitute the system. To the extent that personal rulers are constrained, it is the result not of rules or roles but of the power of these other actors to whom they are linked. Games that these political actors play tend to be zero-sum events, in which there is little, if any, room for compromise. In fact, a compromise is viewed as a loss, never a win, as is typically the case in institutionalized democracies. This reinforces a sense of insecurity on the part of political actors that, in turn, encourages them to plot their next move to safeguard their interests. The result is that politics in these countries is both fluid and unpredictable. This makes it a challenge for all interested in studying it.

Even though personal rule has its own logic, there are differences among these rulers. Jackson and Rosberg (1982:73–82) distinguish between four types: (a) princes, (b) autocrats, (c) prophets, and (d) tyrants. The prince is a clever observer and manipulator of lieutenants and clients. He tends to rule jointly with others by presiding over their struggle for benefits, encourage it, and recognize that it is the source of his own legitimacy. Princely rule is sufficiently flexible to allow for a politics of accommodation. Senegal's first president, Leopold Senghor, is offered as the prime example of a princely ruler.

Autocrats differ from princes in that they command and manage rather than preside and rule. The country is the ruler's estate and the state apparatus is ultimately his to use at his own discretion. Party and government officials are essentially his servants and agents. Any limitations that he faces to his rule are the result of shortage of resources or lack of organizational ability, not the absence of discretionary power. Presidents Banda of Malawi and Bongo of Gabon are provided as examples. Presidents Moi of Kenya and the late Houphouet-Boigny of the Ivory Coast may be other cases in point.[2]

The prophets among African rulers constitute a minority. They are visionaries wanting to reshape African society. They are typically socialist leaders, like Nyerere and Nkrumah, who are impatient with existing conditions and want to see them altered as quickly as possible. All of them have run into the problem of not possessing the means to remove the obstacles to their vision. Their challenge has been greater than the one facing princes or autocrats, because not only have they faced the task of maintaining political order but they have placed themselves in a position where they are expected to steer the ship in a desired ideological destination and mark off some recognizable progress in that direction. Although Nyerere's *ujamaa* was never realized, he

---

[2] It is interesting to see how these rulers often fall back upon references to the divine sphere in justifying their rule. For instance, state radio in Equatorial Guinea reported on July 16, 2003, that President Nguema is in permanent contact with the Almighty and that he can decide to kill without anyone being able to hold him accountable and without him going to Hell. President Banda rejected the need for a political opposition with reference to the absence of opposition in Heaven: God himself does not want opposition – that is why he "chased Satan out" (Decalo 1992).

did survive the disappointments that followed in the wake of losing direction. He was the exception that proved the rule: raising popular expectations to high levels was tantamount to political suicide for the prophets.

The fourth category of rulers in Africa is the tyrants. Idi Amin is the example given by Jackson and Rosberg. Most observers today would probably like to add Robert Mugabe to this category. The reason is that tyranny is a residual category into which any of the other types may deteriorate. Mugabe did not start off as a tyrant, but he has turned into one, because of unwillingness to recognize challenges to his position of power. Tyrants rule through fear. They reward agents and collaborators and turn them into mercenaries. Tyranny, in short, is marked by particularly impulsive, oppressive, and brutal rule that lacks elementary respect for the rights of persons and property.

There are problems with this typology, some of which Jackson and Rosberg acknowledge. One is the classification of the rulers. There is much overlap between the four categories and it is clear that some presidents would fit more than one category. For instance, President Kerekou of Benin was a military autocrat in the early 1980s, but he transformed himself into a civilian ruler in the early 1990s when the country shifted to a democratic system of rule. It is not clear whether he should be treated as a prince or be categorized in any other way after his conversion. Another issue concerns the prophets: Is a socialist vision the automatic criterion for being considered as such? Many socialist leaders in Africa in the 1970s and 1980s had adopted Marxism-Leninism, but it is not evident that leaders like Mengistu of Ethiopia would qualify as a prophet. There are also a number of African leaders who do not fit these four categories because they chose to adopt a more formalized system of rule. Botswana's first president, Seretse Khama, is a good example. Why did he break with the pattern of personal rule that his fellow presidents adopted? How far is his exceptional behavior the reason why Botswana has been able to develop democratic forms of governance that are not found elsewhere on mainland Africa? Finally, a question must be raised about the analytical utility of the typology. There is no empirical evidence that one category of leaders, on the aggregate, produced better development performance records than others. For instance, prophets did no better than autocrats. Nor is there evidence to suggest that princes have a more impressive track record. The only thing that seems certain – although the evidence is not really mustered for that purpose in the book by Jackson and Rosberg – is that tyrants have caused more harm to their respective countries than the other types of ruler.

The conclusion that can be drawn today with the benefit of twenty years of additional experience is that neopatrimonialism, prebendalism, and clientelism have continued to dominate African politics. Analysts like Sandbrook (1985) and Clark (1997) view neopatrimonialism as highly problematic from a development perspective. Personal rule, in their view, is a symptom of underdevelopment. Regardless, it is clear, as Bratton and van de Walle (1997) conclude in their study of democratization in African countries during the first half of the 1990s, that the legacy of neopatrimonialism is a powerful factor in determining the prospects for democratic transition and consolidation.

THEORIZING PERSONAL RULE

The real problem with the use of concepts like Big Man, personal rule, or neopatrimonialism is that they remain undertheorized. They are typically used in historical comparisons in which the premise is that what happened in other parts of the world at an earlier point in history is being replicated in Africa today. Although there is no reason to deny the potential value of such comparisons, it tends to omit a sharper focus on the present. How do Big Men act strategically? Why do they do it? The point is that personal rule produces very different dynamics from that associated with formally institutionalized rule. This is evident regarding the issues of (a) free riding, (b) coalition making, and (c) transaction costs.

Whenever individual choice is treated as independent of what others choose, there is always the possibility of free riding, that is, the assumption that a person does not need to contribute anything in order to benefit from what others do. Pioneering theorists have suggested this is the case with voters in a democracy (Downs 1957) and members of large organizations (Olson 1965). Although the model of a human being in rational choice theory is an oversimplified one, there is empirical evidence, especially from the United States, to suggest that the theory is valid. The question is the extent to which it is universally valid. Students of comparative politics like Laitin (1992) and Geddes (1994) have applied rational choice to the study of both economy and culture, arguing that political actors outside the system of consolidated democracies are no different from actors in those systems.

The rather narrow premises of this model have been criticized by many students of politics in Africa. Their alternative explanation has been structural or a more general reference to the notion that politicians act to maximize their power. How they do it and with what consequences are questions that are yet to be systematically addressed. In situations where formal institutions are either rejected as illegitimate or ignored because they do not correspond to the dominant cultural idioms, the natural tendency is to treat personal relations with other actors as inevitably the most important. The ambition is to build relations of power by relying on controlling access to resources that others need but cannot get on their own. Because it is done on a person-to-person basis, power relations are highly subjective. They require compliance not with formal rules, but with more ambiguous informal rules, as discussed in Chapter Four. This makes power relations less predictable and stable, but such are, nonetheless, the structures of power on which African societies depend.

It is obvious that holding a political regime together based on personal rule is very difficult because each reciprocal relation is essentially direct and, thus, face to face. The Big Man is unable to be personally in touch with everyone, but assumes that his clients and followers will keep their reciprocities with others alive as they radiate out from the apex of the system. This will not happen without the incentives of access to resources. Clients and followers expect something in return for their loyalty. The result is that the Big Man needs to accumulate a lot of resources that he can share with others. He also needs to demonstrate his personal wealth in order to appear credible in his promise to clients (Daloz 2002).

This orientation toward clientelist relations as a key premise of politics creates a dynamic in which free riding is ruled out. To be sure, reciprocities are not demanded immediately, but the expectation of payback is always there and thus, sooner or later, an element of punishment will be introduced into the relationship if it is not reciprocated. The more dependent actors will find themselves at the receiving end. Clients and followers are typically bound by relationships that they can ignore only at a definite cost. This will only happen if there is reason to assume that the Big Man is losing his grip of the situation. A recent example of this dynamic is what happened in Kenya in 2002 when President Moi declared his intention to step down and many political actors decided to invest in relations with those that were most likely to win the forthcoming election. Personal rule is highly opportunistic. Although calls for regime change are usually made respecting universal principles of human rights and democratic governance, in the end, there is no way that informal relations based on direct reciprocities can fail to matter most for the actors involved. Zambia and several other countries that have embarked on transitions to democracy demonstrate this dynamic. Thus, even if elections tend to generate an improved indexing of civil liberties and political rights, as Lindberg (2004) demonstrates, there is still the question of what such an improvement really means. Is it really a greater respect for human rights that is reflected in such a figure? Or is it merely that fewer outright violations of such rights occur? In other words, are we witnessing a process of positive respect for rights and liberties or merely a political truce among contending Big Men and their followers? This is a set of issues that constitute a meaningful follow-up to Lindberg's path-breaking study.

There are African rulers who have gotten away with being effective in power without engaging in conspicuous consumption and the extensive use of public resources to stay in power. Julius Nyerere of Tanzania is the best example. His puritan personal way of life, combined with his persuasive rhetoric, allowed him to rule during much of the 1970s without resorting to massive misuse of government funding. The generosity of the international donors at the time was such that it compensated for the need to prey on the state for its scarce resources. In the long run, however, because his vision of a new socialist Tanzania could not be materialized, his own ability to hold the system together weakened. There was much grumbling in the early 1980s, a failed coup, and his decision to step down in 1985 was at least in part made in order to give his successor the chance to start afresh. The same applies to the new brooms, the new generation of African leaders that was briefly discussed in Chapter Two. Leaders who are fresh in power do not have to institutionalize the networks of clients that typify personal rule immediately because they can ride the euphoric wave of victory. Followers are anxiously awaiting the ruler's decisions and in that transitional moment – the honeymoon period – there is scope for attention to policy and the need to legitimize the new regime in the eyes of the international community. The point, however, is that this window of opportunity disappears sooner rather than later and clientelist relations begin to call for more of the ruler's attention. Museveni's Uganda is a good illustration of this transformation (Khadiagala 1995).

The dynamics of politics in Africa, then, tend to rule out free riding, because it constitutes a threat to the system of rule. The Big Man cannot afford it and neither can his clients who are all dependent on being powerful in relation to their followers. This has implications for how African political systems are governed.

Rational choice theory posits that government leaders will try to rule with a minimum-sized coalition (Riker 1962). In other words, there is no additional value of sharing power with others beyond the minimum 51 percent needed to get policies adopted; the assumption is that the greater the number of actors that have to be placated in any one decision the more difficult and costlier it becomes. Wherever policy and formal rules count, this argument, even if it is simplified, makes sense. It fits much less, however, in polities where personal rule prevails. The rational choice in those places is to maximize the coalition. Rulers cannot afford to operate with just a slight majority because it means that competing reciprocities can easily prevail and pose a threat to their control of the system. Personal rule invites cooptation and other measures that are much more difficult and costly for political actors in policy-oriented and formally institutionalized polities. Thus, uncertainty that follows from not having effective control induces the ruler to extend reciprocities to as many clients as possible. This happened, for instance, in mid-2004 when the governing coalition of President Kibaki was threatened with breakdown and Kibaki decided that it was in his best interest to expand the coalition to include representatives of the opposition parties. That way, he could more easily neutralize the threats from those who were threatening the coalition's existence. In short, the broader the support base, the more powerful the ruler and the more stable the system! Kibaki, like other African leaders, relied on what two authors (Rothchild and Chazan 1988:248–50) call hegemonial exchanges. That is why they adhere to the notion of the supremacy of politics, defend the single-party system, and, in the context of current competitive politics, prefer a dominant party system. One observer believes that the new reliance on competitive elections to decide on who should rule a country may have the effect of creating a preference for minimal rather than inclusive collations (van de Walle 2001:260). This continues, however, to look more like a wishful hypothesis than empirical reality.

There are two threats to democratic consolidation in Africa that would be worth studying more closely and systematically. One is the extent to which political order tends to break down when majorities are slim and unpredictable. The other is the extent to which in systems of personal rule, voter preferences in the absence of a stable party system tend to shift in response to the failures of elected leaders to deliver on their patronage promises. As we have seen in countries like Benin and Zambia, the credibility of the Big Man has a lot to do with the loyalty of his clients.

Transaction costs in systems of personal rule, therefore, tend to be very high. Nurturing the myriad reciprocal relations on which it rests takes a lot of personal energy and resources. Personal accumulation of resources by the ruler becomes necessary in order to sustain these relations. Much of this comes through misappropriation of public funds, but as attempts have been made by the international community to put an end to this practice, rulers have found other ways of accumulating the necessary resources. Members of the Asian minority in East Africa and the Lebanese minority in West Africa have often found it necessary to buy protection from political strongmen. They, like many foreign and local investors, have figured that having the Big Man – or one of his closest lieutenants – as partner or patron is mutually rewarding. It gives businesspeople their opportunity to conduct business as usual and provides the political leaders access to income that may be necessary to keep the majority coalition going. There is no evidence that measures by the international community to improve governance in African countries have significantly reduced the Big Man's predilection to rely on patronage. There is definitely a conflict between the ideal of competitive politics, on the one hand, and the calls for transparency and accountability, on the other. The former invites secrecy and deals behind the official curtains, which is contrary to the principle of a more transparent and accountable political practice. Kenya offers an interesting opportunity for studying this set of issues. Those who came to power in 2002 were in the forefront of demanding transparency and accountability while President Moi was in power. Now that they are in power, there is evidence that these demands are not easily compatible with the dynamics of personal rule.

African rulers and their clients are all rational actors, but their rationality is political rather than economic. Their action strives to embed rather than disembed because no act is pursued without primary attention to the demands that must be met to keep the system of personal rule going. These rulers are not concerned with transaction costs – what they do is allowed to cost as much as is necessary to remain in power – but rather with transgression costs. They watch carefully what the consequences of their own actions are for their clients and followers. They are constrained, as we have noted, not by formal rules, not even by availability of resources, but by the limits of their personal authority and power.

Although the phenomenon of personal rule and the institution of clientelism are not unique to Africa, they are so prevalent that they are a dominant feature of politics there. The question that Africans and the international community have struggled with in recent years is whether it is possible to rein in the powers of the Big Man and make him subject to the law of the land. The remainder of this chapter will be devoted to an account and analysis of these efforts to enhance constitutionalism in African politics.

REINING IN THE BIG MAN

African countries have had their own constitutions ever since they became independent but they have been important largely on paper, not in practice. The independence constitutions that were negotiated in the colonial capitals before power was handed over were nothing like the basic law that is the U.S. constitution. These documents were the product of negotiations between a departing colonial power, interested in doing so honorably, and the nationalist leaders, who were in a hurry to seize power.[3] The latter were aware that once their country had gained independence, whatever they agreed to in the transition would be possible to change. The case of Kenya is quite illustrative. Following no less than three constitutional gatherings at Lancaster House in London, the Kenyans agreed to accept a constitution that would give significant powers to regional authorities, a concession to the one part of the nationalist movement, the Kenya African Democratic Union (KADU), that represented the smaller ethnic groups in the country. Within the first year of independence, the majority in the nationalist movement, made up of the Kenya African National Union (KANU), dominated by the two largest ethnic groups, forced major changes in the constitution to establish a strong central government (Ndegwa 1997:606). This eventually led to the co-optation of KADU into KANU and the establishment of a one-party state, in which the majority for constitutional reform could easily be

---

[3] The situation in Iraq in 2004 greatly resembled the situation at the time of independence in African countries.

mobilized. Hence constitutional amendments have been both easy and frequent in Kenya.

The same story is true for most other African countries where constitutions have been treated rather cavalierly. Incoming rulers, especially if they have seized power by virtue of a coup d'état have often referred to the abuse of the constitution by their predecessor, but rarely, if ever, have these new rulers turned out to be different from those they ousted. African states have lived with what Okoth Ogendo (1991) calls constitutions without constitutionalism; that is, constitutions have been used just as any other instrument to achieve narrow political ends. The basic laws of the land have not been approached with the self-binding moral commitment that we associate with political systems where constitutionalism prevails.

The period since independence may be divided into two phases as far as the treatment of constitutions goes. The first, which lasted until the end of the 1980s, was characterized by opportunism; the second, which coincides with the introduction of multiparty politics, has been characterized by realism. A brief account of each helps explain why the rule of law is such a challenge to institutionalize in African political systems.

The Period of Opportunism

In the period of opportunism, constitutions were treated as utilitarian documents that provided a fig leaf of legitimation for illegitimate governments, as symbols of the political authenticity and uniqueness of particular regimes, and – at best – as minimal frameworks of governance. Experiments with democratic constitutions in Ghana (1969–72) and Nigeria (1979–82) did not last long enough to provide alternatives. Instead, their quick demise only confirmed the attitude political rulers in Africa had toward constitutions as being without a special value.

Amendments were many and often approved without due regard to their substantial implications. For example, when President Milton Obote of Uganda amended the constitution in 1966, members of parliament were told to approve it unseen and then await a copy in their respective mailboxes. When Obote presented the country with a full new constitution the following year, it was again approved without adequate opportunity for parliamentary debate. The tendency in Uganda and elsewhere was to treat the constitution as just another law. Amendments were frequent – on average in Kenya, for example, one a year. In West Africa, LeVine (1994) reports that in the sixteen countries making up the region, there were no fewer than fifty constitutions produced between 1963 and 1989, an average of 3.12 per country. Ghana and Nigeria had five each, Benin and Burkina Faso four each.

During this period of opportunism, the constitution was prized more as a political instrument than as a statement of fundamental principles about how to conduct politics. It was an instrument in the hands of single-party rulers – a revolutionary prophet, a civil or military oligarch, or in the worst of scenarios, a tyrant – and it inevitably became a devalued document. In many African countries, the years of opportunism left a constitutionally bleak and chaotic landscape. With few exceptions, the promises of independence lay unredeemed, overwhelmed by the legacy of rulers who devised their own informal system of rule that omitted public accountability.

Much of this happened in front of the international community that, at the time, had very little to say on this particular issue (except in the most extreme cases, such as those where tyrants ruled). Because the international community tended to treat political issues separate from development, its representatives refrained from asking hard questions about the way these countries were ruled. The competitive atmosphere of the Cold War tended to reinforce this orientation among the donors. The means by which development was achieved mattered less than the fact that there was a rhetorical commitment to the objectives of development, capitalist or socialist.

The Period of Realism

This way of looking at things in the donor agencies has changed since 1990 and is one reason that a more realistic orientation has developed among African rulers. This means that they no longer ignore constitutional issues, but rather respond to them in ways that typically involve only as much behavioral change as is minimally required. The leaders engage the issues in new ways. In most countries, there is a public discourse that they cannot completely ignore. Many countries have also set in motion significant constitutional reviews in order to have a control of the process that it triggers.

The francophone and anglophone countries have chosen different strategies for dealing with constitutional reforms, each reflecting their respective legal traditions, the former within the civil law and the latter within the common law system. The French-speaking countries adopted the national conference as the principle vehicle for engaging rulers and ruled in a dialogue on constitutional and legal principles. LeVine (1994) believes that it is a replica of the French Third Estate, a popular assembly in 1789 that declared itself a sovereign legislative body, and swore its famous Tennis Court Oath to be the sole representative voice of the people.[4] The parallels are especially striking in the cases of Benin and Mali. The national conference in these two countries brought together representatives of the most important social forces, proceeded to assert its own autonomy, and, after having chased incumbent military rulers from power, engaged in drafting a new constitution.

---

4 The Oath was a major event in the build-up of the French Revolution in 1789.

Although these national conferences lacked their AbbéSieyès[5] to realign and manage the Third Estate throughout the process, the churches in both Benin and Mali made their clergy available to preside over and guide the proceedings. The new constitutions are largely reinventions of the French constitution for the Fifth Republic and there is little that someone familiar with the French system does not find (Mbaku and Ihonvbere 1998). It should be added here that the national conferences that were held in other francophone countries about the same time were not as successful as those in Benin and Mali. For instance, in the Republic of Congo, the national conference fueled ethnic conflict. Much the same happened in Chad. In Togo, the military decided to hold delegates to the conference hostage for a long time (Clark 1997).

The trend in anglophone countries has been characterized by more caution. Governments in power have been quick to point out that they are legitimately constituted bodies and that their parliaments are sovereign. This argument has been used in several countries – for example, Kenya, Tanzania, Zambia, and Zimbabwe – against groups in the emerging political opposition that have advocated sovereign constitutional conferences along the lines of what the francophone countries have done. Constitutional amendments, therefore, have remained the prerogative of parliaments in which incumbent governments typically have a comfortable majority exceeding the two-thirds necessary for such amendments. Uganda and Kenya, in addition to South Africa, are the only countries in English-speaking Africa that have appointed independent commissions involving politicians, lawyers, and lay people representing civil society.[6]

The experiences of constitution making in Africa since the early 1990s can be summarized in three main points. The first concerns the challenge of finding a balance between constitutional principle and political practice. The latter has been largely autocratic since independence and there is relatively little in African society itself that can be used as a foundation to construct an African model of democratic governance. There is an interesting difference between francophone and anglophone countries. In the former, there has been little effort to find solutions outside the mainstream French model. Even such a relatively innovative country like Mali has essentially relied on institutional innovations compatible with the overall French system of government that the country inherited at independence. This applies even to

---

[5] Abbé Sieyès was the principal organizer of the Third Estate and a principal catalyst of its concerted action against the monarchy and the other estates – the clergy and the nobility.

[6] Ethiopia and Eritrea are two other countries that chose the mechanism of independent commissions to prepare for constitutional reform. The extent to which these commissions enjoyed autonomy varied. It was very high in South Africa, quite high in Uganda, but much less so in Kenya, and especially in Ethiopia and Eritrea where the process was very much influenced by the agenda of the incumbent regime (Hyden and Venter 2001).

such interesting experiments as the Espace'd'Interpellation Démocratique, a public forum for dialogue on human rights issues, that is quite unique in the contemporary African context (Wing 2002).

As French authors confirm, the French constitutional model continues to be predominant and it is no coincidence that the notion that they use in their writing is *Francafrique* (Dozon 2003). The debate about democratization in those countries, therefore, has been more about putting into practice a model that already exists in the minds of the key political actors than searching for something different.[7] Even though the debate in anglophone countries has also been framed in terms that draw on the British colonial legacy, there has been more openness in the search for new principles. Constitutional reformers, therefore, have looked outside Africa for inspiration and guidance. Members of reform commissions traveled to countries in Europe, North America, and Asia – notably India – in order to learn more about models of governance that would be appropriate in a democratizing setting. Moreover, in most countries, foreign advisors were involved in the preparatory stages. In short, there has been much more struggle over constitutional issues in these countries than the case has been in the French-speaking countries. For instance, in Kenya there has been a long debate about the extent to which the country should embrace a model that involves some degree of federalism (as the independence constitution did) or should remain a unitary state (Ndegwa 1997; Oyugi et al. 2003).

The result is that constitutional reform in francophone countries has typically been carried out within a short-term deadline while in the English-speaking countries the reform process has often dragged on much longer than expected. In Uganda, it lasted from 1988 until 1995. In Kenya, which started in 2001, the process had overshot three deadlines and was still not finished by the time this manuscript was completed. Wherever the process has been dragging on, the temptation to include detail has grown.[8] This inclination to include so much detail indicates the interest and concern that constitutional actors have in the reform process. It shows that they want a constitution that reflects the political realities on the ground. On the other hand, much of the constitution is not likely to last long, because it can be challenged easily. This can become a serious problem, especially if these constitutional rules are not justiciable, that is, possible for an independent court to resolve. In such situations, the issue has to be resolved politically,

---

[7] At least one author is suggesting that France needs to demonstrate its relevance to its former colonies in Africa as a way of also proving that it is a world power (Chafer 2002).

[8] The 1995 Uganda constitution is a document containing 287 paragraphs and is 196 pages long. The Kenyan proposal for a new constitution is also running into a multitude of detailed paragraphs.

which often invites allegations of opportunism and self-interest and thus undermines the legitimacy of the basic law of the land (Oloka-Onyango 2001).

The second point is that constitution making in francophone countries relied almost exclusively on a representative group of elites, while in anglophone countries there has been an effort to also include the public. The latter, therefore, has been a more participatory process with a view to seeking inputs from as many sources as possible. This effort was especially extensive in South Africa, but was considerable also in countries like Uganda.[9] Nonetheless, making the reform process participatory was not always easy. People sometimes questioned the extent to which the offer to participate was genuine or just a show. This became an issue in places like Ethiopia and Eritrea where the leaders who had just seized power tried to control the process as much as they could.[10] It is clear that wherever the constitutional reform process was advertised as participatory, public expectations rose and any indication of central direction, therefore, would easily backfire.

The experience of consulting the public on constitutional matters, however, should not be written off as bogus. Both South Africa and Uganda certainly provide evidence that it helped raise popular appreciation of governance issues in ways that contribute to any effort at promoting more democratic forms of governance. There is a deeper political consciousness that political leaders have to take into account. Much of the public criticism of President Museveni in Uganda can at least in part be attributed to the effects of the civic education campaign that accompanied the reform process in the first half of the 1990s. There is some evidence, therefore, that the notion of popular sovereignty is beginning to mean something to people. Although it may still be a long shot in most African countries, the best that can be said about the constitutional reform process is that the role of the people in legitimizing democracy is not merely fictional. As Chambers (2004) argues in a review of recent constitution making, it is not merely a matter of entrenching the right principles; it is also about including the citizens in the process in the right way.

---

[9] Waliggo (2001:51–52) reports that the Constitutional Commission secretariat received no less than 9,521 written memoranda from the country's 40,000 villages; almost half of Uganda's parishes – the administrative units above villages – submitted their opinion, as did 564 out of the country's 890 subcounties, and 36 of its 39 districts. Together with individual submissions from citizens, the secretariat received no less than 25,547 documents to consider.

[10] Wodajo (2001:139) reports that the inclination in Ethiopia among some participants to consider their own voices to be more important than that of others backfired. People were informed by members of the commission what they had in mind as the principles for the new constitution. Those who listened, therefore, felt that their input would make no difference. The legitimacy of the process suffered as a consequence.

The third point is that reform activists have not always found it easy to retain their personal credibility. The question people ask is whether they have begun to call for reforms because they have been denied access to power or they have a genuine interest in a new system of democratic governance. In countries where the Big Man syndrome prevails, there is a natural tendency to treat politicians with suspicion. Establishing a reputation as genuine reformer is not easy in such contexts. The way many political leaders have acted in relation to proposed reforms has done little to remove that suspicion. Although there are many individuals who have engaged in this process with a high degree of personal integrity and been able to sustain it, there are also a large number of individuals who have jumped on the reform wagon for more opportunistic reasons. For instance, when it became clear that President Moi's regime in Kenya was a sinking ship, many of those who had worked closely with him in previous years crossed over to the opposition criticizing the very government of which they had been part. By virtue of their position as powerful patrons, they still had enough support to get away with such chameleontic behavior, but it added little to their credibility as political reformers. The problem in African countries is that political leaders are ready to resort to calls for constitutional reform to deal with shortcomings that they can identify in the practices of other leaders, but they are far less ready to treat rules as applying to them once they are in power. The notion that constitutional norms and principles are binding on political leaders is still very much in doubt.

This is evident, for instance, in their attitude toward term limits. Many African countries, as part of the new constitutional landscape, have adopted a rule similar to the Twentieth Amendment of the U.S. Constitution, which limits presidents to two terms. Many incumbent presidents have been reluctant to treat it as binding on them. Discussions about a third term took place in Kenya before Moi decided to leave, in Malawi as President Muluzi's second term was coming to an end, and in Zambia where President Chiluba's attempt to win a constitutional amendment on the issue was defeated by the country's parliament. President Nujoma of Namibia, by virtue of a two-thirds control of parliament was able to extend his rule for a third term, changing the very constitution that he promised to honor only a few years ago. It may be seen as positive that these efforts to amend the constitution to allow for a third term have generally failed, but, as the case of Nujoma illustrates, this should not necessarily be interpreted as sign of a deeper commitment to constitutionalism. Much of it has to do with political rivals wanting to come to power and seeing their ambition as being blocked for an indefinite period without the term limit clause in the constitution. The constitutional review process in Kenya has been bogged down by precisely this kind of behavior by leading members of the government.

Another indication that African heads of state are uncomfortable with any attempt to rein in their powers is their unwillingness to criticize each other. It was a cardinal principle in the 1963 Charter of the Organization of African Unity, the reason being that criticism by fellow heads of state could set in motion rebellions that the weak states of which they were heads could not handle (Herbst 2000). This principle was almost always upheld during its close to forty years of existence. Only when someone engaged in an act of unprovoked violence against another country, such as Idi Amin's attack on Tanzania in 1978, did heads of state break ranks. Otherwise, human rights violations and other breaches of rule of law, notably misappropriation of public funds, in a particular African country was really never the subject of criticism by heads of state of other countries. These were issues that sovereign governments had the right to treat the way they wanted. Again, only in extreme cases was there disagreement on this subject. One such instance was the Biafra War in Nigeria 1967–70. Nigerians treated it as a civil war and therefore a domestic matter. Because of the large number of people who were starving to death in Biafra (former eastern region of Nigeria), the international community was divided on the issue. The United States and many European countries were ready to recognize Biafra as a sovereign country. Some prominent African leaders, like Nyerere of Tanzania and Houphouet-Boigny of the Ivory Coast, took a similar position. They received open criticism from their fellow heads of state, however, for not treating the issue as a purely Nigerian affair.

When the African Union replaced the OAU in 2002 as the main regional organization of African states, member countries committed themselves to the idea of promoting better governance. The principal mechanism for achieving this was identified as a peer review process, whereby governments would be allowed to criticize each other in ways that would be constructive and open. In principle, this marked a major difference from the rules that prevailed in the OAU. Trying to put this new approach into practice, however, has not been easy.

At a summit in Kigali, Rwanda, in February 2004, agreement was reached along these lines, which indicates that the mechanism will not be so intimidating for heads of state as the original idea of an open peer review suggested (Anonymous 2004a). The review will be led by an outside panel of experts whose responsibility it is to help countries conduct some form of self-assessment of their governance weaknesses, such as corruption and human rights violations. Each study will last up to nine months. Any such assessment is voluntary and the report is not necessarily going to be a public document. The head of state is not bound by its findings or recommendations. He only needs to consider them.

Given that the terms have become easier for incumbent heads of state to accept, some have agreed to have their country's governance subject to review. Thus, at the summit in Kigali, Ghana, Kenya, Mauritius, and Rwanda agreed to go first and thirteen others indicated that they are ready to accept a review in the future. The success and credibility of the proposed process will depend on how reviewers handle sensitive issues. Judging from what has happened with audits in previous years, for example, reports by the Ombudsman institution that was imported into some African countries after independence, and the Auditor-General, one cannot be too optimistic that the new mechanism will transform governance. Issues such as reducing corruption in Kenya or making elections in Rwanda more democratic are legitimate topics for these reviews, but it is not clear that the outside review panels will be able to nudge the host governments in the right direction. It is reasonable to assume that if these reports are not published, the public will conclude that the government has something to hide. If it is published, it will also invite criticism of the government. None of these scenarios, however, is likely to pave the way for genuine reform, because it will politicize the issues to a point where reform will be blocked rather than facilitated. Donor governments and international finance institutions may be able to exercise some leverage by insisting on conditionalities, but again, judging from experience, there is little evidence to suggest that these external actors are effective. Zimbabwe under President Mugabe is the most obvious case in point but it is generally true that African governments have always found ways of wiggling themselves out of such binds.

CONCLUSIONS

Almost all African countries have gone through some constitutional reform exercise in the past fifteen years. Certain changes in political practice have taken place, notably in the way political representatives and leaders are selected. Competitive elections are now standard, even if practices still fall short of being perfect. There is also evidence that the judiciary in many countries has become more independent and assertive. These are important incremental steps that should not be overlooked at this stage. Yet, the problem is that the uncertainty that continues to characterize African politics is not one stemming from a veil of ignorance but from arbitrary and sometimes impulsive personal rule.

Democracy, as Przeworski (1991) has argued, implies the institutionalization of uncertainty. This involves first and foremost the readiness of political actors to accept that no one stands above the law, that every one must engage in some form of self-binding behavior (Elster 1997). Such behavior only comes about in situations where the actor is able to step out of his own shoes and place himself in those of someone else. In such situations, the individual is able to see the logic of abstract rules that regulate social interaction. He realizes that personal legitimacy comes from subjecting oneself to such rules. He also sees that the costs of not doing so exceed the benefits.

Where such rule-oriented behavior exists, we speak of the presence of rule of law.

Africa is still struggling to move in that direction. The most serious obstacle is the prevalence of primary forms of reciprocities. They preclude the opportunity for empathy. The Big Man is always on one side, the client or the rival on the other. Because they deal with a premodern social reality, their interests are tied to a social space that has not yet been distanciated from the local place or socially differentiated to produce significant economic interest groups. African rulers continue to see their interests as tied to local communities rather than to systems of abstract rule. They act at the level of state as they do in their community. They rely on investments in personal reciprocities that are self-enforcing and hence not a matter for a court or any other third party to judge. They act in ways that go contrary to the principles of transparency and accountability.

Africans fed up with personal rule and members of the international community have assumed that improved governance is possible through a combination of rewards and punishments aimed at changing the behavior of the political elite. The idea of getting politics right through a restructuring of the incentive structure has been pursued through a variety of new governance measures. The experience of the past fifteen years indicates that putting an end to Big Man rule is quite complicated. Political actors in Africa do not respond to the incentive structures provided by economic and governance reform efforts, because their rationality – and thus strategic action – is embedded in personalistic relations of reciprocity. Because the political sphere is not independent of society, it can only be fully understood in the context of prevailing premodern social structures. As long as they continue to be dominant, certainty is going to be sought in personal and direct reciprocities even if the costs will be high and a heavy burden for both private and public finance. The idea that who you are matters more than what you are is a product of social structures that are not changed merely by governance measures being brought in from the outside.

The continued presence of Big Man rule also means that governments will be more interested in accumulating resources for patronage than in designing good policy. New projects will continue to be preferred over concerns with maintaining existing ones. The latter carries none of the glitter or benefit that goes with new money or "pork" to the constituents. In fact, the importance of serving one's constituency has grown in recent years as politicians learn from the experience of competitive elections. This means that the cost of being elected keeps going up. In relative terms, it exceeds what it costs to be elected to the House of Representatives in the United States. Having no party to back them financially, opposition candidates are typically forced to rely on their own resources or whatever they can raise from friends and supporters.

Their chance of competing with incumbents is not very good, because the latter can usually fall back upon support from government or other public sources. Being involved with individuals who control key resources remains the main purpose of political life. It is as much embraced by those in politics as by those who aspire to be part of it. Being part of the political opposition is a losing strategy.

6

The Policy Deficit

When Americans and Europeans think of policy, they usually associate it with a measure to solve a particular problem within the limits of what public resources permit. Making policy involves a careful calculation of how means relate to desired ends. It is about such principles as feasibility, sustainability, and efficiency – all in one. Policy analysis, as conventional textbooks confirm, is the application of economic principles to the political process. But, as the African experience suggests, policy making does not have to be based on an economic rationale. As the previous five chapters have shown, where politics is supreme and power not effectively reined in, policy making is more typically made on purely political grounds. Policy objectives become ends in themselves as the calculation of costs to achieve them are ignored.

There are three factors in the international environment that help explain why policy making in Africa has tended to be void of economic thinking. One is that African countries originally saw themselves as being caught in the process of catching up with the developed societies. In such circumstances, thinking economically meant going slower than was deemed desirable. The second reason is that African governments have often viewed the rest of the world, and especially the former colonial powers, as having a moral responsibility to pay for African development because of all the suffering that colonialism caused. The third reason is that development assistance provided by donor agencies, Western as well as non-Western, for example, China, has tended to make policy makers less cost-conscious. The attitude of most African governments has been to appeal to donors to provide funding for specific projects and programs. In this process, the notion that there are real budgetary limits to what the government can do has waned.

It is important to point out that most African governments don't lack professional competence to make cost-benefit or feasibility types of analysis. In fact, such analysis is often prepared alone by local professionals these days, and only sometimes with input from expatriate expertise. Rather, the problem is that those at cabinet level making the final decisions tend to ignore the policy analysis that was done. Thus, what passes as policy in most African countries is being pursued with little thought given to costs, depreciation of assets, and maintenance. For instance, roads are being built, but allowed to deteriorate to a point beyond repair. New ones have to be built instead. Despite pressures from outside funding institutions, this is a pattern that repeats itself in Africa to this day.

If Nkrumah set the tone for how politics should be used to penetrate all other sectors of society in the postindependence period, it was Julius Nyerere of Tanzania who became the leading architect of development policy changes in this period. In the 1960s, it was Asia, not Africa, that was generally perceived as the most vulnerable continent in the world. Population pressures on the land, hunger, and poverty, as well as the soft state, were identified with the former region, as the seminal work by Myrdal (1968), *Asian Drama*, among many volumes, confirms. In Africa, by contrast, optimism reigned among nationalists as well as expatriate development advisors. By being freed from the shackles of colonialism, African countries could finally chart their own path to human progress while benefiting from the resources, both technical and financial, provided by friendly donors. Nyerere's success lay in his ability to ride the wave of optimism and confidence that the rest of the world had in African leadership while he simultaneously created a home-spun development ideology – *ujamaa*. It emphasized two principles that were broadly embraced by the international development community in the first two decades of independence: self-reliance and equality. Nyerere became an influential voice among developing nations, both in and outside of Africa. It can be argued that no other African, including Nelson Mandela, has matched Nyerere's influence on the global development scene. He was highly influential in shaping the debate about a new international economic order through the Brandt Commission in the 1970s and the realignment of north-south relations in the South Commission in the 1980s, which he chaired.

Nyerere's international stature allowed him not only influence over the development agenda, but also how it should be carried out. He was of the opinion that African countries could avoid committing the mistakes made in developed countries. Above all, he saw no need for these countries to go through the painful processes of social change associated with the spread of capitalism. His firm belief was that an African form of socialism could be an adequate basis for the emergence of modern forms of socialism as identified in classical texts by either Utopians like Saint Simon or Marxists.[1] His conviction came from a strong sense that political independence provided the Africans with an opportunity to radically redefine their own conditions

---

[1] There were, of course, those who criticized Nyerere for his view that there was something called African socialism. They included scholars but also some intellectuals who had shared the struggle for independence with Nyerere. See, for example, Babu, *African Socialism or Socialist Africa?* (1981).

and make human progress. There was no time to lose; hence his notion that we must run while others walk.[2]

I have suggested elsewhere (Hyden 1975; 1979) that this metaphor also captures the essence of one prominent form of policy making in African countries after independence, especially among regimes that adopted a vanguard model of politics. The idea that we-must-run contradicts the prevailing principles of policy analysis and was certainly a challenge to the prevailing notions of planning for development that existed in the 1960s and 1970s. In Nyerere's mind, it was political mobilization rather than economic calculation that produced policy success.

This chapter will take as its starting point the development planning context of the first two decades after independence and place Nyerere's approach in a comparative perspective. In addition to presenting its main features, this chapter will discuss the implications of the strategy and why eventually it was difficult to sustain. It will proceed with a discussion of how the international community in recent times has tried to direct policy making into better economic strategies. It will conclude by placing the issues associated with improving policy making in African countries in a broader conceptual and theoretical perspective.

PLANNING, SELF-HELP, AND DEVELOPMENT

One of the defining issues of postindependence politics in African countries was who should be allowed to control the resources needed for national development. One aspect concerned indigenous versus foreign ownership. Another was the question of how far local actors in the villages and towns across the continent, as opposed to government, would have a say in the process. The choices that policy analysts and policy makers faced in the early days of independence came down to whether (a) national development required central planning and control, (b) it was best pursued through local self-help efforts by the people themselves, or (c) some combination of both was feasible.

Development analysts in the 1960s and 1970s were strongly in favor of some form of comprehensive national planning. They argued that development problems can be effectively tackled only by paying systematic attention to the temporal and spatial dimensions of getting things done.

---

[2] Nyerere coined several metaphors to describe the policy challenges facing his country; one was *while some are reaching for the moon, we must reach the village.* See the volumes containing his speeches from the 1960s and early 1970s: Julius K. Nyerere, *Freedom and Socialism,* 1968, and *Freedom and Development,* 1973. It is noteworthy that the only real biography that has been written on Julius Nyerere uses as its title the words: *we must run while other walk* (see Smith 1971).

In the abundant literature on planning and policy making at the time, the extensive volume by Tinbergen (1964) stands out as among the most influential. His analysis of what goes into preparing a national development plan starts from the premise that there is a sovereign political body that specifies the social and economic objectives of development. In the African context, the state, now controlled by a nationalist movement, was typically regarded as the body that would set these goals. Subordinated to this political entity would be a group of planners with responsibility to formulate the actual plan, a process that Tinbergen divided into seven distinct phases: (1) a general overview of the national economy, (2) a tentative choice of the optimum growth rate, including expected rate of savings, (3) an estimation of the expansion of demand derived from the expected rate of growth, (4) a survey of manpower and, thus, educational requirements, (5) revisions of the first four steps in view of incoming data, (6) specification of tasks for the public as well as private sector, and (7) the means to get everything done – public investments, taxes, subsidies, foreign aid, and so forth.

This type of planning has been referred to as synoptic problem solving because it presupposes good enough information for analysts to be able to find optimal solutions to specific problems through various modeling exercises. The majority of development economists who were hired to formulate national plans in Africa during the 1960s came from Western countries – ironically, only a sprinkling came from socialist countries that had extensive experience with this kind of planning. An influential publication on development planning in East Africa by an American economist bore all the features of this synoptic approach to policy making (Clark 1965).

Because development planning was treated as an exclusively economic exercise, it remained largely aloof from day-to-day political considerations. In fact, one of the early criticisms of the process was its inability to accommodate itself to prevailing circumstances in developing countries, especially the tendency to consider politics supreme. Nor did it consider the fact that reliable information on the economy was available only for some activities, but not others. These and other related criticisms were made quite convincingly in a World Bank–sponsored review by Waterston (1965). Even though some efforts were subsequently made to incorporate assumptions about the political process into the planning exercise, economists failed to come up with assumptions that really and truly reflected the way policies are made in African countries (Killick 1974).

The lack of fit between politics and planning was not the only challenge to development analysts and policy makers in Africa after independence. Equally difficult was the question of what to do with the mushrooming self-help movements. Self-help was not a new concept in African circles. It has its roots in community life. Ever since they began their proselytizing and development work on the continent, mission societies had taken advantage of African communal self-help as a means for constructing schools and health care dispensaries, as well as for creating famine strategies. The colonial administration, albeit on a more limited scale, had also promoted self-help as a low-cost approach to social and economic development. Finally, during the process of decolonization, nationalist movements had used the concept to mobilize support for alternative approaches to development.

During the 1960s, self-help activities throughout the continent increased substantially. Kenya's *harambee* movement is a particularly notable case of self-help promotion after independence. From a national development perspective, one would have expected general agreement that self-help was an important complementary activity. Such was not the case, however, as both politicians and planners raised questions about its implications for politics and policy making. Planners objected because self-help activities were difficult to assess in terms of contributions to the national economy. Many were not formalized and official figures providing budgetary estimates of inputs and outputs were typically absent. Even more seriously, self-help activities were often started as a means to ensure the prospect of matching funds from government sources. Such requests were not planned for and approval by political leaders of such matching support subverted budget assumptions made by the economists. This became a particularly serious issue in countries like Kenya with large numbers of community-based projects. Holmquist (1970) has referred to this as a preemptive development strategy because communities try to preempt the field of competitors by demonstrating to political leaders and officials that they are more deserving of support than other communities. In Kenya, politics and planning grew increasingly apart in the late 1960s; this discomfort in both planning and political circles with spontaneous forms of development activities continued into the next decade.

The tensions between macro- and microlevel concerns for development took a particular turn in Tanzania as a result of the early conscientious effort made to combine a local self-help strategy and national development policy. Already in 1962, the new government decided to create formal channels through which local schemes initiated by village development committees would be included in the broader development planning exercise. From a national point of view, agriculture was treated as the basis for development, a prerequisite for financing industrialization. More specifically, development of the rural sector was expected along two lines: (a) continued incremental improvement of existing small-scale agricultural plots, and (b) transformation of the agricultural sector through establishment of highly capitalized settlements in which farmers would have titles to their own land and work closely, hand in hand, with agricultural extension specialists. This two-pronged approach, relying on simultaneous improvement and transformation, had been defined in a World Bank report to the colonial government; it was inherited and adopted by the new government (International Bank for Reconstruction and Development 1961).

In spite of the deliberate efforts to bring microlevel development concerns into the planning process, practice fell far short of promise. There were at least four principal criticisms directed at the process. First, there was a skewed allocation of resources in favor of those select farmers that agreed to move to new settlements. At the same time, these settlers constituted a very small percentage of the rural population. Second, benefits to the national economy from investments in the new settlements did not match the costs incurred especially through the importation of expensive mechanical equipment. Third, progress in the rural areas was still much slower than the new government had expected. In spite of being organized into successful marketing cooperative societies, farmers, on their own, were unable to make the headway that Nyerere and his government ministers had hoped. Fourth, as Bienen (1967) and Leys (1969) have pointed out, the planning process may have been integrated as far as macro–micro relations are concerned, but it still existed apart from the real political process. Neither the formulation of goals nor the choice of means for implementation of policies was grounded in the political process.

These failures are the reasons that, in the latter part of the 1960s, Nyerere decided to chart his own path to development; he broke with the conventional planning model that his country had relied on since independence and that was being promoted elsewhere on the continent. Because of sharing a similar sense of frustration with development planning, many African leaders found Nyerere's notion that we must run emancipating. They saw it as an incentive to do something different. The next section will provide further information about the new strategy, focusing on what its main features and implications are.

THE WE-MUST-RUN STRATEGY

There are at least a couple of good reasons why this strategy made sense to Nyerere and many Tanzanians supported him in his effort to develop the country. As a poor country and latecomer to the community of sovereign states, Tanzania had a lot of catching up to do. A predominantly rural country, made up of relatively independent smallholder peasant farms, Tanzania's database for more systematic economic planning was largely absent. It made sense, therefore, to emphasize the political rather than the economic aspects of development. With his *ujamaa* ideology, Nyerere provided a new sense of direction that could be easily comprehended by fellow Tanzanians because it was cast in cultural idioms familiar to them. Although he stressed the urgency of collective action, Nyerere also accepted that the race would be a long-distance one, full of hurdles that had to be overcome before it was over. Using this language, he was anxious to hold back expectations so that they did not run too high while, at the same time, he enforced the need for discipline and restraint. Much of what he tried to get others to accept was a reflection of his own puritan lifestyle.

Even if Nyerere was a master pedagogue and highly persuasive to compatriot Tanzanians in his political rhetoric, he also realized that people were not going to change their lifestyles merely because of his words. The task of making people ready to accept a sacrifice in the interest of national development also required a strong political organization that could oversee and implement the new ideology. In Nyerere's original version of the strategy, the leadership of the nationalist movement played the role of a coach standing on the sidelines to ensure that the runners would not lose their stamina.[3] Its role was to constantly reaffirm that the race is worth pursuing.

Main Features

The we-must-run strategy has at least four features that are worth discussing here. The first is the strong urge to do everything and do it at once. There is no attempt to think sequentially nor to introduce feasibility considerations. Instead, policy making is focused on maximizing as many social values as possible through mobilization of human resources. In Tanzania – and in other socialist African countries where a similar strategy was adopted – this approach manifested itself in frontal attacks on development problems that were perceived by the political leadership as standing in the way of the country's development. For instance, in Tanzania the villagization campaign that began in 1973 is one such example. *Kilimo cha kufa na kupona* – a campaign effort to raise agricultural production in the early 1970s as a matter of life and death (*kufa na kupona*) – is yet another such case. Because the social values that were pursued were never really disaggregated and operationalized in advance, the aspiration to maximize implies the assumption that not everything will necessarily be achieved at once. Even a suboptimal outcome, however, is acceptable given the many hurdles that each campaign faces. In this respect, the approach is similar to that of a fisherman who throws his net into the water knowing that as he pulls it in, some of the fish may escape.

A second feature of Nyerere's strategy is that policy makers act without first obtaining any detailed sense of the possible consequences of their decisions. They start running and take the consequences as they come. The

---

[3] It is worth reminding the reader that the nationalist movement in Tanzania – the Tanganyika African National Union (TANU) – was totally unopposed in the preindependence elections in 1960. Although the country is made up of some 120 ethnic groups, they all united behind TANU. Following a military mutiny in 1964 and some unexpected political turbulence in its wake, Nyerere and other leaders in the party decided to turn the political system into a constitutional one-party state in 1965. The *ujamaa* ideology was launched with the Arusha Declaration in 1967, so named after the town in which it was adopted by the party's national conference.

strategy resembles what Hirschman (1965) with reference to Latin American countries called the motivation-outruns-understanding style of policy making. An attempt at fully understanding what can or cannot be achieved with a particular policy intervention is not sought as a precondition for action. Instead, the political decision is made first, typically under dramatized circumstances, to produce a sense of urgency. In this approach, ends are used to justify means; the ultimate goal is deemed so important that the costs of attaining it become a secondary matter. Two political resolutions adopted in the early 1970s may serve as illustrations. The *Mwongozo* (Leadership Declaration) was adopted by the ruling party in order to preempt exploitation of workers by private and public corporations on the ground that human dignity is more important than business efficiency. The Musoma Resolution was similarly adopted to bring forward the date for universal primary education in the country from 1989 to 1977. In these cases, as in others, one social value was pursued at the expense of other potentially competing values. The task of trying to sort out any problems arising from this approach was left with the implementers.

A third feature of the strategy is the unwillingness of policy makers to use the past as a source of guidance for the future. Being associated primarily with colonial rule from which the leadership was seeking a break, the past was in the minds of the leaders largely irrelevant. Dror (1969) identified this way of approaching problems as a prominent feature of policy making in many ex-colonial countries. Policy makers, therefore, are rarely trotting on familiar grounds but rather making frequent moves into the unknown, the assumption being that the right policies are not necessarily chosen from the realm of what is presently known or economically feasible. The solution to a problem is not always found where there is light; it may well be hidden in the dark. The task of those making policy, therefore, becomes, in Hirschman's language, one of zeroing in on a new policy that would have been ruled out if considered in terms of conventional criteria of efficiency or feasibility. In Tanzania, one case in point is what happened to the cooperative movement in 1976. After years of failing to reduce corruption in the movement, the ruling party decided to cancel all member organizations and restructure rural cooperation by designating *ujamaa* villages as the new primary units. The community model was chosen over the collectivity one.

The fourth feature of the we-must-run strategy is that those responsible for implementing policy constantly have to work in a context where the expectations of their political masters exceed what is possible to accomplish. Civil servants in government ministries, for instance, are forced to constantly stretch themselves to the utmost, leaving them with a sense of anxiety, even insecurity, because they are never certain that their job has been done. This approach flies in the face of conventional organization theory that emphasizes the notion of equilibrium between contribution and reward (for example, Blau 1965). It is more in line with the argument of Frank (1964) that over-defined roles, where role expectations exceed what role incumbents can accomplish, often produce better results than where they are too narrowly defined. Nyerere was of the opinion that in order to get Tanzania going, every official had to lift himself (or herself) by the bootstraps, so to speak.

Implications

The notion of we-must-run was adopted by African leaders who found that political mobilization rather than economic calculation made more sense in tackling development problems in the still undeveloped or underdeveloped circumstances of their countries. Its widespread use, especially pronounced among the many governments that adopted a socialist approach to development, created an increasingly serious gap in the 1970s between African policy makers, on the one hand, and Western or African advisors trained in conventional policy analysis, on the other. In order to appreciate more fully what happened in those days, it is worth focusing on four specific implications.

Conventional policy analysis focuses on overcoming constraints. African leaders, on the other hand, emphasized the importance of seizing the opportunity while it exists. This made a lot of sense in the years after independence. To most Africans, colonial rule had meant being prevented from doing what they wanted. Political independence brought them the opportunity to pursue preferences that they had been denied earlier. Especially the leaders of the new nation-states in Africa wanted to show that they were not being intimidated by uncomfortable or incomplete information. In fact, civil servants and advisors that insisted on more comprehensive information were typically brushed aside as having a colonial or capitalist mind. Political leaders were breathing optimism and their spirited commitment to making a difference spread to friends and supporters in the international community, especially if they echoed values that the latter could identify with. For example, many donors, especially from friendly European countries, were ready to give the African governments the benefit of doubt. They bought into the notion that politics is supreme at any cost.

Chambers (1969) provides an interesting illustration of how opportunity rather than constraint determines what policy is pursued. His case study – the Mwea Irrigation Scheme in Kenya – was developed in response to the opportunity that decolonization created to provide land to people who had earlier lost it to white settlers in the Kenyan highlands. He shows that the scheme was started under almost unbelievable ignorance about its physical, technical, and economic aspects, but it became a success story thanks to bold initiatives by policy makers and an imaginative and effective followup. As Chege (1972) noted about this and other cases of rural development initiatives, inadequate preplanning is not necessarily the paramount cause of faulty implementation that it is usually made out to be. There are ways of sorting out unresolved issues once the work of getting something done has already started. Seizing a political opportunity at the right time is often more important in countries where information is inadequate than trying to assess technical and economic feasibility first.

The problem that so many African governments eventually ran into came from another source: their unwillingness to learn the lessons as they went along. Hirschman (1965) stressed that wherever motivation is allowed to outrun understanding, it must be accompanied by a readiness to accumulate knowledge and make continuous assessments as implementation progresses. In short, incomplete knowledge may be all right upstream, that is, at the point of policy formulation but becomes a serious liability if not corrected in the implementation or downstream stage. Van Rensburg (1974) confirms this observation in a study of development projects in Botswana. Government officials did not give themselves the time to assess results of these projects. Instead of learning the relevant lessons, these officials rejected them as criticism. Thus, in Botswana as in many other countries, governments often failed because officials did not realize that even if a policy or a project was started to seize a political opportunity, it required attention to technical and economic aspects once it was being implemented.

A second implication of the dominant policy making strategy in Africa after independence follows from its emphasis on rhetoric rather than analysis. The two always go together but there is a big difference between conventional policy making in which analysis plays a crucial part, on the one hand, and the we-must-run strategy where rhetoric dominates, on the other. The first generation of African nationalists flourished by seizing the moral high ground. For them, the ultimate objective – that of eliminating imperialism and colonialism – was beyond question. They all were strong believers in the idea of progress. As Coleman (1960:285) noted in his account of the first generation of nationalists, they treated progress as linear and inevitable, reflected in such slogans as "Forward Ever, Backward Never." They demanded men and women to commit themselves to this vision with discipline, dedication, and selflessness. By asserting "truths" that they present as inescapable and by defying the need for argumentation and dialogue, they also preempted the need for corroborating evidence. These leaders eschewed the canons of an instrumental type of rationality and instead adhered to what Weber calls an expressive or value type of rationality (Weber 1978). In short, African leaders preferred to assess rationality in relation to intrinsic values – ends in themselves – rather than calculation of how ends relate to means. Much of what they wanted to do was justified, but they eventually ran into serious problems with their assertive rhetoric by stifling any debate about critical development issues. In justifying their positions, they typically invoked the imminence of a crisis or an external threat so that the need to ask any questions was essentially preempted.

A third implication is the tendency to rely on power rather than on planning to get things done. Again, it is obvious that both power and planning are important for successful policy implementation. Western textbooks tend to assume that the two can be blended in ways that lead to positive-sum outcomes. The we-must-run strategy, by contrast, treats the two as opposites. For Westerners, planning typically has a positive connotation whereas power has a negative one. In African societies, things tend to be different: The conscious manipulation of social relations involving a high turnover of goods and services for a net gain in political support was, and still largely remains, the ideal of these societies (Uchendu 1969). Political success is counted in terms of the number of followers. Adapting this ideal to the new nation-state meant the need for a strong political authority to enforce and legitimize decisions in the minds of as many people as possible. During the first few years after independence this task was facilitated by the general sense of euphoria associated with being politically independent. The honeymoon, however, gradually waned and was eventually lost, forcing African governments to rely on naked power to remain in charge. In many instances, this process resulted in excesses, because unlike societies in which humans have become slaves of their own technical creations, in Africa, as indicated in previous chapters, there are few domestic structures or institutions to restrain leaders from using their power in a personally discretionary manner. Thus, the relative role of power and planning is shaped by a human's relation to the forces of production and, more specifically, to their ability to tame these forces for purposes of preempting uncertainties in their physical and social environments. The more developed a society is, the more it will rely on planning and coordination; the less developed it is, the more it will rely on hierarchy and power.

The fourth implication concerns the preference in African governments to rely on social transformation rather than on administrative routinization, on movement rather than on state. Many African nationalists became inspired by the Chinese political experience in the 1960s. They tended to close their eyes to the downside of the Cultural Revolution and other excessive interventions to limit the influence of the party and government bureaucracy. Instead, they latched on to the notion that they could imitate the "Great Leap Forward" that Mao Zedong suggested China was in the process of making. The Chinese influence was especially prominent in Tanzania. Although Green (1974) cautioned against too much optimism that Tanzania could replicate the progress attempted in China because of the differences in historical experience, government organization, and social discipline, others, like Hyden (1968), Kunz (1973), and Tschannerl (1973), found a close ideological affinity between the ideas of Mao and *Mwalimu* (Teacher) Nyerere.

The preference for a social transformation approach caused special problems for the agencies responsible for implementing policy. The emerging literature on development administration had advocated the need for a new style of administration that emphasized innovation and adaptation rather than rule orientation and routinization. Administrative reforms were attempted in many countries, but they tended to have bureaucratizing rather than debureaucratizing effects. Schaffer (1969) pointed to the difficulties of reducing the negative influence of bureaucracy on efforts to accelerate development. Both Moris (1973) and Collins (1974) confirmed this observation with reference to Tanzania; Rweyemamu (1974) concluded that public managers and administrators in that country preferred to dodge rather than solve the problems people face.

The Demise

The idea that African countries must run while others walk peaked in the 1970s, but by the end of that decade costs seemed to exceed its benefits in terms of outcomes. Although many blamed it on government bureaucrats, others attributed it to the absence of the kind of vanguard political party that had facilitated the social transformation in the Soviet Union after the Bolshevik Revolution in 1917. This point had been made with reference to Tanzania even before it embarked on its socialist transformation (Bienen 1967). His observation seemed to be corroborated by the experience of the 1970s, which suggested that the party had the power to temporarily impose its will but lacked the means to sustain a socialist transformation. To fully understand its gradual demise, however, it is also important to examine the issue in the light of local African conditions.

Apart from the point made in Chapter Two that the social relations and structures in Africa are not really congenial to the kind of modernization that was attempted in the Soviet Union, there is also the problem of sustaining an ideologically inspired social mobilization. Nationalist leaders insisted that national unity was a prerequisite for national development. The issue that arose in a state of social mobilization was how much criticism to tolerate. Most leaders were intolerant and did not wish to be challenged in public by others. The call for national unity, therefore, was often interpreted as a justification for insisting on ideological uniformity. This was particularly the case with the liberation movements like FRELIMO in Mozambique and the Marxist-Leninist regime in Ethiopia after 1974, but the tendency to muzzle dissent occurred in all regimes regardless of ideology. And as ideology failed to deliver on its promise, the result was not a greater respect for the importance of economic rationality but rather a turn toward political tug-of-wars between factions within the ruling party. Elsewhere, in an analysis of policy making in Kenya, where politics has always been pragmatic, I have referred to this mode of policy making as we-must-pull-while-others-pause, a reference to the more conflicting political process in that country (Hyden 1979). What happened in Kenya – and gradually elsewhere in Africa – was the emergence of groups or factions within the ruling party, which tried to preempt the opportunities for others while also maximizing their own gains. In Kenya, this was quite evident during the reign of the first president, Jomo Kenyatta (1963–78), who very directly favored members of certain ethnic groups, notably his own. The same pattern was repeated after his successor, Daniel arap Moi, took over. For the twenty-five years that he stayed in charge of Kenya, he allowed some groups – including his own Kalenjin people – to benefit at the expense of those who had benefited during the Kenyatta days.

This mode of policy making has something in common with the disjointed incrementalism that Braybrooke and Lindblom (1963) wrote about as characteristic of pluralist political systems like the United States. Both have in common the need for political bargaining between groups with interest in accessing public resources. What they bargain about and how they do it, however, differ. In the United States, any attempt to pull while others pause is focused on specific policy issues by insisting on special favors before the adoption of a given policy package. This logrolling allows for the approval of a set of benefits that are very important to a certain group of voters, but in the context of the overall policy package is a marginal extra cost. In Africa, by contrast, the idea of taking advantage of one's political strength translates into more categorically preemptive moves that alienate others and are being pursued regardless of cost to the public purse. Although there are limits to what may be possible in individual cases, the tendency is for the winner to insist on all, leaving the loser with nothing. With such an approach to policy making, one can easily see that being in opposition carries no real incentives in African countries. That is why its members can be easily co-opted by the ruling party and why a maximum rather than a minimal coalition makes most theoretical sense as a governing mechanism in these countries.[4]

The politically driven policy-making modes that African leaders developed and sustained during the first two decades of independence eventually were called into question not so much by local citizens in these countries as by international donor agencies that felt there was no attention to cost, including the expenditure needed to maintain a particular facility of project. Most of what had been funded in the days of optimism by external donors and banks tended to cease operations once the outside support was withdrawn. They were not sustainable because design had ignored politics or politicians had ignored their responsibility to make calculations of costs associated with keeping the activity going. By the end of the 1970s, therefore, Africa had become a graveyard of donor-financed projects. It was becoming increasingly clear that policy making had to be reformed in ways that allowed greater consideration of cost, feasibility, and sustainability than had been the case in earlier years.

---

[4] For a discussion of the theoretical case for minimal coalitions in competitive democracies, see, for example, Riker's *The Theory of Political Coalitions* (1962).

POLICY REFORMS

In the eyes of the international finance institutions and many bilateral donors to African countries, the issue in the early 1980s was how they could stop the governments on the continent from running away from concerns about efficiency as well as effectiveness. These governments were seen to have operated beyond their means for too long and in the interest of long-term sustainability of the economies, radical measures, they argued, were necessary. In short, they wanted to bring in an element of cost-benefit analysis that had been lost in the development race during the previous two decades. Given the tendency in African political circles to ignore these issues, any attempt to stop the running implied an intervention into the internal affairs of these governments. For governments that still remembered the paternalist and patronizing way their people had been treated in colonial days, this was bound to create controversy in many countries. The more the government had been committed to a socialist strategy of development, the greater the probability that such controversy would arise.

Getting Prices Right

The policy reforms that were being demanded of African governments in the 1980s consisted of a broad range of interventions, but may be summarized as focusing on getting prices right. The focus was on removing the state from the market and providing incentives for a process of resource allocation driven by economics rather than politics. More specifically, it involved stabilizing public finances by reducing inflation, reducing public expenditures, and devaluing domestic currencies. The structural adjustment that was seen as accompanying the surgical interventions in the public sector was meant to give incentives to producers, and reduce the subsidies that had been the consequences of past policies that ignored cost-benefit and feasibility considerations. Although these reforms could be convincingly defended on economic grounds, they were politically painful, especially on a continent where the perception of national sovereignty was so highly valued because of its colonial experience. As Bratton and van de Walle (1997) claim, political leaders saw a relationship between conditionalities issued by the IMF, on the one hand, and decreasing regime legitimacy, on the other. The structural conditions of the African economies, however, were such that governments could not completely ignore the demands placed upon them by the international finance community.

Clapham (1996:176) has identified three different types of response to these demands: (a) resistance, (b) acceptance, and (c) acceptance but with subversion. To this can be added a fourth, which is best characterized as acceptance but with substitution. Given Nyerere's prominence in defining a policy process driven solely by political leaders with no interest in the economics of their actions, it is no surprise that the Tanzanian government put up the most vocal critique and resistance to the new economic policies. Nyerere's anger was directed first and foremost at the IMF, which he regarded as exploiting his country's balance of payment difficulties following the collapse of the East African Community in 1977, the war with Uganda 1978–79, and the second oil shock of 1979 (Mukandala 1999:49). His calling into question the legitimacy of the IMF to serve as some sort of International Ministry of Finance, however, was not tenable in the long run and his government, with advice from friendly Scandinavian governments, opted for the fourth option: substituting the IMF package with a set of financial stabilization measures developed by economists based in Tanzania. This was a politically acceptable strategy, but the substitute measures did not go far enough to cause a noticeable change in the health of the Tanzanian economy (Elgstrom 1999:131–35). Rather than swallowing the bitter pill of having lost to the international finance institutions, Nyerere eventually decided to step down as head of state and let his successor, Ali Hassan Mwinyi, take responsibility for signing a far-reaching agreement with the IMF in 1986. At the continental level, the initiative taken by the UN Economic Commission for Africa to develop a substitute approach – the Lagos Plan of Action – also faded in the mid-1980s. The international finance institutions prevailed and soon there was a reference to the Washington Consensus, the idea that developing countries were best served by unanimity in the donor community about the principles that needed to be implemented in economic reform programs.

Although the international finance institutions had their way across Africa, the francophone countries were initially much less affected by structural adjustment policies, because their currency was pegged to and supported by the French franc. Governments in those countries lived in a false sense of security until the 1990s when their financial conditions had worsened to a point that a significant adjustment had to be made in their overvalued currency – the CFA (the local currency in French-speaking Africa that prior to the introduction of the euro in 2002 was pegged to and backed by the French franc) – in 1994. These economic reforms came at a time when the countries were simultaneously asked to introduce political reforms. The dual call complicated matters and left analysts uncertain about the feasibility of doing both at the same time (Clark and Gardinier 1997). In the end, however, those countries have had no choice but to accept the bitter pill. Although some, notably the Ivory Coast, have suffered political turbulence that, at least, may in part be attributed to the reform programs, the francophone countries have gradually accommodated themselves to the new economic reality (Alibert 1996).

Among other African countries, the third option of accepting the reform policies on paper but subverting them in practice was quite common.

Sometimes, as in Kenya, the position taken by the government was that of outright sabotage of these policies. President Moi engaged in a cat-and-mouse game with the IMF and the World Bank in which he would agree to their demands when pushed against the wall, but later renege on his commitments, an approach that eventually created a vicious circle for that country's economy. Much the same happened in Zambia. Based on this experience, Bayart (1993:26–27) has suggested that sometimes the puppets themselves can pull the strings.

It would be wrong to assume, however, that the fault lies only on the African side. Structural adjustment packages were often quite rigid and even though they may have worked in Latin America or Asian economies, the structural conditions in Africa are sufficiently different that it is necessary to consider the problem of design of these policies. Mkandawire and Olukoshi (1995) argue that these policies rest on a misdiagnosis of Africa's problems. For instance, they would maintain that the real problem is not a bloated public sector, but the failure of measures to improve bureaucratic effectiveness. In short, there was too much emphasis on a one-size-fits-all approach (Olowu 2003).

The African criticism of economic reform policies otherwise tends to follow two main lines. The first is the absence of ownership. The international finance institutions have quite arbitrarily imposed these policies on African governments without having first won them over to their side. As Botchwey (1998:24) notes in a review of policy reform in African countries, if ownership implies voluntary adoption of donor-driven programs, it is clearly in question because most African governments fundamentally disagreed with the financial premises of these programs.

Perhaps the most striking aspect of this reform process, as discussed in Chapter Two, is that the two governments that were most ready to introduce an economic policy rationale were – ironically – run by former Marxists: Jerry Rawlings of Ghana and Yoweri Museveni of Uganda. Both realized, once they were in power, that it was in the best interest of their respective countries to adopt structural adjustment as an economic philosophy and do whatever they could to make it work. Although they kept tight reins over the political process, they initially conceded considerable autonomy to economists and technocrats who were free to design neoliberal economic policies that reduced state involvement and encouraged private investments. The reason for their initial success has been attributed to different factors. One is the presence of a strong executive authority, an observation that has been made about both Asia and Latin America by Haggard and Kaufman (1992). According to this argument, reforms succeed initially because rulers have personal control over economic decision making, the security to recruit and back a cohesive reform team, and the political clout to override bureaucratic or political opposition to reforms. This explanation, however, is not enough to understand what happened in Africa. Most leaders were in a position to have done what Rawlings and Museveni did, but the vast majority chose not to do so.

It is important, therefore, to examine the extent to which there was something special about these two rulers. From a purely ideological point of view, they had a long distance to travel as Marxists, intellectually speaking. Without their own full explanations, it is impossible to know exactly why they became such strong advocates of structural adjustment policies. Maybe ideology, after all, was only a cosmetic cover for their political ambitions and it was not hard to throw aside. Maybe they were genuinely convinced that socialism had run its course and it was time to start afresh.[5] Whatever the reason for making this intellectual journey, both of them had one thing in common: They wanted to make a break with the past. Bienen and Herbst (1996) make the point that a new leader, whether freshly elected with a popular mandate or in office because of a coup or rebellion (as the case was with Rawlings and Museveni), has the great advantage of not being beholden to established patron-client relations that form a major reason for poor economic performance. As they come to power, they can get away with things that were impossible before. They are the "new brooms" (see also Kjaer 2002:40–43). Although the new-broom thesis is typically applied to democratically elected leaders, who enjoy a honeymoon period immediately after coming to power, it is relevant also in these two cases, because both leaders came to power using coercive means, making the break with the past especially dramatic.

The problems that such leaders face, however, begin to surface after some time. Their relative autonomy and the discretionary powers that come with it may eventually make them less interested in building coalitions; instead, they rely on media and other means to impose policies on the public. It can be argued that given the relative weakness of organized interests in African countries, it is easier to get away with discretionary power than it is in more developed societies, where Evans (1995) as well as Haggard and Kaufman (1995) maintain that different approaches other than reliance on a strong executive are necessary to sustain reforms.[6] In spite of such structural

---

[5] Museveni has given a lot of thought to the African predicament. He is of the opinion that the forces of production in Africa remain undeveloped; therefore, African countries need not only a strong central executive, but also a political system that reduces ethnic competition and conflict – at least until social classes have been formed. In this respect he may be described as a Marxist in neoliberal clothing. For further information, see Museveni (1997).

[6] There are observers who disagree with the premise that interests in African countries are not well organized and of little consequence. Kjaer (2002:155) cites the report of a senior consultant on civil service reform in Uganda, George Okutho, as showing that unions of civil servants, teachers, and other professionals were quite vocal and influential when it came to finalizing reform packages, especially as they affected their pay.

variations, however, it is evident that sustaining reform in Africa is difficult beyond the point of initial adoption and implementation. The new-broom thesis has also been questioned more recently on other grounds by Kjaer (2004a), who suggests, using both Kenya and Tanzania to provide illustrations that old brooms can sweep too. In her view, President Moi and his successor, Mwai Kibaki, in Kenya as well as President Mwinyi and his successor, Benjamin Mkapa, in Tanzania have, over time, succeeded in doing as much as the new generation of leaders, like Rawlings and Museveni.

Getting Politics Right

The reforms that were begun in the 1980s focused almost exclusively on the economic arena. More specifically, it was aimed at restructuring state-market relations. In reducing the public sector and enhancing the private sector, agencies in the international development community sought to win the African political leaders on their side. They were at best only moderately successful. By the 1990s, the international agencies realized that it was no longer possible to treat policy as if it were independent of politics. Politics was part of the explanation why African countries tended to stall in their development efforts. Reform since the early 1990s, therefore, has been aimed at getting politics right. More specifically, this means reforming political and administrative structures so that they are better attuned to an economy that is market-based. The code word that members of the international community have used for these reforms is governance–good governance referring to systems that incorporate the essential features of a democratic polity. In the remainder of this chapter, the focus will be on administrative reforms; other aspects of governance are discussed in Chapter Twelve.

Administrative reforms in the 1990s differed from earlier attempts at civil service reform in African countries in that they were placed in a broader economic and political context. Previous reforms – and they were many[7] – had treated the civil service as a closed shop. Relations to other sectors had been largely ignored. A fair amount, however, was already known about the problems facing African civil servants.

For one, there was the lack of professional qualities. Studies had shown that there was little concern with organizational mission, issues of professional integrity, and readiness to take risks. A study of managers in southern Africa confirmed that they were little interested in the goals of their organization. Policy issues were only in fifth place on a list dominated by money and turf as the main causes of bureaucratic conflict (Montgomery 1987). Although extensive efforts have been made to train African administrators

---

[7] Some of the most well-known reports on civil service reform in Africa include the Ndegwa Commission Report in Kenya 1970 and the Udoji Commission Report in Nigeria in 1975.

and managers, the influence that training programs and institutions have had is quite limited, as Kiggundu (1991) notes.[8]

A second issue that had been noted for a long time is the politicization of the civil service. It was a recurrent complaint among civil servants attending the annual Ford Foundation–funded seminars[9] in the 1960s and 1970s that their political masters did not appreciate their professional advice and preferred them to be just sycophants (Rweyemamu and Hyden 1975). The same problem also affected public enterprises that were many and powerful in the days that the state dominated development. Both Mukandala (1988) and Grosh (1991), studying such enterprises in east and southern Africa, point to the many instances of political interference in operational matters that managers reported.

A third issue, perhaps the one that civil servants felt most strongly about, was poor remuneration. Although in the 1960s and 1970s the private sector in African countries was quite small and most people saw employment in the public sector as more prestigious and rewarding, they felt underpaid. The salary reforms that were introduced by the first generation of public service reforms in those days were not really linked to performance assessments. They were given for other reasons such as compensation for inflation or boosting staff morale.

None of these issues were tackled very well by reforms in the first two decades after independence. It is no surprise, therefore, that they reoccur in the 1990s, this time, however, cast in a different light. The interest in governance means that civil service reforms are not ends in themselves. They are related to specific objectives that society (read also: international community of donors) demands: (a) better performance, (b) greater effiency, and (c) public accountability. Reflecting key elements of what are called the new institutional economics (NIE) and the new public management (NPM), this second generation of civil service reforms is much more ambitious and also more complex.

Improved performance, according to the new philosophy of reform, implies first a reduction in size of the civil service. African civil services during the 1970s were allowed to hire far too many employees in relation to tasks performed. Moreover, in most countries there was a considerable

---

[8] Many observers involved in capacity building in African countries have noted the preference for formal certificates or diplomas rather than the substance of learning. Trying to deal with this, one of the more innovative training programs was conducted by John Cohen under the auspices of the now defunct Harvard Institute of International Development (Cohen 1991). It provided highly focused training without providing a certificate and therefore limited the risks that the trainees would leave the organization upon completion of the program. As Leonard and Scott (2003:45) note, however, it purchased commitment by reducing outside options and may therefore also have discouraged risk-taking.

[9] These seminars led to the creation of an all-African association of civil servants, AAPAM – the African Association for Public Administration and Management.

Because power is being held in a personal rather than official capacity, it is being exercised in a dispersed and unpredictable fashion. Individual politicians with a strong charisma may achieve things that would otherwise be impossible, as the case of Julius Nyerere in Tanzania suggests. Sustaining such enthusiasm, however, is difficult, because power is not formalized into corporate structures. The weakness – in many 'countries virtual absence – of indigenous corporate power structures explains why policy outcomes almost always tend to fall so far short of promise. Growing involvement by international actors, not the least the international finance institutions but also bilateral donor agencies, through economic and governance reforms has only marginally helped create a more predictable policy environment. Their increased presence may be a necessary ingredient in any effort to sustain the reform process, but it is also clear from experiences reviewed in this chapter that it serves as a source of opposition to necessary changes. Politicians know that standing up to external actors is the most effective way of gaining political legitimacy quickly. In a multiparty political setting, the temptation for quick and easy gains grows and the inclination to sidestep official policy objectives consequently becomes even greater.

7

The Agrarian Question

Social exchange theory, as discussed in Chapter Four, posits that power is manifest in relations between people. It is the interdependence thus created that generates the possibility of exercising power. The more symmetrical these relations are the less likely that they will be perceived as one person exercising power over the other. The more asymmetrical they are, however, the more probable that the persons involved in these relations will subjectively perceive them in terms of power. As suggested already, relations between people can be formal or informal. The more formal they are, the more corporate their character is likely to be. What determines these relations, in other words, are the roles people play rather than their own personal attributes or character. For instance, relations of power in an organization are constituted by the hierarchy of positions contained in the organogram. A regulation or contractual agreement certifies who can tell whom what to do and who in the end has the ultimate responsibility for what is decided and done. The more informal these relations are, the more personal their nature. As previous chapters have indicated, relations between people in African society tend to be highly personalized. For instance, power relations are constituted by patrons linking up with clients. Furthermore, more symmetrical relations are also informally constituted in response to needs of individuals and households, for example, pooling labor or saving money in small groups. In short, they are based on primary and direct reciprocities that need no contractual confirmation but rely on face-to-face measures to achieve compliance. Power does not reach very far in social terms because its base is personal rather than corporate.

This is the issue at the very root of both governance and development in Africa. Herbst (2000) makes it a main focus in his analysis of states and power in Africa. The paradox is that in Africa politics is supreme but the result is a definite power deficit at the state level. Because the state is embedded in society, the political economy lacks many of the characteristics that can be found in countries where relations of power have been formalized and the state enjoys a higher degree of autonomy vis-à-vis society. Perhaps nowhere else does this become more evident than in the relations between the state and the peasantry. Ever since colonial days, this has been a contentious issue in Africa as officials have tried to subordinate the agricultural producers to their policy commands. The issue of what to do with a multitude of smallholding peasants who are largely subsistence producers is not unique to Africa. This was labeled the agrarian question in nineteenth-century Europe when urbanization and industrialization created new social classes based in the urban areas, and agricultural production had to be modernized and commercialized to meet their demands for food.

The issue was resolved in different ways in various parts of Europe. As agriculture was mechanized and land ownership privatized, as in Britain, surplus labor moved to the cities in search of jobs. In countries like Sweden, where industrialization came late – the beginning of twentieth century – surplus labor among the peasants migrated to North America. In yet other places, notably Russia, a social revolution helped transform relations of power in the countryside. What happened there is of special relevance to Africa as both colonial officials and postindependence nationalist leaders tried to copy measures used by the Bolsheviks after their 1917 revolution. To fully understand this link it is necessary to recall that the intellectuals who theorized about development in those days all had a condescending view of the peasants. The latter were good for nothing when it came to modern development. Rather, they had to be extinguished as a class because their subsistence orientation made them more interested in the parochial concerns of the local household than the modernizing ambitions of the state. This was also the position taken by the colonial officials and – interestingly – the postindependence nationalist leaders. Both had an approach to development that implied modernization of the agricultural sector as the highest priority.

This chapter is about the agrarian question in Africa. The first part, beginning with the experience during colonial days, is a review of how officials have tried to reorganize relations with the peasantry. It will highlight the problems of creating relations of dependence that facilitate the exercise of power over this group. The second part will deal with the implications of these failures for what is a fledgling civil society in the region.

THE CHANGES IN AFRICA'S RURAL AREAS

With the exception of southern Africa – and notably South Africa – there has been no structural transformation that has turned the reliance on small-scale peasant agriculture into modern forms of agricultural and industrial production. Small-scale production continues to prevail, leaving the economy fragmented into myriad independent producers whose contribution to the national economy is both cumbersome and costly to secure.

Twenty-five years ago, I argued that Africa's peasant producers remain uncaptured and that this phenomenon is a challenge for the region's economic development (Hyden 1980). My argument centered primarily on the failure of the state to capture the peasants: Twenty years of independence had not produced a situation in which peasants – as a social class or category – had been effectively subordinated to the corporate demands of the state. Structural adjustment and its focus on economic liberalization was meant to be the policy response to the ineffectiveness of the state. The market would achieve what the state had failed to do. As Schultz (1964) had argued earlier, if provided with the right incentives, traditional smallholder farmers would constitute the basis for agricultural – and national – development.[1] In the eyes of the policy analysts in the international finance institutions this was viewed as a win-win situation: the peasants would earn more and thus the national economy would grow and eventually provide a viable basis for development. Today, there is much more skepticism about the effectiveness of the market. Neither peasant producers nor African economies are markedly better off. As agricultural producers, the peasants remain uncaptured in the sense that they have failed to respond to the new policies. Instead, they have acted rationally by diversifying their sources of income outside the farm. Off-farm income has become more important to rural households than earnings from sales of agricultural produce. Studies done in the 1990s estimated the non-farm source to be approximately 40 percent of the total (Bagachwa 1997; Reardon 1997; Ellis 1998); a more recent study puts the estimate as high as 60 to 80 percent (Bryceson 2002). Although Africa remains largely rural, agriculture appears to be waning in significance. This is also evident in the international development community, in which there is much less interest in investments in agricultural development than there is in measures to alleviate the more general poverty (World Bank 2000).

One of the lessons learned from fifty or so years of research in development economics and political science is that conventional ways of conducting political economy analysis are not the most appropriate for understanding the nature of the agrarian question in Africa. Political economy analysis that draws its inspiration from a rational choice theoretical perspective tends to overemphasize the autonomy of human agency. Moreover, it assumes that we are all like *homo economicus*, that is, ready to make autonomous decisions as if the marketplace is the only relevant locus for establishing what is rational. Political economy analysis that is inspired by Marxian theory, in contrast, tends to exaggerate the importance of structure, notably what happens in the relations of production. Furthermore, because

---

[1] His book on how to transform traditional agriculture was issued in a second edition in 1983 in response to the interest neoliberal reformers showed in his ideas.

of its reliance on historical materialism, its analysis easily becomes too deterministic.

A political economy analysis that is relevant to the African situation has to be tempered in two important respects. The first is that it recognizes that choice is not autonomous but made in regard to how it affects relations with others. In this respect, it differs also from conventional neoinstitutional analysis, which interprets formal institutions as the outcome of human conduct in respect to written rules. A political economy analysis that is relevant to the African situation also needs to transcend the Marxian notion that the economic base explains the social and political superstructure. Because the economy is still embedded in social relations, values other than the material are causative.

Smallholding peasants are crucial to what is happening in Africa not only because of their mere numbers, but also because of what they do – or not do – in agriculture, usually considered the backbone of the African economies. Many would argue that peasants hold the key to Africa's future. Because they are poor and sometimes marginalized, the fact that their contribution to national development has been so limited is usually blamed on bad policies or exploitation by those in power. There has been much less attention to their role as autonomous agents. Even when caught in confining social relations, their agency in the African context is not insignificant. From a national development perspective, therefore, peasants are not just victims without opportunity to influence their destiny; they are also actors that shape the destiny of their country. As such, they are potentially part of both the problem and the solution to the region's predicament. A look at what has happened in Africa since colonial days provides a sense of how peasants have acted in response to shifting structural constraints and opportunities. This discussion will be divided into the three subsections: (a) the colonial period, (b) the statist years after independence (1960–80), and (c) the market reform years (1981–present).

The Colonial Period

African systems of agricultural production were prescientific in the period prior to colonization, relying on simple technologies of cultivation. Neither the horse nor the plow was employed in the use of land for reasons related to geography and politics (Goody 1971). Most of Africa was unsuitable for the horse, which is more sensitive to tsetse flies than other livestock. It never really penetrated the tropical zones of Africa. Where it was introduced, for example, in the semiarid parts of the Sahel, only the nobility was allowed to use it. It was employed more for ceremonial than for productive purposes. These systems were also denied the benefits of scientific advances made in Asia and Europe because African emperors and kings sustained their regimes not by subordinating their subjects on the land to heavy taxation, but by collecting revenue primarily from taxing long-distance trade, requiring tributes from surrounding states and forced contributions from slave settlements. Thus, agriculture was not a source of national income as much as it was just a source of livelihood. Agriculture was first and foremost a subsistence activity. Production strategies emphasized resilience and robustness. Various forms of shifting cultivation developed in response to constraints like the shortage of humus and soil nutrients. In many places, intercropping was practiced to deal with such and other constraints. All innovations came out of practical experience, not scientific experimentation.

To the European colonizers, these forms of agriculture were regarded as primitive and backward. The purpose of agriculture to them was to extract wealth from the African soil. They wanted to introduce efficient systems of production centered on crops that were in demand by the increasingly industrialized and urbanized Europe. The result of this approach to agriculture was intensification of land use in certain parts of Africa, the reliance on monocrop regimes, and the development of new technological packages. These innovations, however, were not brought about by market competition, but by administrative fiat or law. They did not come from the farmers themselves, but from the colonial officials. The Africans were told to discard their own knowledge of agriculture in favor of new insights derived from agricultural research and communicated through the extension service. This turned African farmers into imitators rather than innovators (Hyden 1988).

Toward the end of the colonial period, African farmers had developed an uneasy relation of dependence on the agricultural experts. It worked well as long as their advice proved to be correct and yielded positive results. It became controversial in those instances when advice contradicted existing local practices and was deemed wrong or too risky. With the growth of the nationalist movement, there was a venue for channeling objections to these policies. For instance, Cliffe (1964) shows how resistance to colonial agricultural policies in Tanganyika helped the nationalist movement gain a foothold in certain parts of the countryside.

The peasant producers were also helped by the presence of a cooperative movement in which they were members by virtue of their sale of crops. The colonial authorities recognized that the best way of organizing the many small producers was by creating membership organizations that could be used to tax their crop sales. Such organizations flourished especially in areas with notable increases in production of export crops like coffee, cocoa, tea, cotton, and groundnuts. The cooperative movement in these places was constituted at three different levels. The primary was the cooperative society, in which producers were members. The secondary tier was the cooperative union, made of the primary level societies. The third tier – or apex – was the federation of cooperative unions, which existed at the national level. Though the movement was set up as a convenient economic management instrument, it did also have the effect of educating members in a civic and political sense. They became aware of their rights and realized that they could speak out against wrongdoings by government officials and other leaders. Many political leaders started their career in the cooperative movement. Mamdani (1996) tends to ignore or underestimate the extent to which the rural cooperatives were part of what he calls the civil society that he sees as essentially confined to the urban areas.

In the more successful instances, the colonial authorities could rely largely on the carrot to induce African producers to participate in the market economy by selling their crops to cooperatives or specifically designated crop authorities. In countries like Kenya, parts of Tanzania and also Senegal (Cruise O'Brien 1975), cooperatives constituted viable membership organizations with positive roles in rural development. In areas where agriculture was more marginal, however, the stick often became necessary. Wherever the participation in the market economy was marginal, the colonial authorities tried to increase their control over the peasantry by forcing them into settlements (Kjekshus 1977). By bringing families that had hitherto lived in scattered homesteads into village settlements, they would make these families more reachable with national policy. It was an attempt to capture them by making them dependent on what the state would take in the form of revenue and give in terms of services. Keeping these settlements together proved quite difficult because settlers often left to return to their original homesteads. Much effort, therefore, was devoted to simply controlling them. In economic terms, they turned into a liability rather than an asset to the colonial state.

The most important thing to say about the colonial state in this chapter is that it constituted a viable system of control of the peasant producers on the land. Although it was typically a poor replica of the state in Europe, and much criticism can be directed at its way of approaching agriculture (see e.g. Dumont 1966), it had the basic features of a formal system based on rules and regulations. Even if it did not always practice what it preached, it constituted a system that manipulated and managed the African population to serve its interests. Africans found it hard to escape the arm of the state. Because of integrating them into the world economy through export crops, even the majority of the many smallholder producers were quite effectively captured by the colonial state. In this sense, the colonial state was both quite firm and strong.

The Statist Years

The irony to which I have already alluded in earlier chapters is that while the nationalist leaders preached the inevitability of a centralized state-driven approach to development after independence, the first thing that they did was to destroy the institutional edifice that was the colonial state.

The fully understandable ambition to replace colonial officials with Africans placed people in public office who often lacked experience and who felt more accountable to a political patron than to the public. The whole system that the colonial authorities had put in place to run the country was called into question. Rules were abandoned because they prohibited the interest leaders had in practicing clientelism. Policies that had been successful in colonial days were thrown out because they were seen as potentially damaging to the local population. Most seriously, nationalist leaders abandoned the local head taxes that had served as an important component in the link between state and citizen in colonial days. The formal relations of dependence that the colonial authorities had painstakingly put in place were deliberately subverted.

What happened in Africa more specifically with regard to agriculture in the 1960s and 1970s is that the official ideology stressed the value of modernization, but the institutional practice was the opposite; it aimed at recreating premodern and local values that undermined any effort at modernizing agriculture. Political leaders, as discussed in Chapter Six, did not see that policies require attention to ends as well as means – and especially how the two relate to each other. In trying to expand agricultural production, and thus the revenue of the state, government leaders spoke as if nature and producers could be tamed at will. Big was more beautiful than small. Hoe cultivation was primitive; tractorized agriculture, advanced. It became necessary, therefore, to take advantage of Africa's surplus of land and expand production to those areas that were not already occupied. If land was opened in a contiguous manner and producers settled in a systematic fashion, the use of mechanized tools for production would be possible.

Settling people on new land became a policy in socialist as well as nonsocialist countries in Africa. Many of these schemes were quite capital-intensive and typically launched in the euphoria that existed in the first decade or so after independence. In places like Nigeria with its considerable revenue from oil, such schemes continued long into the 1970s. Nowhere did they succeed. The original investments could not be sustained because there was little or no attention paid to the tasks of managing and maintaining the infrastructure and equipment. Managing on a large scale proved to be beyond the direct reciprocities that Africans were used to and, therefore, unsustainable. There was no readiness to see the tasks in systemic terms and to attend to the issues accordingly. Instead, managers and others would react only when there was a breakdown or problem to which their attention was called. Preventive maintenance based on the premise that what they deal with is a system of many interactive parts was overlooked (Moris 1977).

The African experience stands in great contrast to what took place in most Asian countries at the same time. They made great headway in agriculture through their Green Revolution – the introduction of new seeds and technologies that allowed for a major development breakthrough. The importance of the Green Revolution goes beyond its contribution to increasing agricultural yields. Equally, if not more important, as Djurfeldt (2004) argues, that Green Revolution technologies made the farmers dependent on scientific knowledge developed outside the farm and outside the farming community. The state in Asia succeeded in incorporating the agricultural producers into both the national and international division of labor and thus widened the geographical scope of agricultural circuits of reproduction from local to national or global chains. It managed to capture the peasants in ways that the state in Africa did not. The result was that African agriculture – from having been on the verge of transformation at the end of colonialism – reversed to dependence on prescientific methods of cultivation.

Agriculture in Africa remains largely prescientific to this day in that intensified cultivation is the outcome of spontaneous processes in response to increased pressure on land. As Netting (1993) has demonstrated, such preindustrial methods of cultivation are historically not unique to Africa and have developed in many locations around the world independently of each other. These methods have been the result of the farmers' own ingenuity and typically caused by demographic pressures.

Alexander Chayanov, a Russian economist who studied the life and work of peasants in that country in the early twentieth century, offers an explanation, sometimes referred to as Chayanov's Rule (Chayanov 1966), that has been labeled relevant to contemporary Africa. His proposition is that farmer productivity increases as the ratio of dependents to producers rises. In short, the larger the family a particular producer has to support, the more probable that he will work harder to satisfy this need. Internal household composition, therefore, is key to understanding what drives agricultural intensification. Although Chayanov's own analysis dates back almost one hundred years, it is relevant to Africa today given that peasant agriculture in Russia at that time was characterized by the same prescientific circumstances. Sahlins (1972) and Norman et al. (1981) are among those who have shown that Chayanov's Rule applies to the African cases.

Boserup (1965), a Danish economist, offers another complementary explanation by demonstrating that rising population densities induce technological change and transformation. In Africa, studies show that a rise in population density leads to increased production through more intensive use of the land (Turner et al. 1993; Tiffen et al. 1994; Wiggins 2000). There is disagreement about how sustainable these gains are. Lele and Stone (1989) show that aggregate gains are offset by land degradation and fertility loss, causing greater impoverishment. Turner et al. (1993) suggest that intensified land use tends to have more positive effects on livelihoods wherever farmers have access to urban markets and opportunities for income diversification exist.

One may argue, therefore, that agriculture in Africa changed and developed after independence, not thanks to the state but in spite of it. Social reproduction rather than policy incentives drove agricultural production. Efforts by the state to develop peasant agriculture backfired because they were often ill conceived and heavy handed. It is no surprise that the power of the state over the peasants weakened as the relations of dependence in the market economy, which had been built in colonial days, were much weakened. Nor is it a surprise that by 1980, the international community decided that the market rather than the state would be the instrument to get peasant producers to become more responsive to national and international circuits of reproduction.

The Market Reform Years

The conventional wisdom in international development circles is that policy matters. Changes can be attributed to specific policy interventions. This is a questionable assumption in the African policy environment, which lacks the instruments that allow policy makers to make a difference. The scientific and rational assumptions that need to be shared and respected by all actors are not institutionalized. For such reasons, it makes sense to rely on the invisible hand to achieve what the visible imprint of the state cannot do. But how far is the market capable of making a difference in rural Africa? What are its consequences for agriculture?

There is a good deal of literature on the effects of structural adjustment on peasant agriculture in Africa, most of it overwhelmingly critical (e.g. Bigsten and Kayizzi-Mugerwa 1995; Mkandawire and Soludo 1999). They point to the marginalization of the rural producers and their inability to make headway because of negative terms of trade. Thus, even if the prices paid to producers for some crops, especially locally consumed food crops, have gone up, so have the prices of inputs that are necessary for increasing productivity. For instance, in many countries, peasant producers have been encouraged to adopt high-yield varieties such as maize (corn). These new varieties rely on the use of fertilizers and, often, pesticides. Fertilizers, for instance, used to be available at reasonable prices thanks to state subsidies. Economic liberalization, however, has forced governments to abandon such subsidies, which means that peasants have to pay market prices for their fertilizers, something that only a few of the well-endowed farmers can afford.[2] This means that global market structures deny the African farmers the opportunity to make productivity gains and force them to consider alternative options to make a living. This search for alternatives has been further spurred by declining world market prices

---

[2] Fertilizer prices in African countries are five times as expensive as they are in Europe or the United States.

for many traditional export crops, for example, coffee, cocoa, sisal, and groundnuts.

Peasant response to market prices for agricultural produce has followed two lines. Wherever markets function reasonably well, especially in the vicinity of urban centers, producers have shifted to new crops, notably vegetables and other crops. This has created the impression that the market works and that agriculture has a future in Africa. A second option has been to look for income outside the farm, either in the rural community or in the city. Market reforms in Africa have not set in motion a transformation of agriculture, but a transfer of people from agriculture to other sectors. Analysts adhering to this view are more pessimistic about the future of agriculture in Africa.

The optimists place their confidence in the ability of market and technology to work for development. Their argument is that agricultural systems of production are not static; they continue to evolve in response to market incentives and new technologies. Haggblade (2004) identifies three broad categories of technological change that have been important in Africa: (a) development of improved genetic material, (b) increased use of collateral modern input, and (c) improved management practices. Improved genetic material has proved central in the cases of cotton, maize, and especially cassava. Use of purchased inputs has also helped raise yields of these and other crops. Finally, management changes such as seasonal minimum tillage has led to output gains even with existing genetic material. Haggblade suggests that these innovations vary in degree of difficulty. The first is the easier one, the third the most difficult. Others, like Larsson (2004), agree that the potential for agricultural growth in Africa exists.[3] The problem is that there is not enough consistent effort at national and international levels to realize it. Not enough funds go to research on better crop varieties, and neither is there enough of a commitment to make inputs like fertilizers available to small-scale farmers at affordable prices. Questions must also be raised about the commitment among the African governments themselves.[4]

Whereas many development analysts, especially in the international community, recognize these constraints, their opinion remains upbeat. The problem can be fixed with the right policy interventions. There is obviously a bit more to this than just hope, but the optimists do overlook a number of issues that are also important for understanding the challenges to African

---

[3] Larsson was tragically killed in a road accident in northern Tanzania in October 2004 while this chapter was being revised.

[4] African heads of state and government agreed at the African Union Summit in July 2003 to make agriculture a top priority and to raise budget allocations for agriculture to a minimum of 10 percent of total public spending within five years. Like many other such resolutions, given resource constraints and the fickleness of policy making in most African countries, the probability that this promise can be realized must be considered relatively low.

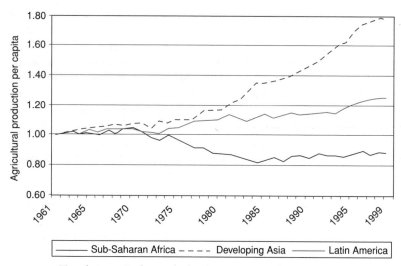

FIGURE 3. Trends in agriculture production per capita by region.

agriculture. The main omission of these people is not to recognize the farm household as a social organization, pursuing many other goals than just enhancing crop yields. African farmers are not subjected to institutionalized poverty in the ways that peasants are when other social groups have effectively captured them. To be sure, Africa suffers from poverty, but it is different from what is found in the Asian and Latin American countryside. In those places, changing one's social destiny is very difficult. Social mobility is much more restricted than it is in Africa. Only Ethiopia, with its long state tradition, resembles the conditions in Asia and Latin America, because there the peasants take their destiny as more or less given. In the rest of Africa, that is not the case. The economy of affection, operating through kinship and other networks, allows for a socially much easier escape from the drudgery of life on the farm, a point made from various angles by other scholars (Downs and Reyna 1988; Guyer 1997; Berry 2002).

This is where the second position on agriculture in Africa comes in. It is much more pessimistic regarding the prospect of making the necessary gains in this sector. Instead, it points to the inevitability that African countries will become increasingly dependent on imports of food from other countries. The facts tend to support this scenario. Figure 3 shows the downward agricultural production trend in the region. In less than forty years, sub-Saharan Africa has gone from a net exporter of basic food crops to a region already dependent on food imports. For instance, between 1966 and 1970 net agricultural export from the region averaged 1.3 million tons per year, one-quarter of which was cereals. By the end of the 1970s, the trend had been reversed. Instead of exporting crops, sub-Saharan Africa was importing no less than

4.4 million tons of food crops, a figure that more than doubled by the mid-1980s (Paolino 1987). A decade later, Wiggins (2000) reports, the import of food crops had gone up to twelve million tons. As Larsson (2004) shows, this is in stark contrast to Asia. Between 1961 and 2001 per capita cereal production in that region grew by 24 percent; in sub-Saharan Africa during that same time, it decreased by 13 percent. There are many reasons why agriculture in Africa is declining. At the global level, continued subsidies of farmers in OECD countries cause an overproduction that presses prices on agricultural produce, not the least cereals, to a level that is unattractive to producers in other countries. The problem with the world market today for Africa's rural producers, therefore, is not that prices are too volatile, but they are too stable at a low level. Another reason is the drudgery of farming associated with an elementary technology like hoe cultivation. Young men, especially if they have gone to school for a few years, will not choose to remain on the farm, but seek employment and income elsewhere, preferably in the city. I am ready to hypothesize that the more governments invest in education in the rural areas, the more they undermine the prospects for growth in agriculture.

Bryceson (1996; 2002) has conceptualized what is going on in rural Africa as a dual process of de-agrarianization and de-peasantization, implying that not only is agricultural production declining, but so is the social coherence of the peasantry. De-peasantization, of course, is not a new process in some parts of the region like southern Africa, where migration from the rural areas to the mining centers has gone on for a long time. In 1913, for instance, 80 percent of South Africa's population was forced into 13 percent of its land area, the objective being that Africans would primarily serve as a labor reserve. A similar policy, albeit on a less ambitious scale, was adopted in Kenya in order to serve the interest of the European settlers. In other African countries, this process of de-peasantization began much later, but has become a significant feature of the social scene that is not identical everywhere. For instance, in countries with high population density, like Burundi, Rwanda, and Uganda, there is less mobility to the cities and greater inclination to find jobs outside the farm while still residing there. This is also true for eastern Nigeria, where villages are turned into townships and market centers because of increased reliance on income from other sources than agriculture. In other countries, off-farm opportunities are often more difficult to come by in the rural areas and people have to go in search of alternative sources of income all the way to the cities.

De-agrarianization refers to the fact that agriculture plays an increasingly less important role as a primary source of income for rural dwellers in Africa. For reasons already discussed, peasant producers find few incentives in the current market situation. Other activities are often more rewarding, even if they do not necessarily offer certainty in the long run. The studies that Bryceson and her colleagues have carried out indicate that rural households do not abandon agriculture altogether. In fact, there is evidence that they become increasingly concerned about securing their own food from the farm. Thus, the old subsistence ethic is kept alive and reduces the costs that they otherwise have to incur for purchasing food. In the absence of large-scale irrigation of the type that is prevalent in Asian countries agriculture in Africa is more dependent on climatic variations. This leaves rural households exposed to high risks in case of drought or any other natural calamity. Food aid becomes necessary to prevent famine. De-agrarianization – and its ensuing emphasis on subsistence – means that a growing percentage of the urban population has to be fed through imports.

Looking at African agriculture through the political economy lens, it is clear that neither state nor market has succeeded in developing, let alone transforming, it. The relations of dependence between state and producer that had been created in colonial days were largely undone in the post-independence periods – ironically, by those who most emphasized the role of the state in development. The informalization of relations of power that followed the nationalist takeover was easier to escape. In spite of being more affected by the market today, the strategy of peasant households has been to diversify their sources of income, thereby leaving them hard to capture for the benefit of national development. The rest of this chapter will discuss the implications of this situation for the formation of a civil society in African countries.

IMPLICATIONS FOR CIVIL SOCIETY

Fifteen years ago, civil society was largely absent from political science literature. The first to really draw attention to it in the context of African politics was Bratton (1989). Today, it is one of the most frequently used concepts. Authors typically assume that civil society is made up of the associational life organized between family and state. The problem with its usage is that authors take it for granted. Most discussions about civil society never really problematize or even operationalize the concept. Furthermore, few examine the underlying social structures on which associations are founded. Hence the concept of civil society is stretched to a point where it could mean everything and, therefore, nothing. With the understanding of African politics and society we have today, there is reason to be more circumspect or careful in the use of the concept. Authors who have expressed this view already include Mamdani (1996) and contributors to a volume edited by Kasfir (1998). The discussion here recognizes the importance of examining associational life in Africa in the light of underlying social structures and identifying the challenges to building civil society in the context of an economy of affection.

Current Social Structures

It may be pretentious to suggest that what has happened to Africa's social structures in the past twenty years can be summarized in a few pages. Being the first to admit this, I will, nonetheless, attempt to identify what I consider to be the principal features of African society today. I try to do it with reference to the following points: (a) growing social instability, (b) greater social stratification, and (c) continued informalization.

Growing social instability manifests itself in different ways. Urban migration is one such important manifestation, but equally important is the concentration of people into city slums where crime in combination with poverty makes living transient and insecure. Although urban-rural transfers have connected urban to rural living for a long time, the literature has tended to treat rural and urban as two separate categories. Mamdani (1996), as late as only a few years ago, laments the absence of a link between the urban and rural areas once the nationalist movement had reached its objective of seizing power from the colonial authorities. This distinction between rural and urban held for the first two decades after independence, but with life in rural and urban areas becoming more challenging after structural adjustment policies were introduced, it is no longer as clear. As suggested earlier, people in the rural areas no longer rely on cultivating the land only. Furthermore, urban residents often grow their own food. Despite the concentration of people, urban agriculture is quite common and residents make sure that they have access to at least a plot for growing vegetables in their immediate vicinity.

People, however, are increasingly unable to cater for themselves. Most people do not earn enough to make a decent living. Traditional family structures are breaking down as the physical distance between members of the household grows with migration. Morris MacLean (2003) noted this with reference to Ghana where the safety net that had always been the extended family system broke down in the 1980s. Diouf (1996:230) quotes the Senegalese newspaper, *Le Soleil*, commenting on life in Dakar:

Senegalese society has known profound upheavals that occasionally have dramatic repercussions for familial structure. The Senegalese family forms a very important social group in a strongly hierarchical agrarian society. Today, with all order of change, the family has been completely transformed and, with it, parental authority is lax, indeed permissive, if not gone altogether.

Despite the positive role that solidarity structures like the Muslim Sufi brotherhoods have played in both social and political life in Senegal, there is a decline in the importance of family and kinship authority when it comes to social discipline (Clark 1999; Villalon 1999). This has resulted in two phenomena. One is the growth of crime and violence, organized or spontaneous. Unemployed youth, many of them educated and frustrated, constitute a fertile recruiting ground for politicians and others in search of groups of people that can help intimidate opponents or enemies. The battles between political gangs in Brazzaville, the capital of the Republic of Congo, have been particularly fierce and threatening (Bazenguissa-Ganga 1999). This increased level of violence has made life, especially in urban areas, more insecure, but it is replicated in the rural areas in many countries. For instance, the sungu sungu vigilante groups that were initially established to stop cattle rustling in rural Tanzania soon became a common way of organizing self-defense in other parts of the country, including the cities (Tripp 1997:12).

The other phenomenon is the increased reliance on religious prophets for personal security. Prophetic movements are not new to Africa and have emerged among Christians as well as Muslims. They have been most likely to rise in situations of crisis. Thus, for instance, early colonialism created the conditions of insecurity that encouraged Africans to seek salvation in prophetic movements. Dini ya Msambwa – a local prophet with his own church – in Kenya is one case in point. Structural adjustment and the uncertainty stemming from greater social mobility, including the threat of HIV/AIDS, lie behind the resurgence of such prophetic movements in recent years. Many of the adherents or members of these movements come from established religious orders, but find that the latter fail to provide the personal salvation that charismatic prophets can offer. The effect of these movements and groups is largely one of escapism. People devote so much time to the obligations associated with membership that there is little, if any, time left for participation in public affairs.

Growing social stratification is another consequence of structural adjustment. People can no longer satisfy their needs or solve their livelihood problems in the village. Off-farm sources of income are available only at a distance and not accessible without a personal connection. Investment in reciprocal relations, therefore, typically involves accepting an asymmetrical relationship of dependence on a patron or broker. Because of the diversification of income opportunities, these patrons or brokers are not necessarily present within the existing kinship structure. It may become necessary to cultivate a relationship with someone more distant, even a stranger. It is not unusual for a European or American living in an African city to be approached by a young man – or, sometimes, a woman – who is requesting a favor, typically in the form of cash money, but at times involving sponsorship of a relative's education. The affective networks that people are ready to invest in today are much wider than in the past, although also more fickle. By becoming more and more vertical, that is, involving a patron and a client, and revolving around issues that cannot be solved locally, there is a greater moral hazard associated with the economy of affection today than was the case in the past. This doesn't mean that pooling within local communities has disappeared. Such practices continue, but they are no longer the only dominant feature of the economy of affection.

The fact that there is a growing social stratification in rural Africa with some peasants having been obliged to sell their farms and already well-to-do farmers taking them over is itself a reason for the expansion of the economy of affection. Landlessness has not yet created a situation of social alienation in which a proletariat is emerging. The poor remain wedded to reciprocal exchanges in which they trust that someone with more resources than themselves will provide the necessary support. This may one day turn out to be all in vain; now, however, Africans prefer to cope within the parameters of an economy of affection rather than removing themselves completely from the prospect of being socially recognized by someone who personally responds to their request for help.

The notion that the objective conditions for social class differentiation exist in Africa today is possible to sustain only if one ignores completely the importance of the informal relations inherent in the economy of affection.

Informalization is the third phenomenon that characterizes the social structures in Africa today. It may at first glance look like an irony, but exposure to the market in the past twenty years has not turned people into autonomous individuals making decisions on their own without regard for others. On the contrary, the uncertainty that market exposure has brought to their lives has reinforced reliance on the economy of affection. Peasant producers in Africa are potentially responsive to prices, but it is not the only consideration that they make. They are quite comfortable having one leg in the market, the other in the social fold that is the economy of affection. Diversification is an important component of a social or political strategy aimed at building or soliciting support. No one wishes to place all eggs in one basket, nor pursue only one option.

This means that people make investments in relations that typically go contrary to formal rules and regulations. A seeks the support of B in order to get a favor, but A does not follow the formal rule that decrees otherwise. From a structural point of view, this informalization is driven by poverty and the sense of urgency to satisfy a need that it causes. From an institutional perspective, it may be explained with reference to path dependency. People know that the economy of affection works and it is the most cost-effective manner to get something done. From a strategic point of view, informal relations make sense because they are direct and in the eyes of the individual actor, therefore, more trustworthy than reliance on abstract rules. Chabal and Daloz (1999) are correct in asserting that there is a social logic in African societies that defeats the conventional notions we have of how political order is being established. Creating

self-enforcing networks that draw on the resources and opportunities provided by the formal institutions has become, if anything, more urgent in the
context of economic and political competition. Multiparty politics invites
actors to engage in the economy of affection in order to maximize their
chances of winning. The question is what the consequences are for building
democracy.

Challenges for Civil Society

Given the prevalence of premodern social structures, what are the implications for the study of civil society in Africa? Where are the boundaries of
the concept in societies in which the line between private and public, formal and informal, is not very precise but, in fact, is very often intentionally
obscured. Drawing on the discussion of what African society and economy is
like today, I shall focus on the following issues: (a) what are the prospects for
associational life? (b) to what extent can this associational life be converted
into a civil society? and (c) what contribution can organizations outside the
state and the private sector make to development?

The first issue is important because it raises the question of how far there
is scope for formally registered organizations in which local people have a
stake. There used to be member organizations such as cooperative societies
and trade unions, but they were by and large neutralized by political patrons
who preferred to treat them as instruments of control in their own hands
(Cruise O'Brien 1975). Not only did this trend facilitate misappropriation of
funds belonging to the members, but it also extinguished the trust that people
had previously had quite painstakingly built up in their own local organizations before independence. Corrupt leaders of these organizations were
often re-elected in spite of such practices because they could use resources
to pacify critics and buy the support of their own clients (Hyden 1973).
Any trust people were ready to extend to others, once political patrons had
penetrated the cooperatives, was based on direct forms of reciprocity. This
meant restricting the social space within which trust would operate and limit
the possibility of using secondary types of organization to achieve objectives
that transcended primary forms of social organization. In short, the opportunities for the growth of associational life were pretty much closed after
independence.

Has this situation changed today? Structural adjustment and demands for
democratic forms of governance challenge the claim to monopoly of power
that political leaders make. In this sense, the structural and institutional
opportunities are more congenial than in the 1970s, when associational life
had been pretty much closed down across Africa. What is clear is that associational life has been slow in rebounding. It remains fragmented, factional,
and sectional in ways that renders its aggregate contribution to development

of new forms of governance very marginal (Lewis 1992). Tripp (1997:199) may be right in questioning the extent to which these new associations are marginal, because, in her view, they mean a lot to their members. In short, these associations should not be underestimated. In Senegal, Ivory Coast, and Zambia, to mention only a few cases, associations have failed to be effective in influencing policy and demanding democracy (Patterson 1998). The most successful example in recent years may be the contribution that voluntary associations have made to constitutional and political reform in Kenya. There are at least two reasons why associations have been so often unsuccessful in bringing about political reform.

The first is the increased diversification of income that characterizes the African household. It means that members are preoccupied with scrambling together an existence in the informal sector. Their self, as Kelsall (2003) notes, is fragmented; their ability to engage in collective action at best sporadic. In short, their everyday activities do not lend themselves easy to organization and coordination with others. This only occurs at a point when the informal activities become formalized, because of legal requirement. The formalization of the informal taxi and bus business in African cities is a case in point. The *matatu* (pirate taxi) vehicle owners in Nairobi have become a significant voice in the discussion about transport in the city after having initially been ignored because of their lack of formal status (Lee-Smith 1989). The majority of people in the urban areas, however, continue to seek a living on their own in small business activities that have yet to develop to the point where association with others make sense (Tranberg Hansen and Vaa 2003). Diversification and fragmentation of economic activities continue to limit the incentives for people to form associations in ways that they used to do when their source of income was more concentrated and permanent.

The second reason is that the level of trust has declined so much in both urban and rural Africa that the interest in seeking out others in order to pursue a joint project is much less than it used to be. There has been a significant loss of social capital, partly as a result of the misappropriation of member funds, referred to above, partly because of the accelerated social change that has taken place in the past twenty years. As will be further discussed in Chapter Eight, women are among the few that show trust in each other, albeit even among them in small circles. Religion provides a foundation for social trust. Muslim brotherhoods and church-based organizations tend to have a vitality and strength that are not found in other contexts. Even in these relative strongholds of social capital, however, not everything is fine. Particularly troublesome to many followers is the extent to which religion has become politicized as a result of an intensified proselytization especially among radical and evangelical sects (Villalon 1999). This may have had the effect of strengthening the internal solidarity of each group, but it has also polarized society and made communications across denominations more difficult.

So, what are the prospects of converting this type of associational life into a civil society? This question is relevant as long as we don't assume that civil society and general society are one. This distinction is made in order to confine the notion of *civil* to the organized activities that aim at articulating opinions on public issues. Moreover, a society is civil if there is sufficient evidence of dialogue and tolerance of others participating in the discourse. Without a specification along such lines, the notion of a civil society makes little sense.

It was suggested at the end of Chapter Four that there is a distinction between the kinds of civic communicative space that Habermas (1979) and others associate with a functioning democracy and the affective space that characterizes African society. The former encourages discourse on issues of principle with a claim to universal validity. The latter tends to foster compliance and a preference for claims to validity based on concrete and tangible results. There is reason to return to this distinction here.

Civic space is the outgrowth of a society in which thinking long-term, accepting abstract rules, and acknowledging interdependence as a positive rather than negative phenomenon comes naturally to the individual. Such a society is inevitably modern, relies on a market-based economy, and rests on the principle of rule of law. Furthermore, it is a society in which there is relative plenty. Civicness is more easily promoted in conditions of plenty than in poverty. For these reasons, civic space is more extensively present in developed societies that are also consolidated democracies. Affective space is more prominent in societies that are still characterized by premodern features in which the formal institutions of a market economy are weak; the idea that there are rules that are independent of human agency is not widely embraced.

This dichotomization of civic and affective spaces amounts to the creation of two ideal types. Reality, of course, is more complex. So most societies function with a bit of each present. Still, there is reason to assume that turning associational life into a functioning civil society along the lines of civic communicative space is going to prove more difficult wherever poverty and premodern features of society dominate. The emphasis on immediate and tangible results tends to make organizations more vulnerable. Because the main reason for their existence is not a universal cause, but serving a particular local interest or preference, these organizations rest on a shallow foundation of legitimacy. Furthermore, they are often dominated by a single individual with persuasive personal qualities. Because of this concentration on the role of the founder, relations in nongovernmental organizations also tend to be easily personalized. Criticism is discouraged and seen as a sign of disloyalty. Rules and procedures are often ignored in order to make things work the way the leader wants it. In short, many of the features that are identified with the Big Man syndrome in politics can be found also in associational life outside government. These problems do not only just apply to development-oriented organizations, but also to many groups that devote themselves to the promotion of human rights. In spite of a rhetorical commitment to a universal principle such as a civil or political right, these organizations often end up being quite parochial and sectional in their practice.

What expectations should we have regarding the contributions to development that associations outside government and the private sector can make? In recent years, Africans as well as agencies in the international community have been inclined to look more and more to the voluntary sector as the answer to the region's development crisis. There are three problems, however, with the current tendency to place so much confidence in this sector. The first is the overemphasis that is being placed on these organizations as service deliverers. The second is the dominance of international NGOs as intermediaries between government and community. The third is the absence in African society of the factors that keep modern organizations going.

It is hard to escape the impression that in many circles, not the least in the international development agencies, civil society has become a mechanism of last resort for development. Many of these agencies, not the least the United States Agency for International Development (USAID), are tired of the ineptness of African governments and they realize that economic liberalism notwithstanding, the private sector in most countries in the region is still a long way away from playing a leading role in development. The NGOs have become especially prominent in the service sector where they play an increasingly important role in education as well as health delivery. According to one source (Semboja and Therkildsen 1995:17), donor funding of the voluntary sector rose from U.S.$1.04 billion to U.S.$2.13 between 1980 and 1988. This growth is almost five times higher than that for total official development assistance (ODA) to governments, which actually declined quite considerably during the 1990s. Although ODA has since rebounded, a large chunk of the overall development assistance is being handled by NGOs.

This means that a heavier burden of development work now rests on the shoulders of these NGOs. Their activities are being funded in two different ways. One is through contracts with a donor government for the implementation of a specific program or project that it is committed to supporting; the other is by contracting with an African government. In both cases, the NGOs become implementation agencies with reporting responsibility to a particular government. Many analysts lament this arrangement because it reduces the role of these organizations as intermediaries on behalf of the people. NGO leaders are usually aware of this critique and try to counter it by engaging in participatory forms of problem analysis before engaging in implementation. Even so, the argument that NGOs are somehow caught in links to governments and, therefore, cannot speak out when witnessing abuses of power and other shortcomings in government operations cannot be whisked aside altogether. As agencies that could contribute to the formation of civic values in environments where they are overshadowed by affective ones, they are not doing very much.

One reason why this does not happen is that most NGOs in Africa are international and lack a local support base. Even those organizations like Oxfam, which raise money from citizens in developed countries, find that they have difficulties reaching the local communities in African countries. The best that they can do is to work with community-based organizations. This means that it is civil society rather than the state that is bifurcated today. The civic values that international organizations bring to Africa from their home base are not insignificant, but the challenge is how they may be disseminated and can take root in this more inhospitable setting. One organization that has experimented with this is Oxfam-Canada, which has run a program to harness voluntarism in countries in the Horn of Africa and, especially, Ethiopia. The experience shows that voluntarism requires charismatic leadership and usually some independent wealth in order to grow. The best opportunities tend to exist in relation to perceived popular needs, particularly in education and health (Hyden and Hailemariam 2003).

The problem that these international NGOs encounter in dealing with local communities is that the latter are quite excited about the attention that they get. As a result, popular expectations climb. Fulfilling them within the specific parameters of a small-scale project may not be overly difficult, but sustaining the effort beyond such a timeline proves to be much harder. Because the local people and their leaders do not have the tools of analysis that their modernist counterparts in the international NGO community have, very little tends to happen once the externally funded activity is over. The real challenge, therefore, is how to develop the mind-set that makes these communities capable of doing development work on a sustained basis.

This takes us to the third problem, which is that in the absence of the basic features of modernity, African society is not a very congenial environment for the growth of social movements that cut across the bonds of primary social organizations. Nor does this environment easily foster other such important values for the growth of civil society as transparency, accountability, and reflexivity. The antiapartheid movement in South Africa is the closest that any popular initiative has come in that direction. It operated in an environment in which people had been sufficiently alienated from their roots so that in the face of an easily perceived common enemy – racism – people could come together and fight for a common cause based on the principle of justice and freedom for all.

In other African countries, it has been much more difficult to mobilize popular support for general causes, be that protecting the environment, promoting human rights, or fighting HIV/AIDS. In communities where local space is what people know, there is a natural tendency to fall back upon the security that lies in not getting involved in anything that implies challenging hegemonic local norms. It is safer to lie low than to stick one's neck out. The exit option is more attractive than the voice option (Hirschman 1970). This is not to imply that people in the local communities are cowards, only to suggest that in the prevailing circumstances it is fully understandable and rational if they shun involvement in the issues that the modern world gets excited about. As Galvan (2002) has convincingly demonstrated, people in the rural areas can relate to their local enviornment in creative ways by reinventing traditions to suit modern demands. The "syncretic" institutions that they so create are meaningful and help them navigate the difficult terrains associated with social change. Yet, these institutional creations remain not only local but also driven by a premodern logic that limits their potential for replication on a national basis.

CONCLUSIONS

The paradox of African society today is that there has been little development but a lot of social change. Most of what has happened in Africa is not the result of grand design but of millions of Lilliputians trying to achieve what is rational from their microperspective. Small is beautiful in Africa; it is untouched in respects that are not found in the world where global capitalism has already institutionalized a system capable of capturing rich and poor alike. Small is problematic in Africa because it has not been fully captured and, therefore, is not forced to respond to manipulations of the system in the same way or to the same extent as elsewhere in the world. For the individual or the local community, this is a blessing. For the country it is, if not a curse, a serious structural obstacle.

One serious consequence of this state of affairs is the decline that agriculture has suffered. This process may be beyond the point at which it can be reversed by better policy or offer more attractive incentives to farmers. There are likely to be only isolated pockets of viable small-scale agriculture left where men and women will share in the task of tilling the land. In most of Africa, agriculture, where it is not going to be taken over by commercial and capitalist-oriented farmers, will be left in the hands of women who have little time to devote to this task other than what is necessary for subsistence. It is impossible to ignore the de-agrarianization argument altogether.

Urban migration and the prospect of capturing the small for the benefit of the system because they live in an environment without the same access to the means of subsistence may at first glance sound more feasible. A closer examination of what happens in urban Africa, however, contradicts any such optimism. The vast majority of these migrants end up self-employed in the informal sector where they are no easier to capture than on the farm. They may struggle to make a living even more than they did in the village, but they prefer the anonymity that urban residence provides. This does not mean that they cease making contacts with others. In fact, much of what people do is investing in relations with others as part of making a living. In the informal sector, the formal system does not reach them easily, so affective networking makes sense. Even if the moral hazard is much greater in any such investments in the open urban environment than it is in the more enclosed rural community, the prospect of gain is higher with direct reciprocal exchanges than relying on formal institutions to deliver the same benefits.

What social exchange theory has taught us in this chapter is that relations of dependence that generate viable power structures for development are cumbersome to create. The power deficit that can be easily identified in African countries stems from the ability of so many people to escape relations of dependence. From a development policy perspective, people in the rural as well as urban areas are largely uncaptured. What is more, there is no corporate system to redress this shortcoming. African countries continue to be ruled through complicated but fragile social networks that cost a lot of time and money to sustain.

It is in the light of these anomalous social formations that the prospect for a civil society should be analyzed. Africa already has a rich associational life at community level, but these many organizations remain generally parochial in orientation. They cater for small groups and deal with demands that require immediate solution. Their rationale, therefore, is generally based on reciprocities, i.e. people trying to help each other, rather than hierarchically organized priorities pursued in a systematic fashion. There is rarely such a thing as a plan of operation and wherever it exists, it is typically the result of demands made by funding agencies. The role of such plans in day-to-day management, however, is minimal. While these features are especially manifest in the countryside, they do exist also in the urban environment, which, as we have seen above, is an extension of the rural rather than a social sphere constituted separately. The main difference is that the urban Africa has far more externally induced organizations than the countryside has. To be sure, there are many urban organizations like the hometown associations in Nigeria that are indigenous but they tend to have a parochial objective – that of helping the home community develop. The urban enviornment in Africa, therefore, is characterized by two types of organizations – the externally induced NGO and the internally induced community service organization. None of these is especially well placed to contribute to the growth of a civic sphere and thus a true *civil* society. Yet, it is in these rather inhospitable circumstances that private and voluntary actors have to try to make progress. A focus on the role of women in public life will help illustrate this further.

8

Gender and Politics

If the analysis of the agrarian question in Africa suggests that peasants can circumvent relations of dependence because their reliance on the state and other external agencies is weak, the opposite tends to be the case in gender relations. A woman may be able to divorce her husband, but even in such a scenario she is likely to be subjected to control by other males. In societies, therefore, where control of women is vital not only for social reproduction but also for economic reasons, their emancipation is fraught with special hurdles. This chapter will analyze the constraints that women encounter and discuss the progress they are making despite these many hurdles. As such, it will draw on social exchange theory to examine both symmetrical and asymmetrical, informal reciprocal relations.

Gender came to the forefront as a public issue in Africa in the 1980s. It was a reflection on what was happening elsewhere in the world. The role of women in politics and development got a special boost from the international conferences that the United Nations organized in Copenhagen 1980 and Nairobi 1985 in order to showcase this theme as a concern of all. The idea of holding the second international conference in Nairobi was deliberate. The situation of women in Africa was generally considered critical. Not only were women poor, but they also carried a heavy burden of work on the land. Furthermore, in a cultural context where group rather than individual rights tended to prevail, their status was generally of secondary importance. They had difficulty gaining the recognition they deserved for their contribution to development.

The literature on gender tends to be as prescriptive as it is analytical; the one that deals with women in Africa is no exception. Most writers are women and the subject matter invites an understandable moral concern. It sets the conditions of women against those of men and points to the long legacy of discrimination, if not oppression, that has characterized gender relations for generations. Much of the analysis is cast in materialist terms, pointing to the adverse consequences the growth of a capitalist economy has had on the status and role of women. The main thrust of this literature is emancipatory: Women should be given equal status with men and the same rights.

Another question in Africa-focused literature concerns the extent to which the conditions of women are the same there as in other parts of the world. Is the gender issue one that is best tackled in universalist terms, or is there a rationale for being culture-sensitive and ready to accept a measure of relativism? This has become a particularly important issue with regard to women's reproductive rights. Because female genital mutilation is practiced in certain parts of Africa but is an issue that feminists elsewhere condemn as a violation of a woman's integrity and rights, the question has arisen: How far is it best tackled? Should it be confronted by African women who understand the cultural context of these practices, or by an international movement of female activists who reject it on principle grounds only?

A third distinction in the literature is between authors who focus on women in development and others who approach the subject primarily from the point of view of their participation in politics. It seems a fair assessment that the literature in the 1980s focused more on the former while, since the 1990s, the interest has shifted more toward the rights of women in public life. As such, it is more political in nature.

The purpose of this chapter is to try to do justice to the variations that exist in the literature, yet arrive, like previous chapters, at some aggregate statement about where it has taken us until today. In accordance with the premise underlying the analysis in this volume, women in politics cannot be fully understood without first looking at the underlying structural conditions that determine the issue. Thus, the discussion will focus on four important dimensions of women in politics and development in Africa. The first is the demographic dimension. Of special importance is the way marriages are transacted because it has implications for property rights and inheritance. The transactions in sub-Saharan Africa are different from those in Asia and Europe, leaving women in Africa with a different structural hurdle to overcome. The second is the economic dimension. Especially important are women's efforts to circumvent hindrances and develop their own means of earning an income, individually or in cooperation with others. The third is the sociological dimension, which acknowledges the fuzzy boundary that exists between things private and public and the implications this has for the role of women in politics and development, especially for the pursuit of their rights. Finally, there is the political dimension, which focuses on women's participation in development as well as in public life. It deals with the ambivalent view that women have toward politics given the low credibility that politicians have and the cost that active participation in politics carries for their personal reputations.

THE DEMOGRAPHIC DIMENSION

The African family is changing in the light of increased social mobility and other factors such as the HIV/AIDS epidemic and the economic reform process. This change affects everyone, but the burden of coping with it tends to fall especially hard on the female members of the family. One sympathetic African observer puts their situation in the following language:

> Forced to contend with the simultaneous omnipresence and instability of the African family, they [women] desperately attempt to fit innumerable obligations into their schedule. They take care of the home and the housework, earn an income, deal with the budget, savings, and investments, negotiate tensions among family members, and ensure the multiple connections between city and village. They have little time for dreams and are often deprived of the minimal amount of solitude that every human being requires. (Monga 1998:131)

Women anywhere in the world would probably find themselves able to relate to this predicament. The purpose of this section is to explore the extent to which the explanation for what happens to women in Africa might be found in the sphere of social reproduction. As various authors mentioned in previous chapters argue, premodern structures continue to exist at the local village level and extend their influence to much of the urban environment as well. The kinship structures continue to be influential when it comes to social and economic behavior. There are at least two respects in which the demographic dimension in Africa differs from that of other regions. The first is the extent to which kinship is of importance not only in terms of social organization, but also as relations of production. The second is the way marriages are contracted in Africa, which differs from the patterns prevailing in Asia, Europe, and the Americas.

Kinship Structures and Women

There are various ways of explaining the role that kinship structures play in Africa. This book has largely explained it in terms of how they affect formal institutions. Being at the roots of the economy of affection, these structures are responsible for capturing formal economic and political institutions and embedding them in a social logic that runs counter to the rationale of modern organizations. Drawing on Marxian ideas, one can also explain the role of kinship structures as applying both to infrastructure and superstructure at the same time. As Meillassoux (1975) argues, social hierarchy in premodern societies without a state system is not based on the control of the means of production. Instead, it is the system of social reproduction that is dominant by allocating authority to those who control the system of marriage alliances through which the basic cells of society are reproduced. Other authors, like Rey (1973) and Godelier (1977) who write in a similar vein, generally agree with the observation that wherever the laborer has not been separated from the means of production, the key to understanding social structures and how they influence behavior must be sought in social ties that are more directly personal. Whether these social relations are taken to be basically egalitarian or inegalitarian – and authors differ on this subject – they must nonetheless be personal.[1]

No one suggests today that the lineage mode of production exists in its pristine form in contemporary Africa. Rather, the point is that it continues to be an enduring influence on society because the kinship structures have yet not been captured and replaced by either market or state. None of these institutions has emerged as dominating society. This means that relations of social reproduction continue to overshadow the importance of relations of production, which manifests itself in various ways. Families are allowed to grow independently of what they can afford. In other words, the notion of the cost of living does not serve as a break on family size in the way it does in societies where families are captured by the market. African governments typically do not have family planning policies that they take seriously, and state influence over social reproduction is virtually nil. The demographic transition that we have seen in other regions of the world is still, at best, a distant phenomenon. More money does not necessarily mean fewer children and nuclearization of the family. It continues to mean the opposite: more children and more dependants.

Another manifestation is the widespread phenomenon of self-employ-ment, especially in the informal sector. Because African families are not closed and nuclearized types of social organization, members do not share an economic destiny. As anthropologists have told us, in the past there was always the possibility of exiting, that is, leaving the place of origin because land was insufficient and then establishing oneself on new and unoccupied land (Kopytoff 1987). This process, if anything, has intensi-fied as land is becoming in increasingly short supply and opportunities have opened up for life in the urban areas. Self-employment in the urban informal sector is in many respects the modern equivalent of the move-ment on the social frontier in precolonial Africa, which colonial author-ities tried to either end or, at least, control by moving people into state-controlled settlements. Since independence, the original logic has come back and explains why urban life for most Africans is foremost an extension of what they learned in the rural areas. Evasion and migration – the exit option – remains very much part of the African political tradition today (Kelsall 2003).

---

[1] Even when classes are attributed to premodern, segmentary societies, these classes are con-ceived in a different way from those that emerge under capitalism. As Terray (1975) argues, whereas elders, juniors, and women may form classes in such societies, they are not antago-nistic in the same sense as are the bourgeoisie and the proletariat (see also Kahn and Llobera 1981).

With relations of social reproduction being dominant – and certainly not yet subordinated to those of capitalist relations of production – the position of women is more influenced by premodern rather than modern institutions. Men acquire women because they are both the means of economic production and the means of social reproduction. They are responsible for ensuring the subsistence of the family, and it is through them that additional labor – in the form of children – can be obtained. It is not the wealth of the woman that matters, but her fertility. Being able to have children remains to this day the sine qua non condition for a woman to stay in her marriage. For a man not to have fathered his own children is still perceived in most circles as a social embarrassment. Even if these attitudes may be changing among members of the younger generation, especially the educated in the urban areas, the majority view of women remains instrumentalist. Romantic love between a man and a woman and respect for her integrity are values that remain the exception rather than the rule in the African context.

Marriage by Alliance Rather than Descent

It is important to remind the reader that land has not differentiated the population in Africa, either within or between clans, into gentry, kulaks, poor peasants, and serfs. The conditions of landlordism or feudalism has not developed, not even in densely populated places like Northern Nigeria (Hill 1972). As Goody (1973:30) notes, the strategy of not letting one's daughter marry beneath her in terms of landed property has never really been an issue in rural Africa. As the same author notes in a case study of the Gonja in northern Ghana, Muslims marry commoners, the commoners marry chiefs, and the chiefs, Muslims (Goody 1969:159). There are a few notable exceptions to this practice. One is imperial Ethiopia, in which landlordism did develop and created conditions under which marriages between lords and peasants were inconceivable. Another is the interlacustrine kingdoms of Rwanda and Burundi where a castelike stratification between the Tutsi aristocracy and the Hutu commoners had developed, and intermarriages between the two were prohibited (Lemarchand 1970).[2] The marriage system in these societies was closed.

Historically speaking, such closed systems have emerged wherever property is differentiated; similarly, open systems have typically been found where property is more evenly distributed. Marriage within specified social circles is a strategy of isolation. Marriages without such prohibitions involve wider exchanges or interchanges, and involve a leveling off because the prohibitions are a form of redistribution. Consequently, what Goody (1973:32–33)

---

[2] It is worth noting at the same time that this stratification in neighboring societies in the same region did not produce an equivalent rigidity. Thus, among the other kingdoms where the Hima aristocracy ruled, chiefs and princes often took wives among commoners.

calls in-marriages tend to be associated with the complex stratification found in European and Asian societies, whereas out-marriages are the norm in societies like those in Africa with a much simpler stratification.

To fully appreciate the difference between Africa, on the one hand, and Eurasia, on the other, it is necessary to also consider how property was transacted in marriages. In the stratified societies of the former two regions, marriage tended to stress ancestry, descent, or filiation, whereas the emphasis in Africa was laid on alliance or affinity. Wherever ancestry is more important, the bride typically brings property to the marriage and is an heir to her father. In this kind of situation, it becomes important to consider whom the daughter is getting married to. The notion of matchmaking becomes relevant. The fact that women are heirs to their father's property tends to push conjugal relationships in a monogamous direction. This individualizing form of marriage is associated with the concept of love. Gluckman (1965) argues that it is love that serves to separate both spouses from their kin, uniting them into a conjugal team. Love has the effect of splitting society into spatially distinct groups based upon monogamous unions. In polygynous societies, love is controversial in the sense that if one wife is favored over others, the task of managing the family unit becomes much more contested.

The position of women, therefore, differs between societies that practice marriage by descent and by alliance. The conjugal union tends to be closer in the former case, leaving the wife a captive of social pressures, but giving her some clout by bringing property into the marriage and having access to inheritance from her father. In the latter case, the union is looser and may involve more than one wife. The woman is not incorporated into her husband's lineage – as in marriages by descent – but is linked with him in a crosscutting conjugal unit in which she retains her identification with her father's lineage. Because the husband and his family pays the bridewealth, he tends to have less commitment to a monogamous relationship and to exercise stronger pressure on her to perform her dual role as an instrument of production and social reproduction. Boserup (1970), from an economic and technological perspective, has come to the conclusion that wherever shifting cultivation prevails and the majority of agricultural work is done by women, one can expect to find a high incidence of polygamy, and bridewealth being paid by the future husband or his family. In contrast, wherever plow cultivation is predominant and women do less agricultural work than men, monogamous marriages are most common and the woman's family usually pays the dowry.

We can conclude this section by noting that in Eurasia, the wife has historically been more dependent on the husband's economic support, because she has not been allowed to do anything besides being a homemaker. In Africa, the situation has been – and still remains – different in the sense that women continue to spend a lot of time cultivating the land while, at the same time, being compelled to have many children and responsible for their well-being. The structural constraints operating on the African woman, therefore, are especially heavy and make her social and political emancipation doubly difficult.

THE ECONOMIC DIMENSION

The fact that women in Africa work longer hours than men, in housekeeping, caring for their children, fetching fuel wood and water, and tending the fields, should come as no surprise given the demographic structures outlined here. Women typically work sixteen hours per day due to their numerous and diverse responsibilities (Kaul 1989). Another study shows that women contribute three-fourths of the labor required to produce the food consumed in Africa (Food and Agriculture Organization 1985). Further, aggregate data indicate that African women provide about 90 percent of the labor for processing food crops and providing households with water and fuel wood, 80 percent of the work in food storage and transport from farm to village, 90 percent of the work in hoeing and weeding, and 60 percent of the work in harvesting and marketing (Lele 1991:50). Peasant men's incomes rarely augment the family diet and, even in the city, women provide significant contributions to household budgets (Walu 1987; Schoepf and Walu 1991). As Goheen (1991:244) argues in a study of the Nso in Cameroon, the point is not that men are necessarily uninterested in the welfare of their families, but rather that they are not held socially responsible for the family's basic food security. The men rarely purchase items routinely used on a daily basis to prepare the family meals. When they purchase consumables, they tend to select prestige supplements such as sugar, tea, white bread, or meat.

In economic terms, the average household in Africa is quite inefficient. Men and women work independently of each other instead of cooperating in ways that enhance its cohesiveness. Much of this inefficiency is at the root of Africa's current predicament. It is increasingly clear that wherever husband and wife try to work together more closely as they do, for instance, among the Chagga in Tanzania, the households are more successful and the ethnic group itself benefits. It is no coincidence that the Chagga are often compared to the Asian minority in East Africa precisely because they have tighter family solidarity than among most other ethnic groups in the region.

The policy reforms that have enhanced the role of the market in development have been at best a mixed blessing for Africa's women. The new economic situation has increased the insecurity of most households in both rural and urban areas, which has translated into an even heavier burden of work for women. The same trend that accompanied the growth of a capitalist economy and the emergence of a bourgeoisie is not applicable to Africa. In Europe, this trend had the effect of making an example of the wife as a homemaker, loyal to her husband within the confines of a monogamous marriage. The neoliberal reforms in Africa have come at a time when precapitalist features of the economy continue to prevail: there is no real bourgeoisie to speak of, and gender relations remain embedded in premodern structures.

What we have seen in recent years is not an embrace of the opportunities for income that the market provides but a backing into it by force of circumstances. Women have had no choice but to enter the market in order to supplement their own and their family's income. Almost all of this supplementary income activity is in the informal sector and is typically very small in scale. Cooking and selling food on the sidewalk in the urban areas is one such income-earning activity; dressmaking is another. Those who do not earn enough from such businesses may have to sell their bodies in order to make enough money to provide for their families. This is especially true for single or divorced women but applies in extreme cases also to married women. Because women enter the market out of poverty, they have little clout, and often have no choice but to succumb to demands for sex by men with money. All these women are fully aware of how they contract HIV/AIDS, but in a situation of dependency, they are ready to take the risk rather than face their family's starving at home. Short-term rationality prevails over longer term implications of behavior and choice.

One positive thing about the new situation is that women have realized that they share a common predicament and that there is value in cooperating with one another. Reference was made in Chapter Four to rotating credit and savings societies as a phenomenon that has increased in popularity among women. Such groups are particularly valuable because they provide a lump sum that is often important for members who need to make an emergency payment at a hospital, or pay school fees that are higher than what the everyday cash balance permits. Because of its simplicity, this form of cooperation is easy to sustain. No one really ever runs away with the money and the level of trust is high. The problem with the rotating credit and savings model is that there is no real value added to the economy at large. It does not contribute to economic growth, only to the sharing of existing resources. Thus, women use it primarily as a coping mechanism. It allows them to stay afloat.

Some women are more ambitious and another positive phenomenon in the African economies today is the rise of an entrepreneurial cadre of women. Some of these entrepreneurs operate in the domestic market only, but often network in order to make more money. A study of women traders in Tanzania showed that they established networks with friends and acquaintances to solve specific business problems and to make their businesses more profitable by assisting one another with transport, storage of goods, and even household work. This pooling of resources was all done on an informal basis but worked quite effectively (Mattila 1992). Other female entrepreneurs have taken up the import business. They go to the Middle East, Europe, or Asia to purchase goods, for instance, textile materials and assorted specialized products, such as hair creams, that are in demand in their local African markets. The women can buy these goods at sufficiently low discount prices so that their travel costs are covered and they can still make a profit.

The more ambitious the business venture, the greater the probability that it will be pursued on an individual instead of a cooperative basis. This proposition seems to apply to the fledgling capitalism in Africa, in general, as well as to women entrepreneurs, in particular. This does not mean that women are not members of professional business associations. They are, but they run their businesses as a private affairs. A study of African-owned businesses in Kenya showed that pooling of resources, especially finance, occurs only rarely (Marris and Somerset 1971). In Zambia, even the largest and most successful businesses were run with solo-management and ownership (Beveridge and Oberschall 1979). The main reason for this reluctance to establish pooling arrangements seems to be the widespread fear that partners will cheat in some way or try to take over. Related to these concerns, entrepreneurs fear that people who have made investments in their businesses will interfere in the detailed management of the day-to-day operations and thereby make efficiency difficult to sustain. Further, the investing partner could regard the so-called disappearance of their money into a common fund as evidence that the entrepreneur-manager partner has squandered or stolen their assets (Kennedy 1988:166). Indigenous African corporate businesses are few and far apart. The Big Man mentality prevails also there.

Although many women have emerged as successful entrepreneurs they have not escaped the difficulties that their male counterparts face. The vast majority of these businesses are characterized by what Akeredolu-Ale (1975) calls the profit-for-self-and-family approach, which he contrasts with the profit-for-business-growth model. The former involves a focus on consumption and subsistence; the latter is based on the desire for expansion and growth. One is precapitalist in orientation, the other capitalist.

African society relies on direct reciprocal exchanges that are face-to-face and most actors have great difficulty in placing their trust in abstract market arrangements. There are very few precedents even for genuine family businesses based on continuous, joint activity and ownership. Thus, it is no surprise that there is even greater unwillingness to establish true corporate forms of business arrangements as, for instance, Trulsson (1997) found in a study of successful entrepreneurs in Tanzania. Chronic economic and political insecurity in many African countries has often exacerbated this phenomenon, but it is clear that it exists whether or not the country is characterized by political stability. It has much more to do with the path dependency of informal institutions associated with a premodern society. The lineage system remains, as Hart (1982) puts it, a fertility machine that is being fueled through injections from more successful members of the organization; the urban elite still actively supports a wide circle of less privileged kinsmen. Dependency on others is the order of the day for both men and women.

There are attempts by members of the elite to break out of this pattern, but the lack of trust in others and the presence of relatives and friends expecting a share of the cake mean that the scope for capitalist development from within Africa is limited (Iliffe 1983). Structural and institutional constraints remain such that the evolution of indigenous corporate business organizations is still not a very likely scenario in the near future. To be sure, there are some African entrepreneurs who are ready to cooperate with foreign investors, but even these ventures have been characterized by problems. There have been difficulties in establishing mutual trust and few of these relationships have lasted very long. It is worth noting that male African entrepreneurs have attempted such collaborative ventures more often than women. The latter have preferred to operate individually.

In summarizing the points made in this section, there is much to suggest that the economic burden of the majority of African women has grown in the past two decades. Life has become harder for them and their chances of doing something positive for themselves have diminished. Their daily life is a continuous struggle to make ends meet. At the other end, there is evidence that women with access to starting capital have entered the market as entrepreneurs with a measure of success, although their contribution to the strengthening of a modern economy is still marginal. They may run profitable businesses, but like their male counterparts, they do not translate into corporate structures that have the power to transform the social and economic landscape in Africa.

THE SOCIOLOGICAL DIMENSION

Even though educated and successful business-minded women are trying to emancipate themselves, the lives of the vast majority of women in Africa continue to be dictated by a deeply entrenched tradition of patriarchy. This tradition is particularly insidious in Africa because it is not formalized as in other societies where laws for the domestic and the public realm have been regularized. Formal laws in Africa have a very limited reach. Customary law continues to dictate most social life. This means that there are always ways around the formal legal system, especially on civil matters such as the relations between husband and wife in a marriage.

Patriarchy typically refers to the deference due to males, but in the African context reflects more specifically the relations of reproduction and production that mandate that men have the right to control the property and lives of women and juniors. This is endorsed in customary law throughout the continent. Men continue to see their rights in these terms. The Big Man phenomenon, described in Chapter Five, permeates both politics and society from top to bottom. Such is the power of patriarchy, writes one analyst of the southern African scene, that female activities are almost always judged inferior to men's: Where men deliberate and judge, women intrigue; men exchange information, women gossip; men intercede with supernatural forces, women are witches (Bennett 1995:80–81). This is the kind of social reality that women live in and find hard to break out of. They have few rights, if any, in the customary law. They have rights in the common or civil law system that has been established by the colonial powers, but only a small percentage of women are in a position to claim these rights. In fact, a major problem for women in Africa is that more than one set of laws applies to such issues as marriage and inheritance. Like state and civil society, the legal system is bifurcated (Noergaard and Hilmer Pedersen 2002).

Customary law today has evolved over the years, but there are two problems that continue to afflict its application today. One is that judges in colonial days did little to challenge the existing patriarchal tradition and with social change brought about by capitalism and urbanization, the conditions of women often deteriorated. As colonial officials tried to understand and codify specific customary laws, they relied on senior men who were believed to have the relevant information. They did not question the fact that these elders interpreted the situation from their vantage point. The result was that many intrafamilial rights and duties that had existed in precolonial days were overlooked. Judges after independence have done little, if anything, to challenge this legacy.

The second problem is the failure to unify the codification of customary law. There are significant differences between ethnic groups due to variations in the way that family and inheritance are socially organized. One such difference is between matrilineal and patrilineal societies. In anglophone Africa, only Tanzania has succeeded in this effort of providing a unified system of family laws based on customary principles. This is a compromise product in the sense that it reflects basic features of most individual customary law systems – and there are over a hundred of them in Tanzania – but it is also different from local customs in some respects. Although it is now some thirty years of age, the unified customary family code in Tanzania is a reinterpretation of old principles with a view to making them more relevant to modern practices.

Even so, women who seek emancipation from their status as secondary citizens in their own country, find customary principles – whether unified or not – to be a hindrance to their cause. The struggle to overcome these obstacles has been particularly intensive in southern Africa. In Zimbabwe, the battle was initially over the *locus standi* of women in courts. According to customary law, women were treated as minors, that is, like children who could not appear before a judge without someone else speaking on their behalf. An Age of Majority Act was passed in Zimbabwe in 1982, two years after majority rule had been introduced, applying to persons subject to customary law (McNally 1988). In Botswana, the battle for women's rights crystallized around a clause in the country's constitution that prevented children of Tswana women married to foreigners to become citizens of the country. Led by a few prominent female lawyers, women created a movement to fight this clause, which they identified as discriminatory. After concerted efforts to raise public consciousness and to lobby lawmakers in the parliament, the constitution was changed to allow children in such circumstances to become Botswana citizens (Leslie 2003).

The constitution-making process in South Africa in the first half of the 1990s that produced the country's new constitution in 1996 is especially instructive here, because it brings to the fore the sharp differences between modern and premodern principles that afflict all African countries. South Africa is, of course, not typical of most of Africa, because for over three hundred years, a white immigrant minority ruled the country. This meant that there was a Roman-Dutch legal tradition in place that applied to Europeans and with some modifications to Coloreds and other immigrant minorities, for example, from India. The process, which was highly participatory, produced a very liberal constitution, one that in language goes much further with regard to principles of justice and equality than most other constitutions around the world. This outcome can be explained only with reference to the particular dynamics inherent in this process. Although there were many conservatives among both European and African groups participating in making the constitution, there was a majority in favor of producing one that was universally applicable and transcended the conservative strands in both the Roman-Dutch tradition as applied in the apartheid era and the various customary law traditions in the country. The African National Congress (ANC), which was the most influential organization on the African side, and many whites who realized the opportunity to create a more liberal political order, drove the process – in tandem – away from the traditional leaders and the right wing groups among the whites. They found common ground in a set of principles that reflected the cosmopolitanism of the educated and modern-minded cadres among both the ANC and the whites (Hyden and Venter 2001).

This was not, however, an easy process, especially for the women who wanted to use this opportunity to emancipate themselves. Even within the ANC, male delegates to the constitutional negotiations queried why women should participate in this process. During the struggle against apartheid, black men and women had fought together; gender had never emerged as a dividing issue (Geisler 2000; Goetz and Hassim 2003). This changed when negotiations began for a new constitution. One prominent female delegate representing ANC tells how frustrating and difficult it initially was to convince male delegates about the significance of the full emancipation of women. She tells of how male delegates did not allow women to complete their intervention before they would butt in with what they wanted to say. She also quotes the case of one female delegate who was physically abused by her husband at home because when he saw her on television participating in the proceedings, he thought that she had a relationship with the male delegate sitting next to her – without realizing that he treated her with contempt because she was a woman delegate (Mbete-Kgositsile 2001:34–35). She also shows how women within the more liberal-minded delegations had to fight the traditional leaders who were interested in using culture and tradition in order to continue subjecting women to male dominance. By forming a women's caucus that united them across party lines, they were able to get approval for an equality clause that applies to every one regardless of gender. The chiefs were not happy about this, because they felt that within the new constitutional framework they could potentially lose their power.

Women in South Africa made definite progress in raising public consciousness about the rights of women in their country, but it did not come without costs. Traditional leaders were able to strike a deal whereby the constitution prescribes the formation of provincial Houses of Traditional Leaders and the national Council of Traditional Leaders. These bodies are organs of government and as such they can debate bills pertaining to their own powers as well as to customary law. Their influence can be traced in the Recognition of Customary Marriages Act that was passed in 1998. Whereas it granted customary marriage partners equal rights, it did not specify the legal future of polygyny or bridewealth even though women had been fighting to have those two practices removed (Geisler 2000:625). In short, the new constitution in South Africa has provided a platform for the continuation of a bifurcated legal system that can be used to discriminate against women. It is for this reason that politically conscious women in that country are aware of the need to continue fighting so that they do not lose the gains they made in the euphoric days when the new constitution was negotiated.

The African Charter of Human and Peoples' Rights professes that human beings are inviolable but with a cultural tradition of patriarchy derived from the continued influence of premodern economic relations, the cultural climate is rarely in favor of women's empowerment. Von Doepp (2002), for instance, found in a study of the role churches in Malawi play in providing democratic space for women that the hierarchical Catholic church provided a more cosmopolitan atmosphere, in which women could progress, than the lay-dominated Presbyterian church, in which local patriarchal values prevented women from making any gains.

There is a strong tendency throughout the continent to treat women more as objects than as citizens with their own rights. This continues to be true with regard to their economic rights in marriage and at its dissolution by divorce and death. Social practice diverges not only from international conventions, but often also from national laws. Men continue to be able to divorce women at will, for example, for barrenness or adultery, but women cannot leave their husbands for the same reasons. In this context, Muslim women are often under even greater legal disability than those who contracted marriage under customary law (Howard 1986). Regarding divorce and custody of children, women in the customary sector are at best dependent upon family negotiations and the assumption of goodwill between the two families. Finally, regarding violence against women, the practice is still commonplace. The cultural traditions of most ethnic groups condone wife beating (e.g. Gutto 1976; Mushanga 1978).

THE POLITICAL DIMENSION

Athough women continue to be oppressed economically and socially, at least they constitute a potentially political force that cannot be ignored. Male political leaders recognize this and wish to handle the gender issue in such a way that it maximizes their own power. In the light of growing international pressures to achieve greater equality for women, their discretion today is more circumscribed than it was before the gender issue was globally politicized. Thus, there have been concessions to allow greater participation by women in legislative and executive offices. This section begins by providing some statistics to demonstrate the extent to which women are involved in higher office today. It will continue by offering some explanations for this. The final part will discuss the problems and challenges that women continue to encounter in the political realm.

Women in African Politics

The expanded role that women play in politics is recent; before 1990 women may have held positions as government ministers or parliamentarians, but they were scattered and attracted little attention. It is different today. The gender issue has become more prominent and women more visible, both nationally and internationally. What is going on in Africa with regard to gender and politics is no different from what happens elsewhere. During the 1990s, women sought nomination for president in no less than a dozen countries although they were able to secure nomination as candidates only in two. Even so, this was a great step forward. Africa's first female head of state in modern times was Ruth Perry of Liberia who served as chairperson of the country's collective presidency in the mid-1990s. Dr. Specioza Wandera Kazibwe of Uganda became Africa's first female vice-president in 1994 and served as such for eight years.[3] Women were appointed to the position of prime minister in at least three countries during this period: Burundi, Rwanda, and Senegal. By the end of the 1990s, Ethiopia, Lesotho, and South Africa had parliaments with women speakers, and both Uganda and Zimbabwe had women in the position of deputy speaker (Tripp 2001:141).

[3] Dr. Kazibwe was herself a frequent victim of domestic violence and after having gone public with the issue was divorced by her husband, a civil engineer.

There has been an especially marked increase of women in legislative bodies. In the 1960s, women were very few indeed, but the proportion of women in legislatures grew rapidly during the 1990s. According to one survey, women constituted 9 percent of the total in the lower houses of Africa's forty-eight parliaments (Reynolds 1999:2).[4] It is especially high in three southern African countries – Mozambique, Namibia, and South Africa – where women occupy between one-quarter and one-third of all the seats in parliament. Following the election in Rwanda in 2003, that country now has the highest proportion – 40 percent – of women in parliament. The percentage of women cabinet ministers across Africa was slightly lower at 7.8 percent. Tripp (2001) reports that women on average held 12 percent of parliamentary seats compared with just half of that a decade earlier. The African figures are somewhat below the global average and also a little below the figures for Asia and the Americas. The average for Africa, however, is considerably above the figure for Arab states. Even if Africa trailed all other regions but one, it exhibited a faster growth since 1960 than any of the others.

In most instances, women's representative gains have taken place within established political parties, but there are also examples of women who have started their own political parties because they found that existing parties were not responsive enough to their demands and interest.[5] In addition, there are a number of women's organizations across Africa working for an increased presence of elected women in parliaments. These include a variety of national NGOs and global bodies like the Inter-Parliamentary Union (IPU), the world organization of national parliamentarians.

The main women's organizations prior to the 1990s were generally affiliated with the ruling party and lacked an independent voice. This has changed in recent years with a growing number of women's NGOs getting involved to address specific women's issues. In Tanzania, the party-led women's organization – Umoja wa Wanawake – was transformed into a council-type of organization, Baraza la Wanawake wa Tanzania (BAWATA), which took on the general challenge of increasing women's registration for elections. In other countries where such a catchall organization had not existed, professional bodies, like Femmes Entrepreneurs and Femmes Juristes in French-speaking countries, became particularly important. In many countries, women organized themselves also to lobby parliament and government. The nonpartisan National Women's Lobby Group in Zambia is one case in point, the National Committee on the Status of Women in Kenya, another. The number of autonomous women's organizations was particularly high in South Africa and Uganda, where they played an important role as complements

---

[4] This survey includes legislative bodies also in North Africa.

[5] Examples of women who started their own political parties include Inonge Mbikusita-Lewanika in Zambia, Margaret Dongo in Zimbabwe, and Limakatso Ntakatsane in Lesotho.

to those women who served in parliament (Tripp 2000; Goetz and Hassim 2003).

These organizations were often quite successful in bringing about changes in constitutions, laws, or policies. The Women's National Coalition in South Africa, drawing on support from eighty-one organizations and thirteen regional alliances, lobbied hard in the early 1990s to have the special Women's Charter adopted. The National Women's Lobby Group in Zambia, in collaboration with six other NGOs, succeeded in getting the Constitutional Commission that was sitting in the early 1990s to incorporate a separate section on women's rights in the draft constitution. In Uganda in the mid-1990s, a special, nonpartisan Women's Caucus played a crucial role during the debates in the Constituent Assembly, which was charged with approving a new constitution for the country. The caucus worked with other women's organizations on requiring that gender equality was being written into all laws passed by parliament. Further, this women's group required parliament to prohibit laws, customs, and traditions that undermine the position of women, and to form an Equal Opportunities Commission (Tripp 2001).

Women have also been in the forefront of criticizing corruption and sectarianism in politics. Margaret Dongo in Zimbabwe and Wangari Maathai in Kenya[6] have been particularly prominent in attacking corruption in public office. Not surprisingly, they have also had their lives threatened. Women have found it easier to oppose sectarianism because their support has relied less on manipulation of ethnic constituencies. Charity Ngilu in Kenya, Winnie Byanyima in Uganda, and the late Agathe Uwilingiyimana, Rwanda's Prime Minister 1992–94, are among those who have gained a reputation for their antisectarian stands. In fact, Ms. Uwilingiyimana's support of ethnic tolerance was a contributing factor in her murder by the Presidential Guard at the onset of the mass killings that devastated the country in 1994.

Reasons for Progress

Given the progress that women have made in politics in the short span of ten to fifteen years, it is tempting to suggest that politics is ahead of society, that is, the norms applying to political representation are more progressive than those of society at large. How does that proposition tally with the earlier argument in this volume that politics is supreme?

Reynolds (1999) has carried out a survey of women in African legislatures and executives, trying to find what accounts for the changes that have taken place since the 1990s. His conclusion with reference to women in the legislatures is that neither level of democracy nor the previous length of

---

[6] Maathai was the recipient of the Nobel Prize for Peace, issued by a special committee of the Norwegian Parliament, in 2004.

experience with multipartyism and women in politics, not even the socio-economic position of women in society, matters. Instead, women are elected in significant numbers when the national culture and religion are not overly hostile to women in positions of power, there are a small number of polit-ical parties that dominate elections, and the electoral system does not pro-vide undue barriers against women candidates being elected. Dominant or majority Christian countries in Africa have, on average, 11.2 percent of legis-lative positions filled by women members of parliament. Countries where traditional religion is dominant or embraced by at least a majority of the population score 8.5 percent, whereas the Islamic countries have a corre-sponding figure of 5.9 percent. Party system fragmentation, which Reynolds measures – like Laakso and Taagepera (1979) – by counting the number of effective parliamentary parties, proves to have significance for women's elec-tion to legislatures in Africa. This confirms the global finding that wherever there is less competition for the bulk of the parliamentary seats, the prospect for women being elected is greater.

Electoral system is also important in determining the number of women elected to parliament. Systems based on some form of proportional repre-sentation are most hospitable, whereas the two-round system, producing a majority candidate, as practiced in the majority of French-speaking coun-tries, tends to suppress the number of women more than any other system, including the plurality system of first past the post. The closed list system practiced with the proportional system has the advantage of allowing parties to independently decide to include names of women in electable places on these lists. For instance, this is what ANC did in South Africa, thereby com-pelling other parties to do the same, and eventually helping to significantly enhance the prospects for women being elected. FRELIMO in Mozambique, as the incumbent ruling party, did the same. As these examples indicate, the closed proportional representation list system is by far the most effective in terms of accelerating the number of women in elected bodies.

Many African countries using other types of electoral systems have been reluctant to go as far as changing in order to accommodate a greater number of women in parliament. Instead, they have chosen to adopt a system whereby women are appointed to a number of reserved seats in parliament. What matters in such a scenario is who has the right to appoint: the head of state or the legislature itself? Wherever the head of state has the preroga-tive to make the appointment, as the case is in Burkina Faso and Tanzania, the mechanism favors the ruling party and is perceived by many as a token. Where, on the other hand, the parliament itself appoints the women, as the case is in Kenya, opposition parties have a greater say. However, as Reynolds (1999:11) notes in both scenarios, women are likely to be more beholden to their male party bosses than to the electorate.

The final point in this subsection concerns the question of how this progress in female representation in legislative bodies tallies with the notion that politics is supreme. Can women change the character of politics in Africa in ways that make it more tolerant and respectful of the rule of law? The answer at this point is that it cannot be ruled out in the long run, but there is little evidence that it is happening enough in spite of gallant efforts by women activists. South Africa, where the women's constituency is considerably more autonomous from and critical of the ruling ANC, the prospect may be greater, because there the inclusion of women is treated as a right. In other countries, however, including Uganda with its impressive figures, women's inclusion in politics is interpreted more as a favor extended to them by the president (Goetz and Hassim 2003:17).

Problems and Challenges

The political advancement of women has not come easy. On the contrary, it has been achieved at a considerable cost for the many women who have been ready to fight for their cause. Like students, workers, and human rights activists, women have often been in the forefront of opposing repressive regimes. Such was the case in Kenya in the early 1990s when women protested against imprisoned human rights activists (Press 2004). Thousands of women demonstrated against the military rule in Mali in the same years. Many of them were shot at and killed. In Niger, several thousand women demonstrated against the exclusion of women representatives from a preparatory commission charged with organizing the country's constitutional conference in 1991 (Tripp 2001:142–43). Governments have not hesitated to use force to quell any attempt to mobilize opposition to its stand by women. They have also been ready to use more subtle means to achieve the same end.

There are at least three different methods that governments have used to neutralize or marginalize women's organizations. One is to depoliticize them by confining them to development work. Here I will use the 31st December Women's Movement (DWM) in Ghana as a case in point. The second is to co-opt the organization and appoint leaders who are ready to echo the view of government rather than advocating an independent position. The Maendeleo ya Wanawake Organization (MYWO) in Kenya will serve as an illustration. The third method is to outright suspend the organization so that it can no longer speak on behalf of women. The Baraza la Wanawake wa Tanzania (BAWATA) suffered this fate and will be briefly discussed here.

Many a head of state in Africa has tried to control women politics by giving his wife an organization that she can use to attract funding and distribute among women as patronage. This way, the First Lady is able to demonstrate her contribution to women's development. Attacks against her by women activists are easier to deflect. The DWM in Ghana was started after Jerry Rawlings seized power by force in 1982. He initially portrayed himself as a revolutionary. The DWM was referred to as a mass organization – the women's wing of the revolution. The movement, therefore, was seen as being closely aligned to the PNDC, the political organization that Rawlings had started. His political rhetoric initially included the liberation of women, but it became increasingly clear during the 1980s that what he and other leaders in the PNDC wanted was for women to engage in development activities. He made his wife, Nana Konadu, the president of DWM so that the money collected for development from local or foreign sources would come through an organization over which the incumbent government had some control. What was originally supposed to be the political empowerment of women, therefore, eventually turned into support of social service programs. Particularly prominent was the idea of establishing day care centers in the urban areas so that women engaged in trade could earn their livings more comfortably. The DWM played an important role in helping Rawlings and his party to win the 1996 election by providing matching support for various rural development activities (Ayee 1999). No one will deny that Konadu was an effective leader of DWM, but her reign as president of the movement had the effect of depoliticizing the main women's organization in the country.

The story of MYWO in Kenya has much in common with what happened in Ghana. The leadership was not tied to the wife of the president, but the most prominent of all chairpersons of the organization, Jane Kiano, who served from 1971 until 1984, was the wife of a prominent cabinet minister. Like Konadu, Kiano herself would be the epitome of a liberated woman, but she preferred to direct women's activities toward development and other issues that did not necessarily antagonize men. For that reason, during the 1970s, MYWO became an example in Africa of a successful women's self-help movement. Its high profile, however, eventually got the organization into trouble with government leaders. President Moi used a major financial scandal in MYWO as an excuse to appoint a trusted civil servant as chairperson. Subsequent leaders of the organization in the 1990s became vocal advocates of the policies of the ruling party and ignored issues specific to women. As Aubrey (1997) shows, the MYWO leadership went out of its way in 1992 to argue that Kenyan women were against multiparty democracy, a position that Moi had taken at the time, despite the fact that many female activists had been in the forefront of demanding it. MYWO was simply co-opted by the ruling party to echo the master's voice.

BAWATA in Tanzania was an attempt to create an independent women's organization after multiparty democracy had been reintroduced in Tanzania in the early 1990s. Its birth came at a meeting of Umoja wa Wanawake wa Tanzania (UWT), which had served as the women's mass organization during the days of socialist one-party rule. The leadership of UWT was defeated and BAWATA was established with a new cast of women, drawn from the ranks of educated and professional groups, in charge. In preparation of the first multiparty elections in 1995, BAWATA organized a countrywide campaign to make women conscious of their civil and political rights, something that the leaders of the ruling party interpreted as an activity supporting the political opposition. It was eventually accused of having overstepped its mandate and engaged in politics. Government took the organization to court and suspended its activities. In order to further frustrate the leadership of BAWATA, the case was allowed to drag on for years in the court without resolution until the martyrdom that the leaders were seen to have incurred had vanished. BAWATA was allowed to resume its work after the 2000 elections, but its original leadership is gone and its role in association life in Tanzania is much less prominent than it was in the first few years of its operations.[7]

These three examples demonstrate two things that are significant about women in politics in Africa. The first is that women's organizations that earn a national significance as a mouthpiece for women's issues are easily accused of being political in the sense of opposing the government. There is little room for an independent women's voice if it becomes too prominent. The other is that government leaders like to confine women's organizations to the nonpolitical sphere. These organizations are acceptable as long as they contribute to improving the conditions of women without entering the political realm by calling into question what government is doing.

This has left women in a dilemma: Should they accept the status quo and work within the limited confines of Big Man politics on the assumption that they can get at least something done, or should they challenge the status quo and demand more political space as a prerequisite for not only women's progress but also national development? Educated and professional women's groups tend to be in forefront of battling patriarchy (see e.g. Mama 1996; Nzomo 1997; Tripp 2000). They believe that the contribution women can make to development in Africa is being held back by their lack of recognition by male political leaders. Their stand is not only in favor of greater gender equality, but also supports a fuller utilization of female skills and competence in public life. Other women accept that civil society is an arena where they can make a difference, even if it doesn't mean explicitly challenging the patriarchal order. They prefer to work quietly taking one small step at a time, hoping that the recognition of women's rights and their contribution to national development will come from social and economic instead of political action.

CONCLUSIONS

The interesting thing about the analysis of women in politics in Africa is that the state appears as a powerful instrument of control (e.g. Parpart and Staudt 1989). The literature on this theme differs markedly from other accounts of

---

[7] With the permission of Tanzania's president, Benjamin Mkapa, the first chairperson of BAWATA, Dr. Anna Tibaijuka, was appointed executive director of Habitat, the specialized UN agency in Nairobi that deals with urban and housing development issues.

the state in Africa that, as indicated in previous chapters, portray it as weak, soft, or unable to broadcast its power over the full territory of the country. This should not be a surprise, however, given the premodern features of society and the fact that rule in Africa is perceived as being over people rather than land. As this chapter has tried to demonstrate, most women in Africa still live and work in conditions under which they are treated as mere instruments of production and social reproduction. Their status and rights are in many respects even more marginalized than women elsewhere in the world who, even if they are subordinated to patriarchy, suffer it largely within the confines of the household. In Africa, where the boundary between what is private and public is much more diffuse and fluid, the arm of the state can be used to strike at women with greater impact. The fact that rule is personalized means that the discretionary use of state power by men is also more difficult to challenge in court. Women in Africa, therefore, experience the power of the state in more insidious ways than the case typically is in Europe, Asia, and the Americas where marriage transactions allow women to bring something to the husband's home, they have the right to inherit from their father, and there is a reliable judicial system. Women in those regions may find themselves in relations of dependence too, but they can more easily achieve emancipation without having to challenge the political order at large. Women in Africa are caught in dependencies that are more complex. Although many female activists and others have broken out of these bonds, this can only be achieved by either polarizing politics along gender lines or exiting from politics in order to pursue a career in the private or voluntary sector. In fact, many of the latter get employed in international organizations where their career prospects are often better than in national organizations, which are more easily prey to predatory patriarchs.

9

Ethnicity and Conflict

Africa's informal institutions, as suggested in Chapter Four, may be distinguished by the extent to which they are symmetrical and inclusive. Within these parameters, however, the most striking thing about these institutions is their malleability. They are constantly being reoriented and reshaped in response to emerging constraints and opportunities in society. That is why they are also tenable. They constantly recur to meet new challenges. Most Africans are used to this way of life. Constant social maneuvering, if not fun, is at least what they are ready to excel in. This is a reality that is very different from what people know in countries where formal institutions dominate. In Europe as well as in North America, certainty and predictability are among the most highly held values. Where the state is consolidated, it becomes an economic planning and steering instrument aimed at minimizing threats to the system. The public is being socialized into believing that society can manage itself through formal institutions without harm to individuals and groups. Therefore, when something goes unexpectedly wrong, it is common practice that the official ultimately responsible steps down. Where the state is still being formed, as in Africa, the challenges are different. Uncertainty is not only greater, but also curbed differently – notably, by seeking out the support of other individuals. Whereas Europeans and North Americans can rely on the welfare state or some private corporate arrangement to take care of their basic needs, it is the *Kernkultur* of primary reciprocities of the economy of affection that are being called upon in Africa.

This means that members of the same family, clan, village, and ethnic group constitute the core of these relations. Dependencies within these primary social organizations have existed for generations and are more effective to rely upon than those that involve socially more distant individuals or groups. The cost of not responding to a distress call from a kinsman is much higher than if that call comes from a stranger. The economy of affection, therefore, is at its strongest when examined at this level of social organization.

As the analysis in the two previous chapters indicates, however, African society is in the midst of extensive social change with repercussions for its future development. One of the key questions is how African countries, which are typically made up of many primary social organizations, can be more effectively integrated into corporate wholes. National integration is still an issue in virtually all these countries. The role of ethnicity in this process continues to attract primary interest among scholars and popular analysts alike.

Ethnicity is not a new concept in the study of African politics, but it has gained widespread prominence, especially since the 1990s. Much of it can be attributed to the increasing number of conflicts within African countries. These intrastate conflicts have been interpreted as ethnic in nature, although they are much more complex and, in some instances, they are not ethnic at all. The orientation toward ethnicity among political scientists, like that of colleagues in the other social sciences, has been ambivalent. There are those, on the one hand, who have tried to avoid it altogether, as if it were a false category, and those, on the other, who have been inclined to explain too much with the help of ethnicity. Revisiting the subject in the light of its recent notability, therefore, is important.

Before proceeding to a more systematic analysis of the relevant issues, it is necessary to say a few words about why ethnicity has been met with such ambivalence. Much of it stems from its connotation with *tribe*. The latter has a condescending connotation in European and North American parlance, even in places like East and South Asia. A tribe is a group of people who live outside the mainstream civilization, be that Christian, Hindu, or Muslim. There is something primitive, even uncivilized, about being a member of a tribe as compared to a major religion. Thus, in societies with a predominant civilization, tribal people are marginal or exotic, as the case is in China, where the indigenous peoples are offered special state-sponsored parks in which they can display their customs.

In African countries where local customs continue to be important and no single civilization has erased them, the situation is different. Africans feel free to identify themselves by tribe and they use the concept without any particular restraint in everyday discourse.[1] After all, all people are expected to be members of a tribe if they are natives of the continent. Its common usage among Africans does not mean that it is the only identity that they have, nor is it a very deep one. Like everyone else, Africans have multiple identities and how they see themselves depends on whom they address. They are typically quite pragmatic in their approach to the subject of identity.

---

[1] Anthropologists preoccupied themselves with the notions of tribe and tribalism in the years after independence, making the point that the former refers to a distinct cultural group, and that the latter refers to political actions taken in the name of such cultural groups. See, for example, Gulliver (1969) and Southall (1970).

What makes the concept of tribe controversial in Africa is the legacy of the colonial powers, which tried to freeze the identities of their African subjects so that society became more legible and easier to administer. Furthermore, the way Europeans addressed the subject reflected their own preconceptions that tribe is something primitive. Not surprisingly, Africans felt disparaged. Ethnicity emerged after independence as a surrogate concept for tribe in the scholarly community in Europe and North America because its members were anxious to distance themselves from the vocabulary of the colonial governments. It is politically more correct in academic circles than tribe and it has given everyone a license to address the issue of identity more openly (Ekeh 1990).

Ethnicity, however, remains a contested concept, because scholars have disagreed about its meaning. It is important, therefore, to provide a brief overview of how the concept has evolved in the social sciences and how it has been used. With an increasing number of conflicts inside many African countries in the past fifteen years, the tendency among scholars and popular analysts alike has been to fall back on ethnicity as an explanatory variable. The second section of this chapter will examine the extent to which these conflicts are really ethnic. The third section will look at what the causes are of the many conflicts that have affected African countries. It will provide a discussion of reasons other than ethnicity.

DEFINITIONS

The literature on ethnicity is very rich and it is impossible to do justice to every contribution that has been made to our understanding of what the concept stands for. My own reading of it suggests that these contributions can be categorized in response to two major questions: (1) how much is it the result of human choice? and (2) how far is it an end in itself or a means to accomplish other ends? The answers to these two questions provide us with four types of approaches to the definition of ethnicity, as indicated in Figure 4: The vertical axis indicates the extent to which the choice is interpreted as made free from structural or institutional constraints by a particular person. The notion that it is autonomous is on one side of spectrum, the idea that it is embedded in cultural or social relations, on the other. The horizontal axis points to the degree of significance that people attach to ethnicity. Some are ready to consider it so important that they cannot see themselves giving up any part of it. Others have a more pragmatic view and are ready to make trade-offs in order to achieve other ends. The first of these two groups may be referred to as essentialists, because of their inclination to stress the importance of cultural and symbolic factors, the second as existentialists because they argue that the definition of identity is situational. It would be wrong to suggest that any one of these approaches exists in pure form in reality. The two axes are best seen as continua. In practice, people are likely

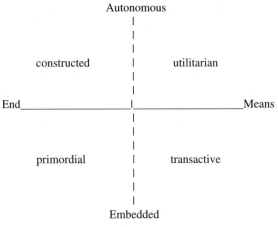

FIGURE 4. Definitions of ethnicity.

to lean toward one of these approaches, but may also be influenced by the others. The purpose of this matrix, therefore, is to indicate what the various definitions present in the literature are. It is also offered here as an alternative to the relatively elementary distinction that many authors make between primordialism and constructivism or instrumentalism. How far one of these categories is present in a particular society is, of course, an empirical question. In the African context, it is an important one, because the significance of ethnicity is still a contested subject. To ensure that the four definitional categories listed above are fully clarified, I shall offer a brief account of each.

Primordialism is the oldest of the four categories and dates back to the 1950s and 1960s when modernization was a leading approach to the study of politics and development. Geertz (1963) was the most influential source on the subject at the time. In his analysis of the new states in Africa and Asia, he argued that primordial attachment is not only a critical variable explaining human behavior, but also a source of legitimacy. Geertz's premise was that the old multiethnic societies would cause problems of integration into the new states that were coming into existence after the demise of colonialism. The capacity of the state to act independently would be hampered by the extent to which people's sense of self would remain bound up in blood, ethnicity, race, language, locality, religion, or tradition.

As is evident from this list of factors, primordial attachment stems from the givens of social existence. Family, kinship, ethnicity, and language, in this perspective, are the most influential formative factors in life. Individuals are captured by these social and cultural givens to such an extent that their behavior and choices are a direct reflection of these attachments. Many scholars, for example, Young (1976), Kasfir (1979), and Eller and

Coughland (1993), have criticized this definition and the effects it has on the study of politics. They believe that these attachments are not as overpowering as Geertz implies. The primordial approach does not recognize that ethnic and similar ties may have a social origin. In short, primordialism is both static and ahistorical because of its reluctance to explore where ethnic attachments may come from.

There may be those who see primordialism being reinvented in the context of religious fundamentalism, whether Christian or Muslim. If this perception is correct (the exit polls from the 2004 U.S. presidential election indicated that a great many American voters were motivated to vote for President Bush because of his stand on moral values), there is reason to examine the extent to which primordialism is reasserted in response to challenges posed by the more secular culture that has dominated the American scene for at least a couple of generations. It certainly suggests that primordialism is not the prerogative of suicide bombers and other religious zealots in the Middle East. Globalization may have brought people around the world closer, but in the cultural realm the distance may in fact have increased. The clash of civilizations (Huntington 1997), in this perspective, cannot be treated as a mere myth.

The constructivist approach to the study of identity assumes a greater degree of autonomy by implying that individuals are not complete captives of their cultural environment, but use pieces of it in creative ways to define who they are. This postmodernist approach to the study of identity is apparent in many current studies, for example, Anderson (1983), Chabal (1992), Bayart (2000), and Mbembe (2001). Using such features as language, religion, and ethnicity, people imagine the essence of the community of which they want to be part. In this approach, culture is the primary ingredient in the definition of ethnicity, but the assumption is that it can be disaggregated at will by members of a given community and put together in ways that reflect their choice of what is significant. Traditions are not given but constantly reinvented thereby giving culture a more dynamic character than what is implicit in primordialism. People assert their community, whether in the form of ethnicity or locality, when they recognize in it the most adequate medium for the expression of their whole selves. At the same time, the constructivist approach can be criticized for being too culturalist or too dependent on symbolic factors. It overlooks the possibility that people behave and make choices in response to a wider range of variables than just culture. Above all, it does not take into consideration that ethnicity may be just a means, not an end in itself.

The utilitarian approach to ethnicity assumes that individuals will act together to maximize their common preferences, interests, or purposes when the benefits from doing so exceed the costs (Banton 1993). Ethnicity will feature in social or political action as a means to achieve a higher end.

This shared sense of preference or purpose may come about as a result of people feeling marginalized or excluded from access to resources. People become aware of their common identity by virtue of a shared experience of exploitation, oppression, or exclusion. Ethnicity, however, does not necessarily become a factor in politics without someone first being able to articulate a common identity and mobilize action based on any such claim. This common sense of grievance may be genuine but sometimes generated to serve more narrow interests shared by only a few members of the political elite (Bates 1981). This more cynical view of utilitarianism has been articulated by students of political leaders in Africa who are seen to use cultural differences and tribalism to advance their own agenda while pretending to act on behalf of the whole group (see e.g. Mafeje 1971). The point about the utilitarian approach to ethnicity is that it assumes a very pragmatic or instrumentalist view of things cultural. It is subsumed under the general premise of utilitarianism and, as such, ethnicity is treated as an exogenous variable, that is, one that does not need to be explained. Individuals are ready to make cultural trade-offs in order to achieve materialist or other tangible gains. It can be argued that it omits the role that socialization plays in fostering preferences and values that people may not be ready to trade. Cultural tradition, as a variable, disappears from the calculation (Laitin 1992).

The transactive approach to ethnicity assumes that identity is determined in the context of social interaction. Self-identification is not enough to understand how a particular identity such as ethnicity or nationality comes about (Eriksen 1993). It draws its inspiration especially from the work of Barth (1969) who has argued that we cannot ignore the ascriptive nature of ethnic groups. In understanding how these groups are sustained, however, there is a need to shift from their essentialist components and how they are internally constituted to how the boundaries of these groups are maintained with the help of language, dress, food, and other types of symbols. These phenomena become important in social exchanges and determine what is perceived as distinct about a particular person or group of people. The point about this relational approach is that ethnic boundaries are maintained not for cultural but for social or political reasons. An ethnic group is constituted not because of some essentialist factors, but because of having interacted over time with other similar groups. Members of the group are social actors capable of adapting their identities to changes in circumstances. Some may even transcend existing boundaries and change their identities by moving from one group or community to another. This is a dynamic approach to the study of ethnicity that fits the main thesis of this book: that face-to-face reciprocities are important in determining social and political outcomes, not just in Africa, but in particular there.

Horowitz (1985) adds to the transactive approach to ethnicity by emphasizing the importance that affective elements and forces play in shaping ethnicity and relations among such groups. Conflicts between ethnic groups are neither the result of modernization or the pursuit of economic advantage nor do they stem from irreconcilable primordial factors. Such conflicts, however, may also be explained with reference to the apprehension that members of a particular group experience as they interact and compare themselves with other groups. These comparisons provide a sense of worth – inferior or superior – in relation to others. As Horowitz (1985:228) writes:

Merely to know the position of a group, in terms of worth and legitimacy, is probably to be able to forecast what political claims it makes, what idiom it speaks in, what issues divide it from others, what counterclaims others make, and generally, how each will behave in and out of power.

Institutions may help to constrain conflicts between groups, but these relations are often spontaneous and driven by affective forces that at times could be so strong they overthrow the institutionalized system in place. The transactive approach goes beyond the utilitarian approach because it recognizes the outcome of social interaction and, in so doing, also includes the role that spontaneous and informal human behavior and institutions play in determining ethnicity.

The argument here is not that any one of these four definitions is necessarily more useful than the others. It is rather that the preference of one definition over another should be based on social and temporal context. There is no single ethnicity or one way of studying it. It is necessary, therefore, to choose a definition that fits time and space. Given the knowledge we have accumulated over the years about the state and society in Africa, there are at least three good reasons today for studying ethnicity as relational and thus in the context of a definition that stresses its transactive aspect.

The first reason is the competitive conditions that neoliberal economics and political reform in the 1990s have created. It is not clear what exact effects competition in the market or in the political arena has, but one can profitably hypothesize that these effects may be both positive and negative. For instance, with growing competition comes the possibility that groups become more aware of their relative worth and tensions among them increase. The insecurity that is often associated with enhanced competition easily translates into greater social consciousness. Alternatively, competition, especially in the market, may spur greater social mobility – as discussed in Chapter Seven – and this may have consequences for the effectiveness of the gatekeeper factors to maintain ethnic boundaries.

A second reason is the relatively small size of most ethnic groups in Africa. The gatekeeper function is likely to weaken especially in those groups, because they have to compete with others. Building alliances with others, whether socially or politically, becomes a rational strategy to pursue. The same decline may apply also to the larger groups. Their boundaries open up so that they can accommodate newcomers by marriage or by other means of co-optation. Growing numbers of interethnic marriages as well as interethnic socialization in educational institutions, professional life, and similar contexts contribute to fostering greater social interaction across ethnic boundaries. In a country such as Tanzania, the ethnic markers have lost much of their significance because of the availability of a common lingua franca – Swahili. In the Democratic Republic of Congo (Zaire), Lingala has had a similar integrative effect. Other examples abound across Africa where indigenous languages have spread across ethnic boundaries and become means of communication among many groups. Hausa in West Africa is one such case in point. Furthermore, as Posner (2004) has demonstrated, the salience of ethnicity depends in part on the size of a particular ethnic group relative to the country as a whole. In other words, ethnic consciousness becomes a viable factor for political mobilization where size counts, but typically not otherwise.

The third reason for studying ethnicity as relational is that ethnic consciousness in African society is not particularly deep. In other regions of the world with a longer literate tradition, the burden of history weighs more heavily on each individual group. Ethnicity is often steeped in religion, which means that the cultural differences among groups tend to go deeper. The conflicts between Hindus and Muslims over control of Kashmir as well as between Tamils and Sinhalese in Sri Lanka are two relevant cases in point, as is the conflict between Israelis and Palestinians in the Middle East or the one between Serbs and Albanians in the Balkans. Religion sometimes infuses ethnic relations also in Africa. This has happened on more than occasion in the Sudan and Nigeria as Islamic groups in the north have clashed with Christian members of ethnic groups coming from the south of these countries. With enhanced tensions between Christians and Muslims also in other parts of Africa, this could become more widespread. Nonetheless, religion is a much more serious dividing force in other regions of the world than it is in Africa. Because ethnic and other cultural forms of identity such as religion and language do not go very deep, ethnic relations are more fluid. People are more open to other influences and the notion that ethnic attachments or ties are primordial in Africa is usually highly misleading. As Mozaffar and his colleagues (2003) note in their study of ethnopolitical cleavages in Africa, neither language nor religion has acquired the same political salience as it has in other regions.[2]

---

[2] The same authors discovered that the frequently used Ethno-Linguistic Fractionalization Index (ELF) was not a helpful tool in their analysis because it assumed that ethnic groups are primordially fixed, and thus measures ethnic rather than ethnopolitical cleavages. World Bank analysts have used this index to assess the relationship between ethnic heterogeneity and economic growth in Africa (see Easterly and Levine 1997). Posner (2000) has subsequently helped develop a new instrument – the Politically Relevant Ethnic Group Index – which proved more applicable to the conditions in Africa. This index disaggregates ethnic groups that are politically divided and combines others that act together politically. It has its own

We can summarize the discussion above in the following manner: Ethnicity in Africa is more social than cultural in nature. Ethnic awareness stems more from interaction with others than from a long-standing tradition. Compared to people in other regions of the world, Africans are generally less burdened by the cultural baggage that they carry with them. The boundaries that have distinguished one ethnic group from another are losing some of their significance. At the same time, it would be a mistake to dismiss the fact that ethnic relations are socially embedded. People's choices are not completely autonomous, but take into consideration the consequences that they may have for their relations with others. Social cleavages based on ethnicity are diminishing in significance. Still, Africa in the past decade or so has suffered from more domestic conflicts than before, most of which have been blamed on the ethnic factor. This apparent anomaly is the subject of the next section.

CONFLICTS AND CONFLICT PATTERNS

There are many ways to think about and define conflicts. One such distinction is between manifest and latent conflicts. A conflict manifests itself in the use of force or violence leading to human casualties. Latent conflicts are hidden in societal cleavages but have not broken into open confrontation. Analysts interested in conflict prevention tend to be especially concerned with these latent conflicts. Another distinction is between social cleavages that are either vertical or horizontal. The former are based on ethnicity, race, or religion, whereas the latter are based on control of or access to economic resources. Horizontal cleavages would usually be described in terms of class. Modern societies often have crosscutting cleavages, that is, people are not consumed by a single identity but combine more than one within themselves. The premise is that persons characterized by such crosscutting cleavages are more tolerant of others because they can more easily empathize with people coming from perspectives different from their own. The point that we have made about Africa in previous chapters is that the region really lacks institutionalized social cleavages based on class. As suggested earlier, African societies are generally multiethnic, but these cleavages are not as deep as they are in other regions of the world. I will build on that argument here as I compare conflicts in Africa with those in other regions of the world.

If cleavages are at the root of conflicts, there is still a need to distinguish among them. Domestic political conflicts include a diverse amalgam of civil strife, ranging from protests, strikes, riots, plots, assassinations, coups d'état, to civil wars (Henderson 2002:104). The argument has been made, for

problems but it is, at least with regard to measuring ethnopolitical cleavages, a more suitable instrument.

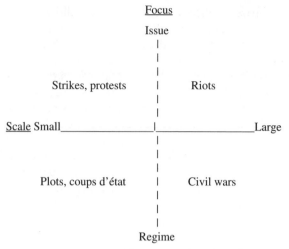

FIGURE 5. Types of domestic political conflict.

example, by Gurr (1970), that civil wars are a particular kind of conflict, because they typically entail greater coordination and cause greater destruction. It seems reasonable, therefore, to think of political conflicts along two different spectrums, one distinguishing between scale of destruction caused by the conflict, the second identifying how far the conflict involves a particular issue as opposed to the regime at large. Drawing on these distinctions, the typology in Figure 5 is helpful for the analysis of domestic political conflicts. This typology does not preclude the possibility that in reality more than one type may occur together with others listed in the matrix. The purpose is to highlight the need to distinguish between conflicts with limited or widespread consequences in terms of focus and human life. One common thesis in the literature is that the more consolidated a democratic regime is, the less likely that it will be subject to violence associated with challenges to its core (Gurr and Lichbach 1979). Not only are democracies less likely to fight each other – the democratic peace proposition – they are also less likely to suffer widespread violence stemming from rebellions or other forms of popular resistance aimed at the regime level. Domestic conflicts will be confined to protests, demonstrations, and strikes and concentrate on the resolution of an outstanding issue rather than on constituting a challenge to the system. There is also evidence that economic development reduces the likelihood of large-scale conflict. Instead, it appears to increase the probability of lesser forms of domestic conflict.

More recent conflict research has called into question some of these findings. Henderson and Singer (2000) bring the new findings together in two important propositions. One is that the conflict-dampening impact of democracy is not linear. The other is that autocracies are as capable as democracies in maintaining domestic peace. They also suggest that the most vulnerable regimes are what they call the semidemocracies, that is, those that strive to become democracies but still suffer from a democratic deficit. The relationship between democracy and civil war is curvilinear, approximating an inverted U-shape with both autocracies and democracies relatively less prone to civil war and semidemocracies the most prone to it (see also Henderson 2002:105). I shall examine the African situation in the light of this proposition.

A common impression is that Africa is the most conflict-ridden continent in the world. Much of this opinion stems from a memory of the collapse of Somalia in the early 1990s, the genocide in Rwanda in 1994, or the more recent civil conflicts in the Democratic Republic of Congo, Liberia, Sierra Leone, Sudan, and the Ivory Coast. Looking back over the past forty years, there is evidence that civil wars have afflicted several African countries and caused considerable harm to local populations. The worst such event was the civil war in Nigeria – the Biafra War 1967–70 – that was internationalized before it was brought to an end. At least two million people died – a large percentage from hunger caused by the blockade of the rebellious Eastern Region of the country (Biafra). Other civil wars that have been destructive to people as well as development prospects of the country include Sudan, Somalia, Angola, and Mozambique. The conflict in Sudan has lasted over thirty years and displaced and impoverished large numbers of people in the southern regions of the country. At the time of writing (late 2004), it had officially been brought to an end following an exceptional UN Security Council meeting in Nairobi to enhance the prospects for compliance by all parties to the conflict. A new conflict, however, has erupted in the Darfur region of western Sudan and is still brewing.

The civil war in Somalia began in the late 1980s in reaction to the arbitrary rule of President Siad Barre. It is especially instructive because the Somalis are a single ethnic group, but divided into powerful clans with a long tradition of antagonism. Some of these clans took up arms against the government, and the state gradually collapsed. The country turned into a conflict between powerful warlords and their followers. Although peace negotiations have been going on for a long time, the conflict in Somalia has not yet been resolved. Similar conflicts have since occurred in the west African states of Liberia, Sierra Leone, and Ivory Coast where warlords have played a significant role in reshaping the political landscape (Reno 1998, Akindés 2004). The civil wars in the former Portuguese colonies of Angola and Mozambique were fueled by external powers – South Africa and the United States on one side and Cuba on the other – and can be labeled products of the Cold War. Both countries suffered tremendously from the civil war before it was resolved, first in Mozambique in the early 1990s and ten years later in Angola. The exact number of casualties in these four civil wars is not known, but estimates put the number of dead between five hundred thousand and one million (Stedman 1996).

One of the problems with analyzing conflict is reliable data. Another is to define the conflict in a meaningful manner. A domestic conflict may cause the deaths of a few thousand people; in another such conflict, the number may rise to the hundreds of thousands. A particular definitional issue arises when domestic conflicts are internationalized through involvement by troops from other countries. A recent data set produced by the Department of Peace and Conflict Research at the University of Uppsala distinguishes between three levels of conflict: (a) minor, (b) intermediate, and (c) war (Gleditsch et al. 2002).[3] The same data set also makes a distinction between three types of conflict: (a) intrastate, (b) internationalized intrastate, and (c) interstate.

Between 1946 and 2002 there were a total of 226 armed conflicts. No less than 116 of those – or just over half – occurred between 1989 and 2002 in seventy-nine different locations around the world. In 2002, there were 31 conflicts active in twenty-four places (Eriksson et al. 2003). Out of the 31 active conflicts in 2002, 13 were in Africa. The data set makes two important points. The first is that there was a spike in the number of conflicts worldwide beginning in the late 1970s that peaked in the early 1990s. This is especially true for intrastate wars or internationalized intrastate wars. For instance, the figure for all types of armed conflict in 1991 and 1992 was 54; ten years later it was down to 31. In fact, with the recent decline in armed conflict worldwide, the probability of a country being immersed in conflict is no higher today than it was at the end of the 1950s, and lower than it has been any subsequent time during the Cold War (Gleditsch et al. 2002:621). Because the data set codes not whole countries but actual geographic locations, the second point that can be deduced is that armed conflicts in Africa tend more easily to engulf whole countries, whereas elsewhere they are often more localized. The conflicts in Chechnya (Russia), Kashmir (India and Pakistan), and Mindanao (The Philippines) are cases in point (Eriksson et al. 2003:594). Even though the number of casualties may not be higher in any single African case, the escalation of the conflict across a wider geographic area tends to make the conflict more costly in economic terms. In short, the national development prospects are hampered by armed conflict especially in Africa. Collier and Hoeffler (1998) as well as de Soysa and Gleditsch (2002) provide empirical verification of a strong bivariate relationship between poverty – as measured

---

[3] The criteria they use to produce these three subsets are the following: *minor armed conflict*: at least 25 battle-related deaths per year and fewer than 1,000 such deaths during the course of the conflict; *intermediate armed conflict*: at least 25 battle-related deaths per year and an accumulated total of at least 1,000, but fewer than 1,000 in any one year; and *war*: at least 1,000 battle-related deaths per year.

in gross domestic product (GDP) per capita terms – and internal armed conflict.

With this review of recent data on armed conflicts, it is time to return to the semidemocracy thesis. It is clear that the rise in armed conflicts from 1978 to 1992 coincides with the *Third Wave of Democratization* (Huntington 1991). Countries in transition from autocracy to democracy, as Henderson and Singer (2000) argue, are more likely to suffer from armed conflict than consolidated democracies or autocracies. The fragility associated with regime transition appears to be especially great in Africa. There is an interesting difference between Africa, on the one hand, and Asia and Europe, on the other, when it comes to the relationship between democratization and armed conflict. In the latter two regions, democratization tends to generate calls for secession, as the former Yugoslavia and Russia demonstrate in Europe, and Indonesia, Philippines, and Sri Lanka show in Asia. In Africa, by contrast, democratization seems to produce armed conflicts associated with control of the state. At first glance, this looks like a paradox given the weakness of the state but because it is the main resource for development in most countries, it becomes more easily the prime target of the battling parties. Given that it is so deeply embedded in society, the conflict also easily expands to all corners of the country. It spreads more spontaneously and, as a result, is also more difficult to contain.

The question that remains to be addressed in this chapter is how far this tendency for African countries to be prone to armed conflict can be attributed to ethnicity. Is it really the cause of so much of the human suffering that follows in the wake of armed conflict or do we have reason to downplay its significance?

CAUSES OF CONFLICT

As suggested in the beginning of this chapter, scholars have an ambivalent attitude toward ethnicity in Africa. Because of its prevalence, it is hard to ignore, yet there are those who believe that blaming the continent's woes on a cultural variable like ethnicity overlooks the fact that most conflicts have an economic or materialist rationale. Furthermore, a cultural variable is more difficult to use for explanatory purposes. In order to cover the controversies in the literature, I have made a threefold distinction. The first is the cultural explanation that focuses on ethnicity itself as an explanatory variable. The second set is structural or economic and sees ethnicity only as a background factor that does not really say much about the causes of conflicts – or development, for that matter. The third is social in nature. It recognizes agency without ignoring the importance of structural conditions. It argues that ethnicity is secondary to other considerations, including political ones.

Ethnicity as Causal Variable

Let us begin with those who blame Africa's development problems on ethnicity. Foremost among more recent publications along these lines is the article by Easterly and Levine (1997) that claims that ethnolinguistic fragmentation is significantly correlated in a negative way with such development indicators as school attendance and number of telephones per worker, but positively correlated with the presence of black market phenomena. These factors in turn, according to the two authors, have negative consequences for overall economic progress, accounting for 25 to 40 percent of the growth differential between the stalling sub-Saharan Africa and the fast-growing Southeast Asia. Africa's growth tragedy is the outcome of cancerous ethnic rivalry that holds macroeconomic reform perpetually hostage to sectarian interest. Ever since independence, it is ethnic fragmentation that has wreaked havoc on African development.

A closer examination of their analysis, however, shows that their generalization does not bear them out. Ethnic homogeneity as well as heterogeneity works both ways in Africa. Although it is true, as Easterly and Levine maintain, that Botswana is economically successful and ethnically homogeneous, there are other countries with a similar ethnic setup, for example, Burundi, Rwanda, Lesotho, Somalia, and Swaziland, where the development record falls far short of that of Botswana. Similarly, as Chege (1999) demonstrates, the six African states, which according to the World Bank in 1994 showed the strongest macroeconomic improvements in the 1980s, had a mean distribution of forty-eight ethnic groups, more than twice the average figure of those that had suffered economic decline during the same period. Subsequent cross-national studies, also supported by the World Bank, have rejected the claim that ethnic diversity is detrimental to Africa's political stability and development (ElBadawi and Sambanis 2000). Trying to blame lack of economic development on ethnic fragmentation, therefore, is misleading. But what about societies with just a few ethnic groups?

Collier and Hoeffler (1998) address this issue and argue that it is ethnic concentration, and especially polarization, that is likely to be the principal culprit behind conflicts in Africa. In other words, wherever two relatively equal but distinct cultural groups account for most of a country's population, the probability of conflict is higher than in societies with more diverse and dispersed groups. Their basic assumption is that where rebels are bound by a common identity distinct from that of their adversaries, coordinating and conducting an insurgency is easier. Henderson (2002:114–16), however, finds that cultural polarization, based on ethnic composition, is not a factor inducing conflict. These contradictory findings may in part be the result of problems associated with coding ethnic groups. For instance, does Sudan have two main ethnic groups – Africans and Arabs – or many because both the north and the south of the country can be subdivided into smaller ethnic groupings? Another question concerns the extent to which the groups are really cultural, and if so, in what sense? Wherever ethnicity is nested in religious differences, or vice versa, it is difficult to disaggregate the cultural content of each group and point to one subset of factors as being more important than another.

This issue comes up in trying to understand the conflicts in Rwanda and Burundi. The standard interpretation of the conflict between the majority Hutus and the minority Tutsi group has been that it is ethnic, like any other in Africa. There is reason to question that premise. After having lived together for many generations – at least three hundred years[4] – these two groups have gradually become a single ethnic group, if we define that by language and shared customs. Assuming, therefore, that ethnic conflicts are evidence of vertical cleavages along cultural lines, the relationship between the Tutsis and Hutus does not really match that description. A more appropriate characterization is to describe it as evidence of a horizontal cleavage based on social caste differences – the Tutsis having traditionally been the upper caste, the Hutus the lower.[5] Although Lemarchand (1994) argues that these status differences are also informed by a perceived ethnic identification, he emphasizes that the relations in Burundi and Rwanda are more social than cultural. The underlying causes of conflict in these two countries differ from the majority of African cases in which each ethnic entity is more discrete. The meaning of *Hutu* is being a social subordinate in relation to someone higher up in the pecking order. The special meaning of Hutu, Lemarchand stresses, must be viewed in the context of gift-giving – or direct reciprocal exchanges – that is part of the basis for exercising power in African societies. Just as power holders are expected to display generosity, the status of dependents or clients is to submit oneself to it. This dependence is not being forced upon the clients, but is perceived as something that the latter seek for their own protection.[6] This relationship of dependence takes on special significance in a society in which the status difference between patrons and clients is reinforced by such rules as prohibition of marriage across status lines (Goody 1976:104). Marriages across such lines were typically allowed in other African societies (cf. Chapter Eight), which meant that the main lines of cleavage were not inside the group but in its relation to others. In the case of Rwanda and Burundi, however, people married within their own status group thus reinforcing the

---

[4] Historians and others continue to study the origins of migration to the Great Lakes region of Africa where the Tutsis and Hima groups established hegemony in precolonial days.

[5] There were also the Twa, but their numbers were so small and their role in society so peripheral that they can for all practical purposes be excluded here.

[6] It is worth noting that the word for God in the interlacustrine region of central and east Africa, *Rugaba*, means "He Who Gives" – the supreme benefactor on whom the well-being of all depends.

social differences between the upper and lower castes.[7] It is worth noting that other neighboring societies in Uganda, Tanzania, and the Democratic Republic of Congo, which share a similar history with Rwanda and Burundi, did not enforce such marriage rules. The result is that there has been much more cultural integration there between the upper caste – the Hima – and the lower one – the Iru.

Structural Explanations

Those who consider ethnicity as just another background factor in explaining conflict in the African context tend to focus on economic variables. They argue that the increased number of intrastate conflicts in Africa since the 1980s must be seen in the light of poor economic performance. The reasons for conflict are seen as structural and caused by the peculiarities of the African economies. Collier and Hoeffler (2001) argue that in economies that are dependent on the export of primary products, the possibility of commandeering these commodities for illegal taxation, or even looting, is quite strong because they have to be transported long distances. This gives an opportunity to those opposed to the state to acquire resources for their cause. In short, the state has little control over economic transactions and, as a result, rebellious groups can quite easily challenge its hegemony. The risk that civil conflict may occur in an African country is, according to Collier and Hoeffler (2001), especially great wherever agricultural and mineral exports make up one-third or more of the GNP. In the view of these authors, conflict in Africa has little, if anything, to do with grievance or ethnicity. Their interpretation rests on the premise that the economic structures provide rebels or resistance groups with the means by which to pursue their cause. The problem with their analysis is that they do not explain why a group would embark on a rebellion or when such an act would start – or end. The structural opportunities for action, they seem to suggest are up for grabs anytime.

Leonard and Strauss (2003:66–82) take the argument about economic causes of civil conflict further by focusing on what they call the prevalence of enclave production. Such production includes diamonds, gold, and oil, all of which are high-value products providing hard currency for many African states. Blaming the legacy of Africa's contemporary position on the global economy, they suggest that countries are especially vulnerable to conflict when elites live off the collection of taxes or bribes from key, geographically confined production without making any productive contribution in return.

---

[7] A similar stratification existed in other places, but the upper caste – or class – was an immigrant minority. In Zanzibar, this group of Arabs, originally from Oman and Yemen, was overthrown in a revolution in 1964. In southern Africa, the ruling caste of European immigrants have either departed or accepted integration on the terms set by the African majority.

These authors go beyond the argument about the rentier state by suggesting that remittances from migrants overseas and foreign aid also contribute to the problem of a productive and publicly accountable state. Like enclave production, remittances and foreign aid are disconnected from the rest of the economy and do not contribute to a society's productive capacity. Whenever rebel groups have access to these resources, they can be successful in waging a war against the state. This is what happened with the many liberation movements in southern Africa, which received considerable support, both humanitarian and military, from external organizations that supported their cause. Diasporic remittances were less important in southern Africa, but played a significant role in supporting the Eritrean liberation movements in their fight against the Ethiopian state.

Rentier states that have depended largely on income from the export of high-value mineral products and oil have been particularly prone to conflict because it has been relatively easy for rebels to seize control of the sites from which these products are extracted. Leonard and Strauss (2003) cite several examples of rebellions sustaining themselves through access to such enclave production. Angola is offered as the clearest example of where it helped sustain a conflict between government and a rebel group – UNITA – for a long period. Although the latter also received military and financial support from the United States for strategic reasons during the Cold War, it was its ability to gain control over territory that produced diamonds that gave the rebel movement its ability to sustain itself for quarter of a century.[8] Another case in point is the Democratic Republic of Congo, also a major producer of diamonds, gold, and other valuable minerals. This enclave production situation had originally allowed its president, Mobutu, to skim off large chunks of revenue without making any reinvestments in the country's infrastructure and development. After 1996 rebels in the eastern part of the country began challenging Mobutu. By gaining control over parts of the enclave production, they could sustain their fight against Mobutu and eventually force him into exile. The new government under President Joseph Kabila, however, failed to unite the country and after a few years, the rebellion started again with groups seizing control of mines. This time, other African governments cashed in on the situation and by supporting Kabila (Angola, Namibia, and Zimbabwe) or the rebels (Rwanda and Uganda), the conflict intensified and the looting of the country's wealth for political purposes reached shameful levels.

Other countries like Liberia, Nigeria, and Sierra Leone also fall into the category of enclave-producing countries that have suffered from civil conflict in which rebels have had access to these strategic resources. There are,

---

[8] Its influence has diminished considerably after the UNITA leader, Jonas Savimbi, was killed by Angolan government troops. Because UNITA has lost its strategic control over diamonds, his successor has agreed to pursue the movement's cause in a peaceful manner.

however, also exceptions. Not all countries with enclave economies have suffered from civil conflict. Botswana is the most obvious case and much of that may be attributed to the honest and effective leadership provided by the country's first and second presidents – Seretse Khama and Ketumile Masire. Cameroon and Gabon also belong to this category, but their case is different. The main reason for the absence of civil conflict is the result of a French determination that rebels must not be allowed to prey on the enclave economies of these two countries. The French have made it clear that they would intervene militarily to ensure that such a threat would not materialize (Chipman 1989; Gardinier 1997).

In an attempt to see how far enclave economies really correlate with civil conflict, Leonard and Strauss (2003) divided African countries into four categories: those with or without an enclave economy and among those two groups, countries with or without conflict. Excluding wars of independence from colonialism, they ended up with fourteen countries having endured a postindependence conflict.[9] Of those fourteen, six were straightforward enclave economies, but because there were a couple of other countries, notably Mozambique, Somalia, and the Sudan, that they label as functionally equivalent of enclave economies, they conclude that the relationship between enclave production and civil conflict in Africa is quite powerful.

When they include state capacity, as measured by its ability to collect taxes – direct or indirect – from its citizens, the structural basis for explaining civil conflict in Africa is further strengthened. Thus, they conclude that a country that has an important production enclave is found on average to have had 6.5 more years of civil conflict than one that does not. But, for every percentage point increase in GDP collected in domestic taxes, the number of years of civil conflict decreases by 0.7 years (Leonard and Strauss 2003:79). The structural composition of the African economies, therefore, cannot be ignored. It is one of the factors conditioning conflict in Africa.

Ethnopolitical Explanations

One of the drawbacks with the cultural as well as the structural explanations of civil conflict or development is that they are static. In order to make ethnicity a meaningful variable, cultural explanations have to treat its various features as frozen in time. They tend to become no different from those that treat ethnicity as primordial. Structuralists go too far in overlooking the potential role that ethnicity plays and focus instead on other factors, notably economic variables. In so doing, they focus on formal institutions and structures. There is no recognition that these formal entities are embedded in

---

[9] Conflicts included here are defined as those in which there were at least 1,000 fatalities in a single year. Enclave economies are those in which at least 75 percent of the value of their exports in 1999 was made up of minerals, timber, or estate agriculture.

social relations and that these relations rather than pure economic ones are determinants of conflict or development. In other words, in establishing their correlations between key variables they leave out the possibility that it is the mobilization of social and political relations that dictate what happens to development and the regime.

In the contemporary competitive political conditions existing in most African countries, the ethnopolitical explanations take on particular importance. In this final subsection, I shall first examine what others have said about ethnopolitics and then proceed to show that there is more to what the literature has contributed so far.

The main argument of the transactive approach is that the firmer the boundaries of a particular group are, the more likely that ethnicity will be a determining variable. Exclusivity breeds awareness. The overwhelming part of the literature suggests that ethnic group boundaries in African countries tend to be fluid. They do not generate the same degree of ethnic awareness as relations among groups do in societies in which there is a long legacy of relations of conflict, often captured in literary sources. This is not to imply that Africans lack a history of their own that matters. The point is rather that prior to colonialism, ethnic boundaries were not particularly firm. As Ranger (1983) writes about precolonial societies in Africa, Africans moved in and out of multiple identities. Very often, this meant moving from the area of one ethnic group to another. Furthermore, Africans had their own ways of maintaining peaceful relations among themselves. As suggested earlier, the notion of tribe or ethnicity became essentialized during colonial times. It came to refer to the various rural collectivities that the colonial powers identified in their respective territories. Although these attempts to assert an ethnic consciousness among the Africans did not overshadow other identities completely, they did make the ethnic boundaries more entrenched than what they had been.

Such was the reality that African nationalists had to cope with after independence. Ethnicity constituted a social or political building block that they could not ignore. Social mobilization, therefore, tended to draw on these categories as political leaders engaged in competitive struggles for control of the state. This competition sometimes intensified fear of the other groups, and it could have disastrous consequences as it did in the case of Nigeria in 1966, when people in the northern half of the country assumed that the Igbos in the southeast would try to gain control for themselves of both military and civilian government institutions.

The role that ethnicity plays in African society, however, has continued to decline. This is reflected in the literature, which recognizes that these identities are socially constructed and the outcome of social and political processes that keep changing. Ethnicity is contingent and contextual (see e.g. Young 2002). This is not to argue that modernization necessarily works in detribalizing African societies. It is rather the outcome of the persistence of premodern features in the context of institutions that are officially modern but, as previous chapters have shown, tend to be permeated by relations of affection. The paradox in the contemporary context, therefore, is that while ethnicity tends to decline in significance, relations of affection at large are on the rise.

There is more than one reason why this process is taking place. At the social structural level, there is more fluidity and hence more uncertainty than in previous years. Structural adjustment has loosened up the social categories that Africa inherited after independence. Kinship structures, although still important, are no longer such exclusive forms of social organization. At the same time, the kinship idiom of social organization prevails. People, in villages as well as cities, cope with an increasingly uncertain existence by, as in the past, investing in social relations with others. With the decline of formal associations such as marketing cooperative societies that used to foster ethnic consciousness and pride, people seek out these new relations in more spontaneous and informal manners. This means building social relations where in the past there was none. This is not an easy process, especially since abuse of official positions for personal gains in the formal associations of the past has left a legacy of mistrust. For this reason, some people try to eke out an existence on their own without calling on others to help. Going it alone, however, is most often not a viable option. Faced with limited income and usually unexpected expenditures for illnesses, burials, and other important aspects of life, seeking out others for help becomes a necessity. Traditional social networks have been breaking down and, even if they can be called upon, are often not enough. New relationships have to be developed even if this means a greater moral hazard, that is, the risk that time spent on generating them does not produce expected benefits. In short, the dilemma facing most African households is that past relations of affection, which were more specific to kinship or other local units of social organization, do not always suffice to cope with the demands that come from being more exposed to the market and, simultaneously, having to respond to costs associated with declining health, particularly illness caused by the HIV/AIDS epidemic (AMREF 2000).

Africans have to transcend these old relations. In so doing, they do not for the most part change behavior and start formal organizations, but rather prefer the direct reciprocal exchanges that they are used to and know how to handle. Globalization may have exacerbated this tendency, because, especially among the urban-based younger generation, they can find much in common in the excitement that popular culture, for instance, video games, offers.[10]

---

[10] Names from popular video games are common in everyday parlance and have been used for the purposes of both social and political organization. One such example is from the

The new political dispensation with growing competition among leaders and their followers has also changed the social parameters of conflict in Africa. The ethnic categories that African leaders inherited at independence provided a definite measure of political legibility and could be manipulated for purposes of control. With ethnic boundaries becoming more fluid and people seeing their interest as less confined to existing social categories, this legibility has diminished. Thus, in combination with a more competitive electoral system, politics is more open-ended and uncertain. The social categories like ethnicity or clan that political leaders could take for granted and use in calculating a rational choice no longer exist to the same extent. Winning an election, therefore, means building bridges with representatives of a wider set of groups. This amounts to intensified reciprocal exchanges over a wider and, in many respects, unknown social space. Costs to each candidate go up, as they invest in relations of affection with clients or followers whose loyalty cannot be taken for granted. They try to create dependencies on which they can rely, but these relations are often both unstable and unpredictable.

It is the growing prevalence of these brittle relations that is at the root of civil and political conflicts in Africa today. Their ethnic content is diminishing; it would be wrong to talk about ethnopolitics in Africa today as if it were similar to earlier accounts in which ethnicity is taken for granted and viewed as the principal component (Lonsdale 1994). It is the struggle to build and sustain new and often fragile alliances that induces political leaders to engage in predatory behavior, whether toward the state or the enclave economy. The imperative of rule over people and not over territory carries its own costs that cannot be met from a single private source. It goes beyond that. Although campaigns to collect money from individuals may be part of such an effort, the easier one has been to take advantage of access to public resources provided through the state. Wherever groups have been excluded from such access, they have not hesitated to go for the wealth hidden in diamond and gold mines.[11] As the cases of Liberia, Sierra Leone, and the Democratic Republic of Congo indicate, the rebel groups are not really ethnic in composition, but made up of an amalgam of people, often youngsters, drawn from different ethnic backgrounds.[12] Social relations have become increasingly transethnic. The more common reason for conflict in Africa, therefore, is not that ethnic boundaries are too strong, but rather that they

Republic of Congo in the early 1990s, where Ninjas and Cobras were used as names of militia organizations affiliated with rivaling politicians (see Bazenguissa-Ganga 1999).

[11] The Zimbabwe government under President Robert Mugabe, after having exhausted what it could extract from the state, decided to expropriate the commercial farms of the country's white minority, an important part of that country's enclave economy.

[12] Richards (2004) suggests that the Revolutionary United Front (RUF) in Sierra Leone was made up of young people from rural communities in which domestic slavery existed. RUF, therefore, provided an opportunity for them to escape this exploitation.

are too fluid. Similarly, conflicts in Africa abound not because the state is too autonomous, but because it is embedded in society.

CONCLUSIONS

Scholarship on ethnicity in Africa has moved a long way from early studies emphasizing its primordial nature to focusing on it as something that is socially or politically constructed in response to specific circumstances. As such, it has also shifted from being culturally essentialist to becoming more existentialist, or from looking at ethnicity as a cultural property to seeing it as an outcome of social relations.

When it comes to explaining civil conflicts in Africa, however, there is a need to go beyond ethnicity. Its significance, as has been demonstrated in this chapter, is declining and does not prove to have a strong relationship with incidence of conflict. At the same time, an alternative focus on structural factors is also inadequate because it overlooks the socially embedded nature of the economy in Africa. It is control of people rather than land or territory that matters. This has become increasingly difficult in the past two decades as the need for building social networks or political alliances extending beyond established categories have become necessary. The political order in these countries rest on more brittle ground, and disagreements can more easily break into open conflict and threaten stability. The enclave nature of production is a facilitating factor, but not a cause of this threat to political order. It is the human agency associated with the economy of affection that explains these conflicts.

The exceptions to this conclusion are, interestingly, the countries that historically have been the most stratified. Rwanda and Burundi continue to be deeply divided between Tutsis, who continue to consider themselves lords, and Hutus, for whom escaping from the notion of being mere subjects remains elusive. The point about their inability to create political bridges between themselves, however, is that it is because of social stratification, not ethnicity. The other exception is Ethiopia, the only country with an indigenous imperial tradition in modern times. It has turned itself into an ethnic federation in which the differences among ethnic groups have been formalized, but the informality of the revolutionary movement is what keeps the country together. This has taken the country on a course that differs from other African countries, especially since the 1994 constitution allows states within the federation to secede, something that reflects the precedent set by Eritrea when it voted overwhelmingly in 1991 for independence from Ethiopia.[13] The Ethiopian case is particularly instructive because it demonstrates how the movement legacy perpetuates a form of rule that relies on

---

[13] Eritrea and Ethiopia have since fought a bloody war; its cause is not related to ethnicity but rather to personal differences between the main leaders of the two countries.

informal relations that transcend the boundaries of formal rules. As in most other African countries, these informal relations are less based on the ethnic than on the affective factor. Political mobilization to win an election may still draw on the former, but for effective rule, the more transactive reciprocities identified with the economy of affection have become increasingly important even if they are linked to greater moral hazard.

10

The External Dimension

The reality of Africa in the beginning of the twenty-first century is that its position in the global economy is peripheral. Statistics presented in Chapter One provide evidence of how marginal the region is to global economic transactions. Africa exports almost exclusively unprocessed commodities – be they agricultural or mineral. It imports a large share of all its manufactured goods. Foreign direct investments in African countries are quite small compared to both Asia and Latin America. With the exception of South Africa, this applies in varying degrees to all countries in the region. Those with mineral resources tend to fare a bit better as far as investment goes, but despite Africa's enormous mineral riches, most investors would tend to place their money in operations in other parts of the world where the investment climate is more attractive.

To a large extent, African countries are responsible for their economic predicament, but it would be wrong to attribute its peripheral position only to bad policies or poor leadership, as many economists are inclined to do. The global economy, as currently constituted, is not particularly enabling to the poorest countries of the world, especially those that still rely on agricultural exports for income. There are two problems that African countries encounter. One is the extensive subsidies and protections given to agricultural producers and textile manufacturers in both the United States and the European Union (EU). These have the effect of limiting export opportunities for Africans and keep world market prices suppressed. The other is the fact that in a competitive global economy, the weakest members, especially those that rely on unprocessed commodities, find it most difficult to make real gains. Africa's predicament in the global economy, therefore, is a combination of inadequate agency and structural constraints.

This chapter will trace the way political scientists have looked at Africa's attempt to deal with global economic challenges since independence. It begins by looking at how African governments reacted to the disillusionment that occurred soon after independence when it became clear that its promises were not being realized. It discusses at some length the literature on dependency and underdevelopment before proceeding to an analysis of the new political economy that emerged in the 1980s. The chapter ends with a discussion of the political implications of Africa's position in the present global economy.

DEPENDENCY AND UNDERDEVELOPMENT

The literature in the 1960s focused on African agency, especially as manifest at the political leadership level. Underlying much of what was said in those days was the assumption that development was a matter of catching up. It was generally accepted that an enlightened leadership imbued with the idea of progress and focused on mobilizing the latent resources of the African countries, notably its human population, would be capable of achieving that goal. Thus, the poorer countries of Africa would grow faster than richer ones elsewhere in the world and their levels of income would eventually converge.

The thesis that there is an advantage to being technologically backward because it promises greater scope for rapid advancement, however, was seriously called into question in the 1970s. The language shifted on all fronts: development became underdevelopment, convergence became divergence, forging ahead became falling behind, agency became structure, and optimism turned into pessimism regarding Africa's prospects for moving ahead.

The shifts that took place in the literature were very much the result of a readiness to incorporate into the mainstream the theoretical constructs and concepts provided by Karl Marx and those who followed in his intellectual footsteps. Authors replaced the linear and evolutionary notion of progress with the Marxian idea that it is dialectical and thus inevitably conflictive. They also brought to attention the concept of structure, not as a facilitator or opportunity-enhancing mechanism, but as a constraint or obstacle. In the light of Lenin's analysis of imperialism as the highest stage of capitalism, authors also made a point of looking at the African countries in the context of the world economy at large, emphasizing their dependency on the richer countries and ensuing underdevelopment. The literature on this subject is broader and richer than is possible to do justice to in this section. I shall concentrate on discussing those issues that proved especially important in the studies of African political economy in the 1970s. They can be formulated into three questions: (1) what were the structures of dependence? (2) how important was capitalism in determining African development? and (3) what were the consequences for the African political economy?

Structures of Dependence

The origin of this literature can be found in the analysis of the Latin American economies that began in the 1950s by Paul Prebisch and his colleagues at the United Nations Economic Commission for Latin America (ECLA). Dependence came to refer to a situation in which the economy of certain countries is conditioned by the development and expansion of another economy to which the former is subjected (Cardoso and Faletto 1969). This is how the Latin economists saw the relationship between their countries and the United States in the post–Second World War period. In this power perspective, the dominant economy – the United States – could expand and be self-sustaining, while the dependent ones could do so only as a reflection of that expansion. This was a situation that left the Latin American economies vulnerable. Consequently, their prescription was investment in import-substituting industries as a means of reducing this dependence.

This notion of dependence and its ensuing vulnerability made a lot of sense also in the African context where countries had just emerged from colonialism. By adopting it, researchers shifted their attention from looking merely at the domestic conditions of each country to analyzing the internal situation of these countries as part of the world economy. The unit of analysis changed from being the nation-state to being the world economy. The situation of the underdeveloped countries was not a failure of their slowness or inability to modernize in the economic sense of adopting the efficiency characteristics of developed countries, but rather a consequence of their incorporation into the word economy on unfavorable structural terms. For instance, trade relations, based on monopolistic control of the market, led to the transfer of surplus generated in the dependent countries to the dominant countries. With financial relations based on loans and the export of capital, which generate their own interest and profit, the domestic surplus of dominant powers would increase and strengthen their control of the economies of other countries.

Reflecting the Marxian tradition, the literature on dependency and underdevelopment is both structuralist and deterministic in nature. As, for instance, dos Santos (1970) argued, the capitalist world economy has its own laws of development. Economic relations dominant in the capitalist centers – the core – determine the ways in which they expand outward to the periphery. Economic relations inside these peripheral countries are the product of the way in which the countries are incorporated into these networks of international economic relations. In the African context, the colonial powers had introduced – and enforced – production of commodities that were in demand in their domestic markets: groundnuts for producing oil; cotton for producing textile; coffee and tea for an expanding urban consumer market, and so on. With this exclusive focus on raw materials and agricultural products to accelerate industrialization in the core countries, the internal productive structure of the colonies was a rigid specialization and monoculture, similar to that found, for example, in the Caribbean and northeast Brazil.

This legacy did not change after independence in the 1960s. Because it was the main source of revenue, the traditional export sector had to be retained in order to provide funding for development of other sectors as well. Trade relations, however, take place in a highly monopolistic market and one that is subject to fluctuations in demand. For instance, while commodity prices had been relatively high at the time of independence, they had since declined, leaving the countries increasingly exposed to the economic powers of the capitalist center. To the extent that foreign investments had been made prior to independence, they had taken place in the mineral sector. At independence or soon thereafter, it was followed by investments in extraction of oil and refinement of petroleum products. Gabon, Cameroon, and Nigeria were among the first independent countries to receive such investments. The policy of the transnational corporations making these investments was to retain control of their operations and to ensure a high volume of profit. Again, therefore, the capital accounts of the African countries benefited only marginally from the presence of these corporations. They did not have enough resources to embark on an industrialization strategy aimed at establishing forward and backward linkages within their domestic economy. As the following account of what happened in Niger after independence indicates, countries found themselves in a vicious circle as they tried to make progress in the conditions provided by the world economy at the time:

Groundnut production accounted for 65 per cent of all Niger's very feeble external revenue during the first decade after independence. As of 1976, however, uranium was accounting for the same percentage but of a larger absolute volume.... While this revenue bonanza makes Niger more solvent, and able to overcome some of the distress of the drought period of the early 1970s, it also ties it much more firmly into a dependency situation within the world economy. (Higgot 1980:57)

The African economies had one advantage over the countries in Asia and especially in Latin America that spilled over into the 1970s. Because they were generally poor by comparative standards and they were recent victims of colonialism, they enjoyed an international sympathy that should neither be exaggerated nor completely ignored. African countries badly needed foreign finance for investments in infrastructure as well as development. The answer came in the form of the so-called basic needs approach to development that was produced by thinkers such as Richard Jolly, Hans Singer, and Dudley Sears working with the International Labour Organization (ILO) and popularized by Robert McNamara in his capacity as president of the World Bank (1968–80).

As Leys (1996:112) notes, behind this line of thought aimed at improving the living standards of the poor lay an acceptance, albeit tacit, of much of the dependency viewpoint. The question that critics of foreign aid raised in the

1970s was whether foreign aid merely filled up the holes that dependency had created in the first place by preventing certain social transformations from occurring. A question they did not ask was whether foreign aid in fact reinforced African dependency on the countries in the core of the world economy. Given the large volume of loans that African countries accepted during the 1970s to pursue development activities such as universal primary education and universal primary health care with no immediate returns, that question is also valid.

The point about the dependency literature that must be stressed here is that it is painted with broad brushes. Generalizations abounded because everything was analyzed from the vantage point of unequal exchange (Emmanuel 1972). Another problem was the tendency for revolutionary romanticism or ideological blinders to develop among its protagonists. Frank displays this in his analysis of underdevelopment and the prospects for social revolution in Latin America (Frank 1969). Rodney echoes similar sentiments in his analysis, *How Europe Underdeveloped Africa* (Rodney 1973). If this rather uncritical adoption of underdevelopment theory implies that there is an alternative – however distant in the form of a social revolution – much of the rest of the literature was more realistic in orientation. It assumed that a capitalist world economy would not provide opportunities for change in the relations between the core and the periphery or between the rich and the poor. Leys (1975) made this point in his analysis of the Kenyan situation in the mid-1970s. Amin (1976) adopted the same kind of perspective in his analysis of what happens to social formations in the periphery. Even among those who did not propagate the revolution, however, there was disagreement about how influential capitalism really was in the periphery.

Influence of Capitalism

African politics in the 1970s tended to develop along two divergent lines. There were countries that accepted their destiny in the periphery, and their governments accordingly tried to live with capitalism and get the best out of it; Kenya, Ivory Coast, and Nigeria were prominent examples of this orientation. The other line was taken by those countries that tried to put an end to dependency by nationalizing foreign-owned corporations and emphasizing socialism and self-reliance. Ghana, Guinea, Tanzania, and Zambia were prominent in this group. Given the importance that the Kenyan and Tanzanian cases came to occupy in the literature, I wish to give them priority here.

A colony with a legacy of white settler dominance in the key agricultural sector, Kenya, on the eve of independence, was a place characterized by uncertainty. Would the new African government respect the property rights of its white minority? The president-to-be, Jomo Kenyatta, provided a resounding answer to that question when he said in a speech after he had been released from political detention in 1961 that the government of an independent Kenya would not be a "gangster government." Those who have been "panicky" about their property, he said, should not fear that they would be deprived of anything (Kenyatta 1968:147). In a conciliatory gesture that was quite unique and bold at the time, Kenyatta promised that everyone, regardless of skin color, would be allowed to continue doing business peacefully in order to bring prosperity to the country.

This political transition was facilitated by the British government, which provided funding to buy up some of the white-owned farms and turn them into settlements. This way some of the social pressures on the new government were reduced. By 1970 no less than two-thirds of the old European mixed-farm areas had been bought and approximately half a million Africans had been resettled on that land (Republic of Kenya 1971:76). Most of the Europeans who had agreed to sell their land remained in Kenya and invested in other businesses, notably tourism. In combination with a concerted effort to develop existing smallholder farms, the agricultural sector grew at an average rate of 4.5 percent annually between 1964 and 1969, by no means a record high, but quite an achievement in a comparative African perspective at the time (Leys 1975:114).

While the land-transfer program reduced foreign ownership in agriculture, it was encouraged in both commerce and industry. Some transnational corporations, like Lonrho, bought very extensive local interests in order to establish itself in the Kenyan market (Brett 1972). With a similar trend in the insurance industry, this led to a debate about the extent to which a capitalist transformation like that which had already taken place in Brazil and India would be possible in Kenya. One view, associated foremost with Raphael Kaplinsky, maintained that the structural conditions in Kenya, notably the relatively small market, ruled out the possibility of a broad capitalist transformation of social relations. There are definite limits to capitalist accumulation in peripheral countries and Kenya is no exception (Kaplinsky 1980). Langdon (1987) offers a somewhat different perspective by arguing that it is technology dependence that limits the prospects for a capitalist transformation. He did not rule it out altogether, but saw the Kenyan bourgeoisie's alliance with foreign capital limiting its technology choices and thus disallowing it from taking the lead in a locally driven transformation.

It is clear from the literature on Kenya that there was widespread skepticism among academics about the prospect for capitalist development on terms set by a domestic bourgeoisie. Their interpretation is typically cast in a dependency perspective that focuses on the negative effects of capitalist development in the periphery. It portrays any beneficiaries of this development – foreign capitalists and local *compradors* (collaborators) – as agents of the ills that it brings. With the benefit of some hindsight, one does not escape the impression that this neo-Marxian genre in the 1970s and into the 1980s was quite dogmatic and unwilling to entertain the possibility of alternatives to their own rather rigid form of analysis.

The analysis of socialist experiments in Africa went on parallel with the debate about the limits of capitalism. Many governments in Africa had come to question their ability to develop their country in the context of the capitalist periphery and, beginning with Nkrumah in Ghana and Sekou Toure in Guinea in the early 1960s, had taken steps to bring the principal means of production under state ownership. By the end of the 1970s, a majority of countries in sub-Saharan Africa had adopted one form or another of socialism. Tanzania stands out in this camp because of its persistence in pursuing its socialist policies.

Its program entailed a broad range of measures, nationalization being only one of them. Also significant in the context of what was attempted are income equalization, measures to prevent leaders from accumulating capital, and collective farming. All these initiatives were taken within a short time in the late 1960s, following the adoption of the Arusha Declaration. The one policy that took time to fully materialize was the establishment of collective villages. It was completed only in the mid-1970s.

The general impression conveyed in the literature is that socialism in Tanzania was a failure. Such a broad generalization may be unfair, depending on what angle one uses to analyze the issues. For one, the leadership code that was adopted to prevent party and government leaders from engaging in capitalist accumulation was quite effectively enforced. To be sure, there were those officials who got away with using public funds for private purposes, but in the light of current concerns about good governance compared to other governments in Africa at the time, Tanzania's was refreshingly free from corruption and other means of misappropriation of funds. Another indicator of success was the significant reduction that took place in income levels between the highly and lowly paid in the public sector. These were highlighted in some of the writings on Tanzania at the time, for example, a volume edited by Mwansasu and Pratt (1979), but they have been generally overshadowed by the assessments of nationalization and villagization, both of which have been extensively criticized. The state-run commercial sector was a disaster from the very beginning and created severe shortages that invited black markets in a number of goods, including everyday consumer items such as bread, flour, sugar, salt, and beer. The state-run industries did not do too badly in the first few years but as the economy began to have problems in the late 1970s, they encountered similar problems of being unable to serve customers. Most important, rising costs for imported parts and inputs eventually made locally produced products so expensive that they priced themselves out of the market. For instance, a large number of jointly owned enterprises in which the state held half or more of the shares had to close down as foreigners withdrew or insisted on closure. The result was the shortage of commodities and empty shelves in the stores.

Of all the programs, villagization was perhaps the most detrimental to the cause of socialism. It started off in the late 1960s as a voluntary program, but it was not very popular among Tanzanian peasants. As a result, in 1973, the ruling party declared the move into collective *ujamaa* villages compulsory. Combined with a severe drought in 1974, the villagization program caused a serious food shortage that year, a fall from which the country never really recovered. This drop in output caused a period of intense austerity that lasted into the 1980s. Coercion was continuously used to try to secure a higher level of agricultural output, but it never rose to levels needed to adequately feed the country's growing population (von Freyhold 1977; Boesen et al. 1986). Foreign borrowing and the eventual acceptance of conditional policy input from the World Bank and the IMF became the ultimate consequences of the failures to build socialism.

Two interesting conclusions can be drawn from the socialist experiences as illustrated by Tanzania. The first is that multinational corporations hardly turned out to be the undefeatable mammoths as the dependency and under-development literature had portrayed them. Governments could with relative ease take over their assets and impose fees and other transaction costs that could not be ignored (Herbst 2000). The consequence, not surprisingly, was that most of these corporations left Africa's socialist countries, in some cases with significantly negative economic consequences. The second conclusion is that trading the challenges of a capitalist transformation for those of a socialist one did not make the development equation in Africa any easier. The structural conditions in the periphery that is Africa, if anything, were even more impeding, a point that for example Coulson (1982) makes with reference to Tanzania. As I argued at the time in pointing to the attempts at building socialism by skipping a capitalist stage of development, there are no shortcuts to progress (Hyden 1983). In a comparative perspective, therefore, by the beginning of the 1980s, working within the capitalist world economy, in spite of its limitations for countries in the periphery, looked more reward-ing than trying to outright reject it. But what were the consequences for the African political economy?

Consequences of Incorporation

Much of the literature focused on the question of what the long-term conse-quences of this structural dependence within the capitalist world economy were likely to be for Africa. Would capitalism serve as a progressive or regressive force?

The dominant position, for quite some time, was to write off the emerg-ing local middle class as essentially a comprador class, content to live parasitically as a commission agent for foreign capital. This perspective echoed the view of Frantz Fanon, an Algerian thinker, who had dismissed this class in the following rather condescending fashion:

This native bourgeoisie, which has adopted unreservedly and with enthusiasm the ways of thinking characteristic of the mother country ... will realize, with its mouth watering, that it lacks something essential to a bourgeoisie: money. ... If the government gives it enough time and opportunity, this bourgeoisie will manage to put away enough money to stiffen its domination. But it will always reveal itself as incapable of giving birth to an authentic bourgeois society with all the economic and industrial consequences, which this entails. (Fanon 1967:143–44)

A couple of years later, this view was echoed by Genoud (1969:52) who argued that "in the colonies, there are more bourgeois-minded people than bourgeois," implying that they have the taste of the bourgeoisie, but not the qualities to act in a fashion that resembles bourgeois transformations elsewhere in the world. Anyang' Nyong'o (1989), with reference to Kenya, maintained a similar view. He argued that instead of being able to develop institutions to organize its collective class interests and attaching other classes to itself through effective political leadership, Kenya preferred to rely on Bonapartism ceding political power to a single individual in return for a piece of the cake. Such categorical dismissals of the African bourgeoisie as merely a petty bourgeoisie historically doomed to play only second fiddle may look overly pessimistic in the contemporary perspective, but it was broadly adopted by local and foreign critics of African development in the 1970s.

World capitalism, therefore, was condemning Africa to the periphery with little, if any, prospect of reversing that position. Most African government leaders had no problem agreeing with this doomsday analysis. They preferred to have a common enemy on whom to blame the conditions in their countries. It allowed them to brush aside any domestic criticism. This condemnation of the rest of the world as responsible for marginalizing Africa in the world economy may also have had the effect of making Western governments more strongly inclined to give increased development assistance to compensate Africans for past sufferings. As suggested above, the World Bank and bilateral donors provided generous aid to African countries throughout much of the 1970s on the assumption that it would relieve these countries from the worst consequences of their neocolonial status.

The debate about the consequences of world capitalism, however, transcended the critique of the African bourgeoisie. Its predicament was, after all, analysts kept arguing, the result of forces beyond the control of these countries. One line of argument was that capitalism tended to freeze precapitalist relations of production as it affected the periphery. Cliffe (1976), for instance, argued this point in an analysis of rural production relations in East Africa. There are at least two problems with that argument. One is that it emphasizes the role of exchange (or merchant capital) at the expense of other aspects of world capitalism. The other is that it implies that capital somehow seeks the impoverishment of the periphery by design.

This overly deterministic perspective on the periphery was dominant in much of the literature, but there were others who provided a more pragmatic analysis of the situation. Marx himself had, of course, accepted the progressive role of capitalism and its inherent ability to transform precapitalist relations. Laclau (1971) builds on this when he argues with reference to Latin America that capitalism does not typically satisfy itself with just restructuring precapitalist relations. It wants to replace them altogether in order to be more effective. In short, the inherent dynamic of capitalism works the same in the periphery as it does in the core countries. Another analyst in the Marxian tradition went as far as concluding that "we have to face up to the unpalatable fact that capitalism has created underdevelopment, not simply because it has exploited the underdeveloped countries, but because it has not exploited them enough" (Kay 1975:55). Hart (1982) applied the same argument in his analysis of the backwardness of West African agriculture.

What happened eventually, therefore, was a gradual shift away from an analysis of Africa's exchange relations with the rest of the world. It was not so much dependence on the world economy that was the problem as the backward nature of Africa's relations of production. Some very important and pathbreaking observations were made. Godelier (1975) noted that economic institutions in premodern societies do not play the same role as they do in capitalist societies. Echoing a point made much earlier by Polanyi (1957) that such institutions are embedded in social relations, Godelier went as far as claiming that there are no purely economic institutions in these societies. Rather, certain noneconomic forms of organization take on economic as well as other functions. The situation is especially distinctive in segmentary societies – that is, societies without a unified central authority – in which kinship determines how relations of production are structured. Meillassoux (1975) put another twist on the same argument when he suggested that in premodern societies it is not the relations of production, but the relations of social reproduction that are dominant. Authority lies not with those who control land but those who control women. Economic cells are reproduced through what amounts to marriage alliances. Rey (1973) as well as Hindess and Hirst (1975), finally, made contributions to the emergence of a new perspective on the African peasantry by arguing that it is ideology that plays the dominant role in distributing the product as well as the allocation of people to different spheres of economic activity.

There was a growing readiness to acknowledge the possibility of a peculiar African mode of production that needed to be the basis for further analysis of Africa's development prospects. Thus, Meillassoux (1975) referred to the prevalence in Africa of a lineage mode of production. Coquery-Vidrovitch (1976) also differentiated the specifics of an African mode of production, and I (Hyden 1980) referred to the same phenomenon as a peasant mode of production. The debate had returned to a renewed focus on the conditions existing in the African countries, regardless of what their relationship was with the world economy. At the same time, the notion of underdevelopment was not completely abandoned but was significantly modified by the renewed emphasis on the precapitalist or premodern features of African societies.

It is against the background of this shift in perception from capitalism to precapitalism as the dominant mode of production in rural Africa that I made the point that the peasantry is uncaptured. It is lodged in relations of production that, in turn, are embedded in relations of social reproduction; hence the subsistence orientation among the peasants and their ability to resist attempts by others to control them (Hyden 1980). Not everyone agreed with this abrupt swing in the intellectual pendulum. Kasfir (1986), Cliffe (1987), and Williams (1987) all questioned the portrayal of the African peasants as autonomous, arguing that they were subjected to the world economy and to a state that was not leaving them alone. My point, as I also clarified in Chapter Seven, was – and still is – that as long as precapitalist – premodern – features of society remain influential in Africa, the peasants can always find ways of circumventing, or ignoring, the commands of their superiors. The African bourgeoisie may try to get at the peasants, but its means of doing so are not very effective when the conditions of smallholder farming under the auspices of kinship prevail. Bates (1981), for example, correctly observes that it is not only that the bourgeoisie are dispersed over large expanses of territory; it is equally important that the rudimentary character of the prevailing social formations limit the capacity of the African bourgeoisie to transform its societies.

This somewhat lengthy review of the past literature on dependency and underdevelopment is not only important as part of the intellectual legacy on which subsequent scholars have built. It is also significant because it provides an interesting backdrop to the concerns of the neoliberal approach that emerged in the 1980s. As will be shown in this chapter, the latter has committed the same mistake of overemphasizing the mode of exchange at the expense of the mode of production as the basis for development in Africa.

THE *NEW* POLITICAL ECONOMY

The early 1980s marked a significant break with the past as far as the region's relations with the rest of the world go. Whereas the intellectual and political climate in the 1970s had provided African leaders with ammunition to stand up against what they perceived as an unjust and exploitative world economy dominated by the capitalist countries in the West, the crisis that affected it in the late 1970s forced government leaders in the economically powerful countries to redefine their economic thinking. Instead of a generous Keynesian demand-driven approach to economic management, they chose to go back to the classical economic market model. This neoclassical economics was initially adopted in the United States and the United Kingdom with ideological enthusiasm and little reflection. It is reflected in the tone and content of the 1981 World Bank Report on Africa that, despite some editing by more cautious economists in the top management of the bank, echoes the notion of the miracle of the market.

The main argument that challenged African government leaders was the new emphasis on the state as an institution that is more a liability than an asset to development in the region. For example, one objective of the new market orthodoxy was to criticize the tendency for rent seeking in African countries. Rents, of course, are profits above opportunity costs and do not exist in the perfect market. Rent seeking is the effect of distorted markets in which competition is absent or ineffective. The fundamental problem associated with rent seeking is that it leads to distorted incentives. More specifically in the African situation during the 1970s, there were strong incentives to engage in distributional struggles and to seek contrived transfers but, at the same time, very weak incentives to engage in productive and growth-promoting activities. Urban dwellers benefited at the expense of their rural counterparts. That was the message coming out of the seminal book, *Why Poor People Stay Poor*, by Michael Lipton (1977). In a conflict of interest between groups, as Olson (1965) had also argued, the recipe for successful collective action is to concentrate on gains for a relatively small group, and on diffused and preferably invisible losses for a much larger group. In African countries, the rural population is the largest group by far. If the smaller, relatively more privileged urban population can succeed in rigging the terms of trade in its favor, the recipe for concentrated gains and diffused losses is realized. The urban population, therefore, has an incentive for exploiting the rural population. This is also the argument that Bates (1981) makes in his widely cited book on the relationship of states to market in Africa.

Those who argue this way suggest that rent seeking occurs for a variety of reasons. One is the obvious fact that it reduces the cost of living for those who can engage in it. Another is that it is always easier for a politician to build a power base from better organized than amorphous groups. A related reason is that the cost of resource mobilization can be significantly cut by assembling a coalition of previously existing groups or organizations rather than having to bring them into existence in the first place (Oberschall 1973). Yet another is that urban populations tend to be more restless and volatile. It is politically necessary, therefore, to give priority to allocating resources to such groups.

The scope of the urban bias, or the burden placed on agriculture, was quite obvious to outside economic analysts as African countries moved into the 1980s. The 1981 World Bank report recognized the distorted incentive structures and argued for a change in favor of the rural producers, accepting that the problem of poverty in Africa is predominantly rural and not urban as in Latin America. In short, the new economic policies that became part of structural adjustment in the 1980s were meant to lure them into the market more effectively than had been the case with the policies developed in the 1970s. If the peasants were not already captured, the new incentive structures favoring the rural producer would achieve it. Such was the new policy prescription that eventually gained acknowledgement as the *Washington Consensus*, reflecting agreement not only between the World Bank and the IMF, but also between these international finance institutions, on the one hand, and bilateral donor governments, on the other.

Since the 1980s, thinking within the neoclassical paradigm has evolved in the direction of what is generally called the new institutional economics (NIE). It calls into question the notion of the perfect market and starts instead from the assumption that markets generally fail because actors lack complete information and it is too costly to try to obtain it (North 1990). Institutions help rectify these failures and are the important mechanisms for achieving the best possible solution to a given economic problem in the absence of a perfect equilibrium between supply and demand. NIE remains the conventional wisdom in economics circles, although it has been criticized for being too functional, that is, assuming failures automatically generate their own institutional solutions (Bates 1995).

NIE is preoccupied with lowering the transaction costs associated with more efficient decision making. It endorses the notion that refinement of market exchanges is the key to development in developed as well as developing countries. No questions are really asked about whether the premises of the NIE model apply across countries. The miracle of the market has been turned into the miracle of institutions. This approach has proved to be contentious in an environment like that of African countries where the structural conditions for formal institutions are hardly in place. Institutional solutions to make the market more effective are being introduced despite the fact that the social prerequisites for these measures are absent. The approach that the international finance institutions have taken toward Africa in recent years is to assume a market transformation, whereas, in fact, what they should do is to help foster the material conditions in these countries for a market to be constructed.

The double pinch that African countries face is that neither state nor market is already fully formed or developed. Neither is in a mode of consolidation. Both are still undergoing formation. The 1970s convinced many analysts that a development state is a nonstarter in African countries. This concept, therefore, has been compromised in favor of the NIE. This has come with its own costs to Africa. By trying to improve the mode of exchange at a time when the mode of production is still at a very rudimentary stage of development, the NIE is forcing de-industrialization as well as de-agrarianization on Africa. The region slips further and further into marginalization. Africa's share of global output has declined from 3.5 percent in the early 1980s to less than 2 percent today. Similarly, Africa's output of global trade has fallen from 5 percent to less than 2 percent in the past two decades. Further, much of Africa's exports continue to be dominated by primary commodities with limited gains in the diversification and the export of manufactured goods (Kabbaj 2004). This raises the issue of what the process of globalization really does to Africa and how it tries to cope with it.

AFRICA AND GLOBALIZATION

The rest of this chapter will highlight the political implications of globalization in Africa. Before proceeding, however, it may be worth drawing attention to the subtle shift that has taken place in the conceptualization of the economic context. In the 1970s the prevailing term was the capitalist world economy, the assumption being that there is an alternative, presumably a socialist, world economy. In the beginning of the twenty-first century, we use the term global economy, taking it for granted that there is only one – the market (or capitalist) economy. In short, discussion in recent years has omitted the alternative that existed, at least implicitly, in the debate some thirty years ago.

Trends

Comparisons are no longer made in ideological terms, but rather in the context of hard facts, setting African figures against trends in other regions of the world. As indicated in Chapter One, statistics for African countries are generally weak, because national accounts do not necessarily cover all economic activities, or analytical capacity in central statistics bureaus is weak. Yet, much of what we know about these countries stems from figures provided through such channels. The data that go into the World Development Report are compiled from national sources of statistics and typically end up as the authoritative measures of how individual countries and the African region, as a whole, are doing. Although I am not going as far as, for example, Ferguson (1990) to suggest that the World Bank portrayal of Africa is merely a constructed reality, it is obvious that statistical figures, in particular, have to be treated with a grain of salt. Even if there is more to these countries than what the numerical data tell us, however, they do indicate scenarios and trends that cannot be totally ignored.

Expanding on the statistics I have just cited, it is clear that the figures for Africa are not pretty. The macrodata confirm that previous efforts to reduce dependency or underdevelopment have really changed the conditions to the

TABLE 9. *Select Economic Indicators by Region, 1970 and 1997*
(*in 1987 U.S.$*)

Indicator	Africa Minus South Africa	Africa	South Asia	East Asia	Latin America
GDP per capita 1970	525	546	380	970	3,940
GDP per capita 1997	336	525	1,590	3,170	6,730
Investment per cap 1970	80	130	48	37	367
Investment per cap 1997	73	92	105	252	504
Exports per capita 1970	105	175	14	23	209
Exports per capita 1997	105	163	51	199	601
Savings/GDP (%) 1970	18.1	20.7	17.2	22.3	27.1
Savings/GDP (%) 1997	16.3	16.6	20.0	37.5	24.0
Exports/GDP (%) 1970	36.4	32.1	5.9	14.6	17.2
Exports/GDP (%) 1997	33.0	31.0	11.4	27.8	31.8

Source: World Bank data.

better. On the contrary, on the most important scores, the African region has gone backward rather than forward, as illustrated in Table 9.

This table provides us with several observations that bear on Africa's failure to deal with its position in the world economy since 1970. Africa is the only region where the average output per capita, as measured in constant prices (1987) have fallen. There has been notable growth especially in South and East Asia, and in Latin America. A few countries, like Botswana and Mauritius, constitute important exceptions, but more than half the region's forty-eight countries have suffered a decline: some such as the Democratic Republic of Congo, Niger, Sierra Leone, and Madagascar have had a decrease of almost 50 percent between 1970 and 1997.

Africa's share of world trade has also gone down since 1970. It now amounts to less than 2 percent. Three decades ago, African countries were specialized in primary products and highly trade-dependent – a major reason why the critique of dependency and underdevelopment emerged in the literature. Because African countries have fallen far short of their ambition to industrialize, some thirty years later, they remain largely primary exporters. With countries in the other regions having made important strides toward diversifying their economies, those in Africa have become marginalized and thus more vulnerable. To be sure, foreign aid continues to flow – albeit in less generous quantities and with more strings attached – but this aid dependence tends to create the impression that the continent is kept alive thanks to external rather than domestic contributions. Its external dependence is further aggravated by the heavy debt burden that in net present value amounts to more than 80 percent of GDP. It will be interesting to see whether the new commitment to reduce poverty in Africa manifested at the 2005 G8 Summit will help change this situation.

Among all regions, Africa is also the only one that has witnessed a decline in investments and savings since 1970. With rapid population growth – 2.9 percent compared to 1.8 percent for South Asia, 1.2 percent for East Asia, and 1.6 percent for Latin America – Africa's predicament is further compounded in a negative direction. Africa's development challenges go deeper than what these economic indicators reveal, but I will confine my account here to the macro aspects of the region's political economy.

Africa continues to be most dependent on the agricultural sector for any attempt at generating a locally driven development effort; economic trends in this area are particularly relevant here. It is especially striking that while agricultural production continued to grow during the colonial period and in the first decade after independence, it began to decline in per capita terms in the mid-1970s. Because Africa has had to contend with higher population growth rates than other regions in the past forty years, per capita production has fallen although aggregate agricultural output has been positive in many countries. As discussed in Chapter Seven, per capita production performance since independence stands in contrast to what has happened in both Latin America and especially those countries in Asia that can be labeled developing. During this period, Africa's share of world agricultural exports has fallen from 8 percent to a mere 2 percent. Although it used to be a food exporter, it has since become a net importer. This applies to important staple crops on the continent.

There are many reasons for Africa's negative agricultural performance. The one that is most important here concerns Africa's economic relations with the rest of the world. When the dependency and underdevelopment perspective first emerged in the analysis of African economies, it was largely in response to a missed opportunity after independence to replace reliance on export of primary commodities with local processing and manufacturing. Analysts and advocates both in academic and policy circles were convinced that such an alternative was feasible. After failing to significantly reverse that trend, the options are much more limited, especially given the new geopolitical climate that leaves African countries even more exposed to external forces than before. In addition to the global dominance of the United States that limits the ability of African countries to play one power against the other – as they did in Cold War days – the most serious constraint comes from the lack of political willingness, both within the United States and the EU, to cut subsidies to farmers and to stop dumping surplus grains in the world market. These two measures have had the effect of leaving world market prices for food crops at a constantly low level, reducing the incentives for African farmers to expand their production.

Interpretations

There are many interpretations of globalization and what it entails for Africa, the vast majority of them gloomy. It is hard not to share some of the pessimism in the literature, but it is also easy to get lost in this often-generalized hopelessness. Trying to avoid this trap, I have decided to focus on three issues that are real to Africans. All three have implications for policy as well as research.

The first of these issues is the deteriorating terms of trade. As the capitalist world economy has changed into a monolithic global economy, the most relevant terminology, as Mittelman (2000) points out, is no longer the distinction between core, semiperiphery, and periphery countries. Even though the dependency and underdevelopment literature rejected the notion of a linear trajectory of progress – as implied in the early modernization literature and initially embraced by the African nationalist elite – much of it entertained the possibility of progress in the periphery. As suggested above, socialism – or in some instances, communism – was treated as a viable alternative because the international arena was still divided into two camps, one dominated by the United States, the other by the Soviet Union. Thus, not only could countries in the periphery play one camp against the other – as often happened – but they could also exit from the capitalist world economy to join a socialist economy that was organized along different lines. The effort by the Non-Aligned Movement, made up of governments from Third World countries, in the 1970s to help bring about a New International Economic Order (NIEO) was ample evidence of that ambition.

With globalization has come a reorganization of the international scene from an East-West to a North-South divide. For protagonists of a new world order, it is meant to offer more opportunities for countries in the South to sell their products because of lower tariffs and thus freer movement of commodities. With the growth of world trade in the past two decades, there is obviously some evidence to back up such a claim. As critics of globalization have pointed out, however, the global market isn't what one calls a level playing field. The structural hurdles that the South, especially Africa, runs into are twofold. The first is the growing vertical integration of the global division of labor that a more liberalized global economy permits. Transnational corporations, typically based in the North, can more easily establish themselves in new locations without the fear that was real in the 1970s (Herbst 2000:226). The costs that governments in the South incur today by disallowing foreign capital to invest in their countries are much higher and thus less feasible not only from an economic but also from a political point of view. The political lever that these governments used to have in the days of Keynesian economics has pretty much vanished today. Compared to the 1970s, there is virtually no academic – let alone policy – discourse on the issue of state intervention to rectify economic and social imbalances caused by the effects of global market operations.

African governments as well as groups of citizens in these countries are quite suspicious of the current world trade system for good reasons. They find a lot of hypocrisy in the statements political leaders in the United States and the EU make about partnering with Africa because these same leaders fail to deal with the most obvious asymmetries in the system, notably the subsidies paid to farmers in their own countries. They are also upset about the elimination of previous partnership arrangements, such as the Lomé Convention that allowed African countries access to European markets based on the principle of North-South solidarity (Cheru 2002:28–29). The clauses that used to apply to the various rounds of the Lomé Convention, like other regional and trade integration arrangements, have more recently been subordinated under the general principles of the World Trade Organization. This means that the principle of reciprocity now guides trade among unequal partners. It is not surprising that many Africans argue that this arrangement will make the weak only weaker.

The terms of trade are such that there are few incentives, especially for agricultural producers, to embark upon improvements that would enable them and their countries to grow richer. Due to their low savings rate, there is little money available on the local markets for investment. This does not mean that all Africans are necessarily losers. Globalization has its winners in Africa, too. It has expanded market opportunities for entrepreneurial individuals – many are women – who are increasingly becoming global operators. Although much of it is still on a small scale, Africans, as the Indians, Lebanese, and Chinese have been doing already for some time, are engaging in intercontinental trade, mostly with Asia, but also with Europe and North America. The most significant of these activities are the exports of fruit, vegetables, and flowers from East Africa to Europe and the Middle East. Fish from the Great Lakes, especially Lake Victoria, is being flown vacuum-packed to destinations as far as Gainesville, Florida. There are also a large number of itinerant traders from Senegal and Mali who walk the streets in cities like New York, Philadelphia, and Washington, D.C. selling handicraft and other locally produced items from Africa. On the import side, electronics and textile products from the Middle East and Asia dominate. Dubai is a favorite destination for cheap purchases of goods that can be sold with a profit in local African markets. The same applies to the many women who ply the routes to Bangkok in search of textile materials to bring back to sell in city boutiques. All these trading activities are complementary to what multinational trading houses such as the United Africa Company (Unilever) have done for generations. They constitute a new feature of African development, one that suggests agency in spite of overwhelming structural constraints.

The second issue is the loss of national sovereignty that accompanies globalization. Sovereignty entails jurisdiction over all activities, including economic ones, within a state's geographic boundaries. Liberalization of the global economy calls this sovereignty into question and tensions arise between state actors and transnational corporations and other international agents, notably the international finance institutions. This applies to every country around the world that is part of this economy, but the consequences for sovereignty tend to be especially marked in the low-income countries, most of which can be found in the African region (Evans 1987).

The big difference between the 1970s and the beginning of the twenty-first century is that during the earlier decade, the penetration by multinational corporations and the role that other external actors played led to an expanding role of the state. As Evans (1987:344) concludes, the sovereignty-threatening intrusions by these actors may actually have led the state into more development activities than it otherwise would have done. As I have suggested throughout this book, it helped generate the movements that led the development efforts after independence. In today's global economy, the same dynamic is not at play, certainly not to the extent that it was some thirty years ago. Writing from an African perspective, the late Ake (1995:26) argues that the economic forces are shaping the world not only into one economy, but also into one political society. Nations participate in global governance according to their economic strength and – by extension – their rights. This global order, he writes, is ruled by an informal cabinet of the world's economically most powerful countries (cf. the G-8 summits); its law is the logic of the market, and status in this new order is a function of economic performance.

The question is, of course, whether African countries have the internal strength to deal with this less hospitable global environment. In a context of increasingly circumscribed national sovereignty, what scope of agency do African governments have? African analysts tend to see very little hope for their continent. A prominent Nigerian economist believes that the neoliberal economic policies that have been imposed on African countries in the past two decades have only caused misery (Onimode 1992). A Ghanaian political scientist, Hutchful (1989:122–23), was among the first to argue that a parallel government is emerging in Africa. It is controlled by the international lending agencies and is causing the appropriation of policy-making powers, which displaces the role of domestic actors, notably the elected representatives in parliament. Government in African countries becomes more accountable to external agencies than those in the domestic arena. These observations and others by African social scientists tend to dismiss the scope for local agency, and there is little doubt that the latter has declined since the 1970s. The multinational corporations were relatively easy targets for sovereign governments, but international finance institutions and other international agencies, multi- or bilateral, are more difficult to deal with, especially in a context where countries are heavily indebted and prices of primary commodities in the world market remain low.

The nationalist movements needed the multinational corporations on the ground in order to demonstrate their ability to stand up against exploitation by outsiders. Once they acted to seize their assets, however, these corporations withdrew, leaving governments without powerful local targets for social and political mobilization. The current dependence on the international finance institutions gives these governments much less leeway. First of all, African governments are themselves members of these institutions. Second, their investments on the ground in African countries are owned locally. For these reasons, standing up against the World Bank and the IMF becomes merely rhetorical. It may provide political leaders with some short-term political capital by doing so, but because they typically have to eat their own words, the longer-term effects are much more contentious. It is fair to say, therefore, that African governments find it much harder today to mobilize energy from opposing external influences. This is a frustration that they nowadays prefer to deal with by exiting; that is, when they have no choice but to agree, they ignore the implementation of policies with external agencies. The structural constraints to blaming Africa's plight on external forces also means that political leaders are increasingly ready to identify enemies within. Real or fictional, these domestic enemies, e.g. in the shape of political opposition to government, become the target of leaders acting in the name of the movement legacy. These conflicts sometimes get out of hand and are the cause of the increased number of intrastate conflicts in Africa discussed in the previous chapter.

The third issue concerns the effects of globalization of social life in Africa. Globalization has no doubt brought a variety of new influences to the continent. Villagers even in distant corners are exposed to new ideas and products that were totally unknown only some years ago. Modern meets traditional in many new ways and contexts. Africans are adjusting and social life changes accordingly. But what does all this amount to? Is Africa finally being modernized in the sense that we discussed in Chapter Two?

It would be wrong to assume that every African reacts the same way. There are those who are capable of taking advantage of these new influences and modernize their life by latching on to new and distant relations that help turn place into space. They become part of global networks and are among the new, successful entrepreneurs that can be found in most African countries today.

The majority of Africans, however, remain at the receiving end of these new influences. They are mainly reactive and try to cope with an increasingly challenging social environment in which opportunities exist but where many find it hard to take the risk involved in seizing these opportunities. Instead, they prefer the relative security that can be found in relying on others to provide the goods that they need. Human agency is not autonomous, but continues to be embedded in familiar social networks.

The effects of globalization on social life, therefore, are both progressive and conservative (MacGaffey 1987). It has created a new cadre of risk-taking individuals with global connections that they themselves have some control over. These people can be found in business. They typically shun politics because they find it too parochial. Globalization, however, has also had a conserving influence. Many of the continent's premodern social relations have been reaffirmed rather than transformed by this process. The free movement of capital has not been matched by a similar freedom for people to move across borders. Thus, capital has shaken African societies, but forced people to fall back upon relations that are often opposed to official authority. It is no surprise, therefore, that across Africa informal relations and institutions have become the prime mechanisms for coping with the uncertainty and insecurity that globalization has brought to the region.

CONCLUSIONS

Three conclusions can be drawn from this analysis of Africa's external dimension. Its ability to make headway in competition with other regions of the world is more constrained today than it was in the 1970s. By encouraging the majority of African governments at that time to take radical measures against their economic dependence on the former colonial powers, they did in fact weaken their own position in the emerging global context. Turning things around today is a much tougher proposition than it was some thirty years ago when governments had access to Keynesian economic policy tools. In the current global economy, African governments have little, if any, leverage and their economies are very extensively dependent on what happens to more developed and powerful economies. If African economies were ever dependent, it is now.

The second conclusion is that the global environment in which African countries find themselves is not itself a determining factor in the sense that it causes things to happen. It is a conditioning factor, meaning that it provides the parameters within which African agency takes place. The latter is ultimately the determining variable because structures do not act on their own. What African governments and other actors on the scene decide to do is what matters.

The third conclusion is that African governments have responded to globalization primarily in political terms. They have not been very effective in pushing their own economic interests within international organizations like the World Trade Organization or UNCTAD, and not just because they are poor countries, but also because they have rarely come well-prepared to negotiate in economic terms. The result is that they have ended up in political posturing hoping that other more powerful nations would, out of solidarity, pursue their interests too. This has invariably not happened. African governments have been forced to leave without anything because they went for something that was totally unrealistic.

11

So What Do We Know?

In bringing together the different arguments that have been made in this volume, this chapter begins by identifying the main points of full or near-full consensus among scholars of politics in Africa. Building on this baseline of propositions, I will offer my own summary statement of politics unbound. The next section will address the implications of the points made in this volume for future research and Africa's position in the discipline of political science, notably the field of comparative politics. The chapter ends with a discussion of the relationship between area studies and the mainstream of the discipline.

WHAT DO SCHOLARS AGREE UPON?

A main purpose of this volume has been to sift through half a century of scholarship on politics in Africa. Time has come to ask what knowledge we have accumulated and what we agree upon. The process of knowledge generation, not surprisingly, has been winding; the result, therefore, not so easy to capture in brief. This difficulty notwithstanding, there is a need to come up with a coherent profile that tells us what politics in Africa is all about. There is a good deal of consensus on a number of points. Based on my reading of the subject matter, I am ready to conclude that most, if not all, scholars would agree with the ten propositions I offer here. They are all stated in terms of what seems to matter most.

1. Society rather than State. Students of politics over the years have come to accept that African countries by and large lack an autonomous state that acts based on its own logic. As this volume has indicated over and over again, state institutions remain embedded in society. State does not lead society in Africa; and state does not control society. Societal values permeate state institutions in ways that are counterproductive to national development. Most notably, state resources are captured by individual leaders to feed their own communities or constituencies through procedures that go contrary to policy priorities specified in the national budget. The state in Africa, therefore, tends to be both weak and soft.

2. Rule over People rather than Land. African countries are still largely characterized by premodern features – including national politics – that tend to survive not just in the countryside, but also in the urban areas. Progress in Africa is often measured more in terms of how successfully governments can bring people together in a peaceful manner than in terms of exploiting natural resources. Peace and stability are more important indicators of success to people in Africa than the objective economic measures used by the international community. Acquiring followers easily becomes an end in itself both at macro- and microlevels. A government leader does not look for just the minimum coalition needed to rule, but the largest possible such coalition because it provides more prestige and, above all, greater prospect of stability. Much the same logic plays itself out at the household level where to this day the larger the number of women and children a person has, the greater his prestige and power in the local context.

3. Private rather than Public Realm. Because the boundary between state and society is fuzzy, there is also a problem of sustaining a meaningful distinction between what is private and public. Officials in state institutions are not feeling bound by rules of conduct that exist on paper but are typically ignored in these countries. Person rather than role matters. This means that individual officers often use their positions to pursue their private rather than the public interest. It may mean feathering one's own nest or diverting resources for purposes associated with the individual's own personal connections. Public conduct, therefore, is not predictable. Cases are often delayed in order to allow the official an opportunity to extract a bribe before resolving them. People with the right connections get their problems solved without delay; others have to wait indefinitely.

4. Patronage rather than Policy. African countries do not have policy governments, but public institutions operating on the basis of patronage. These governments conduct their business not with a view to implementing officially agreed-upon policies, but look to rewarding individuals and groups that have shown exemplary loyalty or contributed to the political success of a government leader. In short, resources flow along very different paths than those that are identified in official statements, be that a policy announcement or the national budget. The result is that African governments tend to look to the past rather than to the future. To the extent that policies feature in politics, they are more often for window-dressing purposes than for real implementation.

5. Politics rather than Economics. African countries are only marginally incorporated into the global economy. The majority may participate in the market economy, but they are not so dependent on specific policies that they really care about what measures government takes. The strategy adopted by the majority of people in African countries is that of coping with whatever circumstances others create for them – despite the small margins within which they try to earn a living. Developing the right connections with people who can mediate on their behalf is part of this coping strategy. These conditions leave political leaders more interested in maximizing control than engaging in economic calculations; they are less interested in the cost and benefits or feasibility of specific measures that will turn competing private interests into a public policy that fosters national development. Because patronage rather than policy matters, economics does not inform politics the way that it does in countries that are more heavily integrated into the global economy, and thus more dependent on managing their economic relations with the rest of the world.

6. Informal rather than Formal Institutions. Because rule over people is important and patronage prevails, informal institutions tend to be particularly influential in African countries. Their influence permeates society and state alike. They manifest themselves at many different levels in the form of patron-client relations, charismatic leaders, political cliques, or individuals who regularly pool resources in order to get by. They exist side-by-side with formal institutions, but are typically so powerful that it is their self-regulating logic rather than such principles as transparency and public accountability that determine the conduct of state agencies. The extent to which formal institutions are being shaped by informal relations is sometimes a creative and, at other times, a subversive act. In other words, formal institutions may sometimes be mended in such a way that positive results occur. More common, however, is the opposite: Formal institutions tend to show negative performance as a result of the pervasive influence of informal institutions.

7. Concentration rather than Separation of Power. Much of the movement legacy that emerged as African countries struggled for independence lives on today in the sense that political mobilization rather than political pluralism dominates the minds of government leaders. They perceive themselves as involved in nation building for which purpose they want to minimize diversity of views and enhance unanimity. They often use their former colonial powers – or just the West – as an enemy in order to enhance the prospect of unity and agreement. This encourages a political setup in which the notion of separation of power is seen as undercutting nation building and development. Instead, they call for concentration of power and a limit on what others can ask from government leaders in terms of accountability. Even though many African countries have established public agencies that are expected to deal with improper conduct of power, these institutions remain under the control of the head of state and are more often used for damage control rather than independent inquiry.

8. *Control rather than Facilitation.* Political leaders in African countries are generally uncomfortable with critique of their performance. Some react more abrasively to such criticism than others, but they all differ only in degree. The idea that governments should facilitate diversification of views remains foreign to these leaders as does the concept that they should help build viable civil societies on whose inputs they could rely for effective policy making. Because politics is so personal and dependent on patronage, control of both public resources and views of people in power becomes more paramount than in countries in which objective criteria used in making policy serve a mediating purpose. Political compromise in African countries is never a victory – not even a half-victory – but always a sign of weakness that political leaders do not want to reveal. To maintain control, therefore, leaders need to be as restrictive as possible in allowing other views to bear on how they perform.

9. *Compliance rather than Deliberation.* In societies where so much of a person's welfare and security depends on relations with other people, the notion that such issues are open for discussion is foreign. There is no public debate that serves the purpose of identifying a public opinion in favor of or against a particular measure proposed or taken by government. To be sure, public media may open their spaces for different views on specific issues, but these debates do not end up in true policy deliberations. Members of the public are always inclined to, first of all, comply with measures by the authorities. If they cannot escape them, often possible with the help of informal relations, they may engage in spontaneous protest – a sign of frustration with the absence of a public dialogue. Civil society is difficult to build in African countries because there is little of a middle ground between protest action and official calls for compliance.

10. *External Dependency Growing rather than Declining.* In countries where the engagement with the global economy is as limited as it is in Africa, its significance is not taken as seriously in political circles as is the case in more developed countries, including the newly industrializing countries. African leaders, by and large, have not paid enough attention to their country's

relations with the rest of the world. They have taken only a limited interest in key international issues that affect their countries, notably those in the
context of the World Trade Organization. Their own economic management
at home has only exacerbated their marginal position in the world. The result
is that their countries have slipped further and further away from the rest of
the world. The untamed nature of politics has been costly to these countries
and the people trying to make a living there.

None of these propositions is written in stone. It is an empirical
question – and therefore an invitation to further research – to examine how
far they can be challenged by new facts. We know already in a tentative fashion that there may be variations among countries that is interesting enough
to suggest amendments or qualifications to the ten points I have just outlined. For instance, as suggested in this volume, are movements giving way
to political parties? Are parties getting formalized thus giving rise to a party
system? Are professional and economic points of view having more impact
than suggested here?

AFRICA'S UNTAMED POLITICS: A SUMMARY STATEMENT

These ten propositions are meant to convey a composite profile of politics
in Africa. They are the building blocks with which most scholars go about
making their arguments. They do differ, however, in terms of how they put
these blocks together. Not everyone argues the same way. Drawing on the
above consensus, I shall make my own summary statement that offers a
narrative story line that can be used for the rest of the discussion in this and
the next chapter.

Understanding politics in Africa begins by understanding society and
the continued presence of premodern features that determine behavior and
choice. Although the colonial powers tried to modernize African society,
they did not do enough of it. Furthermore, the heavy-handed and patronizing way in which they did so made Africans resist it. Thus, the nationalist
movements that came to power after independence tended to reject modernity as a colonial leftover. Instead, these movements embarked on restoring
and reinventing modes of organization and behavior that reflected African
society as they interpreted it to have been prior to colonization. This resulted
in the embedding of state institutions in society, and a personalization of
politics based on primary face-to-face reciprocities. This movement legacy
has been used over and over again by political leaders on the continent
ever since.

Africa's premodern features are a combination of structural underdevelopment and political choice. They are not historically inevitable, but are
sufficiently ingrained in society today to make modernization a serious challenge. Trust does not reach beyond face-to-face relations. In the African
context, money and expert systems have yet to effectively distanciate space

from place, that is, to allow for the sustained growth of secondary institutions that facilitate transactions across wider social distances. In the way politics is being conducted today there is little, if any, room for empathy and self-reflection. Criticism is perceived as personal rather than institutional. Blame is laid on circumstances beyond one's own control or on an enemy – real or perceived – that is responsible for anything gone wrong. Much political energy is devoted to defeating opponents. Politics, therefore, is typically a zero-sum game and conflicts abound.

In Africa's only partially modernized societies, a rational state apparatus reliant on rule and role compliance is still to emerge. Things public remain immersed in private transactions; state institutions are embedded in society. It is rarely clear where state ends and society begins or where things public become private. Because the state is not really an autonomous institution that acts in the public interest, policy analysis based on cost-benefit analysis or any other known technique is typically ignored in favor of political considerations that stem from the need to manage relations of affection. Politics, therefore, is less concerned with transaction than with transgression costs. Compliance is more important than dialogue, the result being that cost considerations in African countries fall upon the shoulders of external agencies – notably the World Bank – which probably would be much happier if they did not have to take on this responsibility. The lack of fit between the priorities of outside financial agencies, on the one hand, and national politicians, on the other, is a constant source of irritation. It leads to deadlocks in attempted reform processes.

Because there is no autonomous state civil society is also absent. There may be associational life in many African countries, but it still has to translate into a vigorous civil society that helps galvanize and organize public opinion. Where politics tends to have no limits, those with power will want to extend their control to as many corners of society as possible. They have no interest in facilitating the emergence of social forces that are independently challenging their position. Whereas African leaders may tolerate the existence of nongovernmental organizations, especially if they confine their activities to development, they are much less willing to let them organize public opinion. That becomes a political act and these leaders see that as a potential threat to their authority. Those who are not engaged in politics must subject themselves to their political leaders. The fewer individuals to manage in politics, the easier the task of sustaining stability and peace! At least, that is the way most African leaders approach the issue of governance.

Finally, conflicts in Africa abound not because of ethnicity, but because of the fluidity of social relations. It is perhaps the most deeply entrenched preconception about contemporary Africa that ethnic identities are strong and thus the cause of conflict. Scholars have reason to contribute to eliminating such misconceptions. Much has been done, but more can be achieved by adopting a transactive approach to ethnicity, which acknowledges the importance of the ascriptive component of ethnicity without falling into the trap of treating it as primordial. Ethnic identity in the context of a transactive approach is the product of social exchange. It springs out of the relationship between individuals and groups. This approach gives ethnicity the dynamic content that is needed to understand why it is not so deeply entrenched in the minds of individuals, yet gives rise to so many conflicts. By relying on such an approach, it also becomes possible to understand why ethnic conflicts in most instances never last very long and why reconciliation is possible. Conflicts that have lasted long in Africa are not purely ethnic; they are civil conflicts in which ethnicity may feature, but religion or another factor has been the determinant cause.

IMPLICATIONS FOR RESEARCH

The challenge to political science that politics in Africa poses is that it is empirically different enough from politics in other regions of the world to call into question the usefulness of mainstream analytical categories. This forces Africanists into either of three strategies while trying to pursue their research. One is to stay with the original concept; the second is to create a subtype that is more specific to the African cases; and the third is to invent new categories altogether. This volume has demonstrated the value and some of the frustrations associated with these three strategies.

The first of these strategies is the easy one in the sense that, intentionally or unintentionally, the researcher assumes away all the possible issues that arise when it comes to operationalizing key concepts. Rational choice theorists, like those relying on a neoinstitutionalist approach, use this approach, praising it for its parsimony. The model of man as a rational self-maximizing individual applies to every society; hence there is no need to worry about values and where they come from. Culture is externalized so as to make analysis easy. A similar issue arises in the study of democratization in which the model is taken straight out of Western textbooks about democracy and how it is meant to work. The assumptions that are made in studies that do not question the extent to which these are accurate or valid convey the image that the process of democratization follows a single and unilinear track. Yet another concept that is rather uncritically bandied about by political scientists – and many others – is civil society. It has typically become just another conceptual box for capturing all associational life outside the state. Very often it stretches as far as including private sector business enterprises. There is little or no attempt to problematize the concept; even to ask the basic question what "civil" really means in this context.

On balance, one can argue that every piece of research requires a trade-off between a manageable design and adequate attention to how well it captures empirical realities. It is necessary to externalize a number of variables that are potentially relevant. The question is really what is being externalized and how much of the possible explanatory equation it leaves out. The natural inclination when making such choices is to rely on variables that have been used by others. These earlier studies provide guidance as to what is important. Furthermore, by relying on their categories, comparison is facilitated. Thus, variables that are relevant in one region are readily borrowed in order to demonstrate the comparative potential of one's research. Too seldom is the hard question being asked on how well concepts travel across regions. Someone may, of course, object and argue that the answer to that question is possible to obtain only after the empirical research has been conducted. To the extent that a researcher in the field is sensitive to context and ready to adjust the research design, this may well happen, but far too often it does not. The researcher prefers to stay with a conceptual apparatus that has been worked out in advance and in the end allows for a statement about the comparative value of the study.

A preference for concepts that are assumed to be universally applicable leads to an unwitting conceptual stretching. Because a concept is not problematized in advance, researchers go into the field believing that what they are measuring, or assuming to be the motivation for behavior and choice, is beyond question. The framework for collecting and analyzing data remains pretty much unaltered; facts other than those collected within the framework do not count. This volume has demonstrated that narrow parameters and premises, while parsimonious, miss much of what is important. In the specific case of African politics, it is clear that assumptions about human behavior that are formalized into theory from Western culture at best allow for comparisons that are superficial and often misleading. It is precisely for this reason that political science needs its area specialists; people who, if nothing else, serve to correct the images that high-flying models of reality tend to convey.

If too many theorists in political science get away with conceptual stretching by not asking questions because they rely on a tight model based on strict assumptions, area specialists run into the opposite problem: stretching the concept too far! They tend to be too much driven by what they come across in the empirical realm. As they dig deeper and deeper they uncover so much detail that, in order to deal with it, they have to bend existing concepts in new directions. Collier and Levitsky (1997) discuss this problem at length using the concept of democracy to illustrate their points. The latter has acquired its precise meaning based on the experiences of Western Europe and North America. The basic subtypes of democracy, therefore, are, not surprisingly, presidential and parliamentary forms of democracy. With the growing interest in recent years in the issues of democratization, the challenge to students of political science has been the fact that these basic subtypes are not the most appropriate to capture what is happening in Latin America, Eastern Europe, or Africa. The inevitable result is that scholars have coined myriad diminished subtypes such as *illiberal*, *delegative*, and *electoral* democracy, implying that the countries that they study fall short of meeting the definitional requirements associated with any of the regular subtypes.

This means that we now have democracy with a virtually endless number of adjectives, each denominating a specific case or a small number of cases. This proliferation of adjectives attached to the basic concept of democracy is a manifestation of some empirical depth – and should be applauded from that perspective. The other side of this tendency, however, is to reduce comparability. The number of cases to which a given diminished subcategory of democracy applies is limited. There is a tendency to get stuck in area-specific studies. For instance, the tendency among Latin Americanists to invent these diminished subtypes has reinforced the area orientation at the expense of more broad-based comparisons. The few attempts to study the Latin American experience in comparative perspective, for example, Linz and Stepan (1996), have not really managed to transcend the limitations inherent in this area orientation. Comparing Eastern Europe with Latin America, using the latter as the conceptual and theoretical baseline, is a bold attempt but one that goes beyond the issues raised by the authors.

Political science needs both general theory and diminished subtypes to deal with the full complexity of the subject matter. Sometimes, however, the question arises whether either of these strategies works. If the premises of general theory are too narrow or the area orientation too deeply embedded in an empirical richness, there is a reason for coining new concepts to stimulate reflection and rethinking more broadly. The economy of affection is a case in point. The assumption on which it rests – that individuals do not typically make decisions as fully autonomous persons but rather in an interdependent fashion in which relations to other people matters – is, of course, not completely new. In fact, it can be taken out of game theory by which the notion of iterative games implies that individuals make decisions in the light of what they know about other actors. The face-to-face context of direct reciprocities rests on the notion that people do have enough information about each other to make a deal without having first to sign a contract. At a time when scholars are preoccupied with the notion of transaction costs, adverse selection, and moral hazard, it is clear that human behavior, as conceived in the economy of affection, is sufficiently different to warrant a separate conceptualization; it carries no transaction costs at the microlevel. The real transaction costs – and they are considerable – occurs at the macrolevel as discussed in Chapter Five. Relying on dyadic networks of clientelistic relations requires heavy monitoring and significant risks if selection is adverse. It is precisely because there are no transaction costs at the microlevel that individuals act rationally within the economy of affection. It is perhaps the most important explanation for the reason that states in Africa have become rentier states. Ruling an African country does not lend itself to the kind of economistic considerations on which much of NIE rests. The political costs of rule in Africa cannot be ignored. They are in most instances a prerequisite for political stability. African actors know it because they operate in an economy of affection context. Foreign advisors have no or little personal experience of the costs associated with reliance of direct reciprocities. They treat anything other than what their own model informs them as constraints that must be removed.

The economy of affection is by no means confined to Africa. The shortcut that is often provided by informal institutions based on direct reciprocities is tempting anywhere. As suggested in Chapter Four, it can be found in every society. Latin Americanists will recognize it in the form of political clientelism and attempts to seek favors, for example, the *jeitinho* phenomenon in Brazil. Middle Eastern scholars will find the economy of affection manifesting itself in many of the social institutions of Islam. It will also have a familiar ring to scholars of Asian societies who study corruption in government and informal practices that shape both politics and management in countries like China and Japan (Fukuyama 1995). Scholars of American society and politics will find the phenomenon in many different contexts, for example, in the prevalence of illegal migrants and their mode of existence, the unofficial transfer of money by Cuban-Americans in Florida to their relatives and friends on the island, and so forth. Scholars of European politics will also be familiar with informal practices that stem from a state that is often too intrusive or regulatory. Immigrant minorities in the welfare states of northern Europe are often forced to lead a life in which direct reciprocities become a necessary part of coping with day-to-day challenges to their existence. Citizens in European countries often fall back on informal deals to escape the heavy burden of paying taxes on services and other types of transactions. In short, people everywhere can associate with some, if not all, the aspects of an economy of affection.

The concept encounters a problem in current literature, which is so heavily influenced by democratization, good governance, and development: What it stands for is typically condemned and, at best, treated as constraint. As this volume has suggested, however, informal institutions based on face-to-face reciprocities are on the rise. It poses a new challenge to researchers in political science and related disciplines. A sharper focus on the economy of affection and the many informal institutions that it gives rise to is justified. Its prevalence in Africa makes the region a natural starting point for such a new research frontier, hence the attempt in this volume to highlight what the economy of affection is all about, how it is best theorized, and how it empirically manifests itself in informal behaviors and institutions.

AREA STUDIES AND POLITICAL SCIENCE

Nowhere is the tension between contextuality and comparability greater than in the study of comparative politics. That is the way it should be, but it means that many political scientists who are active in other fields within the discipline rarely have an opportunity to experience what this tension is all about; what its full dimensions are. The discipline has become increasingly specialized. Students get only a one-dimensional and thus very partial view of the whole subject matter. This is not only the result of the disaggregation of the discipline into fields or subfields. It is also because some professors and departments, serving as gatekeepers in the discipline, only allow their graduate students to learn what in their view is the most powerful model, theory, or method. This tendency for the discipline to become balkanized is exacerbated by the increased reliance on existing data sets. Students of politics easily become immune to the empirical richness that the subject matter offers.

The fervent but sometimes blind search for empirical regularities makes sense in situations where rule-oriented behavior prevails because of the existence of strong formal institutions. Thus, for instance, it can be fruitfully applied to the study of voting behavior in legislative chambers, especially where party loyalties are strong or ideological divisions predict such behavior. The use of formal models to study legislatures may sometimes be an overkill, because much of what they predict would have been possible to anticipate without so much theoretical fuzz. In fact, in many studies that aim to find regularities in political behavior, the most interesting – and sometimes overlooked – aspect of the findings may be the exceptions – those who do not behave as predicted by the model. After all, the very essence of politics is not regularity or precision, but contestation and ambiguity. Capturing those manifestations in formal models is like trying to catch a fly with the help of a lion cage.

Comparative politics continues to rely on real empirical fieldwork to an extent that students of American politics and international relations do not. Thus, relatively speaking, there is much more sensitivity to empirical variation and the challenges that it poses to the field. There is a healthy tension between studies that draw on historical sociology to explain particular phenomena and those cross-sectional studies that try to generalize across national and cultural boundaries. It is the mutual respect among quantitatively and qualitatively oriented scholars in the field that has given comparative politics its strength. In fact, many scholars realize that relying on one method alone is often limiting the conclusions that can be drawn. Diversity, or pluralism, in approaches to the study of politics is strength, not weakness.

It is in this context that the study of politics in Africa best fits. Time has come to answer the question of what contribution scholars devoted to this topic have made to the discipline of political science, in general, and the field of comparative politics, in particular. Others may have different things in mind, but I believe that in addition to highlighting the significance of informal institutions, the contribution can be divided into four principal parts: (a) the need for problematizing the premises of theoretical models, (b) reliance on multiple methods of data collection, (c) raising the issue of how we study power, and (d) showing the value of political sociology.

Africanists, more than most other area specialists, are sensitive to what they perceive as the limits of general theory or models that presuppose universal applicability. To be sure, there are those who may ignore this issue, but the majority of Africanist scholars would start any investigation with a skeptical view about the extent to which a purportedly general theory or model may apply in their context. This skepticism is healthy and one reason why Africanists have something to offer. Most scholars studying African politics do not outright reject the theoretical ambition to be comparative beyond the boundaries of their own region, but it has become the hallmark of much of the scholarly work on Africa that theoretical premises have to be questioned in advance. Students need to demonstrate that a concept or a theory is relevant for their study, and it is working not just because some other comparativist studying some other region of the world has effectively applied it. This often rather scattered search for theoretical guidance in the field of comparative politics is not enough. Researchers need to demonstrate why a particular concept fits the realities in their particular region. This applies, for instance, to the study of democracy and democratization. With specific reference to Buganda in Uganda, Karlstrom (1996) has demonstrated that the local image and understanding of democracy – *eddembe ery'obunty* – differs significantly from the Western concept. It reflects a long political tradition within the kingdom of Buganda that emphasizes civil liberties – including civil conduct by both ruler and ruled – much more than the political rights and institutions that Westerners associate with democracy. It refers more to freedom from political disorder and the notion that ruler and ruled are engaged in reciprocal rights and responsibilities. Schaffer (1998) has taken the idea of comparing the concept of democracy further by examining what the Wolofs in Senegal and the Chinese mean by the concept. The former have no special local word for it, but use *demokaraasi*. The connotations in the local language, however, are again quite different from the conventional Western meaning. Like the Buganda, the Wolofs emphasize a form of hierarchical egalitarianism based on shared responsibilities between ruler and ruled, but it also encompasses a wide range of interactions among kin and community members. Africans may be excused for being "confused democrats" as they reveal contradictory interpretations of the concept when answering survey questions using standard Western categories (Anonymous 2004b). Their notion, in short, is not formalized into a set of specific institutions that operate to ascertain public participation in elections and other such formal settings. The Chinese, finally, use *minshu* – rule by the people – to talk about democracy. It reflects the Confucian legacy in which the emphasis lies on the innate potential harmony of human beings and, therefore, the responsibility of rulers to ensure it. The concept recognizes political participation as important, but sees it first and foremost as a way of building national unity. It is interesting that in recent history the concept of *minshu* has been effectively used by rulers like Mao and Deng, but also the students who demonstrated against the regime in 1989. Concepts that exist simultaneously in both academic and popular discourse, such as democracy, becomes particularly problematic, but the need for checking on the local understanding of specific concepts is an integral part of any good comparative research. The premises on which many theories rest often need to be relaxed in order to offer a better relation between theory and facts.

This leads to the second contribution that Africanists are particularly prone to make to the discipline: the advantages of relying on more than a single method for data collection. The use of surveys in African countries is fraught with a number of difficulties, some of which have been noted in previous chapters. Sampling is difficult because civil administration data are nonexistent or unreliable, even in urban areas, where the majority live in dwellings without registration. The meaning of concepts in local settings varies. It becomes necessary, therefore, to follow up with more qualitative investigations to get a perspective on what specific answers may really mean. Furthermore, people are not used to being interviewed in private. Westerners typically believe that interviewing someone in private generates more openness and personal easiness. The standard requirements of American universities for conducting interviews with human subjects are all aimed at securing confidentiality.

The social context in Africa, and probably in other societies around the world, often calls for the opposite. People in African societies are used to telling their opinion in public (read: community forums), but are reluctant to speak to foreigners in private. To be sure, women, for instance, may find that speaking out in public is more controversial when men are present, but such reservations notwithstanding, there is more openness also among women in community settings than what typically takes place in a personal interview setting. In the latter, the interviewee is not necessarily going to be more nervous, but he – or she – will be inclined to answer questions to suit what he believes the interviewer wants to hear. Even when such an attitude does not prevail, survey respondents are likely to provide answers that do not correspond to what they really do, because the latter is so much more shaped by the social interdependencies in which they find themselves. For instance, asking people in Africa about whom they would vote for in an election usually bears little correspondence to what really happens at the polls. The average African voter is not bound by commitment to a particular ideology or political party, and will vote on the basis of criteria that have more to do with the tangible benefits any one candidate can offer on or around the day of election.

Even if this may sound like an overgeneralization, the point is that without relying on other means to collect data than a survey instrument, the findings may be far off the mark. This is not unique to Africa. The exit polls in the 2004 presidential election in the United States raise the question also about the reliability of such surveys in a country where they are the standard data collection instruments. It is not difficult – for ideological or other reasons – to advise people to give the pollsters a particular reason for voting while, in fact, the motive was different and certainly more complex. There has long been a rather innocent view of the role of survey respondents: They will tell the truth and full truth because they are protected by confidentiality. The African experience calls this into question for a variety of reasons, but, as the recent U.S. election exit polls indicate, there is reason to be more circumspect. Triangulation, that is, the use of multiple methods to collect data, is not only a safer way of finding these data; it is also more rewarding from an educational point of view.

The third contribution by students of politics in Africa concerns the way we approach the concept of power. Power is typically perceived as vested in offices, institutions, or structures. The mainstream approach presupposes the existence of a system of corporate actors – private or public – with power stemming from their ability to get others to do what they would not otherwise have done. Corporations get us to buy things because of campaigns aimed at convincing the consumers that their respective products are the best. Government agencies force us to avoid certain things through regulations, for example, driving under the influence of alcohol. They also compel us to pay taxes even though many citizens would prefer not to do so – at least not the amount that they are being asked to pay. The exercise of much of this power is viewed as legitimate, however, because in countries with a consolidated system of democratic governance, citizens understand that they have obligations in exchange for their rights. Thus, even if they grumble, the notion of a negotiated social contract between government and citizens helps legitimize the exercise of power.

In societies, like those in Africa, where the presence of corporate institutions is weak and informal relations prevail, power is more meaningfully studied as a manifestation of relations of dependence. As discussed in Chapter Four, these relations are typically nonnegotiated, but rely on a tacit understanding that individuals entering into a relationship with each other do so with an expectation of reciprocating. In a situation where this relationship is chosen by two persons with roughly the same need for the good that brings them together in the first place, there is no real exercise of power. Such a symmetrical relationship leaves both with a mutual satisfaction without leaving the impression that one person got the better of the other. Relations of mutual dependence, however, are more often asymmetrical; that is, one person needs the good more urgently or strongly than the other. This leaves the latter with an advantage when it comes to setting the terms for the relationship. Even though, as we have seen in the economy of affection context, reciprocity is expected, people with a power advantage can, if they so decide, do so at their own discretion much later. For instance, the concept of free-riding loses its meaning in the economy of affection because patrons are only too happy to provide goods to their clients in a benevolent fashion. The exercise of power in the context of informal institutions, therefore, is much more dependent on personal idiosyncrasies. That is why understanding the exercise of power in the context of social exchange theory makes sense; outside Africa, too, this theory has potential applicability to many contexts where informal institutions are important.

The study of power in the context of social exchange relations has its own problems in terms of deciding the parameters of measuring influence and changes in behavior. If, for instance, A spends a lot of time and energy to convince B and eventually succeeds in doing so, should one completely discount the costs that A incurred in exercising power? Such questions and other related problems notwithstanding, the study of power in such contexts of interdependence is important for understanding what really happens in formal settings not only in Africa, but also elsewhere. It allows us to transcend the limitations inherent in the notion that power in organizations is unilateral and hierarchical. It should also make us more skeptical about the notion that the exercise of power is always exploitative or a zero-sum game. In the African context, as suggested in previous chapters, there is evidence that economy of affection failures, that is, the dishonoring of a reciprocal agreement, may lead to zero-sum outcomes but, in most instances, reciprocal relations tend to have the effect of reducing the notion that there are victors and victims (Baldwin 1978). This view of power alerts us to the fact that asymmetrical relations in the context of an economy of affection are not symptomatic of naked power, but rather evidence of legitimate power, that is, authority. In short, the informal exercise of power provides a basis for authority that, in the African context, formal institutions do not. It is an empirical issue to find out how much this is applicable also in many other places.

This does not mean that exchange relations in the economy of affection are always positive, beneficial, and pleasant. There is no "merrie" Africa implied in what is being said above. The economy of affection, like any other political economy, has its positive as well as negative sides. Disaffection is the equivalent in the economy of affection to what conventional economics calls market failures and political scientists have referred to as government or state failures, that is, the inability of these institutions to perform their roles in line with stated objectives. What the emphasis on power as seen through the lens of social exchange offers, finally, is a realization that the exercise of power is associated with its own costs that cannot be measured against a standard like money. In this respect, the current interest in getting development done through institutions that are subject to the pruning of NIE often goes wrong. Because these calculations are made in economic terms with no regard for political rationales, they tend to cause opposition among local actors. Such has been the experience in Africa, Latin America, and many Asian countries where this solution has been attempted with too little attention paid to political factors.

The fourth contribution is the emphasis that the study of politics in Africa places on political sociology. Many researchers in the discipline have got used to thinking of political economy – for example, in the form of rational choice or neoinstitutionalism – as the most appropriate way of studying politics. This type of political economy, however, presupposes the prevalence of economic thinking in the sense of careful calculations of ends–means relations with regard to utilitarian objectives. Rationality has become associated with autonomous choice and the assumption that it has no consequences for the next choice the same person makes. The economy of affection through its various informal institutions demonstrates that behavior can be rational in a utilitarian sense even though it takes into account the implications of choice for other people. It is a form of bounded rationality, although to make the distinction between Herbert Simon's original use of the term and what is going on in the economy of affection, it may be better referred to as embedded rationality. It does not lend itself to the same neat model of *homo economicus* but it shows that in every society where informal institutions exist, behavior and choice are often driven by a rationality that takes into account social implications. Political sociology stresses the importance of social relations as vested with power. It highlights the fact that behavior and choice are embedded in these relations.

The distinction between culture and economy that rational choice and neoinstitutionalism makes needs to be challenged. The social embeddedness of institutions is more often the rule than the exception not only in Africa, but also in many other settings. The question arises, therefore, where the line between the two concepts really goes. The study of the economy of affection demonstrates that the premises on which formal political economy rests are far too narrow. Experience shows that they have to be relaxed in order to better correspond to what is going on in regions like Africa, Asia, and Latin America. Culture, therefore, cannot be so easily dismissed, but needs to be problematized in the sense that if it is the foundation on which not only formal but also informal institutions rise, how do we actually go about handling culture? Can the informal be formalized and, if so, how? Should we accept that things informal cannot be reduced to a single formal theory? Must we pursue them on the assumption that, at best, we can identify a series of conditions as possible explanatory variables behind the rise of informal institutions? The study of African politics, therefore, asks others to think of the extent to which their own model of how people act really captures what is going on in their respective political contexts.

POLITICS AND DEVELOPMENT IN AFRICA

The remainder of this concluding chapter will be devoted to what academics and other influential actors have had to say about the development implications of politics in Africa. The first section will highlight three different positions that exist in the literature and the debate about the African predicament: (a) Africa is best off left alone, (b) the rest of the world must show greater sympathy for the African predicament, and (c) Africa has no choice but to follow the prescriptions of the neoliberal paradigm that currently dominates the international development agenda. This section is meant to set the stage for the discussion in the final chapter where some more practical policy issues will be addressed.

Africa Is Best Off Left Alone

There are two schools of thought that both argue that Africa is best off left alone, one idealist, another postmodernist. The first argues that Africa needs to rid itself of its colonial or neocolonial legacy. The second makes the point that Africa works – in its own ways. The problem, therefore, is the attempt by donors to force African countries to adopt values and institutions that are foreign to these societies.

The idealists start from the premise that Africa will and can develop through the effort of its own people, as Rodney (1973) argued in his analysis of how Europe underdeveloped Africa. Colonialism subverted the indigenous institutions and true independence means restoring their significance. Other authors have written in the same vein without necessarily sharing Rodney's Marxist-Leninist mode of analysis. Ayittey (1991) devoted a whole volume to pointing out the broad range of indigenous institutions of potential relevance for contemporary Africa. He discusses the way that some West African kingdoms were constituted with checks and balances and how in some societies it was possible to "destool" a chief who had not performed satisfactorily in the eyes of his subjects. He refers to the democratic and egalitarian nature of the political system of the Igbo people in eastern Nigeria. Another interesting point of reference is his attempt to draw constitutional lessons from Africa's empires for contemporary efforts to create an African Union – or confederation, as Ayittey calls it. The same concern about greater use of indigenous institutions to transform Africa is expressed in a multidisciplinary volume edited by Robinson and Skinner (1983). The background of their argumentation was the estrangement that many Africans felt with their own leaders. They saw them as still wedded to neocolonial ideas that blinded these leaders to more relevant approaches inherent in African society and politics. This frustration led to a call for a second liberation and a strategy to put it into practice, led by a group of intellectuals and prominent politicians (Hammarskjold Foundation 1987; Ayittey 1992). This is also reflected in the writings of Osabu-Kle (2000), who argues for a democracy compatible with the African cultural environment. What make this group idealists is the scale of their project. They are not satisfied with incremental improvements. They call for a full transformation of the way governments conduct their affairs, an expectation that even in the euphoria of democratization in the early 1990s has appeared unrealistic.

The postmodernist approach is perhaps most closely associated with the position taken by Chabal and Daloz (1999), in which they suggest that there is nothing wrong with Africa – it works. What they have in mind is not that it succeeds within the parameters of conventional development thinking. They are arguing instead that Africa works within a set of well-recognized norms of political practice that do not conform to those we find elsewhere. More specifically, their point is that politics in Africa turns on the instrumentalization of disorder. Leaders benefit from it and have no real incentive to work for a more institutionalized order of society. They even go as far as suggesting that economic reforms aimed at reducing the size of the state – and thereby the opportunities for rent – have been counterproductive. By limiting the means needed to sustain neopatrimonialism, the tendency to link politics to disorder, be it war or crime, has increased.

Their conclusion rests to a considerable degree on the same analysis that has been made in this volume. They argue that individual rationality is essentially based on a communal logic. Relations of power are predicated on the shared belief that the political is communal. Second, they maintain that the logic, political or not, lies in what it induces by way of expectations of reciprocity between the parties involved. For instance, the process of voting in a multiparty election must be understood as part of largely informal relations of political exchange that impinge directly on the electoral outcome. Thus, people will vote for a certain political party, not because of its principles or policies but because of its perceived ability to deliver on expected patrimonial promises. Their third point is that vertical, personalized relations drive the logic of the political system. It is not just that politics are swayed by personal considerations or that the personal is manipulated for political reasons. They go further by stressing that the overall purpose of politics is to affect the nature of such personal relations. In short, the aim of the political elites is not just to gather power, but also to use the resources that come with it to buy the affection of their people. The fourth point is that what counts in

Africa are not the productive investments associated with a protestant ethic, but the immediate display of material gain, that is, consumption rather than production. Ostentation remains a virtue in African politics as long as it is associated with redistributing resources and benefits to clients. In this kind of situation, politicians do not see any real need for engaging the population in debates about the changes required to achieve a higher rate of economic growth or a more sustained development in the country. Fifth, they point to the dominance of the micro- over the macroperspective. The political system can only work if it meets its obligations continuously. Its legitimacy rests with its immediate achievements, not its long-term ambitions. Politicians have an interest in new projects that they can point to as patrons of their clients, but they ignore the maintenance and management that are necessary to make the activity sustainable in the longer run. Further, there is no interest among clients in this kind of political system to accept sacrifices for more ambitious national goals (Chabal and Daloz 1999:156–62).

From a developmental perspective, neither the idealist nor the postmodernist version of leaving Africa alone is helpful. The former option falls on practical grounds; the latter on moral ones. Africa today is as much part of an increasingly interdependent world as any other region even if its links are fragile. Going it alone is out of the question, especially for countries as poor as those in Africa. Thus, we have to dismiss both of these two approaches to the African predicament as unfeasible.

Make the World Serve Africa's Needs

This position is often taken by African political leaders, individually or together in forums such as the African Union. They would argue that the rest of the world, especially the current global economy, is stacked against Africa. In international negotiations, therefore, African leaders engage in politicking aimed at changing the terms of trade and other key variables to their advantage. Realizing that they do not have much clout on their own in such forums, they often seek the support of other countries outside the capitalist core. They tend to overlook the fact that leaders of these other countries, for example, Brazil, China, or India, have their own interests to defend and promote. Adding the cause of African countries may not harm them, but it is not their priority. Instead of considering the economic interest of their respective countries, or the region as such, these leaders engage in acts of political solidarity – typically against the West – in what amounts to no more than political posturing. Their attempt to get the world to treat Africa more generously, therefore, ends up being more rhetorical than practical.

To be sure, there are examples of African leaders having played important and constructive roles in international forums. References were made in

Chapter Ten to the role that Tanzania's first president, Julius Nyerere, played in negotiations about a new international economic order in the 1970s. The conditions thirty years ago, however, were quite different. Socialism was viewed as a viable alternative to capitalism and the superpowers were courting the developing countries for support. Such opportunities do not exist today. There is only one superpower; only one viable economic system; and, above all, countries in other developing regions have embraced modernity and left African countries further behind. The African voice in the international community has become increasingly faint.

It has not been easy for Africa's leaders to accept these new conditions. To those, like Robert Mugabe of Zimbabwe, who have been around for a long time and remember the golden 1970s when the liberation cause was still engaging people around the globe, the adjustment has proved especially painful. They continue to believe that they are right and the rest of the world, especially the United States and the EU, are wrong. In a populist fashion, they try to rhetorically seize the moral high ground while often ignoring the extent to which political practice diverges from their verbal statements. Where politics is untamed, there is no need to reflect on the extent to which political behavior is in accordance with specific rules. Leaders are not under pressure to adhere to a set of self-binding rules as the case is where rule of law or constitutionalism prevails. They do not look at themselves in the mirror, so to speak, to get a perspective on their own behavior and choices. Self-reflection, leave alone self-criticism, is generally absent in these situations.

It is only with a lot of reluctance that African leaders more recently have adopted the idea that they should allow their systems of governance to be the subject of peer review. The New Partnership for Africa's Development (NEPAD), the brainchild of South Africa's president, Thabo Mbeki, is an attempt to allow African governments to take a greater responsibility for the continent's predicament. The international donor agencies take a positive view toward this initiative, but they have made it clear that their assistance will be tied to the willingness of African governments to subject themselves to the peer review mechanism. A few governments have indicated their willingness to accept some form of review of their way of conducting politics, but they seem to have chosen this option as a way of gaining some control of the review process rather than allowing it to proceed under more independent auspices. In countries where the state is not institutionally autonomous and thus there are formal rules that matter, meaningful reviews of governance practices become difficult. Furthermore, they are not likely to be openly debated in public. Political leaders will sift through any possible criticism that these reviews generate. Whether they will really heed any of it, however, is uncertain.

Julius Nyerere, reflecting on the African predicament shortly before his death, suggested that Africa lacks an economic engine in the region similar to the role that Japan played in Asia or the United States has played vis-à-vis Latin America. African governments could have chosen Europe to serve in that position but, for understandable reasons, they have found it hard to accept their former colonial masters for that role. Only the former French colonies have come close to letting the former colonial power dominate their economies, but France is neither the United States nor Japan when it comes to economic power. Furthermore, the conditions in African countries are not as congenial for sustained economic development as they are in Asia and Latin America. As this volume has indicated, one major hurdle is politics. President Mbeki and many other South Africans who may be concerned about the region's future realize this, but have great difficulty in convincing fellow leaders in other countries to make their style of governance more congenial for investments and other measures that are necessary for a sustained economic development.

One can conclude that African governments have too little clout in international forums and are rarely sufficiently well informed and prepared for global negotiations to enhance the national interest of their respective countries. Thus, the idea that the international community will change its own behavior to suit the needs of Africa is, at best, wishful thinking. It is in this light that the NEPAD initiative must be seen. It is an attempt to demonstrate that African governments are ready to take a greater responsibility for their own affairs in the hope that this will also generate more matching contributions from various agencies and governments in the international community. Many observers view NEPAD as a step in the right direction, but as long as politics remains untamed, chances of realizing its promise are dim. The burden falling on South Africa to help put NEPAD's ideals into practice certainly is heavy.

No Choice but the Neoliberal Paradigm

The problem facing African governments today is that if they do not take NEPAD seriously, the pressures from the donor agencies in the international development community to comply with the demands for economic and political reforms will only increase. Although the Washington Consensus in the beginning of the twenty-first century has been considerably watered down and there is more concern about poverty alleviation than twenty years ago, the neoliberal paradigm of economic development is still paramount at the global level. There is no viable alternative in sight. Thus, African governments have no real choice but to live with the tenets of neoliberalism, even if they do not embrace the paradigm.

Because the neoliberal paradigm comes with political conditionalities these days, it is understandably controversial. African leaders continue to see the task of relieving their countries from external domination as priority number one. Demands to improve governance along principles practiced in consolidated democracies, therefore, are treated as undue interference in their internal affairs. Some leaders are more sensitive to this than others, but they are generally all concerned about the costs to their personal legitimacy if they appear to fail standing up to those that set conditionalities for their development assistance.

A couple of African governments have demonstrated that it is possible to make progress within the parameters of a capitalist economy. Botswana and Mauritius have moved to the top of the African development league because of a consistent approach to development that includes identifying their comparative advantage in the international economy and a readiness to compete in the global marketplace. These governments have not shunned foreign advice, but have done their best to make it work for their own causes. Furthermore, they have been able to create an institutional environment in which policy can function and matter.

Virtually all other governments in Africa have been much more reluctant to appropriate foreign advice. To be sure, international finance institutions and donor agencies have usually been able to identify first-rate professionals to work with in preparing policy strategies. The problem is that these international agencies have operated as if it is policy that matters; they do not realize that government leaders make their decisions on grounds other than policy prescriptions. Even if these leaders do not officially oppose the particular advice they get, they do not incorporate it into their final decisions. The result is that the majority of African countries continue to lack the institutional mechanisms that allow for a sustained economic development. When diplomats and representatives of these international development agencies point to the need for a better governance setup, government leaders in Africa will typically listen and agree at a rhetorical level, but ignore the necessary follow-up. They find excuses to explain why, in the end, agreements with the donors never get implemented. In societies where leaders have so little control of the policy environment in the first place, it is not hard to make these excuses quite convincingly.

Because the international finance institutions and bilateral donor agencies provide such a large share of the national budgets in African countries – in most places over half the development budget – it is no surprise that they become concerned when policies are not fully implemented and results fail to show up. Wherever this assistance is misappropriated, bilateral donors threaten withdrawal and, in some cases, act on this threat. The international finance institutions cannot withdraw – even if there are good reasons for it – because African governments are members of these institutions. IMF and the World Bank, therefore, continue to be involved and often take the lead in coordinating development assistance in these countries. The latter, in particular, tends to take an upbeat view of the situation as soon as statistical indicators show positive signs. Because it often sees itself as the catalyst for raising support for specific development projects and programs, the spin in their official statements is usually overly optimistic.

In sum, the problem with the external aid agencies is manifold. As will be further discussed in Chapter Twelve, they have a superficial view of the social realities in the African countries. They fail to understand how politics functions. They are often too impatient, more ready to adhere to their own operational parameters than the needs and capacities of African institutions. Thus, even if the African governments often engage in cat-and-mouse games with these agencies, the donors rarely realize that they are as much part of the problem as the solution to the African quandary discussed in this book.

CONCLUSIONS

Two conclusions seem appropriate to draw from the discussions in this chapter. The first is that by being different in many respects, the African continent poses a challenge to the study of politics that the field of comparative politics continues to adjust to. This chapter has identified some of the reasons for taking Africa seriously. The study of politics in Africa challenges dominant theories and methodological assumptions in ways that are relevant to other regions of the world, including the United States. Africa, therefore, is not marginal but is quite central to the concerns of the discipline. By providing a perspective on politics that is different from the mainstream, it opens up insights into how we do political science that must be constantly open to scrutiny and, therefore, change.

The second conclusion is that the study of politics in Africa invites a holistic and reflective look at what we are doing. Formal theory and mathematical modeling is sometimes regarded as the ultimate frontier of the discipline. The reductionist ambitions of such approaches, however, easily become self-defeating because they deny the very essence of the subject matter they study. Whereas such theorizing and modeling may apply to some real-life situations, they are not the more pertinent and interesting from a broader perspective of the discipline. As the study of politics in Africa – but also in other regions – demonstrates, political science needs better understanding to become more effective in predicting. It requires not only its own mechanics, but also its own inventive and reflective engineers who can help redefine the issues and pave the way for the mechanics. Political science is at its best when it combines the insights from different approaches and different regions. With the growing interest in informal institutions, Africa's place in the discipline should be further enhanced.

For members of the discipline of political science, and especially those engaged in the field of comparative politics, Africa remains a challenge. The debate will continue about how much its politics is adequately understood within the conceptual frames that currently dominate scholarship. The empirical realities in the region will also call for attention to new phenomena such as informal institutions that are important beyond their own geographical boundaries. Africa certainly has the potential of enriching the work on political choice and behavior by showing that not only formal but also informal institutions matter.

12

Quo Vadis Africa?

Where Africa may be heading – the question asked in the title of this chapter – is an issue that has become increasingly urgent and important to Africans and outsiders alike. The vast majority of Africans are no better off than their parents were. Despite struggling hard to make a living, they are caught in webs of relations of dependence that are becoming more and more costly to sustain. Those who really wish to break out of these affective relations are frustrated because there is no formal and predictable system in place to do so. Foreign investors and aid agencies share much of that frustration. They want to contribute, but their funds become constant prey to well-placed individuals – investment partners or public officials – for whom they constitute an attractive opportunity to make a quick gain. Even donors who have maintained a constant optimism about Africa and the difference that their own contributions can make have become increasingly skeptical about the future. For instance, after decades of espousing an almost unbounded optimism regarding the prospects of policy reform, the World Bank (2000) is now questioning whether Africa will really be able to "claim the twenty-first century."

Although they may come at the answer from different directions, when asked today about the root of the problem that the region faces, Africans and foreigners increasingly tend to share the view that it is politics. The political sphere long held the promise of a better future for locals as well as foreigners. By Africanizing it and thus making it more in tune with local values and priorities, everyone thought politics was the solution to Africa's postcolonial predicament. As I have tried to demonstrate, politics is part of both the problem and the solution.

It should be clear from the previous chapters that political science is central to any attempt at dealing with the serious predicament in which Africa finds itself. The knowledge that colleagues in the discipline have accumulated about Africa and which I have used to make my own arguments about the current situation is crucial to any such task. So far, most of this knowledge has not been utilized. African governments do not really reflect on their own shortcomings. Donor governments have tended to treat development as something that must be modeled in economic and social policies; they do not pay much attention to whether these policies will ever acquire some political traction of their own. Recent interest in governance and political reform has been more prescriptive than analytical, often just compelling African actors to adopt Western principles of governance without thinking about how well – or badly – they fit into local political processes. In short, there has been little serious political analysis by those who have to date set the development agenda for the many countries of the region.

This chapter begins by providing a brief review of what policy analysts have had to say about Africa and its prospects for development, especially since the 1980s and 1990s when economic and political reforms were introduced. The chapter continues to examine more critically the main assumptions underlying the NIE. It ends by providing some ideas of what a political science–based approach to reform in Africa would look like if the findings presented in this volume are taken seriously.

THE ROLE OF DONORS

Donors continue to play an important role in the development scene in Africa. Although there was a slight downturn in the flow of aid to Africa in the 1990s, it has increased. This is partly in light of the needs to deal with Africa's problems, partly in response to greater confidence that donors have in the commitment of African governments – at least, in some – in bringing about policy reforms and thus accelerating the process of development out of poverty. The Millenium Development Goals (MDGs) program of the UN is likely to allow development assistance to continue at its current level. In fact, the recommendation in 2005 is to drastically increase the aid to Africa in the next ten years on the assumption that such front-loading would enable these countries to make a significant leap forward and, in the long run, reduce their dependence on the program. If anything, therefore, the role of the donors appears that it will be significant for at least the next ten years, possibly beyond.

Even though foreign aid has become an integral part of the African development scene, its role and character has changed over the years. The first part of this section will be devoted to a brief overview of how it has shifted. The second part considers the question of what difference foreign aid makes to individual African countries.

Changes in Foreign Aid

The role that foreign aid has played in Africa reflects the changes that have taken place in theorizing about development. Thus in the 1960s, when it began in earnest, the emphasis was on project aid that would serve as a catalyst for interventions aimed at complementing domestic African efforts. Although the idea was that capital and expertise would make a difference, the perspective on aid was that it would not be needed except for an interim – albeit unspecified – time.

During the 1970s, donors realized that foreign aid was there to stay. Therefore, it had to be planned and managed at a higher level. Projects were too scattered and lacked the necessary forward and backward linkages necessary to make the wheels of the whole economy turn. By planning a concerted effort at the sector level, donors assumed that in collaboration with African governments, they could reduce poverty. Much greater emphasis, therefore, was laid on administration of rather complex programs, for example, integrated rural development initiatives.

During these two decades of project and program assistance, donor countries dispatched their own experts to work side by side with Africans in various advisory – occasionally executive – capacities. They were all busy on what was perceived as the frontline of development, obtaining valuable field and country experience that they could eventually use in planning development assistance projects and programs in the headquarters of their agency. They had a personal perception of what it meant to work in these countries, and the difficulties the realities in the African countries often posed to success. Although there were the odd exceptions, the interesting thing about this generation of aid workers is that despite hardship and difficulties (or was it because of them?), they retained a great measure of moral and political enthusiasm about their role. It is this generation, now gradually disappearing from the scene, that has been largely responsible for administering development assistance in the past two decades.

In their capacity as planners and administrators, they have overseen a shift away from donor involvement in what may be called the downstream of the policy process, that is, program and project implementation, toward a much greater concern with policy and governance issues. This shift has been especially marked in the lack of support in recent years for agricultural production or research on crop and technology issues relating to advancing African agriculture. These upstream issues do not require field experience. They are essentially issues that call for analytical skills. The result is that the second generation of aid workers is more generalist in orientation. The economics profession has taken the lead, but has been supplemented by others. Lawyers and political scientists for example, use their skills to analyze and evaluate policy interventions aimed at liberalizing the economy and enhancing the institutional capacity of government. These people may have had the occasional field experience, but it is not a requisite for their job. They are at least one step removed from African realities and typically work with models or policy designs that are meant to apply to any country. They get their kick not from solving a practical problem in hands-on fashion in an African country, but rather from hard statistical evidence that their model or policy produces for measurable results at the macrolevel. They do not count beans. They count percentage rates.

This means that the relationship to the African governments has changed. The latter used to be referred to as recipients, but they are now called "partners." Development assistance focusing on policy and governance issues does not lend itself to a dictating mode although it has taken donors time to learn that. The rather rigid conditionalities that characterized foreign aid in the 1990s have gradually been softened and replaced by the notion of dialogue. The latter is a more suitable notion in a partnership than conditioning terms set by only one party. Although there are some donor agencies like the USAID that do not adhere to this new approach, the majority of these agencies with assistance to African countries do.

An accompanying change is from project and program aid to what is called funding of sector-wide approaches (SWAPs) or outright budget support. This means that the bulk of the assistance goes to the partner government in the form of general support. It is paid into the general account of the ministry of finance to use in accordance with priorities agreed upon in annual consultations between representatives of the partner governments. In some respects, this marks a return to the practice in the 1970s, especially among the Nordic donors, of giving aid with no questions asked. It would be simplistic, however, to suggest that the situation in 2005 is exactly the same. The dialogue does raise issues about implementation and use of funds and there are much stricter rules of financial accountability built into SWAPs or budget support today. Nonetheless, the jury is still out regarding how helpful this new approach is. Donors like it because it simplifies their administrative burden. African governments like it too because it allows them to exercise greater control of how external funds are being used. It does assume, however, that these governments are committed to the same principles of good governance as their Western donors and that they really have the financial and operational capacity to keep track of what happens with the funds. Attempts at expenditure tracking by consultants hired by the donors suggest that there are still serious shortcomings in most African countries. This may not be because of outright corruption, but inadequate accounting is enough to cause suspicion in donor circles that the partner is not acting honestly.

These changes in the definition of aid and the role that donors should play are still evolving; however, they are turning bilateral aid agencies, which once were the operational arms of their governments in developing countries, into the think tanks of their foreign affairs ministries. Because these agencies do so much less on the ground in African countries, specialized staffs in operational and advisory capacities are no longer needed there to the same extent. A majority are policy analysts with generalist backgrounds who are responsible for providing advice to the diplomats in the headquarters or in the various country missions. The result is that the bilateral aid agencies have become more focused on being up to date on reading relevant literature and attending interesting workshop or seminars. In short, they have become more interested in becoming learning organizations.

Impact of Foreign Aid

Foreign aid has increasingly become a security plank for African governments rather than a contribution toward development of their countries. Because the policy orientation and policy environment of these countries remain so weak, foreign aid tends to have the effect of reducing the pressure on these governments to take charge of their own destinies. Collier and Gunning (1999) as well as Burnside and Dollar (2000) have shown that official development assistance (ODA) is negatively correlated with economic growth. As Leonard and Strauss (2003:29–35) argue, time has come to take a more critical view of foreign aid and go beyond the conventional manual approach to how it might be improved. The long-term effect of foreign aid is to decrease the overall incentives for economic growth and, instead, make African governments even more dependent on external factors than is the case already. Government officials, instead of looking to the domestic arena for resources or solutions, address themselves to the international community. As Moore (1997) and Kjaer (2002) show, governments in this situation become more accountable to foreign governments and international aid agencies than to their own citizens. At the same time, it must be pointed out that the leverage donors have over African governments is limited. The World Bank and the IMF find their ability to influence policy outcomes in African countries slipping (Dollar and Svensson 2000). Bilateral donors do no better. A volume edited by Hyden and Mukandala (1999) that studied foreign aid to Tanzania by China, Sweden, and the United States between 1965 and 1995 shows that, as currently dispensed, aid – whether tied (as in the case of the United States) or untied (as in the case of China and Sweden) – does not produce any long-term beneficial effects for the recipient country.

As suggested above, foreign aid has its critics on both the right and the left of the ideological spectrum. Their assessment of the impact of aid is generally negative. In relation to results, it costs too much! Or, in relation to growth or poverty alleviation objectives, it achieves too little. There is some truth to these criticisms, but they ignore the achievements that have been made in such sectors as health, education, and physical infrastructure. To be sure, because foreign aid is being used in a collaborative context with personnel from an African country, it is always hard to attribute specific contributions from the donor, but it is precisely where the collaborative relations between local and expatriate personnel have been good that most successes have been recorded (van de Walle and Johnson 1996).

The problems encountered from foreign aid in Africa stem from a range of different sources: (1) unrealistic expectations, (2) a strong disbursement imperative, (3) low levels of sustainability, (4) spiraling recurrent costs, (5) constant aid dependency, (6) declining public accountability, and (7) problematic coordination.

1. Unrealistic Expectations. The problem with much foreign aid, whether in the form of project or budget support, is that it sets highly unrealistic timelines for the achievement of particular developmental objectives. The MDGs are only one recent example of this inclination. This means that from the outset foreign-funded activities are doomed to be assessed negatively. With more realistic timelines, such problems would not have arisen to the same extent. People would have viewed aid with more pragmatic eyes. In the current context, foreign-funded activities are the constant subject of the critical lenses of consultants whose evaluation reports often become the final statement on the fate of a particular activity. The time frame is simply not in line with what is needed to make a success of something. Far too many foreign-funded activities, therefore, are written off prematurely by critical evaluators.

2. Strong Disbursement Imperative. There is often more money available for funding development activities in Africa than there is demand or capacity to use it. Donor agencies operate within annual budget cycles, and there is bureaucratic pressure to demonstrate that money that has been allocated is committed and disbursed within the annual cycle. This means that even where money might be possible to move forward to next year's budget, it is viewed as a weakness if it cannot be dispatched on time. This is why the call for raising foreign aid in all donor countries to the level of 0.7 percent of GDP is controversial. If existing funds cannot be effectively used because of lack of demand or capacity, what is the point of raising the spending level, critics would argue. There is certainly some truth in this criticism, because far too often donor solutions are in search of African problems instead of vice versa. Money is often being committed and disbursed even if only a tiny bit of the answers to possible questions about feasibility and costs/benefits have been obtained.

3. Low Levels of Sustainability. Foreign-funded activities are typically pursued on premises that have more to do with the operational and organizational imperatives of the donor agency itself than with those existing on the ground in the African country. Again, whether it is project or budget support, the premises on which assistance is being extended are those with which the foreign staff members are comfortable. This leads to the implantation of values and principles that can be maintained as long as these foreigners are there or at least keep an eye on what is happening. A review of 366 World Bank projects in Africa with institution-building objectives between 1970 and 1989 found that substantial results were achieved in less than one-quarter of the cases (United Nations Development Programme 1993). Other donor-sponsored evaluations have issued broadly similar assessments (van de Walle and Johnson 1996:44). The result is that once a donor-funded activity has come to its official end, it rarely survives on its own. There is not enough commitment or capacity among local staff members to continue. The move away from project and program support is obviously, at least in part, a response to this rather dismal statistic.

4. Spiraling Recurrent Costs. Donors have had an understandable preference for funding something new instead of going in to fund an ongoing activity or institution. A very strong reason for this is that donors have maintained the assumption that their aid is an investment or development expenditure that is going to be met with matching contributions from local sources. This distinction between development and recurrent expenditures was strictly maintained during the 1960s and 1970s, but since the contraction of state budget outlays, it has become increasingly difficult for many poor African countries to come up with these matching funds. The result is that in countries like Mozambique and Zambia, one-third of all maintenance costs, including wages, come from external donor sources. This incompatibility is another reason why more funding for development is not without its own costs. There is not enough local revenue to meet additional recurrent expenditures. On economic policy grounds, governments in these countries are being told not to increase this type of expenditure. Thus, there is a built-in sanction for bringing on a heavier dependence on outside funding of both development and recurrent sides of the national budget.

5. Constant Aid Dependency. Reducing aid dependency in Africa remains an objective in the international development community but by the way it operates under the auspices of the MDGs, it is clear that it pushes onto Africa a funding package that will actually make this phenomenon more, instead of less, constant. These countries are being encouraged to receive more money in the hope that they will be able to swing their way out of poverty. Given past experience – and even taking into consideration improvements in public sector management in recent years – one must still wonder whether such huge increases in funding as proposed in the report to the UN secretary-general under MDG auspices really are desirable. The Government of Tanzania, for example, has demonstrated that by duly collecting road revenue and placing it in a national road fund, the government has been able to finance its physical infrastructural improvements from its own resources. What is more, Tanzania has been able to competitively hire contractors way below the costs incurred when such projects are subject to international tendering using foreign funds. The best part of the story is that the roads have also been built and completed without evidence of bribery and at a quality that surpasses previous road projects in the country.

6. Declining Public Accountability. Because funds from external sources tend to be relatively easy to come by there is a tendency for government officials to ignore the importance of local revenue collection. Taxing citizens is generally considered to be part of building a sense of civic consciousness: In return for paying tax, the citizens obtain their civil and political rights! It provides citizens with a justification for knowing how government handles their money. It encourages transparency and public accountability – two cornerstone principles of good governance. More foreign aid, therefore, has its political costs. It may in the long run not be compatible with building sustainable public institutions (Moore 1997; Kjaer 2004b). It certainly gives government officials an excuse for paying more attention to negotiations with external actors than to working on how the principles of good governance can be most effectively implemented – the promise notwithstanding that they may have given donors about adhering to the global good governance agenda.

7. Problematic Coordination. Partly because donor funding comes in the form of revenue collected from local taxpayers in the home country, the tendency for these agencies to operate with their own domestic constituency in mind is understandable. This is particularly true about the USAID, which has always been very restricted in its operations by rules imposed on it by the politically elected congress. It is reflected in the way that other agencies operate too, albeit it to a less explicit degree. This means that coordination among donor agencies is difficult. To the extent that it takes place, it does so in the context of specific institutions like the Development Assistance Committee of the Organization for Economic Cooperation and Development (OECD). This coordination, however, is problematic from an African perspective because it overlooks what aid coordination means from the point of view of a recipient government. Coordination among the donor agencies tends to reduce the space for negotiation that recipients have. Some progress has been made toward localizing coordination to recipient-country level by providing budget support and having donor representatives participating in joint annual consultations of government priorities. This is a step in the right direction but it still leaves coordination in the hands of government officials with little, if any, input from other societal actors, be that private sector or civil society.

THE NEW INSTITUTIONAL ECONOMICS

NIE has been the dominant mode of thought within the discipline of economics and among economic policy advisors for almost two decades now. Its significance has been recognized internationally in the form of at least two Nobel Prizes (Ronald H. Coase 1991 and Douglass C. North 1993). Its message is rather simple, but one that was initially overlooked as the neoclassical approach to economics was rehabilitated in the 1980s. Thus, the initial policy prescriptions issued by the international finance institutions under the structural adjustment label ignored institutions and preached the message of perfect market rationality. This more radical edict may be understood as a way of pinpointing as explicitly as possible how dramatic a change was required in countries where the economy had been extensively regulated and managed by the state, as the case was in Africa in the 1960s and 1970s. The problem with the initial phase of structural adjustment – largely through the 1980s – was twofold. By virtue of its strong words in support of market liberalization, it generated a lot of political opposition. African governments, working through the UN Economic Commission for Africa (ECA) in Addis Ababa, came up with their own, softer version of reform – The Lagos Plan of Action. With little or no funding backing it, however, it was a nonstarter. The second part of the problem was its naïve operational assumptions. Especially in Africa where markets were little developed and the prospects for market perfection were dim, the neglect of institutions was particularly damning for the advocates of structural adjustment.

From a purely operational point of view, therefore, the NIE must be viewed as a step forward because it begins from the assumption that institutional structure exerts an important influence on human behavior and choice. It transcends the microeconomics of the more orthodox model, which assumes economic efficiency under ideal conditions of perfect information and foresight. As such, NIE has helped extend the range of applicability of neoclassical theory. Its basic assumptions and terms may be summarized as follows:

It emphasizes that people are different, with varied tastes and preferences; hence the state, firm, or political party could not be treated as individual agents. Individuals are assumed to seek their own interests as they perceive them, and to maximize utility subject to the constraints established by the existing institutional structure. Preferences of decision makers are recognized as incomplete and subject to change over time; hence the notion of bounded rationality, originally attributed to Herbert Simon (whose Nobel Prize award may also qualify as recognition of institutional economics). In addition to rationality being bounded, human behavior may be dishonest in the sense that people disguise their preferences, distort data, or deliberately confuse issues, hence what Williamson (1985) calls self-seeking with guile, and the need for contracts to be regarded as incomplete. A country is able to develop economically only if property rights exist and contracts are respected; society, therefore, must be concerned with the social arrangements that regulate the reliable transfer of property rights. The property rights configuration existing in an economy is determined and guaranteed by a system of rules and the instruments that serve to enforce these rules; hence the concern with governance structures that secure such rights. The concept refers to a set of working rules that are actually used, monitored, and enforced when individuals make choices about the actions they will take; these rules may arise spontaneously based on the self-interest of individuals, or come about as a public authority, for example, parliament, tries to introduce an institutional structure it deems appropriate. Finally, institutions together with people taking advantage of them are called organizations and they require real resources to operate, hence the notion of transaction costs associated with using the market and securing adequate coordination within an organization as well as between such structures.

The NIE raises the question of where institutions are coming from. Its protagonists assume that market failures lead to a more or less automatic response in the form of an institutional solution. Bates (1995) interprets the approach as functional. It does not really tell how such a solution comes about, only that it does. There is a somewhat different answer, however, and that is that economists are responsible for the institutional solutions that market failures create. That is, they believe that they have the answer because they are the only ones with enough information and overview to diagnose the failure and come up with a solution. This point is especially important for understanding how the economic reform process works in Africa and other countries that are dependent on economic policy analysts, especially those working with international finance institutions. Only the latter have the necessary overview of the economic conditions of most African countries. To the extent that local economists have, it is usually the result of sharing the information that the economists of the World Bank or the IMF possess. There is rarely an independent perspective from that offered by the latter. Because it is so dominant, institutional and policy prescriptions to deal with market failures in African countries are by necessity imposed from the outside. Institutional realignments are decided upon by economists with very little, if any, concern about the political feasibility and consequences of such interventions. It is no surprise, therefore, that these efforts rarely pay dividends. Institutions are not likely to get off the ground if its principal architects are economists. Yet, for some two decades, African countries in particular have been obliged to work with that arrangement.

The opposite to this top-down approach to institutions is the argument by rational choice theorists like Bates (1995) who suggest that institutions arise from the need that rational individuals create by pursuing their self-interest. Individuals have a vested interest in finding a way of reconciling their differences with others in the form of a public choice that reflects an aggregation and amalgamation of all private choices. Thus even if individuals do not get all they asked for, they get some of it. It is in economic terms a win-win situation even though the solution is suboptimal for each person participating. This approach assumes a form of civic participation where everyone plays by the formal rules established for how to behave in the public realm. It presupposes a form of dialogue that is inherent in policy making in consolidated democracies. In short, the model rests on premises that are identical to those of Western democracies. I have argued in this volume that such premises are not really very helpful in analyzing politics in Africa. The line between private and public is constantly fluctuating; individuals do not operate as autonomous decision makers; and exit, that is, avoiding conflict and accepting compliance, is the preferred strategy of individuals as they operate in a public setting. Patronage rather than policy is what drives individuals in politics.

The neoinstitutionalist strategies that the international development agencies have relied upon in the past two decades, therefore, do not really capture the social logic on the ground in African countries. Whether conceived by economists or political scientists, they become attempts to realign Africa's institutions along the lines of those that can be found in the industrial societies with their consolidated forms of democracy. Even though we may allow for some level of variation in the experiences among African countries, it is doubtful that many observers are ready to conclude that the attempts to accelerate Africa's development with the help of reforms inspired by neoinstitutionalism have been successful.

One reason for this lack of success is that the reformers have not been very effective in selling their institutional reforms to African policy makers. To be sure, they have had no problem finding support among African economists who can see the logic behind the proposed interventions. They have not changed the incentive structures enough, however, for those who ultimately matter most: the government leaders. The latter have retained a preference for a political rather than economic logic. They have adhered to value rationality as opposed to the instrumental and calculative rationality of the economists. With a few exceptions, like Uganda and more recently Tanzania, the reformers have remained on the outside, failing to penetrate the political realm. Another reason is that the international development agencies have themselves been quite rigid and unimaginative in their thinking. The World Bank and the IMF have often been too confident that their economics model works. The United States has been far too preoccupied with making sure that any assistance given to Africa has tangible benefits for

U.S. voters. The European bilateral agencies have often been more flexible, but they have acted in ways that reinforce existing maladies in the African economies rather than helping to overcome them. This is especially true with their interpretation of partnership and its notion that development assistance to these countries is best delivered in the form of budget support or sector-wide funding arrangements. To be sure, this may be a step forward from reliance on project or even program funding. What it does not achieve, however, is a way of tackling the most serious shortcoming in African politics: its reliance on patronage rather than policy.

A POLITICAL SCIENCE–BASED APPROACH TO REFORM

The final task of this volume is to discuss what a political science–based approach to reform would look like if consideration is taken of the points that I have made in this volume. It is not meant to be another blueprint, but sketches in some of the more important components of reform that come from the analysis in this book. It obviously needs further exploration in the African context. Yet, hopefully, it is a helpful start for rethinking what needs to – and can be – done in reforming the public sector in Africa. It begins by pointing out what may be needed to avoid the mistakes of the past.

The first point is that a longer-term perspective on the issues than what is typically provided must be accepted. In this context, it must be said that the expectations associated with the MDGs are a mixed blessing for Africa. It may keep alive an interest in the continent's fate because it is the most problematic region of the world. At the same time, however, it is unrealistic to assume that the many problems listed in the document can be solved within a specific time period, especially one as short as fifteen years.

The second point is the need to think beyond the argument that more extensive external funding is the best means to solve problems. More external funding is not a general answer to Africa's predicament. As proved by Tanzania's experience, which I discuss in the subsection, Constant Aid Dependency, local revenue collection sometimes provides a better incentive for policy makers to consider costs. Even such expensive investments as those in physical infrastructure, therefore, can be meaningfully funded from local sources.

The third point is the need for more operational flexibility than current blueprints provide. There is no one-size-fits-all solution to Africa's problems. Furthermore, because they are blueprints they do not lend themselves to local ownership and, above all, local learning (Dolowitz and Marsh 2000). The idea that the international development community possesses a series of best practices that can be transferred from one context to another is a misleading strategy for Africa. A much better approach would be to allow local actors to reinvent the wheel – again. This becomes a waste only in the artificial temporal framework of donor agencies that fail to recognize learning as an integral part of becoming better at modernizing and developing society.

The fourth point is that development is not only a simple adding up of all the good values with which it may be associated in the minds of people and policy analysts. The MDG exercise may serve as an illustration again. The international community has set itself eight global objectives in a partnership that assumes that if the rich and poor nations each do their part, somehow the results will show up in relation to all the objectives whether they are oriented toward maximizing growth, reducing poverty, or conserving the environment. There is no recognition of the obvious fact that within the temporal framework for achieving them, these objectives contradict each other in practical politics, and that they are best pursued in sequence rather than in tandem.

The fifth point is that the state in Africa is not really at a stage where it is being consolidated. It is still undergoing formation. This means that the institutional incentive structures that come with the new institutionalism rarely acquire the needed political traction. Political leaders in Africa are concerned with building and managing the state out of chaos and ambiguity. In most countries technology remains rudimentary and the ensuing social formation does not support the emergence of the type of corporate state institutions that we know from Europe or Asia. What Africa needs, therefore, is an incentives arrangement that allows local actors more space to constructively pursue their own institutional development, even if that involves ignoring some of the conditions associated with neoinstitutionalist approaches (Dia 1996).

The sixth point relates to the need for greater recognition that African countries operate according to a social logic that is not captured by conventional Western models. This is by no means a fresh observation. The point has been made over and over again. Yet, it has to be repeated because of the strong inclination in the international development community to fall back on its own pet solutions. Even among economic analysts in many of the international agencies, there is growing awareness that somehow what is going on in informal institutions such as clientelism is what really matters, but no one seems to be able to find a way of dealing with what they are seeing.

The seventh point that needs to be made here is that the agencies in the international development community, especially the bilateral donors, need to do much more to put the partnership idea into practice. So far it has been primarily a rhetorical device. It treats the recipient government with respect and it builds on the idea of regular dialogue. It does not, however, ask any hard questions about what may be required by the donor agencies themselves. For the latter it is very much business as usual. Assisting Africa, however, needs fresh thinking about how these agencies relate to their African partners and, above all, how they channel their financial support to these countries.

It is important at this point to emphasize that many African countries have come a long way in the past twenty-five years. The progress of these countries is quite remarkable in a comparative international perspective. The problem is that because these countries started from such a low level of development, their achievements are not making a significant mark globally. These achievements, however, must also be seen in the context of many setbacks that other African countries have suffered, partly due to their own inability to move forward, partly to factors beyond their control. Political agency in Africa today, as discussed in Chapters Two and Ten, is more confined than ever. Governments have little control over what is happening not only because of their inadequate involvement in both economy and society, but also because of the limitations set by external debt and trade barriers. As Leonard and Strauss (2003) emphasize, these are important hurdles that the international community can do something about. At the same time, it is clear that removing them would not automatically allow African countries to move ahead more quickly. The domestic conditions do matter and they must be allowed to change at their own pace. This is where the role that the international development agencies can play is still important, provided they are ready to think more creatively about their own contribution.

The Need for a Policy Government

The biggest governance challenge facing most African countries today is the prevalence of informal practices, such as clientelism (or neopatrimonialism, as it is sometimes called), which have the effect of rendering formal institutional arrangements less effective. These informal measures are rational from an individual perspective – both patron and client – but they undermine objectives at the macrolevel. They also contradict reform efforts and often serve as the basis for resisting them. The question is whether these informal practices can be transcended and turned into something positive, or whether there are other ways than external conditionalities or mere persuasive appeals to turn the relationship between formal and informal institutions in African countries into a win-win equation.

The implementation of ideas associated with the new public management (NPM) approach has already begun encouraging a stricter division between the political and managerial spheres on the assumption that development activities in African countries suffer from too little professional input when putting policy into practice. This had led to the creation of contractually independent executive agencies, such as revenue and road authorities that carry out their functions outside the regular government administration. Given the historical legacy, it seems these initiatives have been easier to introduce in English-speaking than in French-speaking countries, but the need for addressing this challenge exists regardless of what the colonial authorities left behind.

Policy analysts in donor agencies and multilateral institutions assume that policy is all that matters in government. However, many governments around the world are not what one would call policy but, instead, are patronage governments. This is certainly true in many African countries, where rewarding loyal followers becomes so prevalent that it overshadows the effort to achieve public policy goals. To the extent that governments operate according to patronage, they look backward rather than forward toward achieving a set of corporate goals. Needless to say, this undermines the role of government as an institutional mechanism that can make a developmental difference. This is a problem that is increasingly being recognized but little progress has been made toward tackling it because, as stated many times in this volume, the proposed institutional solutions fail to gather political traction in the African context. Thus, experts believe that they know what needs to be done, but are still searching for how to do it.

Every country in the world that is now developed – or succeeding in getting out of poverty – has been forced to reduce or eliminate informal practices such as nepotism, spoils, and similar discretionary uses of public authority. What remains to be done in African countries, therefore, is by no means unique. What is possibly exceptional is the extent to which these problems appear intractable there. They may, therefore, call for bolder thinking and certainly a broader comparative perspective on how the issues may be tackled.

A policy government is committed to providing and implementing public goals that have been duly approved by institutions with legitimate authority to do so. There is a clear separation between official and personal and the distinction between public and private matters. This means that employees have a self-binding commitment to an organizational mission, its objectives, and the specific tasks associated with particular roles that they play. They are driven by work-related goals, not those that may arise during the workday stemming from the personal problems of one's relatives or friends. In short, there is a work discipline that precludes distractions. On top of that, in the best cases, there is a professional pride in work and achievement.

This idea of government is still in the making in African countries. It needs to be further strengthened if these countries are going to become more efficient and effective in increasingly achieving development goals on their own. It is for this reason that the creation of independent executive agencies should be kept alive and continued. Because the temptation to engage in patronage practices is especially high in relation to economic and social development, there is a strong argument for targeting these sectors for such reforms. Many African governments – and international development agencies – tend to treat them as core functions and seem to imply that they cannot be delegated to independent agencies. However, if, tax collection, which is definitely a core function, has already been given to independent revenue authorities the rationale for reluctance to do so in the social and economic development sectors collapses.

The notion of independent executive agencies is still relatively foreign to many Africans, especially those in government positions, who have got used to working within the system that they inherited from their respective colonial powers. This path dependency, however, has been somewhat lowered already as a result of the economic and political reforms that were initiated in recent years. It should also be pointed out that some of the most effective governments in the world – those of the Nordic countries – are constituted around the dominance of independent executive agencies. NPM usually gets accredited to the emergence of Margaret Thatcher in Britain and Ronald Reagan in the United States – evidence of how much the major Anglo-Saxon countries tend to dominate development thinking – but the truth is that the philosophy behind it has been practised in the Nordic countries for two hundred years. In fact, the system arose in response to exactly the same problem that faces Africa today – how government can be made more professional and thus efficient.

The basic premises of that system still exist in the Nordic countries. Many aspects of it have been further refined. Its most important aspects are that

- a cabinet minister cannot interfere with the day-to-day operations of an executive agency without the risk of being called before a parliamentary constitutional committee with oversight responsibility in this field;
- each ministry focuses exclusively on making policies and monitoring their implementation, leaving the key personnel to focus on charting the future rather than on rewarding past services;
- each executive agency has sufficient autonomy within the parameters of specific policies set by government that it can take its own initiatives, making these bodies both innovative and flexible in their operations; and
- should any agency overstep its mandate or a staff member make a decision that can be questioned on legal grounds or because it shows poor judgement, a citizen or group of citizens can appeal through an ombudsman institution.

The interesting thing about many African countries, especially English-speaking ones, is that they have already taken steps in this direction and have many of the features already in place. The problem is that because of patronage politics, these institutional features have not been allowed to become effective. For example, many countries have the equivalent of the ombudsman but their reports are rarely, if ever, acted upon. Time has come to empower these bodies in the interest of better public sector management.

Shared Control of Public Funds

Patronage politics has the tendency to encourage discretionary control of resources that can be used to reward followers. Individuals in key positions of authority would wish to have personal control over funds at the disposal of their organization. This inclination is at the root of the prevalence of informal institutions in Africa and, in many instances, the prevalence of corruption. This problem is not being solved by merely trying to fix the formal institution through the model of, say, NIE. This is a political governance issue that must be tackled as such.

The objective must be that of insulating public funds from control by powerful individuals who tend to overstep their authority. In the social and economic development fields this may amount to the creation of development funds that are legally public institutions, but so constituted and governed that they are also accountable outside the government system. Some years ago, the African Association for Public Administration and Management (AAPAM) brought together an "expert consultation" of representatives from African governments, NGOs, and the donor community, including the World Bank; it made provisions for what the group called autonomous development funds (Hammarskjold Foundation 1995). Its time may have come because this document provides an outline of how the discrepancy between formal and informal institutions in African countries can be bridged in a nonantagonistic manner.

The principal objectives of such funds would be to

- provide funding on a competitive basis to organizations in and outside of government;
- serve as catalytic mechanisms for mobilizing and allocating funds within sectors identified as priority areas in government policy;
- ensure resource allocation based on professional criteria;
- encourage a demand-driven process of development;
- stimulate local capacity-building; and
- promote donor coordination within African countries based on local institutional priorities.

The assumption with these funds would be that they are institutions with a public mandate, established to cater for demands for development within a given sector or in relation to a specific theme, for example, women and development. Each fund would be open to proposals submitted from executive agencies (or development ministries, if such agencies have not been established), local government authorities, nongovernmental and community-based organizations, and, where applicable, private sector organizations. An important feature is the competition that such a fund can create among different types of organizations. The latter is vital for institutional growth and has the potential of formalizing organizations in an organic manner, that is, without causing the kind of conflict that has prevailed so far between informal practice and formalization efforts.

Many submissions to these funds may in the beginning be insufficiently complete in a professional sense to be approved. It is important that staff employed by these funds take the trouble to return such proposals to their original authors with clear instructions on how they can be improved. Since there will be no shortcut to funding, such feedback will serve an important capacity-building purpose and engage local professionals in an important role that is usually absent. It takes time to become efficacious in development in Africa, but this is a way of achieving this in a constructive fashion involving local actors.

Donors have already abandoned project funding and this is in line with their preference for disbursing funds in large grants. For instance, without having to abandon the preference for budget support, it would be possible for donor agencies to negotiate with their African counterparts to set aside a certain amount for deposit into such autonomous development funds. With the establishment of such funds, there would also be a possibility for donors to place money in a common pool that is subject to local national accounting and audit practices.

Development funds are not new to the international community. In African countries, donors once invested their money in rural development funds controlled by the office of the president or a ministry of planning and development. Following the introduction of structural adjustment programs in the 1980s, the World Bank has supported a number of social action funds aimed at financing social development activities. The problem with these earlier efforts is that little or no attention has been paid to how these funds are governed. Many have easily become slush funds for powerful political figures. In other instances, when supported by a single donor, the control of the fund by the donor has been too rigid and forced upon recipients time-consuming accounting regulations. In short, more time has been spent on reporting requirements than on effective spending of the money. Other shortcomings abound in the literature. For these reasons, the fund idea has a negative connotation in the minds of many analysts and practitioners.

There is no reason, however, to throw the baby out with the bathwater. The fund is a good idea provided it is publicly accountable and governed in ways that reduce, if not wholly eliminate, the shortcomings associated with cases in the past. Thus, some of the key principles that would have to be considered before establishing an autonomous development fund would be

- shared governance among government, civil society, and resource providers;
- board members serving in their individual capacity;
- funds having a national, but sector-specific, mandate; and
- funds as public institutions being accountable to the national legislature.

The composition of the board of trustees or directors is crucial to the success of these funds. The idea of a shared tripartite governance arrangement is meant to reduce the risks of mismanagement of the money. In a game situation where there are three as opposed to just two actors – which is the standard model in donor-recipient relations – the possibility of poor use of resources diminishes. There is always the possibility of one of the three being ready to blow the whistle. Furthermore, with three, as compared to just two actors involved, the power game is less likely to end up in zero-sum outcomes. In short, the sharing of fund governance equally among representatives of government, civil society, and the external resource providers creates a positive atmosphere.

To ensure that such an atmosphere is not threatened by narrow personal or organizational interests, it is important that persons appointed to the board do not serve ex officio. Senior civil servants should not be there merely because of their positions, and neither should ambassadors representing donor countries or directors of NGOs. Government, civil society, and resource providers should be three separate constituencies that get together, each with its own rules, to nominate and elect representatives to the board of such a fund. These individuals should be trusted persons, recognized and respected by the constituency and, preferably, the public. One could imagine that each of these three constituencies would elect three members each to the board of such a fund, making it a manageable size. The chair could rotate among the constituencies on a regular basis.

The resource providers do not necessarily have to be external donors only. Once the demand for resources from these funds has become institutionalized, governments may wish to contribute their own allocations in order to enlarge the total available for allocation among applicant organizations. This would also enhance the image of these funds as public institutions.

There is no guarantee that corruption and other possible malpractices would completely disappear with the creation of these autonomous funds, but they do stand a much greater chance of reducing them than those institutional arrangements that prevail or have been tried in the past. By virtue of being public bodies legally incorporated in an African country, they are more sustainable than institutional arrangements that are more directly dependent on external funding. At the same time, donors who have placed money in any one of these funds do, of course, have the right to withdraw their support if malpractices occur that cannot be immediately corrected. This gives them a right to sanction that in the long run may be a corrective mechanism that turns the fund in the right direction.

The idea of an autonomous development fund is not just academic. It has been put into practice on an experimental basis in several countries. One example that is particularly instructive is the Cultural Development Trust Fund in Tanzania (Mfuko wa Utamaduni Tanzania). It started in 1999 as an autonomous fund for cultural development in the country. It has been able to attract support from three donors and the government. Its board is made up of nine persons, one representing the donors, one representing the government, and seven others serving as representatives of different constituencies within the cultural sector. Thus, performing artists have one, librarians another, writers yet another, and so on. This means that the cultural sector itself is more extensively represented, but it is an arrangement that government and donor representatives agreed to in an initial meeting. It is worth mentioning here that each constituency nominates both a male and female. On an alternating basis decided by the lot, each constituency is thus asked to choose its male or a female to ensure that there is gender equity in board composition. The Cultural Development Trust Fund has helped mobilize funds for the sector. It has responsibly allocated grants not only to activities and artists based in the main city of Dar es Salaam, but also to the twenty other regions of the country. Thus, it has had a catalytic effect while serving as a model for how money can be used in ways that enhance the principles of good governance.

The autonomous development fund is a new concept in development assistance. It invites donors to treat development assistance as an investment, not a charitable grant. They call upon donors to operationalize the concept of partnership by calling for a shared responsibility in the management of these funds. The model entails modifications in operational procedures among governments and donors alike. Everyone realizes that such changes do not come easy. The situation in Africa, however, is so critical that it would amount to moral bankruptcy if ideas such as those presented here were not properly explored at this point. Administrative convenience is no longer an argument for how to give development assistance to African countries. Patronage can no longer continue to dominate government operations in these places. In sum, fifty years of political science research ought to have made it crystal clear that African development will remain hampered until the day that donors and governments in Africa have found a modus operandi that takes into consideration the political and social realities on the continent.

CONCLUDING REFLECTION

There is no reason to downplay the progress that African countries have made in the past two decades under often very difficult circumstances. The distance that they have covered is considerable in many instances. Development, however, is a marathon race. African countries have just begun. A longer distance remains to be covered, and some of it even more challenging than what has already been completed. Building on recent reforms is a good start for those that are needed in the next phase. It would be wrong to assume, however, that these steps can be identified along the lines of a single model. They have to be taken with the practical experience of individual

African countries as the most suitable starting point. Furthermore, they have to take into account that what is needed at this point is not so much economic as political reforms. These are inevitably more contested. That is why the recommendations made in this chapter are presented as an open-ended agenda that deserves deliberation and dialogue on the ground in individual African countries; it is not presented as an expeditious implementation with the risk of causing a backlash.

Donors can become effective in the African context only if they temper their own preference for economic reasoning with a dose of cold political analysis of the local situation. A few agencies, such as the Department for International Development (DfID) in Britain and the Swedish International Development Cooperation Agency (Sida), have begun to be sensitive to the need for a political analysis that goes beyond the general prescriptions of the now battered good governance agenda. They recognize that their assistance will have little effect unless they can relate it more effectively to local political realities.

Becoming more effective obviously involves a better understanding of how power is being exercised and with what consequences. Above all, it may entail an appreciation of the economy of affection and the reasoning behind it. African actors, after all, are rational in their behavior and decisions, but they are also based on a different set of considerations than those that guide economic reasoning in the donor agencies. This volume has offered some indications of these differences and the social distance that donors need to bridge in order to get traction for their ideas. Given that this distance is so big and the opportunities within bureaucratic donor agencies for adaptation to these African realities are limited, is there a possible bridge that can be built so that they meet their African counterparts – partners – halfway?

I believe there is, provided the donor agencies are ready to engage in a bit of self-evaluation and, in so doing, bring African institutions on board in joint endeavors in which the notion of partnership becomes real rather than just rhetorical. These joint undertakings, as suggested in this chapter, have to address the most serious threats to effective management of development funding – neopatrimonialism and all the informal dealings that are associated with it. In short, how money is being channeled for African development becomes the most critical issue.

African governments and donor agencies alike rely on a sensible interpretation of operational procedures in order to function well. The reality in Africa is that governments have paid too little attention to these rules, the donors too much. The former have not been bureaucratic enough – in the Weberian sense of legal-rational authority – the latter have been overly bureaucratic. In the light of this considerable difference, donor agencies have to think of how they can help these governments without becoming involved in never-ending expenditure tracking that only defeats the purpose of their softer funding approach. In governments where accounting is known to be very weak, the fungibility of donor funds is likely to be very high indeed; transaction costs easily become much too high for justifying that approach to development funding.

What has been proposed in this chapter is very much in line with the prevailing philosophy of decentralizing responsibility to organs that can act with an independent professional mandate. The distance that governments and donors have to travel, therefore, from their respective starting points should not be exaggerated. It does require, however, a readiness to think afresh without smashing – once again – against the hard lines of a blueprint. How to set such a process in motion with prospects for significant gains for all parties involved is the most immediate challenge.

So, finally, where is Africa heading? No one can obviously say for sure. Most likely, the scenario over the next couple of decades will indicate variation. Some countries will move in a modern direction; others will continue struggling. Whatever the scenario that may apply to each country, there are many hurdles to overcome. They will have to be tackled in sequence rather than on a broad front. The first obstacle may be the toughest: how to transcend the limits of a movement legacy that implies that renewal – accepting the dictates of Amin in Uganda or Mugabe regarding the European minority in Zimbabwe – is achieved only by mobilizing resistance to foreign advisors and funders or to privileged minorities within the country. Africa needs to transform its movements into political parties that are issue-oriented and focused on constructive problem solving rather than the sweeping transformations that movements to date have attempted.

Tackling this obstacle requires overcoming another hindrance: the absence of corporate power and a public opinion that can drive issues. This means differentiating the social formation so that Africans become used to a division of labor instead of operating indivisibly on a self-employed basis in the informal sector. A stronger indigenous bourgeois or capitalist class that respects the rule of law would be important for such a process. Its role would most likely have to be complemented by foreign capital. A strong and dynamic private sector is an integral part of the path forward even if this means, as it most probably will, that the options for many to deal with their livelihoods will become more circumscribed. It is one of the misconceptions that come from looking only at statistics that poverty in Africa is experienced by people as damning. Of course, people know that they are poor, but they do not see themselves as locked into it forever. Because it is not structural, with the exception of countries like Ethiopia and South Africa, there is always the expectation that with the help of others – through investments in the economy of affection – there is eventually a way out. This does not mean that the situation in Africa is nonproblematic; it is but because of its qualitative, not quantitative, dimension. The bulk of the region's countries have large numbers of poor people because they have not been integrated – and subordinated – to the powers of others. The economic base for social stratification has to be transformed in a direction where this happens.

There will be other hurdles on the way, many of which have been identified and discussed in this volume. They will have to be addressed as the two discussed right here are being tackled. The important thing is that this process will be both painful and enduring. It is not a fifteen-year but a fifty-year perspective that is relevant for understanding and dealing with Africa's social and political transformation. It would be interesting to know what a review of political science literature in 2055 might be saying on the subject of this volume.

References

African Medical and Research Foundation (AMREF) 2000. *Better Health for the People of Africa*. Nairobi: AMREF.

Agbaje, Adigun and Jinmi Adisa 1988. "Political Education and Public Policy in Nigeria," *Journal of Commonwealth and Comparative Politics*, vol 26 (March), pp 22–37.

Ake, Claude 1995. "The New World Order: A View from Africa" in Hans Henrik Holm and Georg Sorensen (eds.), *Whose World Order? Uneven Globalization and the End of the Cold War*. Boulder CO: Westview Press.

Akeredolu-Ale, E. O. 1975. *The Underdevelopment of Indigenous Entrepreneurship in Nigeria*. Ibadan, Nigeria: Ibadan University Press.

Akindés, Francis 2004. "The Roots of the Military-Political Crises in Cote d'Ivoire," Research Report No 128. Uppsala: Nordic Africa Institute.

Alibert, Jacques 1996. "Un bilan de la devaluation du franc CFA," *Afrique Contemporaine*, no 179, pp 16–26.

Amin, Samir 1976. *Unequal Development: An Essay on the Social Formations of Peripheral Capitalism*. New York: Monthly Review Press.

Anderson, Benedict 1983. *Imagined Communities: Reflections on the Origins and Spread of Nationalism*. London: Verso.

Anonymous 2003. "Can Oil Ever Help the Poor?" *The Economist*, vol 369, no 8355 (December 6–12), pp 39–40.

Anonymous 2004a. "African Leaders Invite Criticism: Well, a Little," *The Economist*, vol 370, no 8363 (February 21–27), p 45.

Anonymous 2004b. "Confused Democrats," *The Economist*, vol 370, no 8369 (April 3–10), pp 48–49.

Anyang' Nyong'o, Peter 1989. "State and Society in Kenya: The Disintegration of the Nationalist Coalitions and the Rise of Presidential Authoritarianism, 1963–1978," *African Affairs*, vol 88, pp 229–51.

Apter, David E. 1963. "Political Religion in the New States" in Clifford Geertz (ed.), *Old Societies and New States*. New York: The Free Press of Glencoe, pp 57–104.

Apter, David E. 1965. *The Politics of Modernization*. Princeton NJ: Princeton University Press.

Aubrey, Lisa 1997. *The Politics of Development Cooperation: NGOs, Gender and Partnership in Kenya*. New York: Routledge.

Ayee, Joseph R. A. 1999. "The Transition from Military Rule to Constitutional Government and the Consolidation of Democratic Governance in Ghana" in Dele Olowu (ed.), *Governance and Democratization in West Africa*. Dakar: CODESRIA Press.

Ayittey, George B. N. 1991. *Indigenous African Institutions*. Ardsley-on-Hudson NY: Transnational Publishers.

Ayittey, George B. N. 2002. *Africa Betrayed*. New York: St. Martin's Press.

Babu, Abdul Rahman Mohamed 1981. *African Socialism or Socialist Africa?* London: Zed Press.

Badie, Bertrand and Pierre Birnbaum 1983. *The Sociology of the State*. Chicago: University of Chicago Press.

Bagachwa, M. S. D. 1997. "The Rural Informal Sector in Tanzania" in D. F. Bryceson and V. Jamal (eds.), *Farewell to Farms: Deagrarianization and Employment in Africa*. Aldershot: Ashgate.

Balandier, George 1971. *Sociologie actuelle de l'Afrique noire: Dynamique sociale en Afrique centrale*, third edition. Paris: PUF.

Baldwin, David A. 1978. "Power and Social Exchange," *American Political Science Review*, vol 72, no 4, pp 1229–42.

Banton, Michael 1993. *Racial and Ethnic Competition*. Cambridge, UK: Cambridge University Press.

Barber, Karin 1991. *I Could Speak until Tomorrow: Oriki, Women, and the Past in a Yoruba Town*. Washington DC: Smithsonian Institution.

Barkan, Joel (ed.) 1984. *Politics and Policy in Kenya and Tanzania*, second edition. New York: Praeger.

Barkan, Joel (ed.) 1994. *Beyond Capitalism vs Socialism in Kenya and Tanzania*. Boulder CO: Lynne Rienner Publishers.

Barth, Fredrik 1969. *Ethnic Groups and Boundaries: The Social Organization of Culture*. Oslo, Norway: Universitetsforlaget.

Bates, Robert H. 1981. *Markets and States in Tropical Africa*. Berkeley: University of California Press.

Bates, Robert H. 1989. *Beyond the Miracle of the Market: The Political Economy of Agrarian Development in Kenya*. New York: Cambridge University Press.

Bates, Robert H. 1995. "Social Dilemmas and Rational Individuals: An Assessment of the New Institutionalism" in J. Harriss, J. Hunter, and C. M. Lewis (eds.), *The New Institutional Economics and Third World Development*. London and New York: Routledge.

Bayart, Jean-Francois 1993. *The State in Africa: The Politics of the Belly*. London and New York: Longman.

Bayart, Jean-Francois 2000. "Africa in the World: A History of Extraversion," *African Affairs*, vol 99, no 395, pp 217–68.

Bazenguissa-Ganga, Remy 1999. "The Spread of Political Violence in Congo-Brazzaville," *African Affairs*, vol 98, no 390, pp 389–411.

Bennett, T. W. 1995. *Human Rights and African Customary Law*. Cape Town: JUTA Press.

Berg-Schlosser, Dirk 1984. "African Political Systems: Typology and Performance," *Comparative Political Studies*, vol 17, no 1, pp 121–51.

Berman, Harold J. 1983. *Law and Revolution: The Formation of the Western Legal Tradition*. Cambridge MA: Harvard University Press.

Berry, Sara 2002. "Debating the Land Question in Africa," *Comparative Studies in Society and History*, vol 44, no 4, pp 638–68.

Beveridge, A. A. and A. R. Oberschall 1979. *African Businessmen and Development in Zambia*. Princeton NJ: Princeton University Press.

Bienen, Henry 1967. *Tanzania: Party Transformation and Economic Development*. Princeton NJ: Princeton University Press.

Bienen, Henry and Jeffrey Herbst 1996. "The Relationship between Political and Economic Reform in Africa," *Comparative Politics*, vol 29, no 1, pp 23–42.

Bigsten, Arne and S. Kayizzi-Mugerwa 1995. "Rural Sector Responses to Economic Crisis in Uganda," *Journal of International Development*, vol 7, no 2, pp 181–209.

Blau, Peter 1964. *Exchange and Power in Social Life*. New York: Wiley.

Blau, Peter (ed.) 1965. *The Dynamics of Bureaucracy*. Chicago: University of Chicago Press.

Boesen, Jannik, K. J. Havnevik, J. Kopponen, and R. Odgaard (eds.) 1986. *Tanzania: Crisis and Struggle for Survival*. Uppsala, Sweden: Scandinavian Institute of African Studies.

Boserup, Ester 1965. *Conditions of Agricultural Growth*. London: George Allen & Unwin.

Boserup, Ester 1970. *Women's Role in Economic Development*. New York: St. Martin's Press.

Botchwey, Kwesi et al. 1998. *External Evaluation of the ESAF. Report by a Group of Independent Experts*. Washington DC: International Monetary Fund.

Bratton, Michael 1989. "Beyond the State: Civil Society and Associational Life in Africa," *World Politics*, vol 41, no 3, pp 407–30.

Bratton, Michael and Nicolas van de Walle 1997. *Democratic Experiments in Africa*. New York: Cambridge University Press.

Braybrooke, David and Charles E. Lindblom 1963. *A Strategy of Decision*. New York: Free Press 1963.

Brett, E. A. 1972. *Colonialism and Underdevelopment in East Africa*. London: Heinemann.

Brown, Patrick 2004. "European Colonial Rule in Africa" in *Africa South of the Sahara*, thirty-third edition. London and New York: Europa Publications.

Browne, Robert S. and Robert J. Cummings 1984. *The Lagos Plan of Action vs the Berg Report: Contemporary Issues in African Economic Development*. Washington DC: Howard University Press.

Bryceson, Deborah Fahy 1996. "Deagrarianization and Rural Employment in Sub-Saharan Africa: A Sectoral Perspective," *World Development*, vol 24, no 1, pp 97–111.

Bryceson, Deborah Fahy 2002. "The Scramble for Africa: Reorienting Rural Livelihoods," *World Development*, vol 30, no 5, pp 725–39.

Burnside, Craig and David Dollar 2000. "Aid, Policies, and Growth," *American Economic Review*, vol 90, no 4, pp 847–69.

Caldwell, Jack C. 1969. *African Rural-Urban Migration: The Movement to Ghana's Towns*. New York: Columbia University Press.

Caldwell, Jack C., P. Caldwell, and P. Quiggins 1989. "The Social Context of AIDS in Sub-Saharan Africa," *Population and Development Review*, vol 15, no 2, pp 185–234.

Callaghy, Thomas M. 1984. *The State-Society Struggle: Zaire in Comparative Perspective*. New York: Columbia University Press.

Callaghy, Thomas M. 1988. "The State and the Development of Capitalism in Africa: Theoretical, Historical and Comparative Reflections" in D. Rothchild and N. Chazan (eds.), *The Precarious Balance: State and Society in Africa*. Boulder CO: Westview Press.

Callaghy, Thomas M. 1994. "Civil Society, Democracy, and Economic Change in Africa: A Dissenting Opinion about Resurgent Societies" in J. W. Harbeson, D. Rothchild, and N. Chazan (eds.), *Civil Society and the State in Africa*. Boulder CO: Lynne Rienner Publishers.

Campbell, A., P. Converse, W. Miller, and D. Stokes 1960. *The American Voter*. New York: John Wiley & Sons.

Cardoso, Fernando Henrique and Enzo Faletto 1969. *Dependency and Development in Latin America*. Berkeley: University of California Press.

Chabal, Patrick 1992. *Power in Africa: An Essay in Political Interpretation*. London: Macmillan.

Chabal, Patrick and Jean-Francois Daloz 1999. *Africa Works: Disorder as Political Instrument*. Oxford, UK: James Currey.

Chafer, Tony 2002. *The End of Empire in French West Africa: France's Successful Decolonization?* Oxford, UK, and New York: Berg.

Chambers, Robert 1969. *Settlement Schemes in Tropical Africa*. London: Routledge & Kegan Paul.

Chambers, Simone 2004. "Democracy, Popular Sovereignty and Constitutional Legitimacy," *Constellations*, vol 11, no 2 (June), pp 153–73.

Chayanov, Alexander V. 1966. *On the Theory of Peasant Economy*. Homewood IL: Irwin.

Chege, Michael 1972. "Systems Management and the Plan Implementation Process," Discussion Paper. University of Nairobi: Institute for Development Studies.

Chege, Michael 1999. "Comments on 'Structure and Strategy in Ethnic Conflict: A Few Steps toward Synthesis'" in *Annual World Bank Conference on Development Economics 1998*. Washington DC: World Bank.

Cheru, Fantu 2002. *African Renaissance: Roadmaps to the Challenge of Globalization*. London: Zed Books.

Chipman, John 1989. *French Power in Africa*. Oxford: Basil Blackwell.

Clapham, Christopher 1969. "Imperial Leadership in Ethiopia," *African Affairs*, vol 68, no 271 (April), pp 112–34.

Clapham, Christopher 1996. "Governmentality and Economic Policy in Sub-Saharan Africa," *Third World Quarterly*, vol 17, no 4, pp 809–24.

Clark, Andrew F. 1999. "Imperialism, Independence and Islam in Senegal and Mali," *Africa Today*, vol 46, no 3/4, pp 149–66.

Clark, John F. 1997. "Congo: Transition and the Struggle to Consolidate," in J. F. Clark and D. E. Gardinier (eds.), *Political Reform in Francophone Africa*. Boulder CO: Westview Press.

Clark, John F. and D. E. Gardinier (eds.) 1997. *Political Reform in Francophone Africa*. Boulder CO: Westview Press.

Clark, Paul G. 1965. *Development Planning in East Africa*. Nairobi: East African Publishing House.

Cliffe, Lionel 1964. "Nationalism and the Reactions to Enforced Agricultural Change in Tanganyika during the Colonial Period," paper presented at the East African Institute of Social Research Conference, Kampala, Uganda, December 9–11.

Cliffe, Lionel (ed.) 1967. *One-Party Democracy in Tanzania*. Nairobi: East African Publishing House.

Cliffe, Lionel 1976. "Rural Political Economy in Africa" in Peter C. W. Gutkind and I. Wallerstein (eds.), *The Political Economy of Contemporary Africa*. Beverly Hills: Sage Publications.

Cliffe, Lionel 1987. "The Debate about African Peasantries," *Development and Change*, vol 18, no 4, pp 625–35.

Cliffe, Lionel, J. S. Coleman, and M. R. Doornbos (eds.) 1977. *Government and Rural Development in East Africa*. The Hague: Martinus Nijhoff.

Cliffe, Lionel and John S. Saul (eds.) 1973. *Socialism in Tanzania*, vol 1. Nairobi: East African Publishing House.

Cohen, John M. 1991. "Expatriate Advisors in the Government of Kenya: Why They Are There and What Can Be Done About It." Development Discussion Paper No 376. Cambridge MA: Harvard Institute for International Development.

Coleman, James S. 1960. "The Politics of Sub-Saharan Africa" in G. A. Almond and J. S. Coleman (eds.), *The Politics of Developing Areas*. Princeton NJ: Princeton University Press.

Coleman, James S. and Carl G. Rosberg (eds.) 1966. *Political Parties and National Integration in Tropical Africa*. Berkeley and Los Angeles: University of California Press.

Collier, David and Steven Levitsky 1997. "Democracy with Adjectives: Conceptual Innovation in Comparative Politics," *World Politics*, vol 49, no 3, pp 430–51.

Collier, Paul 2001. "Economic Causes of Civil Conflict and Their Implications for Policy" in Chester A. Crocker, Fen Osler Hampson, and Pamela Aall (eds.), *Turbulent Peace: The Challenges of Managing International Conflict*. Washington DC: United States Institute of Peace.

Collier, Paul and Jan Willen Gunning 1999. "Explaining African Economic Performance," *Journal of Economic Literature*, vol 37, no 1, pp 64–111.

Collier, Paul and Anke Hoeffler 1998. "On the Economic Causes of Civil War," *Oxford Economic Papers – New Series*, vol 50, no 4, pp 563–73.

Collier, Paul and Anke Hoeffler 2001. *Greed and Grievance in Civil War*. Washington DC: World Bank.

Collier, Ruth Berins 1978. "Parties, Coups, and Authoritarian Rule: Patterns of Poilitical Change in Tropical Africa," *Comparative Political Studies*, vol 11, no 1 (April), pp 62–93.

Collins, Paul 1974. "The Working of Tanzania's Rural Development Fund: A Problem of Decentralisation," in A. H. Rweyemamu and B. Mwansasu (eds.), *Planning in Tanzania: Background to Decentralisation*. Nairobi: East African Literature Bureau.

Comaroff, John and J. Comaroff 1991. *Of Revelation and Revolution: Christianity, Colonialism and Consciousness in South Africa*, vol 1. Chicago: University of Chicago Press.

Coquery-Vidrovitch, Catherine 1976. "The Political Economy of the African Peasantry and Modes of Production" in P. C. W. Gutkind and I. Wallerstein (eds.), *The Political Economy of Contemporary Africa*. Beverly Hills: Sage Publications.
Coulson, Andrew 1982. *Tanzania: A Political Economy*. Oxford: Clarendon Press.
Cruise O'Brien, Donald 1975. *Saints and Politicians: Essays in the Organization of a Senegalese Peasant Society*. Cambridge, UK: Cambridge University Press.
Dahl, Robert 1957. "The Concept of Power," *Behavioral Science*, vol 2, pp 201–05.
Daloz, Jean-Pascal 2002. "'Cultural Heritage' and Enduring Mentalities: Reflections on Political Representation and Accountability," paper presented at the Conference on Culture, Democracy and Development, Monte Verita, Locarno, Switzerland, October 6–11.
Decalo, Samuel 1992. "The Process, Prospects, and Constraints of Democratization in Africa," *African Affairs*, vol 91, no 362, pp 7–35.
de Soysa, Indra and Nils Petter Gleditsch 2002. "The Liberal Globalist Case" in Bjorn Hettne and Bertil Oden (eds.), *Global Governance in the 21st Century: Alternative Perspectives on World Order*, EGDI Study 2002:2. Stockholm: Ministry of Foreign Affairs.
de Villiers, Les (ed.) 2003. *Africa 2004*. Canaan CT: Business Books International.
Dia, Mamadou 1996. *Africa's Management in the 1990s: Reconciling Indigenous and Transplanted Institutions*. Washington DC: World Bank.
Diamond, Larry 1983. "Social Change and Political Conflict in Nigeria's Second Republic" in I. W. Zartman (ed.), *Political Economy of Nigeria*. New York: Praeger.
Diouf, Mamadou 1996. "Urban Youth and Senegalese Politics," *Public Culture*, vol 8, no 2, pp 225–50.
Djurfeldt, Goran 2004. "Global Perspectives on Agricultural Development," paper presented at Workshop on African Food Crisis: The Relevance of Asian Models, Nairobi, Kenya, January 26–30.
Dollar, David and Jakob Svensson 2000. "What Explains the Success or Failure of Structural Adjustment Programs?" *Economic Journal*, vol 110, no 466, pp 894–917.
Dolowitz, David P. and David Marsh 2000. "Learning from Abroad: The Role of Policy Transfer in Contemporary Policy-Making," *Governance*, vol 13, no 1, pp 5–24.
Dos Santos, Theotonio 1970. "The Structure of Dependence, *American Economic Review*, vol 60, no 2, pp 231–36.
Downs, Anthony 1957. *An Economic Theory of Democracy*. New York: Harper & Row.
Downs, R. E. and Stephen P. Reyna 1988. *Land and Society in Contemporary Africa*. Hanover NH: University Press of New Hampshire.
Dozon, Jean-Pierre 2003. *Freres et sujets. La France et l'Afrique en perspective*. Paris: Flammarion.
Dror, Yehezkel 1969. *Public Policy-Making Re-Examined*. Scranton PA: Chandler Publishing House.
Dumont, Rene 1966. *False Start in Africa*. London: Andre Deutsch.
Durkheim, Emile 1975. *Textes*. Paris: Editions Minuit.
Easterly, William and Ross Levine 1997. "Africa's Growth Tragedy: Policies and Ethnic Divisions," *Quarterly Journal of Economics*, no 112, pp 1203–50.

The Economist 2004. "How to Make Africa Smile: A Survey of Sub-Saharan Africa," January 17.

Ekeh, Peter P. 1975. "Colonialism and the Two Publics in Africa: A Theoretical Statement," *Comparative Studies in Society and History*, vol 17, no 1, pp 91–112.

Ekeh, Peter P. 1990. "Social Anthropology and Two Contrasting Uses of Tribalism in Africa," *Comparative Studies in Society and History*, vol 32, no 4, pp 660–700.

ElBadawi, Ibrahim and Nicholas Sambanis 2000. "Why Are There So Many Civil Wars in Africa? Understanding and Preventing Violent Conflict," *Journal of African Economies*, vol 9, no 3, pp 244–69.

Elgstrom, Ole 1999. "Giving Aid on the Recipient's Terms: The Swedish Experience in Tanzania" in G. Hyden and R. Mukandala (eds.), *Agencies in Foreign Aid: Comparing China, Sweden and the United States in Tanzania*. Basingstoke, UK: Macmillan and New York: St. Martin's Press.

Eller, Jack and Reed Coughland 1993. "The Poverty of Primordialism: The Demystification of Ethnic Attachment," *Ethnic and Racial Studies*, vol 16, no 2, pp 183–202.

Ellis, Frank 1998. "Household Strategies and Rural Livelihood Diversification," *Journal of Development Studies*, vol 35, no 1, pp 1–38.

Elster, Jon 1997. "Ways of Constitution-Making" in A. Hadenius (ed.), *Democracy's Victory and Crisis*. Cambridge, UK: Cambridge University Press.

Emmanuel, Arghiri 1972. *Unequal Exchange*. New York: Monthly Review Press.

Emerson, Richard M. 1962. "Power-Dependence Relations," *American Sociological Review*, vol 27, no 1, pp 31–41.

Engels, Friedrich 1939. *Anti-Duhring*. New York: International Publishers.

Eriksen, Thomas Hylland 1993. *Ethnicity and Nationalism: Anthropological Perspectives*. London: Pluto Press.

Eriksson, Mikael, Peter Wallensteen, and Margareta Sollenberg 2003. "Armed Conflicts 1989–2002," *Journal of Peace Research*, vol 40, no 5, pp 593–607.

Etounga-Manguelle, Daniel 2002. "Who Are the Africans and What Is Wrong with Them?," paper presented at the Conference on Culture, Democracy and Development, Monte Verita, Locarno, Switzerland, October 6–11.

Evans, Peter 1987. "Foreign Capital and the Third World State" in M. Weiner and S. P. Huntington (eds.), *Understanding Political Development*. Prospect Heights IL: Waveland Press.

Evans, Peter 1995. *Embedded Autonomy: States and Industrial Transformation*. Princeton NJ: Princeton University Press.

Fairley, Nancy J. 1987. "Ideology and State Formation: The Ekie of Southern Zaire" in I. Kopytoff (ed.), *The African Frontier: The Reproduction of Traditional African Societies*. Bloomington IN: Indiana University Press.

Fanon, Frantz 1967. *The Wretched of the Earth*. Harmondsworth: Penguin Books.

Faure, Veronique (ed.) 2000. *Dynamiques religieueses en Afrique australe*. Paris: Karthala.

Fenno, Richard F. Jr. 1966. *The Power of the Purse: Appropriations Politics in Congress*. Boston: Little Brown.

Ferguson, James 1990. *The Anti-Politics Machine: 'Development', Depoliticization and Bureaucratic Power in Lesotho*. Cambridge, UK: Cambridge University Press.

Food and Agriculture Organization (FAO) 1985. *Women and Developing Agriculture*, Women in Agriculture Series No 4. Rome: FAO.

Forrest, Joshua B. 2003. *Lineages of State Fragility: Rural Civil Society in Guinea-Bissau*. Athens OH: Ohio University Press and Oxford, UK: James Currey.

Frank, Andre Gunder 1964. "Administrative Role Definition and Social Change," *Human Organization*, vol 22, no 4, pp 238–42.

Frank, Andre Gunder 1969. *Latin America: Underdevelopment and Revolution*. New York: Monthly Review Press.

Fukuyama, Francis 1995. *Trust: The Social Virtues and the Creation of Prosperity*. New York: Free Press.

Gage-Brown, A. and D. Meekers 1993. "Sex, Contraception, and Childbearing before Marriage," *International Family Planning Perspectives*, vol 19, no 1, pp 37–54.

Galvan, Dennis C. 2002. *The State Must Be Our Master of Fire: How Peasants Craft Culturally Sustainable Development in Senegal*. Berkeley: University of California Press.

Galvez, William (translated by Mary Todd) 1999. *Che in Africa: Che Guervara's Congo Diary*. New York: Ocean Press.

Gardinier, David E. 1997. "Gabon: Limited Reform and Regime Survival" in John F. Clark and David E. Gardinier (eds.), *Political Reform in Francophone Africa*. Boulder CO: Westview Press.

Geddes, Barbara 1994. *Politicians' Dilemma*. Berkeley and Los Angeles: University of California Press.

Geertz, Clifford (ed.) 1963. *Old Societies and New States*. New York: Free Press of Glencoe.

Geisler, Gisela 2000. "'Parliament Is Another Terrain of Struggle': Women, Men and Politics in South Africa," *Journal of Modern African Studies*, vol 38, no 4, pp 605–30.

Gellner, Ernst 1983. *Nations and Nationalism*. Ithaca NY: Cornell University Press.

Genoud, Roger 1969. *Nationalism and Economic Development in Ghana*. New York: Praeger.

Gerlach, Michael L. 1992. *Alliance Capitalism: The Social Organization of Japanese Business*. Berkeley: University of California Press.

Gerth, Hans and C. Wright Mills (eds. and translators) 1958 [1946]. *From Max Weber: Essays in Sociology*. New York: Oxford University Press.

Geschiere, Peter 1997. *The Modernity of Witchcraft: Politics and the Occult in Postcolonial Africa*. Charlottesville and London: University of Virginia Press.

Geschiere, Peter and Joseph Gugler 1998. "Introduction: The Urban-Rural Connection – Changing Issues of Belonging and Identification," *Africa*, vol 68, no 3, pp 309–19.

Giddens, Anthony 1991. *The Consequences of Modernity*. Stanford CA: Stanford University Press.

Gleditsch, Nils Petter, Peter Wallensteen, Mikael Eriksson, Margareta Sollenberg, and Havard Strand 2003. "Armed Conflict 1946–2001: A New Dataset," *Journal of Peace Research*, vol 39, no 5, pp 615–37.

Glickman, Harvey 1997. "Tanzania: From Disillusionment to Guarded Optimism," *Current History* (May), pp 217–21.

Gluckman, Max 1965. *Politics, Law, and Ritual in Tribal Society*. Oxford, UK: Blackwell.

Godelier, Maurice 1975. "Modes of Production, Kinship and Demographic Structures" in Maurice Bloch (ed.), *Marxist Analyses and Social Anthropology*. London: Malaby Press.

Godelier, Maurice 1977. *Marxist Perspectives in Anthropology*. Cambridge, UK: Cambridge University Press.

Goheen, Miriam 1991. "The Ideology and Political Economy of Gender: Women and Land in Nso, Cameroon" in Christina H. Gladwin (ed.), *Structural Adjustment and African Women Farmers*. Gainesville FL: University of Florida Press.

Goetz, Anne Marie and Shireen Hassim (eds.) 2003. *No Shortcuts to Power: African Women in Politics and Policy Making*. London: Zed Press.

Goody, Jack 1969. "Inheritance, Property and Marriage in Africa and Eurasia" in *Sociology*, vol 3, no 1, pp 55–76.

Goody, Jack 1971. *Technology, Tradition, and the State in Africa*. Cambridge, UK: Cambridge University Press.

Goody, Jack 1973. "Bridewealth and Dowry in Africa and Eurasia" in J. Goody and S. J. Tambiah, *Bridewealth and Dowry*. Cambridge, UK: Cambridge University Press.

Goody, Jack 1976. *Production and Reproduction: A Comparative Study of the Domestic Domain*. Cambridge, UK: Cambridge University Press.

Gordon, Joshua 2003. "Appropriating a Sociological Political Science: Explaining the Breakdown of the Appropriations Process in the U.S. Congress," paper presented at the Annual Meeting of the American Political Science Association, Philadelphia, August 28–31.

Gouldner, Alvin 1954. *Patterns of Industrial Bureaucracy*. Glencoe IL: Free Press.

Granovetter, M. 1985. "Economic Action and Social Structure: The Problem of Embeddedness," *American Journal of Sociology*, vol 91, no 2, pp 481–510.

Green, Reginald H. 1974. "Relevance, Efficiency, Romanticism and Confusion in Tanzanian Planning and Management," paper presented at the Seminar on Improvement of Management in Tanzania, Dar es Salaam, February 18–19.

Greif, Abner and David D. Laitin 2004. "A Theory of Endogenous Institutional Change," *American Political Science Review*, vol 98, no 4 (November), pp 633–52.

Grosh, Barbara 1991. *Public Enterprise in Kenya: What Works, What Doesn't and Why*. Boulder CO: Lynne Rienner Publishers.

Gulliver, P. H. (ed.) 1969. *Tradition and Transition in East Africa: Studies of the Tribal Element in the Modern Era*. London: Routledge & Kegan Paul.

Gurr, Ted 1970. *Why Men Rebel*. Princeton NJ: Princeton University Press.

Gurr, Ted and Mark Lichbach 1979. "Forecasting Domestic Political Conflict" in David Singer and Michael Wallace (eds.), *To Augur Well: Early Warning Indicators in World Politics*. Beverly Hills CA: Sage Publications.

Gutto, Shadrack B. O. 1976. "The Status of Women in Kenya: A Study of Paternalism, Inequality and Underprivilege," Discussion Paper No 235. Nairobi: University of Nairobi, Institute for Development Studies.

Guyer, Jane 1997. *An African Niche Economy: Farming to Feed Ibadan*. London: Edinburgh University Press.

Habermas, Jurgen 1979. *Communication and the Evolution of Society*. Boston: Beacon Press.

Haggard, Stephan and Robert Kaufman (eds.) 1992. *The Politics of Economic Adjustment*. Princeton NJ: Princeton University Press.

Haggard, Stephan and Robert Kaufman 1995. *The Political Economy of Democratic Transitions*. Princeton NJ: Princeton University Press.

Haggblade, Steven 2004. "From Roller Coasters to Rocket Ships: The Role of Technology in African Agricultural Successes," paper presented at Workshop on African Food Crisis: The Relevance of Asian Models, Nairobi, Kenya, January 26–30.

Hammarskjold Foundation 1987. "The State and the Crisis in Africa: Toward a Second Liberation in Africa, *Development Dialogue*, Nos 1987: 1–2.

Hammarskjold Foundation 1995. *Autonomous Development Funds in Africa: Report from an Expert Consultation in Kampala, Uganda 4–6 April 1995*. Uppsala: Dag Hammarskjold Centre.

Hart, Keith 1982. *The Political Economy of West African Agriculture*. Cambridge, UK: Cambridge University Press.

Henderson, Errol 2002. *Democracy and War: The End of an Illusion?* Boulder CO: Lynne Rienner Publishers.

Henderson, Errol and J. David Singer 2000. "Civil War in the Postcolonial World, 1946–92," *Journal of Peace Research*, vol 37, no 3, pp 275–99.

Herbst, Jeffrey 2000. *States and Power in Africa: Comparative Lessons in Authority and Control*. Princeton NJ: Princeton University Press.

Higgot, Richard 1980. "Structural Dependence and Decolonisation in a West African Landlocked State: Niger," *Review of African Political Economy*, no 17 (January–April), pp 51–68.

Hill, Polly 1972. *Rural Hausa: A Village and a Setting*. Cambridge, UK: Cambridge University Press.

Hindess, Barry and Paul C. Hirst 1975. *Pre-Capitalist Modes of Production*. London: Routledge & Kegan Paul.

Hirschman, Albert O. 1965. *Journeys Toward Progress*. New York: Doubleday and Co.

Hirschman, Albert O. 1970. *Exit, Voice and Loyalty*. Cambridge MA: Harvard University Press.

Hodgkin, Thomas 1956. *Nationalism in Colonial Africa*. London: Frederick Muller.

Hodgkin, Thomas 1961. *African Political Parties*. Harmondsworth: Penguin Books.

Holm, John D. and Patrick P. Molutsi 1992. "State-Society Relations in Botswana: Beginning Liberalization" in G. Hyden and M. Bratton (eds.), *Governance and Politics in Africa*. Boulder CO: Lynne Rienner Publishers.

Holmquist, Frank 1970. "Implementing Rural Development Projects" in G. Hyden, R. H. Jackson, and J. J. Okumu (eds.), *Development Administration: The Kenyan Experience*. Nairobi: Oxford University Press.

Hoon, Parakh 2002. "The Verticalization of Personal-Reciprocal Relationships: Changes in the Local Political Economy of Eastern Zambia," paper presented at the Annual Meeting of the American Political Science Association, Boston, August 29–September 1.

Horowitz, Donald L. 1985. *Ethnic Groups in Conflict*. Berkeley: University of California Press.

Howard, Rhoda 1986. *Human Rights in Commonwealth Africa.* Totowa NJ: Rowman & Littlefield.

Hughes, S. and I. Malila 1996. "Messages from the Urban Environment: The Social Construction of HIV/AIDS in Botswana," paper presented at the 19th SAUSSC Conference, Mmabatho, South Africa, December 1–6.

Hunt, C. 1989. "Migrant Labour and Sexually Transmitted Diseases: AIDS in Africa," *Journal of Health and Social Behaviour*, vol 30, no 4, pp 353–73.

Huntington, Samuel P. 1991. *The Third Wave: Democratization in the Late Twentieth Century.* Norman OK: University of Oklahoma Press.

Huntington, Samuel P. 1997. *The Clash of Civilizations and the Re-Making of World Order.* New York: Simon & Schuster.

Hutchful, Eboe 1989. "From 'Revolution' to Monetarism: The Economics and Politics of the Adjustment Programme in Ghana" in Bonnie Campbell and John Loxley (eds.), *Structural Adjustment in Africa.* London: Macmillan.

Hyden, Goran 1968. "Mao and Mwalimu: The Soldier and Teacher as Revolutionary," *Transition* (Kampala, Uganda), no 34, pp 24–30.

Hyden, Goran 1969. *Political Development in Rural Tanzania.* Nairobi: East African Publishing House.

Hyden, Goran 1973. *Efficiency versus Distribution in East African Cooperatives.* Nairobi: East African Literature Bureau.

Hyden, Goran 1975. "We Must Run while Others Walk: Policy-Making for Socialist Development in the Tanzania-Type of Polities," Economic Research Bureau Paper No 75.1. University of Dar es Salaam.

Hyden, Goran 1979. "Administration and Public Policy" in J. D. Barkan and J. J. Okumu (eds.), *Politics and Public Policy in Kenya and Tanzania.* New York: Praeger.

Hyden, Goran 1980. *Beyond Ujamaa in Tanzania.* Berkeley: University of California Press.

Hyden, Goran 1983. *No Shortcuts to Progress.* Berkeley: University of California Press.

Hyden, Goran 1988. "Beyond Hunger in Africa – Breaking the Spell of Monoculture" in Ronald Cohen (ed.), *Satisfying Africa's Food Needs.* Boulder CO: Lynne Rienner Publishers.

Hyden, Goran and Mahlet Hailemariam 2003. "Voluntarism and Civil Society: Ethiopia in Comparative Perspective," *Afrika Spectrum*, vol 38, no 2, pp 215–34.

Hyden, Goran and Rwekaza Mukandala (eds.) 1999. *Agencies in Foreign Aid.* Basingstoke, UK: Macmillan.

Hyden, Goran and Denis Venter (eds.) 2001. *Constitution-Making and Democratization in Africa.* Pretoria: Africa Institute of South Africa Press.

Iliffe, John 1983. *The Emergence of African Capitalism.* London: Macmillan.

Imai, Ken'ichi 1986. "The Corporate Network in Japan," *Japanese Economic Studies,* vol 16, no 1, pp 3–16.

Inkeles, Alex and David H. Smith 1974. *Becoming Modern: Individual Change in Six Developing Countries.* Cambridge MA: Harvard University Press.

International Bank for Reconstruction and Development (World Bank) 1961. *The Economic Development of Tanganyika: Report of a Mission Organized by the IBRD at the Request of the Governments of Tanganyika and the United Kingdom.* Baltimore: Johns Hopkins University Press.

Isaacman, Allen F. 1993. "Peasants and Rural Social Protest" in F. Cooper, A. F. Isaacman, F. E. Mallon, W. Roseberry, and S. J. Stern (eds.), *Confronting Historical Paradigms: Peasants, Labour and the Capitalist World System in Africa and Latin America*. Madison WI: University of Wisconsin Press.

Jackson, Robert H. 1990. *Quasi-States: Sovereignty, International Relations, and the Third World*. Cambridge, UK: Cambridge University Press.

Jackson, Robert H. and Carl G. Rosberg 1982. *Personal Rule in Black Africa*. Berkeley: University of California Press.

Joseph, Richard 1987. *Democracy and Prebendalism in Nigeria*. New York: Cambridge University Press.

Kabbaj, Omar 2004. "The Challenges and Opportunities of Globalization for Africa," address at the Center for African Studies, University Copenhagen, November 2.

Kahn, Joel S. and Joseph R. Llobera (eds.) 1981. *The Anthropology of Pre-capitalist Societies*. London: Macmillan.

Kaplinsky, Raphael 1980. "Capitalist Accumulation in the Periphery: The Kenyan Case Reexamined," *Review of African Political Economy*, no 17 (January–April), pp 92–108.

Karlstrom, Mikael 1996. "Imagining Democracy," *Africa*, vol 66, no 4, pp 485–504.

Kasfir, Nelson 1979. "Explaining Ethnic Political Participation," *World Politics*, vol 31 (April), pp 365–88.

Kasfir, Nelson 1986. "Are African Peasants Self-Sufficient?," *Development and Change*, vol 17, no 2, pp 335–57.

Kasfir, Nelson (ed.) 1998. *Civil Society and Democracy in Africa: Critical Perspectives*. London: Frank Cass.

Kaul, R. N. 1989. "Gender Issues in Farming: A Case for Developing Farm Tools Specially for Women," paper presented at the Farming Systems Research Symposium, University of Arkansas, Fayetteville.

Kay, Geoffrey 1975. *Development and Underdevelopment: A Marxist Analysis*. London: Macmillan.

Keane, John 1984. *Public Life and Late Capitalism*. Cambridge, UK: Cambridge University Press.

Kebbede, Girma 1992. *The State and Development in Ethiopia*. Englewood NJ: Humanities Press.

Kelsall, Tim 2003. "Democracy, De-Agrarianization and the African Self," Centre of African Studies Occasional Paper, University of Copenhagen.

Kennedy, Paul 1988. *African Capitalism: The Struggle for Ascendancy*. Cambridge, UK: Cambridge University Press.

Kenyatta, Jomo 1968. *Suffering without Bitterness*. Nairobi: East African Publishing House.

Khadiagala, Gilbert M. 1995. "State Collapse and Reconstruction in Uganda" in I. W. Zartman (ed.), *Collapsed States: The Disintegration and Restoration of Legitimate Authority*. London and Boulder CO: Lynne Rienner Publishers.

Kiggundu, Moses 1991. "The Challenges of Management Development in Sub-Saharan Africa," *Journal of Management Development*, vol 10, no 6, pp 42–57.

Killick, Tony 1974. "The Possibilities of Development Planning," Working Paper No 165. University of Nairobi: Institute for Development Studies.

Kjaer, Anne Mette 2002. *The Politics of Civil Service Reform: A Comparative Analysis of Uganda and Tanzania in the 1990s.* Arhus, Denmark: Politica.

Kjaer, Anne Mette 2004a. "'Old Brooms Can Sweep Too!' An Overview of Rulers and Public Sector Reforms in Uganda, Tanzania and Kenya," *Journal of Modern African Studies,* vol 42, no 3, pp 389–413.

Kjaer, Anne Mette 2004b. *Governance.* Cambridge, UK: Polity Press.

Kjekshus, Helge 1977. *Ecology Control and Economic Development in East African History.* London: Heinemann Educational Books.

Kohnert, Dirk 2002. "The Impact of Occult Belief Systems on Democratization and Development in African Societies: Working Hypotheses and Case Studies," paper presented at the Conference on Culture, Democracy and Development, Monte Verita, Locarno, Switzerland, October 6–11.

Kopytoff, Igor (ed.) 1987. *The African Frontier: The Reproduction of Traditional African Societies.* Bloomington IN: Indiana University Press.

Korten David and R. Klauss (eds.) 1985. *People-Centered Development: Contributions toward Theory and Planning Frameworks.* West Hartford CT: Kumarian Press.

Kunz, Frank 1973. "Notes on Some Aspects of Tanzania's Contribution to Comparative Politics," unpublished manuscript, Department of Political Science, University of Dar es Salaam.

Kuznets, Simon 1955. "Economic Growth and Income Inequality," *American Economic Review,* vol 45, no 1 (March 1955), pp 17–26.

Laakso, Maarku and Rein Taagepera 1979. "'Effective' Number of Parties: A Measure with Application to West Europe," *Comparative Political Studies,* vol 12, no 1, pp 3–27.

Laclau, Ernesto 1971. "Feudalism and Capitalism in Latin America," *New Left Review,* vol 67, pp 19–38.

Laitin, David D. 1992. *Language Repertoires and State Construction in Africa.* New York: Cambridge University Press.

Langdon, Steven 1987. "Industrry and Capitalism in Kenya: Contributions to a Debate," in Paul M. Lubeck (ed.), *The African Bourgeoisie: Capitalist Development in Nigeria, Kenya, and the Ivory Coast.* Boulder CO: Lynne Rienner Publishers.

Larsson, Rolf 2004. "Conditions of Agricultural Intensification – A Farm Level Analysis," paper presented at the Workshop on African Food Crisis: The Relevance of Asian Models, Nairobi, Kenya, January 26–30.

Lee-Smith, Diana 1989. "Urban Management in Nairobi: A Case Study of the Matatu Mode of Public Transport" in R. Stren and R. R. White (eds.), *African Cities in Crisis: Managing Rapid Urban Growth.* Boulder CO: Westview Press.

Lele, Uma 1991. "Women, Structural Adjustment, and Transformation: Some Lessons and Questions from the African Experience" in C. H. Gladwin (ed.), *Structural Adjustment and African Women Farmers.* Gainesville FL: University of Florida Press.

Lele, Uma and S. B. Stone 1989. *Population Pressure, Environment and Agricultural Intensification: Variations of the Boserup Hypothesis.* Washington DC: World Bank.

Lemarchand, René 1970. *Rwanda and Burundi.* London: Pall Mall.

Lemarchand, René 1972. "Political Clientelism and Ethnicity in Tropical Africa: Competing Solidarities in Nation-Building," *American Political Science Review*, vol 66, no 1, pp 91–112.

Lemarchand, René 1994. *Burundi: Ethnocide as Discourse and Practice*. New York: Cambridge University Press.

Leonard, David K. and Scott Strauss 2003. *Africa's Stalled Development: International Causes and Cures*. Boulder CO: Lynne Rienner Publishers.

Lerner, Daniel 1958. *The Passing of Traditional Society*. Glencoe IL: Free Press.

Leslie, Agnes 2003. "Social Movement and Democracy in Africa: The Impact of Women's Struggle for Equal Rights in Botswana," Ph.D. dissertation, University of Florida.

LeVine, Robert A. 1966. *Dreams and Deeds: Achievement Motivation in Nigeria*. Chicago: University of Chicago Press.

LeVine, Victor 1994. "Constitutions and Constitution-Making in West Africa," paper presented at a Symposium on Constitution-Making, Constitutional Commission of Eritrea, Asmara, January 7–11.

Lewis, Peter 1992. "Political Transition and the Dilemma of Civil Society in Africa," *Journal of International Affairs*, vol 46, no 1, pp 31–54.

Leys, Colin (ed.) 1969. *Politics and Change in Developing Countries*. Cambridge, UK: Cambridge University Press.

Leys, Colin 1975. *Underdevelopment in Kenya*. London: Heinemann Educational Books.

Leys, Colin 1996. *The Rise and Fall of Development Theory*. Bloomington IN: Indiana University Press and Oxford, UK: James Currey.

Lijphart, Arend 1977. *Democracy in Plural Societies: A Comparative Exploration*. New Haven CT: Yale University Press.

Lindberg, Staffan I. 2003. "It's Our Time to 'Chop': Do Elections in Africa Feed Neo-patrimonialism rather than Counter-Act It?" *Democratization*, vol 10, no 2, pp 121–40.

Lindberg, Staffan I. 2004. *The Power of Elections*, Lund Political Studies No 134. Lund, Sweden: Department of Political Science.

Linz, Juan and Alfred Stepan 1996. *The Problems of Democratic Transition and Consolidation: Southern Europe, South America, and Post-communist Europe*. Baltimore: Johns Hopkins University Press.

Lipset, Seymour Martin 1959. "Some Social Requisites of Democracy: Economic Development and Legitimacy," *American Political Science Review*, vol 53, no 1, pp 69–105.

Lipton, Michael 1977. *Why Poor People Stay Poor: Urban Bias in World Development*. Cambridge MA: Harvard University Press.

Little, Kenneth 1965. *West African Urbanization: A Study of Voluntary Organizations in Social Change*. Cambridge, UK: Cambridge University Press.

Lonsdale, John 1994. "Moral Ethnicity and Political Tribalism" in P. Kaarsholm and J. Hultin (eds.), *Inventions and Boundaries: Historical and Anthropological Approaches to the Study of Ethnicity and Nationalism*. International Development Studies, Roskilde University, Roskilde, Denmark.

Luhmann, Niklas 1988. "Familiarity, Confidence, Trust: Problems and Alternatives" in D. Gambetta (ed.), *Trust: Making and Breaking Cooperative Relations*. Oxford, UK: Blackwell.

MacGaffey, Janet 1987. *Entrepreneurs and Parasites: The Struggle for Indigenous Capitalism in Zaire*. Cambridge, UK: Cambridge University Press.

MacGaffey, Janet 1988. "Economic Disengagement and Class Formation in Zaire" in D. Rothchild and N. Chazan (eds.), *The Precarious Balance: State and Society in Africa*. Boulder CO: Westview Press.

MacGaffey, Wyatt 1970. *Custom and Government in the Lower Congo*. Berkeley: University of California Press.

Mafeje, Archie 1971. "The Ideology of 'Tribalism," *Journal of Modern African Studies*, vol 9, no 2, pp 253–61.

Mama, Amina 1996. *Women Studies and Studies of Women in Africa during the 1990s*. Dakar: CODESRIA Press.

Mamdani, Mahmood 1976. *Politics and Class Formation in Uganda*. London: Heinemann.

Mamdani, Mahmood 1996. *Citizen and Subject: Contemporary Africa and the Legacy of Late Colonialism*. Princeton NJ: Princeton University Press.

Markovitz, Leonard I. (ed.) 1987. *Studies in Power and Class in Africa*. Oxford, UK: Oxford University Press.

Marris, Peter and Anthony Somerset 1971. *African Businessmen: A Study of Entrepreneurship and Development in Kenya*. London: Routledge & Kegan Paul.

Marx, Karl 1970. *A Contribution to the Critique of Political Economy*. New York: International Publishers.

Mattila, Paivi 1992. "A Study of Women in Informal Markets: Women Traders and Women's Marketing Networks in Mwanga and Moshi Districts in Tanzania," M. A. thesis, University of Helsinki.

Mbaku, John M. and Julius O. Ihonvbere 1998. *Multiparty Democracy and Political Change: Constraints to Democratization in Africa*. Aldershot, UK: Ashgate.

Mbembe, Achille 2001. *On the Postcolony*. Berkeley and Los Angeles: University of California Press.

Mbete-Kgositsile, Baleka 2001. "The Principal Actors in the South African Constitution-Making Process" in G. Hyden and D. Venter (eds.), *Constitution-Making and Democratization in Africa*. Pretoria: Africa Institute of South Africa Press.

McLelland, David C. 1961. *The Achieving Society*. Princeton NJ: Van Nostrand.

McNally. N. J. 1988. "Law in a Changing Society: A View from North of the Limpopo," *South African Law Journal*, no 105, pp 426–36.

Medard, Jean-Francois 1982. "The Underdeveloped State in Tropical Africa: Political Clientelism or Neo-patrimonialism" in C. Clapham (ed.), *Private Patronage and Public Power: Political Clientelism in the Modern State*. London: Frances Pinter.

Meyer, M. et al. 1985. *Limits to Bureaucratic Growth*. New York and Berlin: Walter de Gruyter.

Meillassoux, Claude 1975. *Femmes, Greniers, Capitaux*. Paris: Maspero.

Middleton, John et al. 1996. *Encyclopedia of Sub-Saharan Africa*. New York: Simon and Schuster.

Migdal, Joel S. 1988. *Strong Societies and Weak States: State-Society Relations and State Capabilities in the Third World*. Princeton NJ: Princeton University Press.

Miller, Norman 1970. "The Rural African Party: Political Participation in Tanzania," *American Political Science Review*, vol 64, no 2, pp 548–71.

Mittelman, James H. 2000. *The Globalization Syndrome: Transformation and Resistance*. Princeton NJ: Princeton University Press.

Mkandawire, Thandika and Adebayo Olukoshi (eds.) 1995. *Between Liberlisation and Oppression: The Politics of Structural Adjustment in Africa*. Dakar, Senegal: Codesria Book Series.

Mkandawire, Thandika and C. C. Soludo 1999. *Our Continent, Our Future*. Trenton NJ: Africa World Press.

Molm, Linda D. 1997. *Coercive Power in Social Exchange*. Cambridge, UK: Cambridge University Press.

Monga, Celestin 1998. *The Anthropology of Anger: Civil Society and Democracy in Africa*. Boulder CO: Lynne Rienner Publishers.

Monga, Celestin 1993. "Civil Society and Democratization in Francophone Africa," *Journal of Modern African Studies*, vol 33, no 3, pp 359–81.

Montgomery, John D. 1987. "Probing Managerial Behavior: Image and Reality in Southern Africa," *World Development*, vol 15, no 4, pp 518–34.

Moock, Joyce 1978. "The Content and Maintenance of Social Ties between Urban Migrants and Their Home-Based Support Groups: The Maragoli Case," *African Urban Notes*, vol 3, no 4 (Winter), pp 15–32.

Moore, Mick 1997. "Death without Taxes: Democracy, State Capacity and Aid Dependence in the Fourth World" in G. White and M. Robinson (eds.), *Towards a Democratic Development State*. Oxford, UK: Oxford University Press.

Morgenthau, Ruth Schachter 1961. "Single-Party Systems in West Africa," *American Political Science Review*, vol 55, no 2 (June), pp. 294–307.

Moris, Jon R. 1973. "Managerial Structures and Plan Implementation in Colonial and Modern Agricultural Extension: A Comparison of Cotton and Tea Programmes in Central Kenya" in D. K. Leonard (ed.), *Rural Administration in Kenya*. Nairobi: East African Literature Bureau.

Moris, Jon R. 1977. "The Transferability of Western Management Concepts and Programs: An East African Perspective" in L. D. Stifel, J. S. Coleman, and J. E. Black (eds.), *Education and Training for Public Sector Management in Developing Countries*. New York: Rockefeller Foundation.

Morris MacLean, Lauren 2003. "Economies of Affection in Crisis: How the 'Weak' State Transform Informal Institutions in Africa," paper presented at the Annual Meeting of the American Political Science Association, Philadelphia, August 28–31.

Mozzafar, Shaheen, James Scarritt, and Glen Galaich 2003. "Electoral Institutions, Ethnopolitical Cleavages and Party Systems in Africa's Emerging Democracies," *American Political Science Review*, vol 97, no 3, pp 379–90.

Mueller, Hans-Peter, Wolf Linder, and Patrick Ziltener 2002. "Culture, Democracy and Development: Cultural and Political Foundations of Socio-Economic Development in Africa and Asia." Paper presented at the Conference on Culture, Democracy and Development, Monte Verita, Locarno, Switzerland, October 6–11.

Mukandala, Rwekaza 1988. *The Political Economy of Parastatal Enterprise in Tanzania and Botswana*. PhD. dissertation, Department of Political Science, University of California at Berkeley.

Mukandala, Rwekaza 1999. "From Proud Defiance to Beggary: A Recipient's Tale" in G. Hyden and R. Mukandala (eds.), *Agencies in Foreign Aid: China, Sweden and the United States in Tanzania*. Basingstoke, UK: Macmillan and New York: St. Martin's Press.

Museveni, Yoweri 1997. *Sowing the Mustard Seed: The Struggles for Freedom and Democracy in Uganda*. Basingstoke, UK: Macmillan.

Mushanga, Tibamanya M. 1978. "Wife Victimization in East and Central Africa," *Victimology*, vol. 2, nos 3–4, pp 479–85.

Mwansasu, Bismarck U. and R. Cranford Pratt (eds.) 1979. *Towards Socialism in Tanzania*. Toronto: Toronto University Press.

Myrdal, Gunnar 1968. *Asian Drama: An Inquiry into the Poverty of Nations*. New York: Pantheon Books.

Ndegwa, Stephen N. 1997. "Citizenship and Ethnicity: An Examination of Two Transition Moments in Kenyan Politics," *American Political Science Review*, vol 91, no 3, pp 599–616.

Nelson, Joan M. 1994. *Intricate Links: Democratization and Market Reforms in Latin America and Eastern Europe*. Trenton NJ: Transaction Publishers.

Netting, Robert M. 1993. *Smallholders, Householders, Farm Families and the Ecology of Intensive Sustainable Agriculture*. Stanford CA: Stanford University Press.

Nkrumah, Kwame 1961. *I Speak of Freedom: A Statement of African Ideology*. New York: Praeger.

Noergaard, Ole and Karin Hilmer Pedersen 2002. "Development, Law and Democracy: Exploring a New Relationship" in G. Hyden and O. Elgstrom (eds.), *Development and Democracy: What Have We Learned and How?* London and New York: Routledge.

Norman, David W., Mark Newman, and Ismael Ouedradogo 1981. *Farm and Village Production in Semi Arid Tropics of West Africa*, two volumes. Hyderabad, India: ICRISAT.

North, Douglass 1990. *Institutions, Institutional Change and Economic Performance*. New York: Cambridge University Press.

Nyerere, Julius K. 1968. *Freedom and Socialism*. Dar es Salaam: Oxford University Press.

Nyerere, Julius K. 1973. *Freedom and Development*. Dar es Salaam: Oxford University Press.

Nzomo, Maria 1997. "Kenyan Women in Politics and Public Decision Making" in G. Mikell (ed.), *African Feminism*. Philadelphia: University of Pennsylvania Press.

Oakerson, Ronald J. 1988. "Reciprocity: A Bottom-Up View of Political Development," in V. Ostrom, D. Feeny, and H. Picht (eds.), *Rethinking Institutional Analysis and Development: Some Issues, Alternatives, and Choices*. San Francisco: Institute for Contemporary Studies Press.

Oberschall, Anthony 1973. *Social Conflict and Social Movements*. Engelwood Cliffs NJ: Prentice-Hall.

Okoth Ogendo, Hastings W. O. 1991. "Constitutions without Constitutionalism: Reflections on an African Political Paradox" in I. Shivji (ed.) *State and Constitutionalism: An African Debate on Democracy*. Harare, Zimbabwe: SAPES Press.

Oloka-Onyango, Joe 2001. *Constitutionalism in Africa: Creating Opportunities, Facing Challenges*. Kampala: Fountain Publishers.

Olowu, Dele 2003. "African Governance and Civil Service Reforms" in N. van de Walle, N. Ball, and V. Ramachandran (eds.), *Beyond Structural Adjustment: The Institutional Context of African Development*. New York: Palgrave.

Olson, Mancur 1965. *The Logic of Collective Action*. Cambridge MA: Harvard University Press.

Onimode, Bade 1992. *A Future for Africa: Beyond the Politics of Structural Adjustment*. London: Earthscan.

Osabu-Kle, Daniel T. 2000. *Compatible Cultural Democracy: The Key to Development in Africa*. Peterborough, Canada: Broadview Press.

Osseo-Asare, Francislee Syversen 1991. *We Are Magicians: Chronic Stress and the Economy of Affection in Africa*. Ph.D. dissertation, Pennsylvania State University.

Ostrom, Elinor 1990. *Governing the Commons*. New York: Cambridge University Press.

Ouchi, William G. 1981. *Theory Z: How American Business Can Meet the Japanese Challenge*. Reading MA: Addison-Wesley.

Oyugi, Walter, Peter Wanyande, and C. Odhiambo Mbai 2003. *The Politics of Transition in Kenya: From KANU to NARC*. Nairobi: Heinrich Boell Foundation.

Paolino, L. A. 1987. "The Evolving Food Situation" in John W. Mellor, C. L. Delgado, and M. J. Blackie (eds.), *Accelerating Food Production in Sub-Saharan Africa*. Baltimore: Johns Hopkins University Press.

Parkin, David 1972. *Palms, Wine and Witnesses*. San Francisco: Chandler Publishing House.

Parpart, Jane and Kathleen Staudt (eds.) 1989. *Women and the State in Africa*. Boulder CO: Lynne Rienner Publishers.

Patterson, Amy S. 1998. "A Reappraisal of Democracy in Civil Society: Evidence from Rural Senegal," *Journal of Modern African Studies*, vol 36, no 3, pp 423–41.

Philipson, T. and R. Posner 1995. "On the Microeconomics of AIDS in Africa," *Population and Development Review*, vol 21, no 4, pp 835–48.

Polanyi, Karl 1957. *The Great Transformation: The Political and Economic Origins of Our Time*. Boston: Beacon Press.

Popper, Karl 1962. *Conjectures and Refutations*. London: Routledge.

Posner, Daniel N. 2000. "Ethnic Fractionalization in Africa: How Should It Be Measured? What Does It Explain about Economic Growth?," paper presented at the World Bank Development Research Group Seminar, March 29.

Posner, Daniel 2004. "The Political Salience of Cultural Difference: Why Chewas and Tumbukas Are Allies in Zambia and Adversaries in Malawi," *American Political Science Review*, vol 98, no 4 (November), pp 529–45.

Press, Robert 2004. "Establishing a Culture of Resistance: The Struggle for Human Rights and Democracy in Authoritarian Kenya 1987–2002," Ph.D. dissertation, University of Florida.

Price, Robert 1974. "Politics and Culture in Contemporary Ghana: The Big-Man, Small-Boy Syndrome," *Journal of African Studies*, vol 1, no 2, pp 173–204.

Price, Robert 1975. *Society and Bureaucracy in Contemporary Ghana*. Berkeley and Los Angeles: University of California Press.

Przeworski, Adam 1991. *Democracy and the Market*. New York: Cambridge University Press.

Putnam, Robert 1993. *Making Democracy Work: Civic Traditions in Italy*. Princeton NJ: Princeton University Press.

Ranger, Terence 1983. "The Invention of Tradition in Colonial Africa" in Eric Hobsbawm and T. Ranger (eds.) *The Invention of Tradition*. Cambridge, UK: Cambridge University Press.

Rapley, John 1996. *Understanding Development in the Third World*. Boulder CO: Lynne Rienner Publishers.

Reardon, Thomas 1997. "Using Evidence of Household Income Diversification to Inform Study of the Rural Non-farm Labor Market in Africa," *World Development*, vol 25, no 5, pp 735–47.

Reno, William 1998. *Warlord Politics and African States*. Boulder CO: Lynne Rienner Publishers.

Reno, William 2000. "War, Debt and the Role of Pretending in Uganda's International Relations," Centre for African Studies Occasional Paper. Centre for African Studies, University of Copenhagen, Denmark.

Republic of Kenya 1971. *Economic Survey*. Nairobi: Government Printer.

Rey, Pierre-Phillippe 1973. *Les alliances des classes*. Paris: Maspero.

Reynolds, Andrew 1999. *Women in African Legislatures and Executives: The Slow Climb to Power*. Auckland Park, South Africa: Electoral Institute of South Africa Press.

Richards, Paul 2004. "Controversy over Recent West African Wars: An Agrarian Question?" Center for African Studies Occasional Paper, University of Copenhagen, Copenhagen (January).

Richter, Melvin 1964. "Durkheim's Politics and Political Theory" in Kurt Wolff (ed.) *Emile Durkheim, Essays on Sociology and Philosophy*. London: Unwin & Allen.

Riker, William H. 1962. *The Theory of Political Coalitions*. New Haven CT: Yale University Press.

Robinson, Pearl T. and Elliott P. Skinner (eds.) 1983. *Transformation and Resilience in Africa*. Washington DC: Howard University Press.

Rodney, Walter 1973. *How Europe Underdeveloped Africa*. Dar es Salaam, Tanzania: Tanzania Publishing House.

Rothchild, Donald and N. Chazan 1988. *The Precarious Balance: State and Society in Africa*. Boulder CO: Westview Press.

Rozman, Gilbert (ed.) 1991. *The East Asian Region: Confucian Heritage and Its Modern Adaptation*. Princeton NJ: Princeton University Press.

Rweyemamu, Anthony H. 1974. "The Predicament of Managers of Public Enterprises in Tanzania's Emerging Political Economy," paper presented at the Conference on Development of African Bureaucracies held at Belmont, Maryland, April 24–27.

Rweyemamu, Anthony H. and Goran Hyden (eds.) 1975. *A Decade of Public Administration in Africa*. Nairobi: East African Literature Bureau.

Sahlins, Marshall 1972. *Stone Age Economics*. London: Tavistock Publications.

Sandbrook, Richard 1972. "Patrons, Clients, and Factions: New Dimensions of Conflict Analysis in Africa," *Canadian Journal of Political Science*, vol 5, no 1, pp 1–26.

Sandbrook, Richard 1982. *The Politics of Basic Needs: Urban Aspects of Assaulting Poverty in Africa*. London: Heinemann Educational Books.

Sandbrook, Richard 1985. *The Politics of Africa's Economic Stagnation*. Cambridge, UK: Cambridge University Press.

Sangmpam, S. N. 1995. "Sociology of 'Primitive Societies,' Evolutionism, and Africa," *Sociological Forum*, vol 10, no 4, pp 609–32.

Sassen, Saskia 1998. *Globalization and Its Discontents: Essays on the New Mobility of People and Capital*. New York: New Press.

Schaffer, Bernard 1969. "The Deadlock of Development Administration" in C. T. Leys (ed.), *Politics and Change in Developing Countries*. Cambridge, UK: Cambridge University Press.

Schaffer, Frederic C. 1998. *Democracy in Translation*. Ithaca NY and London: Cornell University Press.

Schatzberg, Michael G. 1980. *Politics and Class in Zaire: Bureaucracy, Business and Beer in Lisala*. New York: Africana Publishing Company.

Schatzberg, Michael G. 2002. *Political Legitimacy in Middle Africa: Father, Family, Food*. Bloomington IN: Indiana University Press.

Schoepf, Brooke and Engundu Walu 1991. "Women and Structural Adjustment in Zaire" in C. H. Gladwin (ed.), *Structural Adjustment and African Women Farmers*. Gainesville FL: University of Florida Press.

Schultz, Ted W. 1964. *Transforming Traditional Agriculture*. Chicago: University of Chicago Press.

Schumacher, Eric F. 1973. *Small Is Beautiful*. London: Blond and Briggs.

Scott, James C. 1976. *The Moral Economy of the Peasant: Rebellion and Subsistence in Southeast Asia*. New Haven CT: Yale University Press.

Scott, James C. 1999. *Seeing Like a State: How Certain Schemes to Improve the Human Condition Have Failed*. New Haven CT: Yale University Press.

Semboja, Joseph and Ole Therkildsen (eds.) 1995. *Service Provision under Stress in East Africa*. London: James Currey and Portsmouth NH: Heinemann.

Shipton, Parker M. 1990. "Time and Money in the Western Sahel: A Clash of Cultures in Gambian Rural Finance" in M. Roemer and C. W. Jones (eds.), *Markets in Developing Countries*. San Francisco: Institute of Contemporary Studies Press.

Shivji, Issa (ed.) 1986. *The State and the Working People in Tanzania*. Dakar, Senegal: CODESRIA Press.

Shivji, Issa G. 1976. *Class Struggles in Tanzania*. New York: Monthly Review Press.

Sil, Rudra 2003. "The Economy of Affection in Comparative-Historical Perspective: The Legacies of the Japanese *Mura* and the Russian *Mir*," paper presented at the Annual Meeting of the American Political Science Association, Philadelphia, August 28–31.

Smith, William Edgett 1971. *We Must Run while Others Walk*. New York: Random House.

Southall, Aidan 1970. "The Illusion of Tribe," *Journal of Asian and African Studies*, vol v (January–April), pp 26–48.

Sparks, Donald 2004. "Economic Trends in Africa South of the Sahara, 2003" in *Africa South of the Sahara 2004*, thirty-third edition. London and New York: Europa Publications.

Stedman, Stephen 1996. "Conflict and Conciliation in Sub-Saharan Africa" in Michael Brown (ed.), *The International Dimensions of Internal Conflict*. Cambridge MA: MIT Press.

Tarrow, Sidney 1998. *Power in Movement*. Ithaca NY: Cornell University Press.

Terray, Emmanuel 1975. "Class and Class Consciousness in the Abron Kingdom of Gyaman" in M. Bloch (ed.), *Marxist Analyses and Anthropology*. London: Malaby.

Therkildsen, Ole 2000. "Public Sector Reform in a Poor, Aid-Dependent Country like Tanzania," *Public Administration and Development*, vol 20, no 1, pp 61–71.

Tiffen, Mary, Michael Mortimore, and Frank Gichuki 1994. *More People – Less Erosion.* New York: John Wiley & Sons.

Tilly, Charles 1990. *Coercion, Capital, and European States, A.D. 990–1992.* Cambridge MA: Blackwell.

Tinbergen, Jan 1964. *Central Planning.* New Haven CT: Yale University Press.

Tobler, Verena 1998. "Kulturwechsel in der Adoleszenz: Der doppelte Kultursprung," in *Symposium Soziale Arbeit. Soziale Arbeit mit Jugendlichen in problematischen Lebenslagen,* edited by VeSAG. Köniz: VeSAG

Trager, Lillian 2001. *Yoruba Hometowns: Community, Identity, and Development in Nigeria.* Boulder CO: Lynne Rienner Publishers.

Tranberg Hansen, Karin and Marikken Vaa 2003. *Reconsidering Informality: Perspectives from Urban Africa.* Uppsala, Sweden: Nordic Africa Institute Press.

Tripp, Aili Mari 1997. *Changing the Rules: The Politics of Liberalization and the Urban Informal Sector in Tanzania.* Berkeley: University of California Press.

Tripp, Aili Mari 2000. *Women and Politics in Uganda.* Madison: University of Wisconsin Press.

Tripp, Aili Mari 2001. "Women and Democracy: The New Political Activism in Africa," *Journal of Democracy,* vol 12, no 3, pp 141–55.

Trulsson, Per 1997. *Strategies of Entrepreneurship: Understanding Industrial Entrepreneurship and Structural Change in Northwest Tanzania,* Ph.D. dissertation, Linkoping University, Linkoping, Sweden.

Tschannerl, Gerhard 1973. "Rural Water Supply in Tanzania: Is Politics or Techniques in Command?" Paper No 52, presented at Annual Social Science Conference of the East African Universities, University of Dar es Salaam, June 6–9.

Turner, Billie L. II, Goran Hyden, and Robert W. Kates (eds.) 1993. *Population Growth and Agricultural Change in Africa.* Gainesville FL: University Press of Florida.

Uchendu, Victor 1969. "Polity Primacy and African Economic Development," paper presented at the Annual Social Science Conference of the East African Universities, University of Nairobi, June 2–5.

UNAIDS 2002. *Report on the Global HIV/AIDS Epidemic.* Geneva: UNAIDS.

United Nations Development Programme 1993. *Rethinking Technical Cooperation: Reforms for Capacity-Building in Africa.* New York: UNDP.

Van de Walle, Nicolas 2001. *African Economies and the Politics of Permanent Crisis, 1979–1999.* Cambridge, UK: Cambridge University Press.

Van de Walle, Nicolas and Timothy A. Johnson 1996. *Improving Aid to Africa.* Washington DC: Overseas Development Council.

Van Rensburg, Patrick 1974. *Report from Swaneng Hill.* Uppsala, Sweden: Dag Hammarskjold Centre.

Vansina, Jan 1990. *Paths in the Rainforest: Toward a History of Political Tradition in Equatorial Africa.* London: James Currey.

Villalon, Leonardo A. 1999. "Generational Changes, Political Stagnation, and the Evolving Dynamics of Religion and Politics in Senegal," *Africa Today,* vol 46, nos 3/4, pp 129–47.

Villalon, Leonardo A. and Phillip A. Huxtable (eds.) 1998. *The African State at a Critical Juncture: Between Disintegration and Reconfiguration.* Boulder CO: Lynne Rienner Publishers.

Von Doepp, Peter 2002. "Liberal Visions and Actual Power in Grassroots Civil Society: Local Churches and Women's Empowerment in Rural Malawi," *Journal of Modern African Studies*, vol 40, no 2, pp 273–301.

Von Freyhold, Michaela 1977. *Ujamaa Villages in Tanzania: Analysis of a Socialist Experiment*. London: Heinemann.

Wallerstein, Immanuel 1961. *Africa: The Politics of Independence*. New York: Vintage Books.

Waliggo, John 2001. "The Main Actors in the Constitution-Making Process in Uganda" in G. Hyden and D. Venter (eds.), *Constitution-Making and Democratization in Africa*. Pretoria: Africa Institute of South African Press.

Walu, Engundu 1987. "La Contribution des Femmes aux Budgets Menagers a Kinshasa," Research Report. Kinshasa: Office of the World Bank.

Warren, Bill 1980. *Imperialism: Pioneer of Capitalism*. London: Verso.

Waterston, Albert 1965. *Development Planning: Lessons of Experience*. Baltimore: Johns Hopkins University Press.

Weber, Max 1947. *The Theory of Social and Economic Organization*. New York: Oxford University Press.

Weber, Max 1978. *Economy and Society: An Outline of Interpretive Sociology*, edited by Guenther Roth and Claus Wittich. Berkeley: University of California Press.

Weisner, Thomas 1976. "The Structure of Sociability: Urban Migration and Urban Ties in Kenya," *Urban Anthropology*, vol 5, no 2, pp 199–223.

Widner, Jennifer A. 1992. *The Rise of a Party-State in Kenya: From Harambee to Nyayo*. Berkeley: University of California Press.

Wiggins, S. 2000. "Interpreting Changes from the 1970s to the 1990s in African Agriculture through Village Studies," *World Development*, vol 28, no 4, pp 631–62.

Williams, Gavin 1987. "Primitive Accumulation: The Way to Progress," *Development and Change*, vol 18, no 4, pp 637–59.

Williamson, Oliver E. 1985. *The Economic Institutions of Capitalism*. New York: Free Press.

Wing, Susanna D. 2002. "Questioning the State: Constitutionalism and the Malian Espace d'Interpellation Démocratique," *Democratization*, vol 9, no 2, pp 121–47.

Wodajo, Kifle 2001. "The Making of the Ethiopian Constitution" in G. Hyden and D. Venter (eds.), *Constitution-Making and Democratization in Africa*. Pretoria: Africa Institute of South Africa Press.

World Bank 1981. *Accelerated Development in Sub-Saharan Africa*. Washington DC: World Bank.

World Bank 1989. *Africa's Adjustment and Growth in the 1980s*. Washington DC: World Bank.

World Bank 1992. *Governance and Development*. Washington DC: World Bank.

World Bank 1994. *Adjustment in Africa: Reforms, Results, and the Road Ahead*. Washington DC: World Bank.

World Bank 1998. *Africans Can Compete! A Framework for World Bank Group Support for Private Sector Development in Sub-Saharan Africa*. Washington DC: World Bank.

World Bank 2000. *Can Africa Claim the 21st Century?* Washington DC: World Bank.

World Bank 2004. *African Development Indicators 2004*. Washington DC: World Bank.

Xerchave, Francois-Olivier 1999. *Dossiers noirs de la politique africaine de la France*. Paris: l'Harmattan.

Xerchave, Francois-Olivier 2000. *Noir silence: qui arretera la Francafrique?* Paris: Les Arenes.

Yeats, Alexander J. 1990. "On the Accuracy of Africa Observations: Do Sub-Saharan Trade Statistics Mean Anything?," *World Bank Economic Review*, vol 4, pp 135–56.

Young, Crawford 1976. *The Politics of Cultural Pluralism*. Madison WI: University of Wisconsin Press.

Young, Crawford 1994. *The African Colonial State in Comparative Perspective*. New Haven and London: Yale University Press.

Young, Crawford 2002. "Pluralism, Ethnicity, and Militarization" in Ricardo Rene Laremont (ed.), *The Causes of War and the Consequences of Peacekeeping in Africa*. Portsmouth NH: Heinemann.

Zolberg, Aristide 1966. *Creating Political Order: The Party-States of West Africa*. New York: Rand McNally.

Index